The
Garland Library
of
War and Peace

The
Garland Library
of
War and Peace

Under the General Editorship of

Blanche Wiesen Cook, *John Jay College, C.U.N.Y.*

Sandi E. Cooper, *Richmond College, C.U.N.Y.*

Charles Chatfield, *Wittenberg University*

Peaceful Change

International Studies Conference

(in four volumes)

Vol. II

Population and Peace

A Survey of International Opinion on Claims for Relief from Population Pressure

by

Fergus Chalmers Wright

with a new introduction
for the Garland Edition by
Chadwick F. Alger

Garland Publishing, Inc., New York & London
1972

Library of Congress Cataloging in Publication Data

Wright, Fergus Chalmers, 1903–
   Population and peace.

   (Garland library of war and peace)
   At head of title: Peaceful change. International
Studies Conference... Vol. II.
   Reprint of the 1939 ed.
   Includes bibliographical references.
   1. Population. 2. Emigration and immigration.
I. International Studies Conference, 10th, Paris,
1937. II. Title. III. Title: Peaceful change.
IV. Series.
HB871.W8 1972   301.32   70-147506
ISBN 0-8240-0301-2

Introduction

The four volumes on peaceful change published by the International Studies Conference after its Paris meeting from 28 June to 3 July 1937 serve several purposes. Reports on the Paris sessions offer rich insight into the character of thought and research on international relations just before the outbreak of World War II. Extensive bibliography is provided on problems of peaceful change, particularly those related to colonial questions, raw materials and demographic questions. The volumes also give information on a highly significant effort of scholars from a number of countries to develop procedures for collaborative inquiry on the most critical issues of their time. Their example offers an important challenge to scholars in the seventies!

Before these introductory comments consider the importance of the International Studies Conference for our time, it will be useful for the reader to have a thumbnail sketch of the development of this institution and a brief overview of the contents of the volumes. The International Studies Conference came into being as a result of initiatives taken by the Committee on Intellectual Cooperation, an activity of the League of Nations. Although it was proposed at the Peace Conference that international intellectual

5

relations should be provided for in the Covenant, this was rejected and the Committee was not created until the Second Assembly of the League. The first meeting of the Committee, originally composed of twelve distinguished scholars in the sciences and humanities, was held in August 1922. Its first chairman was Henri Bergson, and among its early members were Marie Curie, Gilbert Murray and Robert A. Millikan.

Because the Assembly did not provide sufficient funds for the small staff of the Committee, an appeal for funds from external sources was issued in 1924. In response, the French government offered financial support and quarters in Paris. The Paris office came to be known as the International Institute of Intellectual Cooperation whose program was drawn up each summer in Geneva at the annual meeting of the Committee of Intellectual Cooperation which acted as the Governing Body of the Institute.[1] Among the achievements of the Institute were the stimulation of activities that led to the creation of the International Federation of Library Associations, the creation of an International Museum Office, and the formation of an International Committee of Popular Arts. In 1931, in response to a request from the Chinese government, the Institute sent an educational mission to China to advise on the reorganization of the Chinese school system. This extension of the work of the League beyond that anticipated by its founders provided precedents and experiences that were important for the founding of UNESCO after World War II.[2]

At its sixth session in 1925 the Committee passed a resolution advocating cooperation between national and international institutions concerned with international studies and authorized the Institute of Intellectual Cooperation to pursue this objective. The Institute responded by convening in March 1928, in Berlin, a meeting of Experts for the Coordination of Higher International Studies. Attended by representatives of national institutes in six countries and a few international organizations, the Berlin meeting urged two kinds of activities: (1) cooperation in technical matters among national centers and institutes specializing in international studies and (2) joint studies of specific international problems. Out of these recommendations the International Studies Conference developed, holding annual meetings until the outbreak of World War II. Until 1933 the ISC was an intrinsic part of the machinery of the League of Nations. In 1934 the International Committee on Intellectual Cooperation declared the ISC an autonomous and independent organization. Thereafter it was responsible exclusively to its constituent members.

The members of the ISC were national institutions, grouped into national coordinating committees. Direct membership was open only to these committees. In cases where no national institution existed, groups of individual specialists were admitted to direct membership. As a result the ISC stimulated the extension of cooperation within nations of centers and individuals engaged in international studies. While individual experts were sometimes invited to meetings on specific subjects in which they had expertise, they did not participate in the governance of the ISC, a matter reserved for national coordinating committees.

Exceptions to membership rules were five international members who participated in the work of the ISC from its earlier sessions: Academy of International Law (The Hague), European Center of the Carnegie Endowment for International Peace (Paris and Geneva), Geneva School of International Studies (Oxford), Graduate Institute of International Studies (Geneva), and Institute of Pacific Relations (New York).

In the early years the ISC was mainly concerned with laying the groundwork for the development of machinery for international liaison and coordination between affiliated institutions. This led to the compilation of several international handbooks³ and to exchange of information, bibliographies, publications and speakers. The Berlin proposal for joint research was not acted on until 1931 when it was decided that the program of technical collaboration between institutions had been developed as far as resources permitted and that future sessions should include the study of concrete problems in international relations. From 1932 until the Second World War the ISC held each year, in addition to one or more Administrative Meetings, a series of Study Meetings. In the Administrative Meetings delegates represented their national coordinating committees, with one vote given to each national committee. But in the Study Meetings participants took part in their private capacity, with participation by representatives and officials of governments discouraged. At the Study Meetings no effort was made to make recommendations or to arrive at unanimous decisions.

The ISC devoted two years to topics selected for study. The first topic chosen was "The State and Economic Life," with a preparatory study conference held in Milan in 1932 [4] and a general study conference held in London in 1933.[5] The next subject studied was "Collective Security," with a preparatory study conference held in Paris in 1934 and a general study conference held in London in 1935.[6] A preparatory conference on "Peaceful Change" was held in Madrid in 1936, with the general study conference on this subject held in Paris in 1937.[7]

Study topics were chosen by the Programme Committee of the ISC after receiving suggestions from participating groups, with final arrangements decided by a plenary Administrative Session. Preparatory memoranda related to this topic were then prepared by individuals and groups and circulated to all members of the ISC by the International Institute of Intellectual Cooperation. Also distributed was a synthesis of documents received, prepared by a General Rapporteur. This was followed by a Study Meeting. In the case of the meeting of 1937 on peaceful change, ten preliminary meetings of experts were held on specific sub-topics of the conference, in Geneva, London, Paris and Vienna.

The 1937 conference received some one hundred memoranda from Australia, Canada, the United States, and thirteen European countries. The 142 participants came from twenty national institutes and national coordinating committees (Australia, Austria, Belgium, Brazil, Bulgaria, Canada, Czechoslovakia, Denmark, England, France, Hungary, Netherlands, Norway, Poland, Rumania, Spain, Sweden, Switzerland, United States and Yugoslavia). Five other nations were represented through invited experts or observers: China, Germany, Italy, Japan and Mexico. Participants were also present from organizations classed as international by the ISC: European Office of the Carnegie Endowment for International Peace, Graduate Institute of International Studies (Geneva), Geneva School of International Studies (Oxford), Institute of Pacific Relations, and the International Labor Organization.

In the light of the attention given at the 1937 conference to relations between so-called "have" and "have-not" nations, with Germany, Italy and Japan as the most prominent members of the "have-not" group, it is significant that these nations had only minimal representation at the Paris conference. Ger-

many and Japan were not members of the ISC in 1937, but Germany was represented by one observer and Japan by three. Germany had been a member but withdrew in 1933. Nevertheless, individual German scholars continued to take part and several studies prepared by Germans were placed before the Paris conference by the Institute for Intellectual Cooperation. They were apparently inspired by the terms of reference for the conference. While Italy was a member, it was represented by only one observer. Poland, on the other hand (also mentioned as a "have-not" nation at the conference), had the second largest number of participants, ten, surpassed only by England.[8]

The subject of the 1937 meeting, peaceful change, developed out of the 1935 and 1936 sessions devoted to collective security. In words so similar to those often written in subsequent decades, the conferees argued that collective security procedures alone could not prevent war: "If war is to be eliminated, it is indispensable to provide other means of satisfying the profound need for change of which war is the expression and the instrument."[9] *Four subjects were selected as foci for inquiry: (1) the production, consumption, and importation of raw materials, (2) demographic questions (population and migration), (3) aspects of colonies related to peaceful change and (4) problems of countries in the Danube Basin. The conference was organized into round-tables on each of these subjects. The reader having particular interest*

11

in one or more of these topics may find it useful to consult the introductory reports of the Secretary-Rapporteurs of each of these round-tables to be found in Volume I. Providing an integrated overview of memoranda presented to the conference, these reports may be found on pages 78 to 256. The records of the round-table meetings that follow, pages 274 to 481, offer insight into the dynamics of the meetings. Only records of three round-tables are included, since the Danube round-table concluded that "it would be premature to discuss the Danubian problem in its economic and political aspects on the basis of the documentation actually available." [10] Records of the four plenary meetings (pp. 259-273 and 486-580) provide a wider ranging dialogue among the participants across the topics of all the round-tables.

Rather than publishing the memoranda prepared for the conference, it was decided to have surveys published of the materials presented to the round-tables, with the exception of the one on the Danube Basin. Portions of these surveys were assigned to a number of scholars who produced the other three volumes generated by the 1937 conference: Population and Peace, Colonial Questions and Peace, *and* Le Problème des Matières Premières. *The contributions made by these volumes extend beyond the conference itself because authors were asked to "assume responsibility for presenting a conspectus of the main currents of contemporary opinion, on the*

12

principal elements of the problem, expressed in the material of the Conference and, whenever useful, in other relevant sources of information." [11]

While much in these volumes refers to concrete international conditions in 1937, issues are raised that are timeless. An example is Quincy Wright's concern for peace and justice:

> *If I correctly understood Lord Lytton, he said that peaceful change means the changes necessary to preserve peace. This strikes me as somewhat doubtful. I should be inclined to say, rather, that peaceful change means changes in the* status quo *necessary for justice. It is to be hoped that we shall get peace as a by-product of justice, but if we are going to make changes in the* status quo *only because otherwise somebody threatens to make war if we do not, we are likely to be confronted by more serious demands in the future. We cannot buy peace as an immediate political proposition at the price of injustice; our discussions must not proceed on the basis of what we have to do to buy off Powers that are threatening war, but on what is necessary for justice.* [12]

Present discussions about the relationship between peace and justice and priorities between them usually take place with reference to quite different concrete situations. Confrontation of issues of the thirties in the context of current discussion on peace and justice could enrich this discussion by extending the concrete cases examined.

While certain aspects of the debates seem timeless and the progress of mankind since the Paris Confer-

13

ence slight, if there has been any at all, the discussion of colonialism should instill a measure of hope in a generation that is inclined to have little confidence in its capacity to solve major global problems. While colonialism continues, in terms of a variety of meanings, the exercise of supreme authority over non-adjacent territories by nation states has been significantly diminished since the Paris conference. Consider this statement of the purpose of the study group on colonial questions:

> But the conference itself was mainly concerned with changes necessary for the settlement of matters in dispute between sovereign Powers in which some part is played by the distribution of colonial territories and the fair apportionment of any advantages to be derived from them.[13]

Of course, there were spokesmen for the emancipation of colonial populations. But it is not thinkable that a conference in the 1970s would include the following items that were on the agenda of the Colonial Study Group as possible "solutions" to colonial problems:

> Participation of nationals of non-colonial Powers in the colonial administration.
>
> International cooperation in the exploitation of colonial resources.
>
> International cooperation with regard to cultural penetration.

INTRODUCTION

Transfer of territory from a colonial Power to another national sovereignty.[14]

Concentration on inability to complete the job of decolonization in Southern Africa should not be permitted to blind us to the tremendous decline in the number of colonies and the overwhelming change in international norms in this regard.

Whatever judgment readers may make of the intellectual content of these volumes, all will admire the way in which scholars from many countries that were involved in the International Studies Conference were able to pool their talents in an effort to find solutions to the problems that beset the nation state system of the twenties and thirties. There is ample evidence that participants in the Paris conference were aware of the tremendous odds against the development and implementation of strategies for peaceful change as events in the world outside unfolded. Before the last volumes went to the printer, war seemed inevitable to Emanuel Moresco, editor of Volume III: Colonial Questions and Peace. *His plaintive preface, written in 1939, evokes empathy and sadness:*

> *Seldom will a book have seemed so hopelessly out of date on the day of publication as the present volume on the colonial aspects of the problem of Peaceful Change.*

15

INTRODUCTION

In 1935, when the subject for the next two years' cycle of research had to be chosen by the International Studies Conference, the term "peaceful change" seemed clear in itself; it meant the peaceful solution, by modification of the status quo *or otherwise, of certain international problems, – economic, social and territorial, – considered in its material as well as in its formal or procedural aspects.*

Since then, many changes, involving the disappearance of several independent States, have occurred, without formal war, but they have been very unlike the "peaceful change" which the 1935 Conference had in mind. In fact, the term seems to have lost all meaning. In 1939, it no longer corresponds, as far as Central Europe is concerned, to any of the realities of the present political phenomena. It has become extremely old fashioned.[15]

The reader's knowledge of the overwhelming tragedy that would shortly engulf the world adds a significant dimension to his reaction to and evaluation of the volumes. Reading and evaluating the work of the International Studies Conference after thirty-five years also stimulates those with similar concerns today to wonder how our efforts will be evaluated in 2007. I imagine that historians in 2007 will wonder why scholars of the 1970s were not as energetic and creative in developing truly international institutions for inquiry as were those who developed the International Studies Conference. Certainly we now have a considerable amount of scholarly collaboration across national boundaries, and there are a number of institutions that involve scholars from more than one country. And international professional associations in all the social sciences have been established. But there is no present effort similar to the International Studies Conference that attempts to assemble the most competent scholars in all countries for a collaborative assault on significant international problems. Will the historians of 2007 not consider it ironic that those who so often have called on governmental officials to cooperate with their counterparts in other countries in creating a global community have not been able to do the same with colleagues in their own profession — nor have they even tried!

There are important relationships between the organization of inquiry and the products of inquiry. It is doubtful if scholars can reach their full potential in attacking the problems of the nation state system as long as their own organization reflects this system. If scholars cannot overcome the restraints of language, distance and custom in an attack on shared problems how can they expect governments to do so? If scholars cannot liberate themselves from the selective filters that their national form of organization imposes on their thought and action, how can they facilitate intergovernmental cooperation?

The example provided by the activities of the International Studies Conference is a challenge to the UN, as successor to the League that sponsored it, and more specifically to UNESCO as successor to the Institute of Intellectual Cooperation. But it is particu-

INTRODUCTION

larly a challenge to today's scholars concerned with the problems of the nation state system. Why have the experience and achievements of the International Studies Conference been largely forgotten and why has its work not been continued?

June, 1971   Chadwick F. Alger
Ohio State University

INTRODUCTION

NOTES

[1] *In 1926 the League Assembly recognized the existence of an International Organization for Intellectual Cooperation (as a technical body similar to other organs of the League), consisting of the Committee, the Institute and National Committees of Intellectual Cooperation.*

[2] *Information on the Committee on Intellectual Cooperation and the Institute of Intellectual Cooperation is taken from,* League of Nations: Ten Years of World Cooperation. *Geneva: League of Nations, 1930, pp. 313-329; Walter H. C. Laves and Charles A. Thomson,* UNESCO: Purpose, Progress, Prospects. *Bloomington: Indiana University Press, 1957, pp. 10-13; and, "Intellectual Cooperation," League of Nations Questions, 6, Geneva: League of Nations, Information Section, 1937.*

[3] Handbook of Institutions for the Scientific Study of International Relations *(1929), mimeographed supplement (1932);* Handbook of Reference Centres on International Affairs *(1931); and "Annual Surveys and Periodicals on International Affairs" (1931), mimeographed.*

[4] A Record of a First International Study Conference on the State and Economic Life with Special Reference to International Economic and Political Relations. *Paris: International Institute of Intellectual Cooperation, League of Nations, 1932.*

[5] A Record of a Second Study Conference on the State and Economic Life. *Paris: International Institute of Intellectual Cooperation, League of Nations, 1934.*

[6] *Maurice Bourquin, ed.,* Collective Security: A Record of the Seventh and Eighth International Studies Conferences. *Paris: International Institute of Intellectual Cooperation, League of Nations, 1936.*

[7] *Information on the development of the International Studies Conference has been taken primarily from,* The International Studies Conference: Origins, Functions, Organization. *Paris: International Institute of Intellectual Cooperation, League of Nations, 1937. Compiled by F. Chalmers Wright, former Secretary of the ISC, this volume of 123 pages contains appendices providing much information on the*

19

NOTES

ISC: lists of members, sessions and meetings, participants in sessions and meetings, scientific studies and memoranda, publications and documents.

[8] *Data on conference participation taken from Volume I:* Peaceful Change, *pp. 620-633.*

[9] *Maurice Bourquin, in "Introductory Report," Volume I:* Peaceful Change, *p. 18.*

[10] Ibid., *p. 484.*

[11] *Volume III:* Colonial Questions and Peace, *p. 8.*

[12] *Volume I:* Peaceful Change, *p. 477.*

[13] *Volume III:* Colonial Questions and Peace, *p. 18.*

[14] Ibid., *p. 19.*

[15] Ibid., *p. 13.*

POPULATION AND PEACE

A Survey of International Opinion
on Claims for Relief from Population Pressure

PEACEFUL CHANGE

POPULATION AND PEACE

A Survey of International Opinion
on Claims for Relief from Population Pressure

by

FERGUS CHALMERS WRIGHT

B. Sc. (Econ.), Ph. D. (London),
formerly Secretary of the
International Studies Conference

INTERNATIONAL INSTITUTE OF INTELLECTUAL CO-OPERATION

League of Nations

PARIS 1939

FOREWORD

This volume is issued by the International Institute of Intellectual Co-operation as one of a series of studies on Peaceful Change carried out by the International Studies Conference[a] in the course of an enquiry into 'the basic difficulties in, and the procedures for, the peaceful solution of economic, social and territorial problems, with special reference to questions of : (i) population, migration and colonisation; and (ii) markets and the distribution of raw materials '.   It is published in pursuance of a recommendation made by an Editorial Board appointed by the Conference and composed of Professor Maurice Bourquin, General Rapporteur on the Conference's study, Mr. Malcolm W. Davis and Professor Etienne Dennery. The first volume in the series, issued in 1938,[b] contains a record of discussions on " peaceful change " which took place at a session of the International Studies Conference held in Paris in the summer of 1937, together with introductory reports giving synoptic statements of material previously assembled by the Conference.

The Editorial Board decided to issue, side by side with this general record, special surveys of certain aspects of the problem of peaceful change to which the Conference had devoted particular attention, *viz* : colonial questions, raw materials and markets, and population problems.

---

[a] ' The International Studies Conference is a permanent organ of co-operation, liaison and co-ordination for national institutions engaged in the scientific study of international affairs.   Its principal objects are to develop a system of technical collaboration among its affiliated institutions and to organise collective research on specific problems in international relations.   The constituent members of the Conference are linked together through an international machinery of which the principal elements are periodical plenary sessions, an executive committee, and the administrative services of the International Institute of Intellectual Co-operation ' (*The International Studies Conference : Origins, Functions, Organisation* (Paris : International Institute of Intellectual Co-operation), 1937, *q. v.* for general information on the activities, methods of work, publications and membership of the Conference).

[b] *Peaceful Change : Procedures, Population Pressure, the Colonial Question, Raw Materials and Markets* : Proceedings of the Tenth International Studies Conference, Paris, June 28th - July 3rd, 1937 (Paris : International Institute of Intellectual Co-operation), 1938.

The present volume is one of these surveys; it is devoted to demographic questions.

In the course of its study of these questions, the Conference assembled a great mass of material, including a large number of mimeographed documents and several comprehensive publications. It would have been physically impossible to reproduce the whole of this abundant material. The Board decided, however, that its essence could be presented in a form that would be convenient to the reader, without detracting too seriously from the value of the original documents, by issuing these special surveys, the preparation of which would be entrusted to individual authors who would be invited to assume responsibility for presenting a conspectus of the main currents of contemporary opinion on the principal elements of the problem expressed in the material of the Conference and, whenever useful, in other relevant sources of information. It was thought that this method, which facilitates a freedom of selection and arrangement less appropriate in formal records of international scientific conferences, achieves the practical end of providing, in conformity with one of the fundamental aims of the International Studies Conference, ' a publication capable of exercising some influence on public opinion ', by making available the results of scientific and technical investigations, not only to the narrower circles of specialists, but also to the general reader interested in topical international issues.[a]

The compilation of a survey of opinion on some of the demographic aspects of the problem of " peaceful change " examined by the International Studies Conference was entrusted to Dr. F. Chalmers Wright, formerly Secretary of the International Studies Conference. In the course of his work, Dr. Chalmers Wright had the advantage of obtaining expert advice and guidance from Professor A. M. Carr-Saunders, Director of the London School of Economics and Political Science, who, as one of the authorities who took part in the Conference's enquiry, made a number of suggestions which were taken into account by the author of the survey.

Companion surveys of opinion on the colonial problem and on raw materials and markets, as well as a volume on peaceful change procedures, are in course of preparation.

---

[a] Any expressions of opinion contained in these surveys are those of their authors and do not necessarily represent the views of the Conference.

CONTENTS

PREFACE

In the summer of 1937, an international conference of specialists in the study of contemporary international affairs brought to an end a joint enquiry into the question of " peaceful change " upon which its members had been engaged since 1935. The study had ranged over a diversity of current problems deemed to be at the root of certain demands for adjustment in the *status quo* of international relations. Among these problems, " overpopulation " had been regarded as one of the principal sources of grievance of several " discontented " Powers; an enquiry into the basis of claims for relief from pressure of population could not but occupy, therefore, a position of prominence in the conference's investigations. Which are the demographically " dissatisfied " nations ? What is the substance of their grievances ? Can their claims and aspirations be satisfied peacefully ? And what international changes are involved in the solution of their population problems by non-violent means ? To use a convenient neologism, what, in a word, is the nature of the problem of international " decrowding " ?

* * *

The preparation of the present volume was undertaken in the spring of 1938 at the request of the Editorial Board of the International Studies Conference, whose intentions are stated in the Foreword. Its object is to provide, in a form accessible to the general reader, a synthetic statement of the main currents of expert opinion on a problem which, although it has already given rise to an ample literature, is frequently distorted in political discussion by partisan bias or by an imperfect acquaintance with the facts.

While the task of extracting the essence of many hundreds of pertinent passages in a large number of sources has been laborious, the compiler's own contribution to the survey has been confined to a discharge of the modest functions of selection, compression and articulation. So far as possible, the text has been composed with the experts' own words, their authorship being clearly indicated in each instance (with an apology to the reader for the typographical necessity of relegating to an index at the end of the volume bibliographical references which would have overloaded the footnotes), so that the reader may see for himself precisely where the compiler's pen has been exchanged for scissors and paste. While the compiler's freedom of choice has necessarily been exercised to an extent which might have been inexpedient in the preparation of an official record of an international conference, a careful attempt has nevertheless been made to introduce into the survey every competent argument and responsible opinion which seems to have been brought to the conference's notice. In the absence, however, of any known process of total individual detachment from the conflict of multi-national interpretations of contemporary politics, it is not suggested that he has succeeded in wholly divesting himself from national partisanship or in repressing the expression of subjective reactions to current political events. Certainly no claim is made to have achieved the measure of intellectual disinterestedness and of international abstraction which was manifested in their loftier moments by many of the eminent authorities whose views are surveyed in this volume; but it does not seem likely that any normally biassed layman would read through the original documentation of the conference without reaching the comforting conclusion that demographic considerations impinge on some of the least objective elements of national policies and sensibilities and that vitally important population phenomena still lie in a deep outer penumbra of common human prejudice beyond the focal range within which the dispassionate scientist can gaze serenely on current affairs.

It is due to the specialists on whose original work the survey is founded to point out to the reader that responsibility for the line of argument on which their opinions have been threaded lies solely with the compiler and that the passages chosen for reproduction may not always reflect, when divorced from their context, the thoughts which their authors have more amply expressed in the documents themselves. On the other hand, it is due to the reader to warn him that an effort to minimise instances of accidental misrepresentation has led here and there to more copious citation than the requirements of the argument rendered strictly necessary; but, wherever possible, the distracting effect of over-prolonged discussion of special points on the reader's visual attention has been mitigated by recourse to the typographical expedients of footnotes and smaller type which he may generally disregard without much loss of continuity in the argument.

The ordinary reader for whose use this survey is primarily destined is invited to bear in mind that the treatment of the problem which forms the central theme of the volume is by no means exhaustive and that there are other relevant factors which, though they have been neglected in these pages, cannot be ignored in any formulation of a rational demographic policy. In the first place, in the course of its study, the conference was led to shift its attention from one aspect of the problem to another in response to swift changes in the international political scene during the progress of its enquiry; in the process of adapting its programme to the exigencies of external events, the conference had to break off its study inconclusively at several points which could not subsequently be knit together into a coherent pattern of consecutive thought. It was inevitable, also, that, in a study of limited duration, the conference should have laid more emphasis on some elements of the problem than on others. Hence the material produced by the conference is in some respects discontinuous. Through the use of complementary sources of information, an attempt has been made in this volume to bridge one or two of the principal gaps; but it has not been possible in the time available for the preparation of the survey to undertake any systematic research into aspects of the problem which were not considered by the conference. It is, therefore, essentially as an interpretation of the conference's own study that this volume is issued. In one respect, however, the survey protrudes beyond this boundary. Since the termination of the conference's study in the summer of 1937, not only has new knowledge come to light on important aspects of the questions discussed in these pages, but the central theme of " peaceful change " upon which the conference grafted its enquiry into demographic problems .has also been the subject of much subsequent discussion and speculation. These recent developments could not be wholly ignored; nor could they be taken so fully into account as they may deserve without straying extravagantly outside the field of the conference's own enquiry. A partial reconciliation of these divergent considerations has been effected by preserving the summer of 1937 as the *terminus ad quem* for the main trend of the argument and by advancing into periods more proximate to the date of this publication wherever more recent information and events seem to impair seriously the validity of the conference's findings.

* * *

The writer wishes to express his sense of obligation to the Director of the International Institute of Intellectual Co-operation, M. Henri Bonnet, under whose inspiring guidance he was privileged for a number of years to gain some insight into the practice of international administration and to whose long experience of international affairs he has had recourse in establishing the general framework of the survey and in overcoming certain difficulties of presentation; to the Director of the Migration Section of the International Labour Office and his collaborators, who have given him the benefit of far more specialised knowledge than he has been able to utilise; to the Librarians of the International Labour Office and of the Royal Institute of International affairs, who have kindly facilitated his work; and to members of the staff of the International Institute of Intellectual Co-operation, for their technical assistance at various stages of the work.

No layman could have embarked unaided upon the preparation of a survey of contemporary opinion on so complex a question as "overpopulation". If the present volume succeeds at all in presenting a connected summary of the International Studies Conference's many-sided enquiry, the result is due in large measure to the opportunities which the writer has had of seeking the authoritative guidance of the Director of the London School of Economics and Political Science, Professor A. M. Carr-Saunders. The writer wishes also to acknowledge gratefully his debt to Professor Carr-Saunders for having consented to read through a draft of the survey and for a number of criticisms, comments and suggestions which, though they could not be specifically indicated in each instance in the text, have determined both the form and the matter of much of the survey which is now submitted to the reader.

F. C. W.

Paris, December Fourth, 1938.

INTRODUCTORY

The sources of the passages quoted in the text of the Survey (reference numbers in small type) and in the footnotes (reference numbers in italics) are indexed at the end of the volume.

References to footnotes are indicated alphabetically.

Chapter 1

Collective Security and Peaceful Change

I. THE IDEA OF COLLECTIVE SECURITY

In the summer of 1933, on the eve of the World Economic Conference and at a time when, it was confidently believed by many, the Disarmament Conference ' had entered a stage of its work which held out real hopes of concrete results ',[14] [a] the International Studies Conference, having just completed a two-year study of state intervention in private economic enterprise,[b] opened an enquiry into the notion of collective security and into the principles and methods of a system for the organisation of peace.[c]

' The idea of collective security ', wrote the Conference's General Rapporteur two years later in the closing stages of the enquiry, ' no doubt exercises — especially since the World War — a powerful attraction on men's minds; but that is not a sufficient reason to justify it. It is possible that, in spite of its apparent seductiveness, the idea may prove, in the last analysis, to be false or dangerous '.[12] The statement epitomised a fundamental difference of attitude towards the concept of collective security which, from the outset of the enquiry, had deeply divided the experts taking part in the Conference's study.[d]

---

[a] See the note on the page opposite.
[b] See *231* and *232*.
[c] See *1*.
[d] 'The majority was large and the minority small but . . . . the majority contained representatives of . . . . only three of the seven great Powers ' (*228*), two of which — Japan and the U. S. S. R. — were not actively represented in the Conference. Although it is a fundamental principle of the Conference's methods of work that no attempt shall be made at its study meetings ' to reach conclusions, to make recommendations or to arrive at unanimous decisions . . . . [or] to formulate findings capable of leading to concerted action ' (*230*), yet ' the absence of the points of view of some of the Powers . . . . makes the Conference from the point of view of anyone seeking realism rather less successful than it is, perhaps, from the point of view of those who approach it purely academically ' (*228*).

There were those who considered that the notion needed no demonstration; they apparently assumed, 'explicitly or implicitly..., as a sort of postulate, the necessity of working toward this goal'.[12]   'I do not know how it may be in other lands', said Sir Austen Chamberlain at the opening of the Conference, 'but... among the questions of foreign policy which most preoccupy us is the question of Collective Security'.[13]   Others challenged the validity of this assumption.   In a vigorous repudiation of the legitimacy of the notion, the most resolute of these critics asserted that :

It is undeniable that, since the war, this myth of security, this vaguely-outlined nightmare, has disturbed and distorted political intelligence throughout the world and especially in Europe; that it is a paralysing burden on European politics; and that it thus constitutes one of the greatest obstacles to the establishment in the world, and especially in Europe, of a veritable peace, that is to say, a peace not only diplomatic and legal, but political and psychological as well...   It is absurd and impossible to establish by means of a universal text and a universal guarantee what is called " collective security ".   To persist in making this anti-historical and impossible " collective security " the first condition of a genuine peace is to distort the historical intelligence of the nations and at the same time to render practically impossible the establishment of peace not only diplomatic but real.[3] [a]

Two years of co-operative research, conducted along lines as rigorously scientific as the current political implications of the question permitted, neither diminished the hostility of the opponents of collective security nor seriously shook the faith of its partisans.   The Conference brought its study to an end without having either " justified " the idea of collective security or shown it to be manifestly " false or dangerous ".

---

[a] In the course of the Conference's closing meetings in 1935, the author of these remarks energetically re-affirmed his distrust of the notion of collective security in speeches (see *15*) in which, as the President of the International Committee on Intellectual Co-operation declared at the close of the Conference, ' he defied us all and put forward ideals which were totally different from the ideals most of us were pursuing ' (*30*).   It is true that, with one possible exception (see *27*), these speeches were not directly endorsed by any other speaker at the Conference (cf., however, the preceding footnote).   Nevertheless, it is unlikely that anyone who followed the debates of the Conference would deny that this almost single-handed defiance was one of the factors which was to influence the Conference's decision (see below, pp. 10 and 12) to enquire more deeply into the nature of the gap between two apparently irreconcilable attitudes towards the notion of collective security by initiating a study of the question of " peaceful change ".

Both sides, however, had admitted ' the necessity of an energetic struggle against war ', and it had likewise been ' recognised that this struggle requires concerted effort and cannot be carried on successfully by purely individual means '.[28] [a] Even the Conference's most uncompromisingly antagonistic censor of the ' anti-historical ', ' anti-human ' and, consequently, ' absurd and impossible ' fancy of establishing a universal system of collective security had emphasised that the effort to avoid war must not be abandoned.[3] The cleavage of opinion which the Conference's examination of the concept of collective security had disclosed did not prevent, therefore, a fruitful exploration of the problem of finding an alternative to the use of force in the conduct of international affairs.[b]

II. THE PREVENTION OF WAR

Three sets of measures were considered by the International Studies Conference when it turned its attention to the practical problem of discovering a substitute for violence in the settlement of international disputes, *viz.* measures for the prohibition or renunciation of recourse to force; measures of repression; and preventive measures proper. While it was generally recognised that ' the principle of " non-recourse to force " . . . has a place in any system of collective security ', there was ' some hesitation about making this principle absolutely rigorous ', since, ' to proclaim non-recourse to force, without setting up methods capable of filling peacefully the rôle which, historically, had been that of war, would only be a limping solution, ill-balanced, and headed, in the long run, for certain failure '.[12]

Nor did the Conference feel that the adoption of repressive measures would go to the root of the problem. ' Our attention ', said one speaker, ' ought to be turned first of all to the causes of war '.[20] ' To avoid war ', said another, ' we must not organise the repression of war by force . . . [but] must apply ourselves to eliminating the causes of war ';[3] for ' all of these methods do not prevent war . . .: they are merely methods of postponing war '.[21]

---

[a] See also *12*.
[b] That the Conference's failure to discover a commonly acceptable interpretation of " the concept of collective security " did not sterilise its efforts to enquire into " the principles and methods of a system for the organisation of peace " was largely due to the General Rapporteur's careful insistence that the Conference's primary aim was to plan the construction of a system for the elimination from international relations of recourse to force. See *12* and *28*.

It was while investigating methods of eliminating the causes of war that the Conference opened a discussion which, its Chairman thought, was destined to break new ground and which, instead of lagging ' behind or following the various Governments and Foreign Offices of the world which had been examining this subject [of collective security] from every aspect for a period of years ', would be ' leading and not following any governmental initiative ' and might ' add a real and lasting contribution to world thought and possibly to world action '.[29] [a]

III. CAUSES OF WAR

What, then, are the causes of war ? In the inexhaustible discussion of the causes of war, it has been said that ' the things for which nations profess to fight are of two kinds : those which they believe they are entitled to as a matter of law, and those which they do not claim as of legal right but want on some other ground '.[55] In either case, it would appear that an examination of contemporary national needs, grievances, aspirations and claims might reveal situations containing the germs of potential wars in the future. The discovery of the causes of war is, however, only a first step towards its prevention. For, while no disagreement seems possible on the principle that, if violence is to be abolished in the conduct of international affairs, it is necessary to organise peaceful methods as a substitute for the use of force, opinions differ ' when the question arises as to what should be the rôle of these peaceful methods '. Are the peaceful substitutes for war ' destined to ensure the application of the law now in force or to ensure the modification of that law ' ?[12]

In considering this question, the Conference concluded that, from the political standpoint, the great difficulty does not lie in the organisation of peaceful methods ' which aim at the settlement of international disputes of a legal character, i.e. which have no other object than to ensure the correct application of the law already in force '.[28] The primary aim of a State, it was suggested, ' is not the fulfilment and application of positive law, but, on the contrary, a change in the present state of the law '.[11] According to views which were held to ' coincide with those of a very large number of partisans of Collective Security ',[12]

----

[a] Cf. below, pp. 11-12.

' it is possible . . ., if not to avoid war for ever, at least to make it more and more rare . . . by substituting for the system of rigid equilibrium . . . the system of elastic equilibrium, or better, of *flexible equilibrium* . . ., [that is], by giving the peoples . . . effective means . . . of satisfying their essential interests, their vital needs, without resorting to war '.[3] Politically, it was felt, the difficulty lay ' rather in the very complex, very serious and very delicate problem of the transformation of the existing law ',[28] yet it was much more in this rôle, ' as a force of upheaval, of transformation, than as an instrument of coercion in the service of the *status quo* ' that war had ' often played in history '.[12] Hence it could be said that ' the chief problem confronting international relations . . . [is] the need for a more flexible structure than that which identifies justice with the *status quo* '.[183]

In studying peaceful means of changing the legal arrrangements which govern international relations, the Conference considered ' changes not of international law but of situations provided for in international law '[19], that is to say, it distinguished between ' objective, general and impersonal rules ' and ' subjective situations '. In the first case, it was pointed out, changes ' can generally be carried out without directly involving the vital interests of any given State', but ' the problem appears in quite another light when it is a question of adjusting or modifying subjective situations, peculiar to certain States and which, usually, are based on treaties '.[28] [a] ' Here ', said the Conference's General Rapporteur, 'is the crucial point. No one ignores either its importance or the difficulties which it raises '.[28]

Two contradictory tendencies mark the Conference's study of peaceful methods of modifying the *status quo*. ' One of them, attentive primarily to the dangers which may be presented by the organisation of a dynamic system, even by peaceful methods . . . is inclined to seek collective security in the maintenance and the guarantee of the establish-

---

[a] The explicit reference to situations based on treaties appears to have been a reflection of the preoccupations of certain sections of the Conference with territorial situations (frontier revision); subsequent discussion tended to show, however, that frontier problems are often merely symptomatic, in part at any rate, of other and deeper problems arising out of situations which are not based on treaties (cf. below, pp. 10-11). It may be noted here that, when examining, on a later occasion, the meaning to be attached to the term " *status quo* " in the context of the Conference's enquiry into " peaceful change ", the General Rapporteur, while suggesting that the term applied ' to the existing legal order in the field of international relations ', specified that ' this legal order is not determined solely by treaties '; but he expressed the view that, ' in order not to extend unduly the limits of our subject, it is preferable to consider as " changes in the *status quo* " only those changes which derive from their international legal character certain minimum guarantees ' (*188*).

ed order . . .[a]   The other tendency, on the contrary, without ignoring
the complex and delicate character of the problem, sees with especial
distinctness the danger involved in regarding security as a system
destined to immobilise historical development '.   It is not possible to
examine in this brief outline of the chief elements of the Conference's
discussion the grounds on which both these conflicting tendencies were
based; but, if attention must now be turned exclusively to the second
tendency, it is not because it was ' visibly that which . . . found the
greater response among the Members of the Conference ',[12] but because
it was in the discussion of this tendency that the Conference broke the
' new ground '[b] which led it to embark upon the study, *inter alia*, of the
questions to be examined in the present survey.[c]

IV. PEACEFUL CHANGE

The futility of attempting to stem the tide of history was sharply
denounced by some of the Conference's experts;[d] but, ' while the necessity of seeing to it that the *status quo* be made more elastic and that it
be modified by peaceful means ' may be said to have been generally
recognised in the course of the Conference's study of collective security,
the question of ' how, by what methods, and following what procedures
this may best be accomplished ' was left largely undefined.[12] [28]   Nor
was any attention given to the actual international situations which
might be held to stand in need of change.[e]   Conscious, however,
that an examination of these questions must form an essential part of

---

[a] For expressions of this tendency, see, e. g., *2, 4, 6,* and *10.*

[b] Cf. above, p. 6.

[c] The first tendency was, moreover, associated more particularly with territorial
situations.   Cf. above, p. 7, note *a.*

[d] A French memorandum submitted to the Conference argued that ' there is no *lex
in perpetuum valitura.*   A law, even though it be excellent at the moment of its enactment,
may become inapplicable . . .   It is just because law is a rule of life that it cannot oppose life,
that it must evolve with life in order to be able to continue to adapt itself to life.   Law
is not the indefinite prolongation of a particular right of enjoyment, the maintenance of the
status quo after profound changes have taken place in the state of society ' (*5*).   It is obvious,
contended a Canadian expert, that ' effective machinery for the peaceful alteration of the
status quo is essential to the organisation of a permanent peace ' (*9*).   ' It may turn out ',
thought a Norwegian authority, ' that the peace of the world depends on . . . [successfully]
organising international ways for the revision of existing situations, and for peaceful reforms
in international law ' (*17*).

[e] Brief allusions were made, however, to labour standards, currency fluctuations,
tariffs, distribution of raw materials, dumping and shipping subsidies (*9*) and to restrictions
upon trade, movements of people and movements of capital (*24*).   See also below, p. 20,
note a.

any comprehensive enquiry into the problem of collective security, the Conference made arrangements to devote a further period of two years to a study of " peaceful change of the *status quo* " for the purpose of throwing light, not, of course, upon all the causes of war, since among the causes of wars there may be some which do not give rise to claims for changes in the *status quo*,[a] but at any rate upon certain causes which, it was thought, were particularly important[b] and were associated with specific current needs, grievances and aspirations expressed in certain claims, that is, the demands of ' those States which — rightly or wrongly — considered that they occupied a situation which was unfair, unjust and perhaps unendurable '.[17] After insisting that the problem of peaceful change has ' been neglected all too long by students of international organisation ',[8] the author of one of the papers submitted to the Conference pointed out that security was not an end in itself :

Security is not a particular system of social organisation. It is rather a *state of things*, which allows communal life to unfold itself and to develop without being periodically and violently dislocated ... Once we realise ... [that the organisation of security must be commensurate with the social life which it is to render secure], we shall more readily appreciate the voices which say in effect : " What interest have we to provide security for a state of things which we dislike, and which is unjust to us ? " To them, a reliable system of security, without simultaneous provisions for peaceful change, seems not a promise but a denial of better times ... The answer [to the question whether security and peaceful change are independent of each other and can be pursued separately] is that they are both equally vital links in the same chain of progress, and that the chain cannot hold and run until they are both wrought stoutly together ... Security, peace, is a set and constant mechanism; change is a dynamic and continuous process. They are not interchangeable, the one is no substitute for the other. As acts of government they will vary in tempo and emphasis; as constitutional devices they must be set up together.[8]

Yet it was not without resistance on the part of some of its participants that the Conference, after an examination of the effectiveness

---

[a] Cf., e. g., *39*.
[b] ' I can think ', said one speaker, ' of no subject more useful to discuss, or the results of which discussion would prove more fruitful ' (*22*). ' You cannot have peaceful change without collective security ', he declared two years later, ' and equally you cannot have collective security without some organised system of peaceful change ' (*191*).

of the existing procedures for the peaceful settlement of international disputes and of the utility of the existing methods of modifying the *status quo*, reached the position in its enquiry when, logically, its next step appeared to be an investigation of the difficulties lying in the way of a peaceful settlement of international conflicts having their source in the needs and grievances of non-satisfied peoples and giving rise to aspirations and claims for changes in the *status quo*. In the first place, the legitimacy of, and the expediency of enquiring into, certain claims which, while they were not specifically mentioned, were nevertheless tacitly assumed to be present in the minds of all the participants in the Conference, were called in question. As one speaker said :

It is not enough that someone should say : " I want a certain thing " for the other to be obliged to give it to him; it is not enough that an active propapanda, a well-organised movement should demand a piece of property from someone else with cries and threats; it is necessary that the universal conscience judge that this demand is just.[18] [a]

Similarly, in discussing the provision in Article XIX of the Covenant of the League of Nations for the re-consideration of international situations endangering the peace of the world, a Polish speaker declared that :

[There can] be no question here of a State, which has demanded something from another State, being allowed to argue that failure to satisfy its demands might endanger the peace of the world. In this case, indeed, it is those demands themselves which would endanger world peace.[4] [b]

These objections, however, clearly sprang essentially from the fear that the Conference might be about to enter what was then deemed by many (as it is still deemed by some) to be the blind-alley of enquiry into the territorial provisions of the Peace Treaties. But "peaceful change of the *status quo*", though it was undoubtedly conceived by some of the Conference's experts as a problem of frontiers and of territorial sovereignty, is not always, and perhaps never essentially, a

---

[a] Cf. this test of legitimate claims with the tests (see below § V) of claims which it would be expedient for the Conference to examine.

[b] There is truth, the same speaker added, ' in that French proverb which applies also to wars and to international politics in general, and not only to the excellent French dinner tables : " L'appétit vient en mangeant " ' (*19*).

synonym for territorial revision. Indeed, as one of the Conference's experts insisted, a principal reason for studying " peaceful change " was precisely that it had hitherto ' been left to be trailed about by national propagandists . . . [whose] main concern is with some revision of frontier — the thing that divides; peaceful change would rather concentrate on the things which bind and unite '. Until then, he said, revision of frontiers, ' instead of being discussed as a vital part of any system of international peace ', had ' been stridently and discordantly pressed as a matter of certain momentary and limited national grievances '.[8]

It was also argued that countries with grievances already had a perfectly simple remedy at hand, since there existed in the League of Nations ' a general association of the States for the discussion of those matters '. It should be said, therefore, to these countries : ' Come into conference; tell the world your grievances; put them before the public opinion of the world . . . Let us know what these grievances are; then perhaps the public opinion of the world may be brought to bear on them '.[26] This suggestion was countered, however, by the assertion that, for example, Germany had ' talked for seven years between 1926 and 1933 ' and had ' made definite complaints especially in the field of disarmament ' — complaints which had been ' very modest '.[16] ' It is quite good to talk about these problems, but when ', it was asked, ' will the talking end ? '[25]

Some misgiving might also be felt lest the enquiry should open the door to a flood of claims. This apprehension might be stilled to some extent, however, with the argument that ' when you give a particular country a right to raise a claim to a certain change, you also impose upon it the obligation to substantiate that claim before the international forum '.[23]

On the whole, it may be said that the Conference, in the words of its General Rapporteur, ' had become convinced that, in order to fight with any chance of success against war, it is not enough to proscribe it nor to set up in the face of it a system of constraint. It is above all necessary to attack the causes of war, by seeking to substitute for it peaceful methods of settling conflicts, of clearing up disputes, and of providing legitimate means of satisfying the aspirations which provoke it '.[188]

In thus setting the problem of the peaceful settlement of international disputes in the context of unsatisfied national claims and aspirations for modifications of the *status quo* in international relations, the International Studies Conference was formulating a hypothetical explanation of some of the causes of war which, upon verification, might throw light upon factors of the problem that the study of collective security had not revealed.   Its next task, therefore, was to test its hypothesis by enquiring into the basis of the national aspirations which it had postulated and by examining the content of the claims for change which these aspirations had generated.   The Conference would then consider the legitimacy of the claims and it would analyse the difficulties which may stand in the way of the contemplated changes.   Finally, on the basis of its findings, the Conference might consider the methods to be followed in overcoming these difficulties with a view to a peaceful solution of the ultimate problems giving rise to national aspirations.

V. PEACE OR JUSTICE ?

In the course of the International Studies Conference's enquiry into the problem of peaceful change, attempts were made in various quarters to introduce into the scope of the study an examination of the claims and grievances, not only of strong military states, but also of smaller, less powerful countries.   These attempts, however, were resisted on the ground that, whatever may have been the basis of claims by weak states in terms of justice and international equity, they were not germane to the Conference's primary object of clarifying situations likely to contain the seeds of future wars.

It was admitted, of course, ' that an accumulation of grievances may end by provoking gestures of despair ', but it had to be recognised, as the Conference's General Rapporteur pointed out, that, ' normally, a grievance which, in the case of a large State, would constitute a danger of war, . . . lacks that character ' in the case of ' a claim made by a weak State, having no means of backing up its claims by force of arms '.   Indeed, looking ' at the matter solely from the viewpoint of the maintenance of peace, it may even be said that such a claim is only of minor interest ' and that ' taken by itself, it is inoffensive '.[188]

It was not, however, without protest on the part of some[a] and

[a] Cf., e. g., *26* : ' [The question of the revision of Article XIX of the Covenant of the League of Nations is] not brought up because there are a number of small countries whose grievances do not secure proper recognition.   It is brought up because there are certain powerful countries, who are inclined to make us feel that if they are not allowed to have their own way, they will find their way in some other manner.   The plain word to apply to that is blackmail '.

reluctance on the part of others that the organisers of the International Studies Conference's enquiry were permitted effectively to limit — with some exceptions[a] — the general scope of the enquiry to situations generally believed to present the contingent danger of war. Germany, it was pointed out, ' is not the only country involved in this matter . . . A large number of other Powers are far from declaring themselves satisfied with the economic régime throughout the world, and in particular with the economic régime followed in the colonial field . . . The Powers which possess no colonial territory are not the only claimants, but certain Powers which possess colonies as well. [In] the case of . . . [Belgium, for example], it must not be imagined that because Belgium has a colony — and a colony which is not without importance — she is satisfied with the present régime. She is by no means satisfied; she would like a régime marked — and not only in the colonial territories, but in the whole world — by more liberalism, by a broader conception of equality. Only on this condition will peace reign in the world; at least it is one of the essential conditions of a generalized state of peace '.[218]

According to a speaker at one of the meetings of the Conference :

If we attempt to reach solutions on the exigencies of a particular moment or a particular area, we shall never get anywhere, because the special interests of our countries will bias our scientific objectivity . . . [It has been] said that Peaceful Change means the changes necessary to preserve peace. This strikes me as somewhat doubtful. I should be inclined to say, rather, that Peaceful Change means changes in the *status quo* necessary for justice. It is to be hoped that we shall get peace as a by-product of justice, but if we are going to make changes in the *status quo* only because otherwise somebody threatens to make war if we do not, we are likely to be confronted by more serious demands in the future. We cannot buy peace as an immediate political proposition at the price of injustice; our discussions must not proceed on the basis of what we have to do to buy off Powers that are threatening war, but on what is necessary for justice.[225]

Such views were not contested. Indeed, it was fully admitted that ' the problem of peaceful change is not limited to eventualities which involve the risks of war ' :

[a] See below, pp. 59-61.

It is much broader, and covers all the transformations which it may be necessary to make in the *status quo* for whatever reason. It concerns the general problem of dynamism, of movement in the legal realm, and this problem arises independently of any wish and of any possibility of aggression.[188]

On the other hand, it was argued that, although ' the grievances which are likely to receive attention are those of such dissatisfied Powers as are well armed ', yet ' what seems cynical to anyone approaching the problem with any idea of justice in mind seems mere common sense when we consider the actual practice of nations '.[101] [a]   The case in favour of a restriction of the Conference's enquiry to grievances associated with the contingency of war was summarised as follows :

From an objective point of view, it is probably a mistake to suppose that every legitimate grievance must be redressed if stable peace is to result. This assumes too readily that continuing injustice is necessarily fatal to peace.   Though sentimentalists are wont to make some such assumption, it is probably as ill-founded as it would be in reference to social situations at home.   For unredressed grievances to imperil social stability they must be not merely deep, or even legitimate : more depends on the strategic position and numerical importance of the persons aggrieved . . .   In the interest, then, of peace, though not of course of righteousness, attention may be fixed on the grievances of those States which, because of the present or potential strength of themselves or their friends, are so situated as to be possessed of " nuisance-value ".   By the same token it is not necessary that grievances be particularly well-founded, if only they be keenly enough felt . . .   If our reflections should lead us to conclude that sometimes peace can be safeguarded only, so to say, at the expense of justice, it behoves us candidly to record our finding, leaving it to the statesmen and the peoples to say whether the maintenance of peace is in all contexts an absolutely desirable object of diplomatic solicitude.[7] [b]

[a] ' For instance ', wrote a Canadian expert, ' Japanese are much better treated in Canada than Chinese although ethically the latter have just as good a claim to courteous treatment ' (*101*).

[b] ' To imply, in the manner of some, that peaceful change is necessarily change for the better, change in the interests of justice, and change accepted freely, is, I submit, to obscure rather than to clarify the question.   If candid in our thinking we must surely concede that a change might be definitely unjust, assented to under protest, and intrinsically a change for the worse, yet, because not the outcome of actual hostilities, technically entitled to rank as peaceful change.   Note that I am not expressly advocating this kind of change : I am merely classing it ' (*177*).

It was also suggested to those who seemed disposed to attach greater importance to justice than to peace that the claims of small States differed from those of powerful countries ' by reason of the way in which the controversy is likely to be settled ' :

Does not the weighing of the difficulties to be overcome coincide up to a certain point with the weighing of the opposing forces ? Does not the desire to settle a conflict peacefully give rise to an inclination to sacrifice the interests of the party which we are sure will not disturb the peace to the interests of the party whose means of action, or even whose tendencies or mood are such as to instil into the situation a sentiment of anxiety ? In other words, is it not to be feared that peace will be purchased at the price of justice ?

This was admittedly ' a redoubtable question ', but its examination would have taken the Conference far beyond the limits of its study. For ' what is Justice ? How can it be defined, especially in international relations ? By what signs may one recognise it, apart from the sub-jective judgments of which it may be the object ? '[188] And is it not true that ' abstract justice may be an imperfect guide to the change that will exorcise the danger of war ' ? [7] ' It is not desirable ', concluded the Conference's General Rapporteur, ' that the Conference should enter upon this ground, where the exchange of ideas, however interesting, would doubtless lead only to highly uncertain results '.[188] If ' the peace of the world is not imperilled ', one of the Conference's experts insisted again at one of the meetings in 1937, ' then the question does not concern this Conference '.[200] [a]

*　*　*

In the course of the debate which took place during the Interna-tional Studies Conference's session in 1937, a point of view put forward implied that " peaceful change " could not properly be discussed in the context of an issue between peace and war. In a discussion on the transfer of colonial areas as a method of settling grievances, a speaker

---

[a] For reasons of the same order, various other demographic problems which were alluded to in the course of the Conference's enquiry must be excluded from this Survey, e. g., the immigration into Palestine of Jews, whose ' exodus gives some relief to the country of origin, viz., Poland and Germany ' (44; cf. below, pp. 59-61); the case of the Italians in Tunis, which tends ' to create international difficulties ' (38); etc.

stated that he ' would be particularly opposed to such transfers if they were considered mainly because of the threat of the use of force by countries making the demands '.[a] ' If ', he said, ' we live in a world of power politics we know exactly where we stand; we hold what we have and we do not give it up unless forced to do so '.[221] This attitude was rejected by another speaker. ' Is it not significant ', he suggested, ' that interest in peaceful change has become most acute just at the time when there is the least possibility of making peaceful changes, and is not one of the reasons why conferences are being held at the moment the fact that there is a threat of war if changes are not made ? It is, therefore, precisely this threat of war which it is most necessary to avoid by making some sort of concessions . . . Certain problems have arisen at the present time just because the threat of war exists, and the question for the future will be how to avoid the occurrence of such problems '. It seemed to this speaker, therefore, ' that even though changes are being demanded as a price, let us say, for the avoidance of war, that is not necessarily a reason why they should be given no consideration at the present time '.[224]

---

[a] Cf. above, p. 12, note a.

PART ONE

THE PROBLEM STATED

Chapter 2

National Needs, Grievances, Claims and Aspirations

I. THE CLAIMANTS AND THEIR CLAIMS

The introductory chapter of this survey has described the circumstances which led the International Studies Conference, in 1935, to undertake a two-year enquiry into the substance of certain national aspirations which had been expressed in specific claims for changes in the international *status quo*, into the difficulties obstructing the achievement of such changes, and into peaceful methods of overcoming those difficulties. As a result of the Conference's study, facts might be brought to light which would have a bearing on the solution of the fundamental problems constituting the needs, or occasioning the grievances, which give rise to claims and aspirations. What were those problems and which were the claims?

Now 'it must be admitted that the terms employed by the Conference to express its intentions leave those intentions somewhat obscure'.[188] [a] In the light of subsequent declarations, it is clear enough that the Conference contemplated an enquiry into demographic problems, on the one hand, and into marketing and raw materials problems, on the other hand; but the Conference gave no explicit indication either of the specific national claims and aspirations to which these two sets of problems had given rise or of the particular changes in

[a] The terms of reference adopted by the Conference for its study of " peaceful change " are quoted in the Foreword, p. vii. ' The ambiguity, or lack of precision, in that formula reflected . . . a compromise between some who had favoured a treatment of population problems, as such [see *33*], and others who wanted . . . a study of the peaceful change problem in general' (*177*); the former proposal was partly prompted by the circumstance that a study of " state measures affecting international migration ", which was originally placed on the agenda of the International Studies Conference in 1931 (see *231*), had had to be postponed.

the *status quo* which were demanded.   It may be presumed, however, that, inasmuch as ' the International Studies Conference is influenced in the choice of its subject by world public opinion ',[186] the claims and changes which the Conference had in mind and which it apparently assumed to be mat ers of common knowledge[a] were those to which authoritative exponents of international affairs in various countries, and particularly in Great Britain, where the Conference was holding its session,[b] were then directing their attention.

In 1935, public opinion was fastened on the grievances, real or alleged, of certain countries which were represented as being dissatisfied with the position that they occupied in a community of nations composed of two numerically unequal categories of Powers : ' on the one hand, there would be the satisfied, well-provided, satiate, bourgeois, possessor nations, *die Besitzenden, die befriedigten Nationen*, the *sodisfatti*, and, on the other, the unsatisfied, unprovided, hungry, proletarian nations, *die Habenichtse*, the *insodisfatti* '[376] — or, to use a terminology which had become current in the English-speaking countries, a large number of " haves " and a few " have-nots ".   These " dissatisfied " countries were held to have put forward various claims, the satisfaction of which was designed to remove the sources of their grievances. According to contemporary statements of the nature of these claims as it was apprehended outside the " dissatisfied " countries themselves, the principal " have-not " Powers were Germany, Italy and Japan (with the possible addition of Poland), and the principal claim was a German demand for a re-consideration of the colonial re-arrangements which had been made in 1919.[c]   It was suggested, more specifically, that ' three types of claim — to *terre irridente*, to outlets for emigration, and to industrial markets and sources of supply — perhaps cover, between them, most of the concrete grievances of the discontented Powers '.[185]

---

[a] Cf. above, p. 8, note e, and the reference to the substance of the question made at one of the Conference's meetings in 1935 in an allusion to ' claims . . . regarding raw materials, population, food stuff and so on ' (*23*).

[b] The spokesmen of the Conference's member-institutions in Great Britain — the British Co-ordinating Committee for International Studies — and in the United States — the Council on Foreign Relations — had taken a leading part in the discussions of a sub-committee of the Conference which prepared the formula defining the scope of the " peaceful change " study.   See *31* and *32*.

[c] For illustrations of such statements, see, for example, *131, 176* and *185*. Among the studies of " claims " which have been published since the conclusion of the International Studies Conference's enquiry on " peaceful change ", the following have been utilised in the preparation of the present survey : *328, 348, 376, 394*.

The proposition which flows from this interpretation of the Conference's intentions is that population, marketing and raw material problems in the " dissatisfied " countries are at the root of grievances giving rise to aspirations expressed in claims for changes in the *status quo* and that the preservation of peace may be a function of the satisfaction of those claims. This proposition may be a legitimate premise upon which to institute an enquiry into the question of " peaceful change "; but, since the first object of an enquiry destined to culminate in an analysis of the difficulties which may obstruct the peaceful solution of problems which are considered to be a source of international friction must be to consider the nature of those problems, it is a proposition which must be tested in the light of definite instances of claims and demands authoritatively formulated in the so-called " dissatisfied " countries. For, if they have not been formulated by the alleged claimants, they may be fictitious; and, if they have not been authoritatively put forward, they may be misleading.

The Conference itself, however, was content to postulate by implication that the statements of claims attributable to publicists in England and in other " satisfied " countries were founded upon palpable evidence that such claims had been authoritatively formulated in the " dissatisfied " countries themselves. With a view to ensuring an early verification of the validity of this postulate, several members of the Conference expressed a fear, at the outset of the enquiry into peaceful change, lest the subject be treated *in abstracto*, and they insisted that ' a study of concrete problems would constitute the most useful contribution towards a better understanding of the problem of " peaceful change " '.[a] The Conference's General Rapporteur likewise took an early opportunity of warning the Conference against a danger which might vitiate its work — ' the danger of generalities and abstract reasoning '. It was necessary, he pointed out, ' to concentrate upon real issues, to deal with the proposed subject in the light of certain special questions, certain particular claims '. The Conference, he added, was not concerned with questions of population, etc. as such, but ' only in so far as they gave rise to claims, needs or aspirations which imply a modification of the *status quo* of the existing international relations '. If, he said, the Conference's analysis of the problem was to lead to substantial results, ' it is necessary that it should rest upon

---

[a] I.I.I.C. document no. K. 68. 1936, p. 5.

cases which are borrowed from real life . . .; [the Conference] should not shirk current problems . . .' [34]

Yet, although the General Rapporteur's recommendation was subsequently repeated by him[40 a] and endorsed by several Members of the Conference,[b] it was not carried out. A two-year plan of study was elaborated which gave no clue to the concrete instances of claims which were to be the pivot upon which the whole of the Conference's enquiry would turn; and, when the study of peaceful change came to an end, no systematic survey had been made of the claims tacitly postulated at the opening of the enquiry.

A silence so long preserved is too odd not to arrest attention. It cannot be explained on the ground that it was superfluous to state claims which might be assumed to be matters of common knowledge; for, although this assumption was undoubtedly made when the Conference opened its enquiry in 1935, it transpired in the course of the enquiry that the interpretation of international affairs which had become generally accepted outside the " dissatisfied " countries, and upon which the assumption rested, was not itself based upon any direct evidence of officially formulated demands advanced by those countries but was largely derived from the unverified hypothesis that a country with a grievance is, *ipso facto*, a country with a claim. This hypothesis proved, however, to be largely illusory. Except in the case of the Conference's member institutions in Poland — a country which, as some thought at the time and as recent events have shown, might legitimately be assimilated to the category of " have-not " Powers disposed to exercise warlike pressure for the purpose of bringing about

---

[a] The General Rapporteur did not himself specify, either then or at any later stage in the enquiry, any instances of " claims ", " needs " or " aspirations ". The only exception to the consistent reserve exercised by the central organs of the Conference in specifying the concrete situations which the Members of the Conference were invited to investigate is a belated allusion to two of them made in a plan of discussion for the 1937 session of the Conference which was prepared on June 12, 1937, by a Programme Committee which recommended that ' particular stress be laid on . . . specific cases of overpopulation (e. g., Italy, Poland) ' (*54*).

[b] e. g. : the Centro Italiano di Alti Studi Internazionali, which suggested that each national group taking part in the study should produce ' a statement of the needs and claims of its own country . . . and also an indication of the means which that country proposed to adopt in order to satisfy these needs and claims ' (*37*), but which subsequently withdrew from active participation in the work of the Conference; the Central Committee of Polish Institutions of Political Science (*36*); the British Co-ordinating Committee for International Studies (*35*); etc. The need for ' a brief statement of the changes in the *status quo* demanded by the dissatisfied Powers ' was also emphasised in a note addressed to the International Institute of Intellectual Co-operation by Lord Lugard (see *43*).

a modification of the equilibrium of international relations — none of the institutions in the " unsatisfied " countries whose position was held to be relevant in the context of the Conference's study of peaceful change produced any confirmation of the view taken outside those countries that their Governments were prepared to stand as formal claimants before the forum of satisfied nations.[a] On the contrary, as will be suggested in a moment, such evidence as was forthcoming from those countries tended to show that, whatever might be the sense of grievance under which they laboured, it was no part of their policy to translate their aspirations into official demands capable of being weighed in the international scales either of justice or of political expediency.[b] The essential difference between an official claim and a presumption that a claim exists was subsequently admitted parenthetically,[c] but the implications of the vital political distinction between a formal statement of a claim and an attitude which contrives to convey the impression that a demand has been authoritatively expressed do

[a] It is proper to point out, however, that, owing to the relatively scant collaboration which the International Studies Conference obtained from German, Italian and Japanese scientific institutions, the Conference found itself unable to make a systematic study of the problems which it had associated with the expansionist policies and aspirations of the three countries commonly regarded as the principal " have-nots " demanding changes in the *status quo*. On the other hand, it does not appear that this circumstance accounts for the Conference's failure to obtain evidence of the form of claim referred to in the text.

(German institutions withdrew from membership of the International Studies Conference in December 1933; since then individual German scholars only have taken part in the work of the Conference in some of its aspects but several studies prepared in Germany on subjects relevant to the Conference's enquiry and, apparently, inspired by the terms of reference of that enquiry, were placed at the disposal of the Conference through the International Institute of Intellectual Co-operation. The Italian institutions affiliated to the International Studies Conference did not participate actively in the study of " peaceful change " except in its earliest stages; with one exception (*178*), none of the Italian studies which were reported to be in course of preparation was made available to the Members of the Conference. No Japanese institutions are affiliated to the International Studies Conference, but individual Japanese scholars have taken part in sessions of the Conference and Japanese studies relevant to the problem of " peaceful change " were prepared for the Conference. *Note by the I.I.I.C.*).

[b] Cf. below, pp. 29-34 and 51-52.

[c] See, for example, *96* : —' The German demand for colonies has been developed only in recent years, though in 1926 a book by Hans Grimm, entitled *Volk ohne Raum*, attracted some attention. In *Mein Kampf* Herr Hitler declared that for the National-Socialist Party the pre-war commercial and colonial policy of Germany was a closed chapter ... But there has always been a demand for equality of status in the colonial field, and certain assurances appear to have been given to Germany at the time of the Locarno Treaty that when Germany became a member of the League she would, in fact, be eligible for a mandate if at any time one should be conferred. *There has, however, been no diplomatic request from Germany for the return of her former colonial possessions.* Diplomatic documents have said no more than that the German Government expected that " within a reasonable time the problem of colonial equality of rights ... will be clarified in the course of friendly negotiations " ... ' (The writer's italics).

not appear to have been generally recognised. On the contrary, it was re-affirmed, apparently without challenge, in the course of the Conference's enquiry, that ' among the most disturbing factors in international relations to-day are the claims for revision of the *status quo* put forward by certain dissatisfied States, based on alleged over-population within those States and underpopulation in other parts of the world ' and that ' there is considerable apprehension that, if earnest attention is not given to this source of dissatisfaction, it may become a grave threat to world peace '.[48]

Must one conclude, therefore, that, notwithstanding the International Studies Conference's tentative adoption in 1935 of the new analytical doctrine that the trend of contemporary international affairs can be most clearly apprehended by examining the ascertainable claims of Governments in the dissatisfied countries, the national aspirations which were intended to form part of the materials of the Conference's study are, not merely ' often not clearly formulated ',[154 a] but that, in fact, the postulated claims cannot be traced farther back than in the theoretical inferences of private students of international affairs ? (And may it not be that ' grievances are real in proportion as they are felt rather than with reference to their ultimate validity ' ?[183]) While answers to these questions do not properly fall within the scope of a survey concerned with one aspect only of the Conference's investigation, it may nevertheless be pointed out here that the Conference's General Rapporteur himself refrained, at the close of the enquiry into peaceful change, from endorsing the conclusion reached by the Conference at the end of its study of collective security that international conflicts ' are in most cases connected with claims for the modification of the *status quo* '.[b]

---

[a] Cf. *176* : — ' It is to be noted that . . . [Sir Samuel Hoare, in his famous declaration to the Assembly of the League of Nations in September 1935] was careful to limit his constructive proposal to . . . the better distribution of raw materials ' as a basis of claims, and that he did not refer to the demographic basis, namely ' pressure of population and the need of colonies to which surplus population can migrate '. In fact, he did not even refer to " claims ". Cf. also *366* : — ' As far as we knew, the German demand had never been precisely formulated '.

[b] Summarising the results of the Conference's study of collective security at the outset of its study of peaceful change, the Conference's General Rapporteur expressed the view in 1935 that it had demonstrated that, ' on the one hand, in order to fight against war with any chance of success, it is necessary to concentrate upon its causes by searching for the means of pacific settlement of disputes which lead up to war, and, on the other hand, that these conflicts are in most cases connected with claims for the modification of the *status quo* or with aspirations which, failing to find satisfaction in the existing juridical order, turn against it and attempt to change it ' (*34*). The reference to claims is omitted from the similar statement (see above, p. 11) made by the General Rapporteur in 1937.

II. POPULATION, MARKETS AND RAW MATERIALS

In the absence of evidence of claims, the task of surveying the results of the Conference's investigations presents an embarrassing difficulty.[a] The difficulty is not mitigated by the circumstance that,

---

[a] The difficulties of exposition consequential upon the adoption of the "claims" method of stating international problems are illustrated in a memorandum submitted to the International Studies Conference (97), the preparation of which appears to have been prompted by the consideration that ' there is a growing consciousness that peaceful change is the alternative to serious trouble ' (p. 51). In the opening sentence of this memorandum, the object of which is to ' provide a basis on which to judge how far the purely economic difficulties of the dissatisfied Powers could be cured or mitigated by the colonial adjustments to which they lay claim ' (p. 51), it is stated that ' the principal source of present unrest undoubtedly lies in the claims for change which are being put forward by the three so-called "dissatisfied" Powers—Germany, Italy and Japan" (p.5). The basis of the claims is stated to be ' partly ... psychological, partly ... economic ' (p. 5) and their nature is indicated in the statement that ' prominent among them is a demand for colonial expansion ' (p. 5). The aim of the three Powers in putting forward such claims is also suggested : ' possibly the Powers in question concentrate upon this [colonial] issue because they see in it the greatest chance of success in achieving change of any kind; possibly it is because they feel that it will fulfil their chief needs — increased prestige, strategic gain, and relief from their economic plight ' (p. 5); and it is asserted that ' undoubtedly it [colonial expansion] would help to satisfy the first two needs ' (p. 5), the relationship between colonial expansion and the satisfaction of the third need being left to the reader's judgment (p. 5), though with the assistance, as will be indicated below, of the memorandum's conclusions. But the four-fold proposition that claims are of a specific character (' *the* claims '), that they have been formulated by the "dissatisfied" countries (claims ' put forward '), that the ' present unrest ' is attributable to the attitude or action of three particular countries (' *the* three ... Powers '), and, finally, that ' Germany, Italy and Japan ' are ' " dissatisfied " ' — propositions upon which the whole memorandum rests — are accepted without verification.

As to the first proposition (that specific claims are causing unrest), while it is implied in the memorandum that they are not exclusively colonial, colonial demands being merely ' prominent among them ' (p. 5), elsewhere it seems to be suggested, on the contrary, that they are exclusively colonial : ' since colonial claims are being put forward ...' (p. 7). As to the second proposition (that colonial claims have been ' put forward '), the only evidence given of any such action on the part of the claimants seems to be derived from rhetorical declarations made in the course of public speeches delivered in Germany and Italy by General von Epp (p. 7), Count Schwerin von Krosigk (p. 8) and Signor Mussolini (p. 9), from a diatribe by the Fascist Confederation of Industrialists against the failure of the allies to honour their treaty obligations to Italy (p. 9), from the suicide of two Japanese on the steps of the American Embassy in Tokyo on the announcement in 1924 that the United States had cancelled the Gentlemen's Agreement concerning migration and had bracketed the Japanese with Chinese by including them in the Oriental Expulsion chapter of the Immigration (Restriction) Act (p. 10), from a quotation in a London newspaper of a statement in *Nichi Nichi* on the policy of Mr. Hirota's new government (p. 11), from a presumption (perhaps warranted in fact, but perhaps not warranted in fact) that a statement by Sir Samuel Hoare to the League Assembly on September 11, 1935, was ' an official pronouncement ' by Great Britain on the subject of ' the prevailing discontent ' (p. 12), and from the threatening exclamation uttered by Dr. Goebbels in the course of a public speech delivered in Germany that ' it is dangerous for the world not to concede such demands, because some day the bomb will explode ' (p. 58). As to the third proposition (that there are three particular claimants : Germany, Italy and Japan), while the creation of a category of three "dissatis-fied" countries flows logically in the memorandum from the evidence just quoted in relation to the second proposition, the possibility that other countries also may be fittingly placed

in the case of the most important of the alleged claims, namely the German claim for a return of her former colonies, a discussion (reproduced at the end of this chapter) which took place at one of the Conference's concluding meetings[a] tends to show that German scientific opinion is disposed to repudiate, first, the suggestion implied in the Conference's formulation of the problem of " peaceful change " that official demands invested with the formal character of a diplomatic *démarche* have been put forward, and, secondly, the Conference's hypothesis that Germany's expansionist policy is attributable essentially to demographic, marketing or raw-material difficulties.

To meet this difficulty, it will have to be assumed, throughout this survey, that the " dissatisfied " countries are, if not open claimants, at any rate potential claimants to a modification of the *status quo* and that their claims are founded on the grievance that they are faced with demographic, marketing and raw-materials problems which, if not solved peacefully by means of international adjustments, must force them to pursue a policy of expansion.

n such a category is not considered.   Finally, as to the fourth proposition (that Germany, Italy and Japan are " dissatisfied "), the memorandum reaches the conclusions that, ' from the strictly economic point of view, any colonial changes must be of limited efficacy ' (p. 58), that ' undoubtedly the dissatisfied Powers tend, consciously or unconsciously, to overestimate the economic advantages of colonial change ' (p. 58) and that ' the cure for their difficulties is world-wide rather than colonial in scope ' (p. 58).   If these conclusions may be accepted on the basis of the facts presented in the memorandum, a question arises as to the evidence for the statement that the dissatisfied Powers overestimate advantages of changes which they are not shown to have demanded.   Moreover, the effect of these conclusions is to reject the memorandum's own implied postulate that Germany, Italy and Japan have chosen to stand as petitioners before a forum of satisfied nations, since " satisfaction " is not the same thing as " satiety " and it is clear that, in theory, the " satisfied " Powers might also be held to stand to gain or to lose from an extension or contraction of their colonial possessions.   Furthermore, is it a useful approach to the problem to postulate a psychological breach between certain " satisfied " and other " dissatisfied " countries in the context of an enquiry which concludes that the cure for difficulties is world-wide, since difficulties are not monopolised by the " dissatisfied " and since " satisfied " and " dissatisfied " alike can avail themselves of cures of a world-wide character ?

A further hypothesis upon which the memorandum is based, that the raw-materials issue constitutes ' a likely starting-point ' (p. 12) for the consideration of the question of peaceful change, seems to support the view here submitted that the preparation of the memorandum was prompted by a fictitious abstraction, generated by motives as well-intentioned on the part of those who resort to this analytical device as they are resented in the " dissatisfied " countries themselves, than by an immediate apprehension of concrete realities.   That this view is not without foundation seems to find further justification in the admission made in the memorandum that ' at the time of writing . . ., the British press and numerous pamphlets published by well-known writers are full of suggestions for possible colonial change, some of which ignore or under-estimate certain of . . . [the] important economic facts ' (p. 51) which the memorandum is designed to bring to light.

    [a] ' The discussions were . . . somewhat disorganised through the inevitably late statement of the German case ' (*229*).

It has already been indicated that, of the various postulated claims, the one which held the International Studies Conference's attention was the German claim to a colonial empire. It was not the intention of the Conference, however, to carry out a special enquiry into this specific claim. The Conference's object was, rather, to make a general study of the economic basis of expansionist policies, whether these aimed at the acquisition or extension of colonial possessions or at an enlargement of metropolitan boundaries. From the economic point of view, the main case, in simple terms, for a policy of colonial or continental expansion or, in other words, the ground upon which the real or alleged claims associated with those policies are based, is commonly stated to be that it is only in the acquisition of colonies or in the extension of territories at home that an effective remedy can be found for the unfavourable situations caused by pressure of population, on the one hand, or by restricted export markets and inadequate access to sources of raw materials, on the other hand.[a] Colonisation, pointed out the Conference's General Rapporteur, ' may serve to solve . . . the demographical difficulties resulting from overpopulation . . . [and] those connected with the problem of raw materials. Colonisation is therefore related to each of the two other topics '.[40]

Accordingly, the Conference organised separate enquiries into these two groups of problems. Had its study proceeded along these two main lines, it must have furnished an effective test of the validity of the argument that colonial and territorial expansionist aspirations are largely attributable to population pressure, on the one hand, and to marketing and raw-material maladjustments, on the other. In fact, however, the Conference pursued another course. Instead of regarding territorial and colonial claims as the expression of a need for relief from overpopulation, for larger and freer export markets and for easier access to supplies of raw-materials, the Conference instituted, side by side with its population, marketing[b] and raw-material studies, a special study of colonial questions (though not of other territorial questions)

[a] ' Over and above . . . [the concrete grievances of the discontented Powers] there remains a psychological demand which is assuredly the most insistent and formidable, as well as the most elusive and difficult, of any. And this psychological demand is the craving for equality of status with one's peers ' (*185*). Colonies and wide territories may also be coveted for political and military reasons. These non-economic aspects of the problem had not been specified in the Conference's terms of reference and they were not studied otherwise than incidentally.

[b] The enquiry into marketing problems was subsequently overshadowed by far more detailed studies of demographic and raw-material questions.

from which, broadly, the consideration of demographic, marketing and raw-material grievances was excluded.

In taking this step, the Conference, passing over the objections of the methodically-minded[a] and yielding to the pressure of those who were obsessed by the clamour for colonies, was broadening its enquiry beyond its original scope; for there may be, of course, demographic, marketing and raw-material problems giving rise to claims for change which cannot find their solution in the acquisition or expansion of colonial possessions, just as, on the other hand, there may be colonial problems giving rise to " peaceful change " claims which are unrelated to questions of population, marketing and raw materials. At the same time, in consequence of the modified organisation of its study, the Conference was side-tracked into lines of investigation bearing no perceptible connection with the narrowly circumscribed problem of " peaceful change " which had preoccupied it at the close of its study of " collective security ".[b]   Its doors were flung open to an abundance of memoranda and reports, not a few of which, whatever their intrinsic interest, are not relevant to either of the two main divisions of the enquiry, while, in the resulting competition for notice, several important aspects of the problem were either overlooked or inadequately investigated.   One of the purposes of the present survey is to attempt, within the limits of its subject-matter, to establish some balance between the

---

[a] At a meeting of the Programme Committee which drafted the terms of reference for the Conference's study of " peaceful change ", one of the members of the Committee had protested with some success against a proposal to place territorial questions on the same logical plane as population questions and raw-material questions (33), but the Committee ultimately accepted a compromise formula encumbered with the ambiguous inclusion of the terms " territorial" and " colonisation " (see above, p. 19, note a).   The point was raised again during a Preparatory Study Conference on Peaceful Change held at Madrid in the summer of 1936, one of the participants pointing out that ' neither logically nor chronologically ' did the problems present themselves in that order (47), while another speaker expressing a preference for the original division of the subject, argued that, in the context of peaceful change, the only relevant problems of colonisation were mainly related either to the availability of areas suitable for migration or to sources of raw materials or markets for manufactured goods (46); if, he afterwards conceded, there were other aspects of colonisation falling within the scope of an enquiry into peaceful change, they might be considered separately (ibid.).   These objections, however, were over-ruled, but it may be observed that the use of the term " colonisation " which had been given in the original terms of reference was discontinued thereafter and that it was replaced by the broader expression : " colonial questions ".

[b] Cf. 43 : — ' Some of the theses proposed [by Members of the Conference in response to a request (see 40) by the General Rapporteur] seem to have only a remote bearing on the immediate problem '; and 45 : — ' The subjects of study as proposed [for the Conference's enquiry into demographic problems], though interesting, seem to be little relevant to " peaceful change " '.

material assembled by the Conference and the requirements of a consecutive argument.

* * *

The subject to be treated in these pages, then, concerns the demographic basis of claims assumed to have been made by the " dissatisfied " countries for colonial or territorial expansion. The basis of the allegation that a need for relief from overpopulation is one of the principal economic sources of the claims for changes in the international *status quo* will be examined in the next chapter. On the basis of the evidence of such claims presented in chapter 3, an attempt will be made in chapter 4 to analyse the notion of overpopulation. The legitimacy of claims founded on pressure of population will be considered in chapter 5. The remaining chapters will deal with remedies for population problems in the " dissatisfied " countries; in a supplementary chapter, an illustration will be given of some of the difficulties involved in giving effect to these remedies.

Appendix

EXCERPTS FROM A DISCUSSION ON GERMANY'S CLAIMS
AT A MEETING OF THE
INTERNATIONAL STUDIES CONFERENCE HELD IN 1937

Dr. FRITZ BERBER (Berlin)[212]. — I should like to raise the question of our method of approach to the " solutions involving a change of sovereignty ", and to point out that a scientific or intellectual fallacy is involved in failing to distinguish between the abstract and concrete method. The abstract method of argument or the application of abstract rules is only legitimate if you have a long series of similar cases with analogous conditions to which similar rules can be applied. In political science it often merely results in putting the concrete purpose of the argument behind abstract formulæ and concealing the real issues.

Let me give proofs of this scientific fallacy. In the abstract method of argument allusion is frequently made to " certain countries " without their being specifically named. An interesting definition was given a few days ago of the word " honour " as meaning " to keep your contracts " and when I applied that abstract rule to the Légion d'Honneur I concluded it was an association of merchants which kept their contracts. That is the way you argue when you try to give a definition and discuss it under an abstract formula or when you say, for instance, that international relations are governed by three rules : good faith, no State to be both judge and party at the same time, and the denial of right to the *fait accompli*. It was, as a matter of fact, precisely the absence of those rules which led to the creation of the *status quo* in 1919, and it is because of their absence that the *status quo* is still maintained.

It may be very interesting to lay down an abstract rule such as " it is not legitimate to transfer native people like cattle ", but that was exactly the way in which people were transferred in 1919, which would lead one to suppose that there has been a complete change of outlook since then and that the world has moved towards idealism. That is the deception of abstract formulæ. In the consideration of concrete cases they are more apt to assist propaganda than to lead to the formulation of scientific truths, and I would warn this group of such fallacious reasoning. It is a method often used by States when making laws for specific cases, in order to show that the rule is a general one applying to all conditions when in reality it applies only to a single case.

For the question we are now discussing — " Transfer of territory : Solutions involving a change of sovereignty " — the method of formulating abstract rules is entirely inappropriate, since we are not faced with a situation in which solutions involving a change of sovereignty are necessary for an indefinite number of cases, and it is only in such a situation that abstract rules could have any meaning. Such a situation, for instance, would have arisen in 1919 had an effort been made to apply Wilson's Fourteen Points in the colonial field : i.e. a general readjustment of colonial claims, which would have obliged the Peace Conference to consider whether England, France, Belgium and Portugal should give part of their colonies, for instance, to Poland, a poor country and one that was unable to obtain reparations. For the present situation, however, that is not the problem.

In talking of Peaceful Change, we have in mind change without war — that follows, I think, from the fact that the Conference on Peaceful Change was preceded by one on Collective Security — and the political issues which imply a danger of war. But so far as transfers of territory involving danger of war are concerned, I do not think there is an indefinite number of possibilities or risks.

Countries are classified into " haves " and " have nots "; that is a classification which explains nothing, which is absolutely false, but which nevertheless is used in scientific research and discussion. Italy, for instance, is quoted as a " have not " country, while she was declared by Mussolini, to be no longer a " have not " country after the conquest of Abyssinia. In considering Peaceful Change in regard to Italy, therefore, one is led to the conclusion that a change unfavourable to that country is implied.

Then there is Germany, apparently the main problem in this connection, since a claim for the transfer of sovereignty was made semi-officially in a speech by Hitler on January 30th, 1937.

May I here remind you of the old Roman law notion that " the judge must not go beyond what the parties claim " ?   Now if we look at the Conference's programme, we see that judgment is to be given on claims that have never been made, but is not to be given on claims that have been made; in other words, the problems we are endeavouring to examine are quite different from those that have actually arisen. Germany has never claimed that because she is a " have not " country she ought to have colonies, yet that is the sort of claim it is proposed to consider here.

And here is what seems to be the main fallacy. You start from the point that nations have the right to get colonies from other Powers, or have a legitimate claim to them, if they can prove that they need them for their emigrants, their raw materials, or if the natives will not be transferred like cattle. Germany, however, has never made such a claim, and she, therefore, does not feel called upon to prove compliance with those conditions; nor does she feel that her case would be disproved if those conditions were not fulfilled. In other words, we have a court which examines claims that have never been made but does not examine those which have — a situation that arises simply from the method of using abstract terms for concrete situations.

Now solutions involving a change of sovereignty are really matters of politics; they may or may not be possible according to the general political situation. But there are political solutions, which are not possible when public opinion is against them. There may be an interest in some quarters to prove that certain solutions are impossible; it is therefore easy to start with a programme that seems likely to lead to a point at which changes may prove impossible . . . .

What I wanted to do was to comment on the method of approach to the discussion and to urge the importance of finding a satisfactory method of scientific approach which avoids the practice of disguising propaganda aims in scientific trappings and formulating abstract rules for concrete situations, but follows the lines adoped in all scientific and historical research. In laying down abstract rules there is always the danger that the concrete case itself may be thought to have been dealt with, thus bringing that peace of mind to scientists which has been advocated as desirable in the course of this discussion, but which seems wrong so long as the world is out of order...

Lord LYTTON.[219] — I wish to thank Dr. Berber for having introduced an element of reality into our discussions ... In the course of our discussions we have not yet been told of conditions in the colonial sphere which threaten the peace of the world or of the changes necessary to maintain peace ... I should like to put this point to ... [Dr. Berber] : it would help us very much if, some time or other during the sittings of this Conference..., he would indicate to us the procedure he would suggest as applicable for the consideration of the issue.   He has stated it as an issue of policy, but clearly it is not an issue which this Conference is called upon to determine ...

Prof. QUINCY WRIGHT (Chicago).[225] — ... Dr. Berber objected to what he called the " abstract method " in our discussion and referred to the problem of returning colonies to Germany as a " political " one.   I do not know just what the distinction between an abstract and a political approach is, but it seems to me that if a conference such as this is to make any contribution it must make it on the basis of general considerations.   If we attempt to reach solutions on the exigencies of a particular moment or a particular area, we shall never get anywhere, because the special interests of our countries will bias our scientific objectivity ...

I must say in defence of Dr. Berber that he did not directly state that the reason for returning colonies to Germany was that otherwise Germany would make war ...   He based his belief upon the cause of justice and referred to the fact that injustice was done to Germany in taking her colonies away from her.   On that point I entirely agree with him; it was an injustice. I also think that when America took the Philippines and Puerto Rico from Spain it was an injustice ...   In fact, in the light of history the contention that colonies must be redistributed because of injustices committed in their origin would, I fear, take us a long way ...

Dr. BERBER.[212] — ... I did not ... state the German claims; I merely said they had been made unofficially.   The question of honour is certainly not the principal one; it is more a question of right, of legal justice ... Professor Quincy Wright said that this was a political problem which could not be studied by a Conference such as this, but I do not agree.   I personally could propose twenty or more topics dealing with the problem on a scientific basis . . .

That does not mean, however, that it is because we need raw materials that we want our colonies back . . .

Lord Lytton has asked me to indicate what sort of procedure would be possible for the consideration of the German claims, but I am afraid he rather misunderstood me. I used the term " legal approach " symbolically, to indicate that a body such as this should try to maintain a standard of objectivity not lower than that of a court of law. I would not suggest that there is a possibility of setting up a tribunal of practical policy to adjust the German claims . . . I do not think that in international policy, you can build up an abstract system of, procedure, but that these things are arranged more or less politically.

We must distinguish between the material conditions of Peaceful Change and the formal or procedural conditions. Can we lay down general rules and, if not, can we treat concrete situations and provide different justifications for each ? Justifications can, of course, be of very various kinds; but there is a tendency to overstate the economic justifications and to understate the moral justifications, which are much more important in political life. For instance, if somebody has a legal right he has a moral justification. In our conception there is no such thing as a legal right against morality. Therefore, when Lord Lytton asks what the Conference can do, what sort of approach it should make, I would suggest the examination of the material conditions for the justification of Peaceful Change, and in some cases the formal conditions also.

I said that in so far as the transfer of territory was concerned abstract rules could not be laid down. I did not exclude abstract rules entirely . . . I merely referred to one aspect of the many problems involved and said that I did not think an abstract formula could be found for it. What I wanted to imply was that while the laying down of general and abstract formulæ in justification for the transfer of territory along the lines proposed in the agenda might be very useful for claims by Poland, Lithuania, Esthonia, Austria and Hungary, for instance, it must not thereby be thought that the problem of the German claims has been dealt with . . .

When I referred to Peaceful Change as a change for the avoidance of war, I did not intend to imply that there was danger of war in the event of Germany's colonies not being restored to her, because dangers of war arise from many causes and situations, but not generally from questions of principle. And here I come to an important point. Professor Quincy Wright

4

said that if one tried to apply the principle of justice to all colonial claims, or to remove injustices throughout history, one would never come to an end. I quite agree, but I would remind Professor Quincy Wright that in 1763 the British took away a French colony which the French tried to win back by war. What you are trying to do now is to say : " We are in a new world with a different conception of international relations; we want to create a method of change without war, and it is no use making parallels from history. "

To conclude, I would point out that my contribution has not been one on the German claims, but on the scientific approach to the question; it was made in order to urge the Conference to beware of the danger of basing its work on popular and misleading slogans, such as are current in every country, and to try to find a really objective line of approach.

Chapter 3

Population Claims

I. THE " DISSATISFIED " COUNTRIES

It is said that ' certain nations have . . . the impression that they have too many people in proportion to their territory and resources and that the standard of life of their nationals is thereby prejudiced '.[376] It is also sometimes said that certain countries which regard themselves as overpopulated are justified in their belief. ' It is common knowledge ', affirms an Italian authority, ' that there are certain countries that are overpopulated '.[42] In either case, the disproportions resulting from the unequal distribution of population in the various countries ' give rise to . . . claims among the more populous who, rightly or wrongly, think themselves overcrowded at home. These consider, more or less sincerely, that they are encircled, as if subjected to blockade, and claim that their existence is threatened; hence an extremely dangerous political tension '.[376] It is, therefore, essential, declares the Italian writer just quoted, ' that this demographic congestion should be relieved by distributing this excess population over underpopulated territories . . . The needs of the overpopulated countries ', he insisted in the autumn of 1935, ' are becoming more and more urgent; these needs cannot be satisfied other than by recourse to force . . . or by an organic system of permanent agreements or collaboration '. To obviate recourse to force, ' let the frontiers . . . be thrown open to men '.[42]

Thus, ' one of the types of demand put forward by the dissatisfied countries ' appears to be for ' opportunities for emigration to less densely populated countries '.[185] " Overpopulation " is considered to be ' one of the most effective grounds on which to base claims for changes in the *status quo* '.[55] Which, then, are the overpopulated countries whose demographic tension impels them to envisage the adoption of expansionist policies, who are claiming outlets for the disposal of their surplus numbers, and whose difficulties, if not eliminated by processes of peaceful change, may threaten the maintenance of international peace?

It was pointed out in the previous chapter that, in the absence of authoritative statements of claims from the " dissatisfied " countries themselves, the International Studies Conference's enquiry was largely based upon the indirect evidence of foreign students of international affairs. If one must accept the external testimony of American, British, French and other " neutral " observers, it would seem that the principal victims of population pressure are Germany, Italy and Japan, with the possible addition of Poland, and that the principal claimants for international relief as an alternative to territorial and colonial expansion are Germany and Italy certainly, Japan probably and Poland possibly.[a] ' Germany, Italy and Japan ', writes a French authority, ' complain that they have not enough colonial dependencies to which they can send settlers '.[376] ' Poland, it is said, would like to join the " big three " but she has stopped short of taking up a definite attitude '.[113] The first three countries, states another French authority, are those ' where particular mention is made of overpopulation and where, on the plea of overpopulation, claims are formulated which are deserving of consideration and which, if they are not satisfied, are likely to lead to conflicts, perhaps very serious conflicts '.[200] ' In view of the political situation in the world ', he is reported to have declared on another occasion, ' [the relative overpopulation of Germany, Italy, Japan and Poland presents] the chief threat of trouble. These are countries in which the standard of living is . . . inferior to the standard of living prevailing in neighbouring countries. It is this fact that gives rise to the demands with which one is familiar '.[51]

Apart from Germany, Italy, Japan and Poland, there are a number of other countries who have to face difficulties arising out of demographic maladjustments;[b] but their problems are not thought to raise issues of " peaceful change "[c]. The " big three " have, indeed, them-

---

[a] See, for example, *43, 55, 113, 154, 176, 185,* etc. In each of these studies, pressure of population at home and the need for outlets for surplus population are noted as grounds for grievances, aspirations or claims implying changes in the *status quo* in some or all of these countries.

[b] See below, pp. 59-61.

[c] See above, pp. 12-15.

selves seen to it that the group of "have-not" Powers shall remain small and compact. 'Germany, Italy and Japan have never at any time shown an intention to associate with their desires those of countries of lesser importance, probably because they think that their individual claims would not thereby gain in force . . .; by separate agreement the revisionist Powers have allied themselves in order to group their efforts. The common front of the dictatorial régime thus constituted will probably claim to formulate complaints against international society in a manner more and more forceful and vehement. If there is no way of giving satisfaction to these complaints it is to be feared that their authors will continue to use illegal means to satisfy them and that the *Realpolitik* will achieve new successes — if, that is to say, it does not end by experiencing some striking setback the consequences of which might be no less dangerous. Before the pillars of the temple of civilization are any more shaken an attempt must be made, if there is still time, to find a compromise; practical utility demands this even more than absolute justice'.[376] This is the problem of "peaceful change" which the International Studies Conference sought to investigate.

There are, of course, variations in the foreign interpretations of claims, of their justification, and of the changes which they envisage. Thus one authority considers that 'Germany is much better able than either of her two companions in discontent [Italy and Japan] to maintain her population within her own existing [1936] frontiers' and that 'from an economic point of view . . . [the] grievance of being excluded from colonial markets and sources of supply is perhaps a greater grievance . . . [for all three countries] than that of restrictions upon migration'.[185] Another, writing in 1936, admits that 'the demand of Germany for colonies, and of Italy for an extension of her colonial empire, is based . . . [partly on the ground] of pressure of population and the need of colonies to which surplus population can emigrate', but he repudiates the contention that Japan might need colonies as outlets for her population, though without implying, of course, that Japan is not faced with a population problem.[176]

Some of the views which have been cited were expressed during the earlier stages of the International Studies Conference's enquiry, but the march of events in 1935-1937 outstripped the Conference, so that, towards the close of the enquiry, the "dissatisfied" countries were thought to have been reduced in number or to have shifted the

ground of their claims. Writing not long before the conclusion of
the enquiry, an American authority[55] noted that ' current discussion of
peaceful change is centred primarily on the demand of Germany for
the return of her colonies ', " overpopulation " having been ' vigorously
advanced as a basis for Germany's demands ', but that ' the claims of
Japan and Italy for more territory in order to relieve their population
pressures ' had become ' less pressing at the moment because already
gratified in large part '. Japan, whose ' action ... in causing
Manchuria to be separated from China has been most often justified
on ... [the] ground [of overcrowding] ... is already stressing her need
for access to raw materials and markets ', while Italy, whose ' Ethiopian
adventure ' had also been justified on this ground, ' admits that she is
a " satiated " State for the time being, while digesting her new African
Empire '. On the other hand, Poland now seemed ' to be preparing
to come forth with demands for changes in the *status quo* as a means of
relieving her population pressure '.[a]

Finally, there are those who seem unimpressed by any of these
views,[b] while others seem to think that the acuity of the problem has
been unduly magnified. If it is true, as one observer believes it is,
that, ' outside territorial Russia, Italy to-day ... [is] the only country
[in Europe] in which there ... [is] any rapid increase of population ...,
it ... [means] that one of the most tremendous pressures in the
world ... [is] relaxing '; this, he suggests, is ' a vital factor in the
question of revision '.[175]

Taken as a whole, the testimony of the experts outside the " dissatisfied " countries appears conflicting and perplexing. There is
disagreement on the reality of a problem of overpopulation; some say
that certain countries are overpopulated, others that they merely think
themselves overpopulated. There is disagreement on the reality of
claims for relief; some consider that certain countries have put forward
claims, others that they have been withdrawn. And there is disagreement on the remedies; some look to emigration, others to internal
measures. Thus the external evidence does not seem very impressive;
it hardly bears out the premise on which the International Studies

[a] Cf. *176* : — ' *The Times* correspondent reports that Poland ... has even gone so far
as to name the territories to which she claims rights. Czechoslovakia and Yugoslavia will
doubtless soon follow '.
[b] In a discussion by members of the Royal Institute of International Affairs in London
which followed an address on " claims ", only one allusion was made to overpopulation as
a basis for demands for " peaceful change "; see *185*.

Conference opened its enquiry, namely, that demographic congestion is one of the principal economic sources of national grievances giving rise to expansionist aspirations expressed in demands for changes in the *status quo*; it seems to corroborate the suggestion made in the preceding chapter that, in the absence of authoritatively formulated claims involving demographic re-adjustments, the " claims " approach to the study of international problems is not illuminating.   Yet is has behind it a weight of authority which commands respect.   It is necessary, therefore, to consider the facts somewhat more closely.

II. ITALY

Of the three principal " dissatisfied " Powers, Italy is commonly regarded as the one which suffers most acutely from overcrowding. Not only do Italians themselves insist that ' Italy is . . . an over-populated country and [that] there is no possibility of this surplus population finding room within the country ',[41] but foreign authorities also hold the view that in Italy, where ' the population is fairly dense while the proportion of the inhabitants engaged in agriculture is very high . . ., the evidence goes to show that . . . [the country is] certainly . . . overcrowded . . .   Italy was already showing signs of congestion in rural areas in 1900 . . .   After the War signs of congestion became more evident . . .   Germany and Italy have nearly the same density of population, a relatively high density . . .   But in Italy nearly half the population is engaged in agriculture as against little more than a quarter in Germany; also less of the total area is . . . [land other than arable land, permanent grass and pasture, and wood and forest] in Germany than in Italy.   Clearly more labour is applied to a given amount of land in the latter than in the former country; and this is no doubt due to the fact that the power and raw materials required for industrial development are much scarcer in Italy than in Germany, thus creating relatively few opportunites for industrial employment '.[81]   Moreover, in Italy ' the standard of life is distinctly lower than in Germany '.[113] Furthermore, the overcrowding in Italy ' is not of the kind that can be relieved immediately by a resumption of world economic activity as is the case with such western European countries as may for a time in one sense be overpopulated.   For, owing to paucity of the facilities at present essential to industrial development, no considerable expansion of industrial employment is possible; so long as industry rests upon its present foundations, it is a delusion to suppose that . . . [Italy] can imitate the example of England and find an outlet for an increasing population in industry '.[84] For these reasons emigration is, as has already been indicated, often held to be the only effective solution for Italy's demographic problem.

When the International Studies Conference began its enquiry, it was generally assumed outside Italy that ' Italy considers itself as overpopulated and ascribes the relatively low standard of living to this fact '.[131] Italy, it was said, is a country whence ' there come loud complaints of congestion ',[84] and the Italian author of a paper prepared for the Conference sought to explain that ' there are two possible remedies . . . : industrial development and colonial expansion. Since, however, industrial development is bound up with that of raw materials, the two solutions are complementary '.[41] Subsequently, outside opinions differed as to whether ' new outlets for surplus population are wanted '[131] by Italy or whether Italy, ' having conquered Ethiopia, had satisfied her appetite for territory '.[113] Although, prior to the establishment of the Italian Empire, Italy had ' on many occasions . . . tried to call attention before the League of Nations and the International Labour Organisation to the contrasts existing between the " overpopulated " and the " underpopulated " nations ',[155] now, ' for the time being, nothing further is heard of the aims which she seemed to be directing towards the Balkans and the Near East. To use a common expression that is not quite clear in itself, she is claiming chiefly a redistribution of raw materials '.[113]

III. JAPAN

Unlike Italy, Japan, ' the great " dissatisfied " nation in the Pacific area ',[128] is not so generally considered either by foreign observers or by the Japanese themselves to have a need for emigration outlets. ' Contrary to the widely held opinion that Japan is overpopulated, and that internal pressure is likely to force the Japanese to emigrate on a scale that may constitute a danger to international peace . . ., it is the unprecedented industrial development of the country that has stimulated the growth of the population, and . . . there is no reason, either psychological or economic, for expecting any great increase in the near future in the number of emigrants from Japan '.[306] Moreover, it has been argued that, even if Japan could be shown to have a need for emigration, her claims, 'though frequently bracketed with those of Italy and Germany . . ., are not analogous. She has large undeveloped territory in Formosa, to which emigration has been negligible, and in Manchuria '.[154]

According to one foreign student of Japanese affairs, the reality of a demographic problem in Japan is not open to doubt. After recalling that 'the Japanese population hardly grew at all during the long period of autarky following the failure of Hideyoshi's Korean expedition in the early 17th century ', he notes that, 'when Japan was drawn into the orbit of Western industrialism in the middle of the nineteenth century, the limits of population growth were lifted and a cumulative process of increase began as the increasing number of children passed into the reproductive age-groups '; but he does not envisage emigration as a method of relieving ' the pressure of population upon limited resources in such a case '; he considers it ' obvious that . . . [it] can only be relieved by industrial development, which involves access to raw materials and markets for manufactures '.[154]

Whether Japan is or is not suffering from overcrowding and whether she needs or does not need relief through emigration, from the point of view of the International Studies Conference's enquiry it is relevant to point out that, according to a review of the work of the Institute of Pacific Relations in which authoritative Japanese opinion is given expression, ' we do not find Japan making sweeping demands for territory to which her people may migrate, or for access to sources of raw materials or to markets ';[128 a] on the other hand, ' it was a foregone conclusion that had such demands been made they would have been denied for it lay within the sovereign right of other nations to accord or deny them ',[128] while abstention from the present-ation of claims has not been tallied by abstention from making sweeping acquisitions of territory. But it would seem that, if Japan has any claims, they are of a different order: ' they refer to outlets for her exports, which she would like to be as large as possible and which become more and more closed to her, because the danger that Japanese competition represents for national productions becomes evident almost every-where '.[113]

---

[a] A Japanese plea for an outlet for population and Japanese dissatisfaction with the immigration laws of the English-speaking countries were discussed, however, by the Institute of Pacific Relations in 1925 (see *128*).

IV. POLAND

While the International Studies Conference's enquiry was in progress, a colonial campaign, emulating Germany's colonial campaign, was launched in Poland. In the summer of 1935, when the Conference was opening its study of " peaceful change ", none but the closest foreign observers of Polish affairs was aware that a movement was afoot to make Poland " colonial-minded ". In 1928, there had been constituted an Association of Colonial Pioneers which, two years later, had coalesced with the Maritime and River League to form a Maritime and Colonial League.[376] [328] The new League ' started an active campaign of propaganda on behalf of Polish overseas expansion ',[328] and ' tried to inculcate the colonial idea into the masses, relying on arguments of prestige : Poland will not be a Great Power of world-wide influence until her flag flies in other continents. But the masses remained refractory and the Government was for a long time reserved ',[376] though, in 1933, the argument was submitted to the Diet that, ' by an application of the principle governing the succession rights of states, the new claim was legally linked to the claim of Germany '.[328]

It was not, however, until 1936 and 1937 ' that more frequent and vigorous expression was given to new considerations ' and that the Polish government associated itself with the colonial propaganda.[a] ' Poland's claims with regard to raw materials and to colonies were formulated . . . before the Seym and the Senate, and more particularly at Geneva during the discussions which gave rise to the study of the problem of access to raw materials and the problem of human migrations '.[328] On August 19, 1936, speaking before the Seym, Colonel Beck ' alleged that his country, Poland, was in the same position as Germany from the point of view of the rapid rate of demographic increase and paucity of raw materials, in particular colonial raw materials, and that if colonies were restored to the Reich she would have the right to claim, since she had inherited former German territory, a share in proportion to the area of these old provinces relative to the territory of the pre-war Reich (i. e. about 15%).[b] Moreover, by the devastation

---

[a] The Polish Ministry of Foreign Affairs has compiled a ' recueil de documents relatifs à la politique coloniale ' (see *328*).

[b] The argument that ' Poland, being a country which comprises part of former German territory possesses an " inherited right " to part of the former colonial territory of the Reich and can lay claim to it ' (*345*), has been used in Warsaw as recently as October 1938.

which she suffered during the War and by the sacrifice of sons who put a stop to Bolshevism in 1920, Poland could be said to have acquired a moral right to satisfaction in the colonial field '.[376] [a] ' From the national plane the question passed rapidly to the international plane. On October 5, 1936, in the Economic Committee of the League of Nations and on the following day in the Mandates Commission, the representatives of the Government of Warsaw made a colonial claim which they justified by the two facts that the purchase of raw materials represents half the imports of Poland and that the movement of emigration from the country ... [was] completely stopped ... At home a colonial week was inaugurated in November 1936 in order to propagate the colonial idea and collect funds for colonial activity '.[376]

The Polish claims were now being noticed by foreign journalists[b] and foreign students of international affairs.[c] ' They were referred to quite recently again at Warsaw on January 10, 1938 ... in the Foreign Affairs Commission of the Diet '.[334]

' Although the Polish claim was advanced at the same time as the German claim, it presents certain features which distinguish it clearly from the latter. In the first place, the Polish claim cannot be as definite as Germany's since it refers to no pre-determined territory ...[d] Secondly, the Polish claim is ... bound up in Poland itself with preoccupations of a more general character. The overseas expansion of Poland is regarded not only as an imperative economic " necessity ", not only as a political act — an act of internal as well as of external policy — but also as an effort calculated to give a whole nation a kind of moral training '.[328]

' It would seem that, first of all, the Polish Government expected that Poland's overseas expansion would provide a partial but direct solution of the emigration problem. Emigration from Poland is to-day practically at a standstill. The extent to which it was practised

---

[a] The argument that colonies are a reward for military valour is double-edged. ' The argument put forward in French circles according to which France could not restore to Germany colonies which she conquered at the price of bloody sacrifices gives rise to protests in German circles. The *Boersen Zeitung* maintains that this thesis is dangerous because France replies to the German claim to justice by an argument based on violence. If taken seriously this argument means that France rejects the method of negotiation and shows Germany the way to violence. But Germany has declared that colonies are not a subject for war ' (*257*).

[b] See above, p. 38, note a.

[c] Cf. above, pp. 20 and 36.

[d] Cf., however, the statement by Colonel Beck quoted above, p. 42.

for many years is well known. In 1913, it was estimated that there were more than 400,000 seasonal emigrants who left Poland regularly for other countries, particularly Germany. About 250,000 persons are said to have emigrated each year to overseas countries.[a] In 1920, 116,000 Poles are stated to have left their country. The number of emigrants rose in the years following, reaching 127,000 in 1922, and 200,000 in 1924. The figure fell in 1925 owing to various circumstances, particularly the immigration restrictions applied in the United States, but this fall was only temporary and, in 1929, the number of Polish emigrants rose to over 240,000. The restrictions imposed as from that date by . . . [various countries] on Polish immigration acted as a rather sudden brake on the number of emigrants. In 1931, as against 80,000 emigrants, 90,000 Poles are thought to have returned to their country; in 1935, there were 53,000 emigrants as compared with 55,400 who returned home. Now the natural increase in the population of Poland is held to be about 400,000 per annum. The general desire to find employment abroad for the surplus population has led to an examination of the extent to which colonial lands at present undeveloped could receive Polish workers '.[328]

' This general desire, however, is accompanied by a more specific aim '.[328] In his address to the Seym of August 1936, Colonel Beck had ' added that it was to Poland before any other Power that the mandate over Palestine should have been entrusted, in order to give an outlet for its Jewish population ', and, in October of the same year, Polish delegates to meetings of the League of Nations had called attention to the fact that, owing to the cessation of emigration abroad, ' the problem resulting from Jewish proliferation became daily more serious '.[376] ' The Polish Government seems to be determined to encourage the emigration of at least a portion of the Jewish population of Poland. For a number of years following the war, the movement of Jewish emigrants was directed towards Palestine . . . Without confining their action to directing Jewish emigration towards Palestine, the Polish authorities felt that steps should be taken to find other outlets. There is, in fact, nothing to justify the hope that the Jewish problem

---

[a] Cf. 84 : — ' Up to 1914 some 600,000 Poles had moved from that part of Poland which was formerly included in Germany, to settle in parts of Germany which were not ethnographically Polish, and over a million Poles had left what was formerly Russian Poland to settle in other parts of Russia. There was in addition a strong seasonal movement of agricultural workers into Germany proper which reached a total of 300,000 in some years '.

will become less acute in the future.[a]   On the contrary, it must be expected that the material and moral condition of the Jewish minority will grow worse in the course of the next few years.   Any improvement in the standard of living of the peasant classes encourages an increasing number of young Poles belonging to agricultural families to take up some commercial occupation.   As in Hungary, moreover, the disfavour with which the nobility and middle classes formerly looked upon these same business occupations is dying out.   Access to these occupations, which to-day are almost completely filled by the Jews, is beginning to arouse such rivalry that the outcome cannot but be to the detriment of the Jewish sections of the population.   It should be added — and this would seem to be an essential point — that the efforts that are being made by the Government with a view to centralizing, co-ordinating and even directing the economic activity of the country, the setting up, in particular, of new financial institutions — for the assistance of farmers and artisans — controlled by the State or by the local authorities, the introduction of new systems of production or exchange, e. g. co-operative societies, the change thus brought about in the rôle of middlemen in the Polish population — all these factors result, at least indirectly, in depriving the Jews of their traditional occupations and jeopardize the livelihood of the young Jewish generations.[328] [b]

The view has been expressed that Polish colonial claims ' do not deserve to hold one's attention ', and that Poland ' gives too obviously the impression, by the lack of seriousness in her colonial claims, that they are for her simply an eventual means of bargaining in international conferences '.   It is suggested that ' Poland would be better advised to begin by colonising her own territory which is one of the largest in Europe, which includes immense non-cultivated areas, and the equipment of which still remains largely to be created '.[376]   So far as

[a] Cf. *84* : — ' In most countries the Jewish birth-rate is related to the birth-rate of the people among whom they are living; it is, generally speaking, high in eastern Europe and low in western Europe.   But it is an almost invariable rule that the Jewish birth-rate is lower than the surrounding birth-rate.   [The author of *93*] . . . has collected statistics for sixteen different countries and five large cities ; in every case, with the exception of New York, the birth-rate of the Jews is lower, and in most cases much lower, than that of the non-Jews.   Thus . . . [he] gives the birth-rate for Jews in Poland in 1929 as 20.0 per 1,000, and for non-Jews as 31.1 per 1,000 . . .   If . . . [his] figures are correct, the extinction of the Jews is in sight . . .   But there are not materials for making the calculation . . . [of] specific fertility rates for Jews in Poland . . . .'

[b] ' The Polish Government, moreover, expects that the adoption of a colonial policy will bring about an improvement in the present situation ruling on the foreign exchange market ' (*328*).

the International Studies Conference is concerned, the threatening
language used by the author of a Polish memorandum may account
for his failure to arouse any general interest in Poland's demographic
situation :

Poland — he declared — is faced with [demographic] problems that
cannot be solved by applying the methods used hitherto under the liberal
economic system.   For a nation that has the will to live, however, no problem
is insoluble.   Italy is solving her population problems by the conquest of
Abyssinia.   Poland is not thinking of conquests, but she can adopt a system
of planned economics of a strictly autarkic character by completely abandoning the gold standard . . .   The essential condition for the success of
such a system of planned economy lies in the total emancipation of the
country's monetary and credit policy from foreign money markets.[143]

The difficulties which such a policy would entail, he added, cannot
' deter a nation which has a surplus of labour and which is suffering from
a shortage of gold and opportunities for productive capital outlay ' :

It was the countries rich in gold and sparsely populated — and first
of all the United States — that began to close their doors to immigration
from countries which are overpopulated and poor in liquid capital.   To-
day, sparsely populated countries are already obliged to restrict their agricultural production since they are no longer able to find a market for it
in the overpopulated countries.   The gradual disappearance of international
exchanges will become more and more marked, until the wealthy and sparsely
populated countries or the countries having a low rate of population increase
realise that there can be no free international movement of goods without
the co-existence of a free migration of labour from specially poor countries
towards those well supplied with capital, and of a movement not only of
credits but also of productive capital from countries that are highly industrialised towards those which, industrially, are insufficiently developed.[143 a]

It would be more exact, perhaps, to speak of Polish " aspirations "
than of Polish " claims ",[b] but, in view of the ambiguities and contra-

---

[a] A still more menacing passage in another Polish memorandum submitted to the
Conference may also be held to relate to pressure of population in Poland : — ' If no fitting
solution is found, so much the worse for the "haves" ' (144).
[b] Cf. the title of 328.

dictions characterising the statements of claims held to have been formulated by, or put forward on behalf of, the other " dissatisfied " Powers, on the one hand, and of the recent tangible evidence afforded in Cieszyn (Teschen) of the Polish government's readiness to modify the territorial *status quo*, on the other hand, it seems proper to assimilate Poland in this survey to the category of the " big three " and to enquire in some detail into her demographic situation.

V. GERMANY

Reference has already been made to the difficulties springing from the circumstance that the discussion of Germany's " claims " is not based upon claims formulated by the German government, but mainly upon an arbitrary assumption abroad that such claims have been put forward. It may be objected that, from the point of view of the maintenance of peace, the circumstance that " dissatisfied " countries may not have made any formal declarations of population claims is not in itself reassuring and that account must also be taken of any informal demands made by their political leaders and publicists. In the case of those countries, in particular, where the discussion of public affairs is controlled by the state and where, as in Germany, the system of internal censorhip is so severe that even acceptable foreign news, for example, may be withheld from public communication for as much as twenty-four hours,[a] it might not unreasonably be inferred that every

---

[a] In November 1938, Dr. Goebbels, the German Propaganda Minister, said that ' it was not the business of . . . the Press and the broadcasting system . . . to purvey the latest news to every breakfast table but to fulfil an important function in the life of the State . . . : " During the Four-Power Conference in Munich the public sat at their wireless sets waiting tensely for the latest news of the progress of the conversations . . .   In these critical hours, I could take but little account of inner needs, because in the great decision which was to be made at Munich the existence of the nation was at stake . . .   For the leaders of the State it was of the utmost importance during the whole period of the crisis that so-called situation reports broadcast by the German stations should not give foreign circles the slightest possibility of seeing through the tactics of the German partner to the negotiations and, perhaps, countering them.   So in Munich we attained our objective " . . .   [Referring] to the fact that President Roosevelt's telegram was published in the German newspapers 24 hours later than abroad, he said : — " On the day of the great demonstration in the Sportpalast . . . the message was given out to all the great American newspapers for publication and also for broadcast.   The German Press and radio informed their readers and listeners one day later — and again for good reasons.   In the foreground of German policy stood at that time the speech of the Führer in the Sportpalast, and nothing else.   The attempt of the foreign Press to deprive us of the initiative by intervening with the Roosevelt message had to be repelled by us.   Nothing is more dangerous than to leave the offensive to the opponents in time of crisis " ' (*267*).

" unofficial " statement or expression of opinion on foreign relations is necessarily either a reflection of official sentiment or an officially inspired *ballon d'essai*. ' Is it becoming too subtle ', enquired a speaker during the discussions of the General Study Conference on Peaceful Change in 1937, ' to suggest, in talking of "aspirations", which are at the root of the problem of peaceful change, that we should consider whether in particular cases we mean the aspirations of the people, the aspirations of their leaders, or the so-called aspirations of the State itself ? There is ', he suggested, ' such a thing as manufactured " aspiration " with a merely conventional existence — cultivated, as an instrument of policy '.   The cogency of this objection is, doubtless, a matter of political judgment and of individual opinion.   To the speaker just quoted, it seemed ' that the " attitudes " of States are less a function of collective aspirations than of calculated official policy ', though policy, he admitted, ' no doubt will incidentally take account o such popular aspirations as exist '.[192 a]

Yet, even if the objection were held to be logically unassailable as a general principle, it is possible that, in view of the character of " unofficial " German statements of claims, it would not be relevant to the question of German population grievances; for, although it is true that abundant evidence can be found in Germany's propaganda at home and abroad of a real or simulated belief that the German people are living under an intolerable burden of numbers, yet it is significant that these statements, unlike those which are made on the subject of raw materials, have never been developed into coherent arguments.   Out of the profusion of polemical utterances, the following may be quoted :

We are a country which has too great a population in too narrow a space, and this fact weighs upon us like a nightmare.[181]
German living space (*Lebensraum*) is too narrow for the 70, 80 or 90 million inhabitants that we expect to have.[160]

---

[a] Cf. *328* : — ' One of the essential and one of the most generally recognised features of Germany's colonial claims is that, within the Reich, only a minority of social groups is interested.   This characteristic does not seem to have changed very much since the peace treaties.   The influence individually exercised by these groups and the weight of their activity, however, have not remained the same in the course of years.   External and internal circumstances have given the minority which to-day is *directly in favour* of the adoption by the Reich of a colonial policy, a force which it hitherto lacked; hence the colonial claims, which originally were the outcome of the demands of a minority, have now assumed the character of a common affirmation in Germany '.

Our living room is too small and must without question be supplemented by colonies. . .[354]

We demand land and territory [colonies] for the nourishment of our people and for settling our superfluous population.[a]

The demand for colonies for our densely populated country will again and again be raised as a matter of course.[353]

We shall voice our demand for living room in colonies more and more loudly till the world cannot but recognise our claim.[355]

Peace in Europe and, therefore, in the rest of the world, depends on whether or not the crowded masses of Central Europe will obtain a possibility of life.[389]

Similarly, in a study of Germany's revisionist policy, a German author refers to 'the revision need of overpopulated Germany' and to 'the need of the German people for wider living and working space' which 'arose immediately after the *Diktaten* of 1918-1919, which reduced German living and working space' and which was accentuated, among other things, 'by the expulsion and elimination of Germans from a number of countries, causing a mass return to the overcrowded homeland'.[180] These needs, he suggests, would be met by a return to Germany of her former colonies,[b] but he makes no reference to any officially formulated German demands.[c] He points out, moreover, that German demands for colonies are not made solely on the ground of overpopulation at home but also for various other reasons.[d]

In his well-known statement of the economic arguments in support of Germany's claims to colonies published in the United States at the beginning of 1937,[364] Germany's foremost exponent abroad of his country's economic requirements, Dr. Hjalmar Schacht, carefully

---

[a] Third Point of the Twenty Five Point Programme issued by the National Socialist Party on February 25, 1920 (quoted in *114* and in *348*).

[b] '. . . the German demand for additional space for work and life — such as the former German colonies in Africa can offer . . .' (*180*); '. . . the demand for revision of overpopulated Germany, looking to the return of her colonies, which were stolen from her by means of illegal acts of various kinds . . .' (*180*).

[c] Cf. the statement in *348* that 'the German Government has not, up to the present [May 1938], put forward officially and publicly any precisely formulated requests to the Colonial Powers concerning its colonial aspirations'.

[d] '. . . Germany's demand for colonial revision, which is based on the vital necessities of the German people — overpopulation, lack of raw materials, exclusion from foreign markets through tariff barriers, lack of foreign exchange — and on a complex of legal and ethical arguments . . .' (*180*).

refrains from endorsing the notion so widely held in other countries that Germany's claims are seriously put forward as springing in part from a problem of population.   After recalling the reference in the Fourteen Points to ' the equitable claims of Governments whose title [to colonies] is to be determined ',[a] Dr. Schacht reproduces a statement alleged to have been made by Colonel House[b] that one of ' the " equitable " claims put forth by Germany ' is ' that she needs a field for the expansion of her population '.   Elsewhere in the same article, Dr. Schacht suggests that the feeling of moral responsibility laid on the shoulders of the American people by President Wilson still exists, ' as is shown by the following statement by Colonel House... who recently wrote ... as follows : " Every statesman will admit in private conversation that Germany, Italy and Japan need reservoirs into which to pour their man power and from which to draw those necessities and raw materials which nature denied them ... " '[364]   Since these two quotations are introduced into the article without comment, it is not clear whether their reproduction is to be taken as signifying Dr. Schacht's approval of their economic implications or whether his object was purely propagandist.   Apart from these quotations, the only references which Dr. Schacht makes in this article to demographic questions are in the statements that, before the war, ' emigration and immigration, between the young countries and the old, was open and looked on with favour', whereas now ' strict regulations govern immigration into almost all the countries where formerly immigrants were welcome ... ' and that ' as against these great national economic domains [Great Britain, France, United States of America, U. S. S. R.] stand the countries with large populations but limited territories '.[364]   Are these the most cogent demographic arguments which the head of Germany's financial system can submit to American students of international affairs in a purposeful attempt to convince them of the legitimacy of German colonial claims ?[c]

[a] The Fifth Point in President Wilson's message of January 18, 1918, was as follows : ' A free, open-minded and absolutely impartial adjustment of all colonial claims, based upon a strict observance of the principle that in determining all such questions of sovereignty the interests of the populations concerned must have equal weight with the equitable claims of the Government whose title is to be determined '.

[b] On the curious origins of this statement, see the editorial comment on *364* (pp. 224-5).

[c] According to *114*, 'the starting point of the argument which Dr. Schacht expounded, in 1926 [see *116*] as in 1936, is the overpopulation of Germany.   He does not, however, dwell on the German problem of emigration.   It is on the soil of Germany herself that this surplus population must live.   Hence, the aim, in the first place, of providing Germans

It is true that the absence of a demographic argument does not prove much by itself, but the negative information derived from Dr. Schacht's presentation in January 1937 of the economic case in favour of a retro-cession to Germany of her former colonies is not without significance in the light of the insistence a few months later by another exponent of Germany's views on the colonial question that it was not because, as Dr. Schacht had explained, Germany needed raw materials that she wanted her colonies back, nor even principally on the grounds of honour, but more as a matter of right and of legal justice.[a]   It is, in fact, increasingly obvious, not only that the "population pressure" argu-ment in favour of colonial revision ' has been falling somewhat into the background ',[166] but that all the "scientific" arguments which have been developed in Germany are put forward or withdrawn in accordance with the requirements of political expediency.

Thus the scientific discussion of Germany's population "claims" has to be based, not upon objective evidence of the reality of such claims, but upon subjective estimates of ' what the Germans "might be assumed to want" '[348] derived from inconclusive political declara-tions, unverified popular beliefs, and shifting "scientific" arguments which, though doubtless bearing some of the marks of official inspiration or approval, furnish no more than presumptive evidence of the reality of the demands which they put forward, for they remain essentially individual statements which, notwithstanding their intrinsic interest, may be of no significant relevance in the effective determination and application of a policy of international relations.   Moreover, as has already been suggested and as the following statement seems to indicate, German diffidence in formulating demographic claims is, perhaps not inconsistently, accompanied by some reluctance to have her demo-graphic situation examined :

The research programme of the international study conference on peace-ful change laid special emphasis, out of the wide range of questions relating to revision needs, to the problem of overpopulation.   The choice of this question was prompted by a certain vexatious semblance, i.e. as if over-

with an adequate supply of foodstuffs, and, secondly, and especially, of developing the industrialisation of the Reich.' Cf. the reference in *44* to an article in *Völkerbund und Völker-recht* in which Professor Dr. von Freytagh-Loringhoven 'says that though the question of raw materials and of room for emigration are important the *decisive* issue is that a resti-tution of German Colonies is a question of *Right* and of *Honour* '.

[a] See above, p. 32.

population could be regarded as an outstanding instance of a vitally important want of a nation in which a "legitimate need" could be demonstrated objectively by the application of simple and purely sociological methods. For this theory rests evidently on this assumption — that an international objective enquiry which is tantamount to an objective international recognition transforms a national need for revision into an international one. Now where is the basis for this seemingly sound (both morally and theoretically) assumption which the whole of political experience reveals as pure fiction?

Instead of an answer we put this positive question — a question which must be taken into full account in any scientific examination of the problem of revision or of peaceful change : *which are the conditions under which a people's need for revision (national revision need) becomes an object of international interest — an international problem calling for a revisionist solution?* This opens up for research a broad field which needs to be mapped out and examined from various angles.

In a genuine society the suffering of one member is regarded as the suffering of the whole society ... It is for science to determine how much political weight ... ethico-legal views possess. History, especially the legal history of the problem of intervention on humanitarian grounds, shows that the policy of States undoubtedly does take these ethico-legal considerations into account to a certain extent but that their action is not motivated by them.[180]

The difficulty in answering the question : what does Germany really want? has recently been explained to an English audience as follows :

Students of Anglo-German relations since 1871 will agree that the difficulty with which Great Britain has continually been faced is that of obtaining from the German Government any clear statement of their real requirements. Our repeated demands for some such statement have always been regarded by the Wilhelmstrasse as either insulting or fraudulent. And the reason for this reiterant misconception is, I firmly believe, due to the fact that the German conception of policy is fundamentally different from our own ... The British conception both of policy and of negotiation is essentially a shopkeeper's conception, a mercantile conception. We believe that when powerful interests come into conflict it should always be possible to reach some compromise under which each side sacrifices something to the other side, and by which both will remain content. And we assume that once some such contract has been concluded it will form the basis of stable collaboration in the future and offer reasonable hope of satisfaction and finality. The German's conception, on the other hand, is the heroic or the warrior conception. He regards negotiation as a trial of strength, implying in its results that one side is victorious and the other defeated. Nor is this all. He is apt to envisage diplomacy as a form of warfare, and to employ such military methods and devices as the feint, the surprise attack, the out-flanking movement, camouflage, the *Kraftprobe* or trench-raid and the limited objective. His tendency is to regard any concession as a local retreat and to set himself immediately to consolidate the position thus evacuated with a view to some further advance. Thus whereas to us a negotiation is little more than a bargain between two men of business, the German is apt to regard any such settlement as unheroic or as a *Kuh-handel*, and to assume that any concessions which they may be asked to make are insulting humiliations and any concessions which we may be ready to make are proofs of weakness on our part. In other words, the objective of German policy is something abstract, namely triumph or power ; and the concrete concessions which may be made to them are viewed, not as objects desirable in themselves, but as symbols of this abstract conception. It is this fundamental difference of approach which has always rendered so difficult any permanent agreement between Germany and Great Britain.[341]

The tentative conclusion suggests itself, therefore, that the demographic situation in Germany, which is alleged to give rise to claims and demands, is itself hypothetical and that such population problems as may exist in that country are of no ascertainable relevant interest in a study of " peaceful change ".[a]

Prior to 1935, ' the starting point of Herr Hitler's argument was the notion of the overpopulation of Germany. He was then seeking a solution of Germany's demographic problem ... in a movement for colonisation outside the Reich. It is common knowledge that Herr Hitler was thinking at that time of territories in Eastern Europe. '[114] This is shown in the following passages taken from *Mein Kampf* :[b]

We must again devote ourselves to representing the highest points of view of every foreign policy, that is to say bringing the land into its proper proportion to the numbers of the population ... (p. 735).

[a] The conclusions which flow from this inference are examined in chapter 5.
[b] Quoted in *347*.

As our forefathers did not receive the land on which we live to-day as a gift from heaven but had to conquer it by staking their lives, so in the future no act of grace by any people can assign to us the land, and so life for our people, but only the force of a victorious sword. However much we may all recognise the necessity for a reckoning with France this would yet remain ineffective if it were to become the only goal of foreign policy. It can only have sense if it acts as a cover for an enlargement of the living room of our people in Europe . . . (p. 740).

We finally part with the colonial and trade policy of the period before the War and pass over to the land policy of the future . . . (p. 742).

I freely acknowledge that even in the period before the War I should have held it to have been better if Germany, renouncing her inane colonial policy, her commercial fleet and Navy, had set herself against Russia in alliance with England and so gone over from a weak world policy to a determined European policy of acquiring continental territory . . . (p. 753). Take every care that the strength of our people has its foundations not in colonies but in the land of its home in Europe. Do not look upon the Reich as secure if it cannot give for centuries to come its own piece of land and soil to every branch of our people. Never forget that the holiest right on this earth is the right to land for one's own cultivation and that the holiest sacrifice is the blood that one spills for this land (p. 754).[a]

Again,

The duty of the foreign policy of a national State is to ensure the existence of the race included in that State by keeping a natural and healthy proportion between the numbers and the increase of the nation and the size and quality of the land in which they dwell. Nothing but sufficient space on the earth ensures freedom of existence to a nation . . .   The National-Socialist movement . . . must attempt to remove the disproportion between our population and our area.[b]

It is not to colonial acquisition that we must look for a solution of this question (i.e. extension of Germany's living room) but exclusively to the acquisition of territory for settlement which will increase the area of the motherland.[352]

---

[a] ' No doubt, the interpretation of these texts was subsequently controverted in Germany. It was contested that Herr Hitler, in . . . [the fourth of these passages], should have formally and finally condemned Germany's colonial aspirations ' (*114*).

[b] From a passage in an American edition of *Mein Kampf* (*My Battle*, Boston, 1933, pp. 275-277) quoted in *55* and purporting to be a statement of ' Germany's claims for territorial revision to relieve her population pressure '.

' If further evidence of this fundamental German policy of acquiring territory in Europe ... [is] needed, it ... [is] but necessary to study with care the treaties of Brest-Litovsk and Bucharest ... ' [347]

Thus, although ' there is nothing new in Germany's colonial claims ... they ... retained for many years a character of secondary importance. '[328] ' But expansion eastwards was ... itself but an intermediate step. The extra power acquired by Germany as a result of such expansion was to give her the means of claiming, in various parts of the world, habitable territories suitable for the settlement of Europeans. One recognises here the demographic argument so often advanced by the partisans of colonial expansion; we thus find once more the idea of extra-European colonization by Germany. '[114]

' At the time of the advent of the Third Reich, the colonial policy ', however, ' encountered the indifference and even the hostility of the National-Socialist Party itself '.[114] ' It is only recently ... [that Germany's colonial claims] have been able to acquire their present force ... A twofold movement ... would seem to explain the present vigour of the claims. Firstly, in industrial, financial and commercial circles, which are concerned, above all, with the condition of various branches of national economic life, the colonial policy is receiving very notable support. Secondly, in the opinion of certain circles responsible for the foreign policy of the Third Reich ... it seems that the time has come to expect a more favourable attitude to a colonial settlement on the part of the Empires, more particularly the British Empire; they believe that the new circumstances in international politics would render useful for Germany the affirmation of a firm requirement '.[328]

' Generally, it would seem that the present claims of the Reich should be linked up not so much with the efforts of the past ... as with the work which Germany has now accomplished with the aim of transforming the economic structure of the nation and the conditions of its political power '.[114]

' At the moment when she is claiming her former colonies, Germany asks that the conditions governing her supplies of raw materials should be improved. She asserts that the two claims are inseparable. The effect of this attempt to link up the economic problem with the colonial problem — an attempt that coincides with the patient and tenacious development of the " Gleichberechtigung " policy — is to carry the claim into a far vaster field and to give Germany's colonial ambitions a scope and an ultimate aim to which she has not hitherto been able to aspire. The interest of Germany's present colonial claims seems to lie less in the argument itself than in the scope which is given to it and in the purpose which it serves '.[328]

' Germany's claims have a certain suppleness, and therein lies their strength. The acquisition of colonies is doubtless desirable but not indispensable for the Reich; the claims could be accentuated or withdrawn, according to circumstances, or at least attenuated; one of their essential features ... [is] that they ... [belong] to that class of claim which, if granted, is profitable, but the abandonment of which, at least in part, is not without certain advantages. Besides, what concession can Germany offer to make in a general or limited discussion — a Germany which, in contrast with the Germany under Bismarck, has, since the Great War, been fundamentally in the diplomatic position of being constantly a claimant party — what has she to offer other than an attenuation of some previous claim ? In the course of the last few months, whenever Germany has manifested her contingent readiness to cede a point, she has thereby put herself under the necessity of advancing a fresh claim. Truly, the philosophy of Germany to-day remains the philosophy of tragedy '.[328 a]

Thus, ' the rallying of the [national-socialist] party leaders to the principle of the connection to be established between the problem of raw materials and the colonial question seems to be one of the essential aspects of the recent evolution of German policy '. But ' nothing is

---

[a] Cf. the statement made by the French Minister of Colonies in January 1937 (*115*) : — ' I do not think that the colonial question figures amongst the fundamental concerns of Germany, or even of Hitler. Germany is using it as a means to her political ends and her claims appear or disappear according to the needs of her general, and, above all, European policy ...'. Cf. also *341* : — ' I do not believe myself that present German policy differs in any important respect from pre-War policy. I believe that power is still the ultimate objective, and that the frame of mind is still a warrior frame of mind ... There are many people ... who sincerely imagine that Germany will be " grateful " for a " generous gesture " on ... [Great Britain's] part. To the Germans generosity means patronage, gratitude, humiliation. They do not want us to be kind; they want us to be frightened ... We cannot foresee the nature of her demands ... What Germany wants is power ... What ... [Herr Hitler] desires is *Grund und Boden* or, in other words, territorial and economic acquisitions in Central and South-Eastern Europe. Such acquisitions might lead him into conflict with Russia. If he is to succeed in that conflict he must assure that he is protected in the rear ... In order to sterilise France he must sterilise England. Yet what does he possess wherewith to purchase ... [England's] neutrality ? He has no real assets at all. Therefore he creates an artificial asset, the Colonial Propaganda. He can now offer ... the abandonment of his claim for the colonies in return for a free hand in the East ... The colonial question is essentially a side-show ...'; and *84* : — ' The German demand for colonies may be in part due to a desire for access to raw materials, but it is mainly due to a desire that her size, importance, and accomplishments, relative to those of other countries, should be recognised '.

said to-day of the need for mass emigration to colonial territories . . .
The old colonialism, easily influenced by arguments of a " sentimental "
order and anxious to prepare for a mass emigration of Germans to the
tropics, makes way for a new colonialism . . . Stress is now laid only
on Germany's desire to produce a certain number of raw materials
within areas covered by the Reich's monetary system . . . For
" racial " reasons . . ., the Third Reich is to-day hostile to a doctrine
which, for some years, had found ardent supporters in Germany . . .
Colonisation may lead to a diminution in the " racial " value of the
emigrated populations . . . From the " racial " and social point of
view . . ., it seems desirable to avoid employing Europeans in the same
areas as natives in tropical colonies '. Moreover, a new German school
of thought has ' shown, in what seems to be a peremptory manner,
the difficulties that attend any important settlement of white races in
tropical areas . . . Survival is possible only for . . . small and exclusively
native undertakings, on the one hand, and for major capitalist concerns,
on the other; thus, since it would already be difficult to find room in
East Africa for ten times more colonists than there are there to-day,
a fortiori the idea of a mass emigration of millions of colonists must be
put aside . . . The German studies published on this subject now confine their observations to the advantages which a portion of the youth
of Germany — active young men eager to find employment — would
derive from colonial services... According to the new arguments
put forward, German emigration to the colonies would be no more
than the emigration of *cadres* . . . Generally speaking, the idea of mass
emigration to colonial territories now seems to have been abandoned
in Germany . . . The argument based on the need for opening
up emigration areas for Germany in her former colonies thus no
longer plays more than a secondary rôle in the claims advanced by
Germany '.[114]

VI. HYPOTHETICAL DEMOGRAPHIC CLAIMS

The foregoing review of some of the evidence commonly adduced
in support of the argument that the " dissatisfied " countries are
claimants for relief from population pressure goes to show that it is
partly contradictory, partly hypothetical and largely inconclusive; it
seems to indicate that ' the population question . . . [is] not as serious

as many nations would like to assert '.[a]   The grievances, real or alleged, arising out of demographic conditions have not found expression in any official claims and demands and some of the informal claims with which those grievances are associated are not always consistent with the known policies of the countries concerned.[b]   Moreover, while the nature of the changes in the *status quo* envisaged in the " claims " is in some cases explicitly stated, in others it is either not indicated or expressed in elliptical terms which cannot be accurately interpreted.

If it be held, on the other hand, that it is legitimate to assume, with the Conference, that the claims which it postulated at the outset of its study of " peaceful change " are related to reality and that their impact on the trend of international affairs is a significant factor in the formation of policy,[c] then the various opinions recorded in the evidence brought to the notice of the International Studies Conference tend to show that two principal remedies are contemplated by (or on behalf of) the countries which are suffering, or believed to suffer, from over-crowding and which, therefore, may need outlets for their surplus population.   The first is the direct solution by emigration; the second remedy is sought after ' vicariously by the opening up of export markets ',[154] on the one hand, and by ensuring a readier access to cheap sources of raw materials, on the other.   Both these types of solution are sometimes expressed in claims, real or alleged, for territorial changes and for a re-distribution of colonies, but it is clear that such claims may also spring from aspirations which are not founded on grievances

[a] See the discussion on *176*.   Cf. *111* : — ' Declarations regarding the aims of Germany's claims are numerous, but they are lacking in precision; they are, moreover, contradictory. The majority of these statements merely contain a demand for " colonies " on behalf of Germany and do not go into details.   The colonial claim thus appears to be the present-day expression of an old and more general claim : the claim to the elbow-room — the *Raum* — needed by Germany.   Thus the speeches dealing with colonial claims reproduce the comparisons and illustrations which have long accompanied the assertion of Germany's need for external expansion.   Sometimes Germany is compared with a seething caldron the explosion of which must be prevented; at other times Germans are compared with caged birds clamouring for freedom.   More generally, the demand for a redistribution of the lands and wealth of the world to the advantage of Germany — the demand, in other words, for a revision of the present international *status quo* — corresponds with the general conception of the " non-satisfaction ", the " future destiny " and the rhythm of death and re-birth which are familiar features of the German *Lebensphilosophien* '.

[b] But cf. below, pp. 151 *sqq.*

[c] Since the meetings of the International Studies Conference, the Economic Committee of the League of Nations has also accepted the hypothesis that overpopulation is at the basis of claims : — ' Demographic pressure is . . . the main argument adduced in support of a policy of autarky, of the claim for colonies, and even of certain armed expeditions ' See *317*.

relating to pressure of population. Moreover, territorial and colonial changes, though they may be regarded as short-cuts to the true remedies for overpopulation, are not themselves solutions to population pressure. Suggested remedies for demographic congestion will be considered in later chapters; meanwhile, the nature of the ailment from which the " dissatisfied " countries are said to be suffering must be examined.

Appendix

SOME MINOR ASPIRATIONS

The " big three " — Germany, Italy and Japan — together with Poland are not the only countries which are dissatisfied with their demographic situation, but, with the exception of one or two countries whose claims cannot be backed up with the political weight which is needed to secure the notice of the rest of the world, other overcrowded countries tend to keep their sense of discontent to themselves. ' I have the privilege ', declared a Swiss expert at a meeting of the International Studies Conference, ' of belonging to a State as big as a pocket-handkerchief and divided into small squares. We are a very, very tiny country. For us, the problem of overpopulation exists; but in Switzerland, this problem does not concern peaceful change; you cannot imagine Switzerland mobilizing its ships and its army to conquer new territories. But when the question concerns Germany, or Italy, or certain other countries, that is a different matter, because technical instruments come into play other than those which my country possesses '.[227]

Austria, Czechoslovakia,[376] Denmark, Norway,[a] Hungary, Ireland,[b] Switzerland[c] — all these countries and others besides have at various times been associated with population grievances and aspirations. Brief references may be made here to one or two of them.

The demographic situation in Hungary is the subject of a memorandum submitted to the International Studies Conference by the Hungarian Co-ordinating Committee for International Studies. ' A really effective solution

---

[a] For Danish and Norwegian declarations, see *331*.

[b] ' The best hope for the future of Irish overseas emigration is that her sons can take their due place in an ordered and rational plan of European expansion which will at the same time guarantee the supremacy in Europe of justice and peace ' (*392*).

[c] For Swiss declarations, see *335*; see also *153*.

of the demographic problem of present-day Hungary...', it claims, 'must be sought in a broadening of living and working space'. The " broadening of living and working space " apparently signifies 'to restore to the plain known as present-day Hungary its " place in the sun ", to give it the possibility of living in accordance with its character and mission, and the rôle which it has filled for a thousand years, as the natural centre of the Hungarian basin'. This, in turn, does not appear to mean ' " revision " in the legal sense of the term', but 'something which signifies less but which will lead to more : the impartial, equitable and radical adjustment of an unsound, artificial and trouble-breeding situation'. As to the nature of the demographic problem, the memorandum states that 'Hungary cannot be regarded as being overpopulated, not even relatively so, although a certain feeling of overpopulation (in respect of quantity rather than of quality) is general', and that the type of demographic problem 'approximates most closely to that of agrarian overpopulation.'[127]

While this memorandum may be thought to give expression, if not to a demographic claim, at any rate to a demographic grievance and, though less clearly, to an aspiration, it does not deal with conditions which, if left unremedied, would lead to a situation falling within the province of the International Studies Conference's enquiry.

The status of Austria having been transformed since the conclusion of the International Studies Conference's enquiry, the following summary of a memorandum submitted to the Conference by the Austrian Co-ordinating Committee for International Studies is of academic interest only :

'The prospects for a small State of acquiring colonies — all the more so for a small State without sea-coast — are certainly very slight, in view of the difficulties with which Germany has to contend when seeking mere sympathy for her colonial claims, and in view of the dangerous opposition that Italy had to overcome when extending her colonial empire. Moreover, the internal national impulse in Austria was only slight; the country had to struggle with great business and financial troubles after the war. So for almost an entire decade colonisation remained unmentioned in Austria'.[a] Then, 'with the benevolent support of far-sighted Federal Chancellor Dr. Dollfuss, the Austrian Colonial Society was founded' in 1933. The first aim of the Society was 'the acquisition of a non-European colonial or concession territory for Austria', which would provide 'the most sweeping

---

[a] See *80*, quoting from the constitution of the Austrian Colonial Society.

and radical solution of ... [her] unemployment problem ' by ' settling ... surplus population in an overseas settlement region '. The Society issued a statement to the Austrian public in which it demanded ' from the great Powers and from the League of Nations the granting to Austria of colonial land suitable economically and from the health point of view '.[80]

It was stated at a meeting of the Conference in 1937 that the Austrian Colonial Society ' is supported by the Government ', and that ' conversations took place in 1933 with the French Government concerning Madagascar, and more recently with the Italian Government concerning Ethiopia, with a view to relieving Austrian overpopulation '.[223]

PART TWO

THE PROBLEM EXAMINED

Chapter 4

The Notion of Overpopulation

I. WHAT IS OVERPOPULATION?

' Justice and the interest of humanity require one to tend towards an equalisation of the conditions of life in the various countries, just as they require one to do so in respect of the individuals composing each nation '.[113] Hence ' claims persistently and emphatically stated in terms familiar to the man in the street — be it " justice for the have-nots " or " room for our children " — are sure to find an echo in democratic countries where the rule of law rests on the assumption of justice for all, and where public policy must be shaped in public discussion '.[131] The echo will be all the quicker in the case of claims for relief from population pressure, for ' overcrowding is a notion that is easily grasped by the man in the street and is apt to meet with a sympathetic response from him '.[55] Provided that his vital interests are not too patently threatened, he may even be disposed to condone disturbances in the equilibrium of international relations if they appear to him to have been prompted in despair by unbearable pressure of population. The dread spectre of overpopulation unites the nations in a solidarity of alarm. A public conscience, haunted by the fear of congestion, is not utterly shocked when the burden of dense numbers tempts one people to covet another's sparsely inhabited territories.

But while sympathy is an amiable virtue and, as the Japanese proverb says, will come back to the giver like an echo, it is not a remedy for overpopulation. As an attitude taken up by the " satiated " democratic countries towards the difficulties of the " dissatisfied " nations, it might have the emollient effect of removing some of the asperities of international life but it will not solve a problem. If the claims of the " dissatisfied " countries are to be sympathetically considered, it is not

6

enough that they should be grasped by the man in the street; it is indispensable that the problems which have given rise to them should be stated so precisely as to leave no room for doubt as to their nature.

The various statements of grievances giving rise to aspirations and demands which were reviewed in the preceding chapter show that 'the term " overpopulation " plays an important part in public discussions. In everyday life, however, we use terms which, when they are clearly examined, are not quite so clear as they seemed to be at first sight and which, precisely for this reason, exert a strong influence on the mind and actions of men '.[151]   Such terms are " overpopulation " and its multiple variants — " overcrowding ", " pressure of population ", " lack of space ", " demographic congestion ", " surplus numbers ", etc. — all of which are used indiscriminately in the discussion of claims in contexts which are sometimes so obscure and ambigous as to give the impression of masking the real intentions of the claimants.   Yet, unless a clear meaning can be attached to the notion of " overpopulation ",[a] it will not be possible to answer the pertinent questions which were raised at the outset of the International Studies Conference's enquiry into " peaceful change ", namely : — ' At which point . . . does the growth of population of a . . . State give the appearance of a legitimate need for expansion ?   What exactly does this need consist of ? '[34]

' Overpopulation ' is a term which ' is used in current literature with very different meanings '.[179] [b]   It is ' one of the most unstable, daring, dangerous and difficult demographic or, rather, economico-demographic concepts '.[127]   ' If we refer to the definitions given by demographic science, we find . . . a great variety of conceptions of the essential character of overpopulation '.[151]   But ' a clear definition of the meaning of overpopulation is . . . necessary because it is used in political arguments whose purpose of influencing the accumulation of power and territory affects the world very deeply '.[129]

A study of the concept of overpopulation occupied an important

[a] It was pointed out several years before the Conference began its enquiry that ' " overpopulation " and " underpopulation " are fundamental terms, which it is important to define with precision . . .   Through lack of such precision, much discussion, even between the most distinguished persons [— ' the controversy between Sir William Beveridge and Mr. Keynes . . . in *Economic Journal*, December 1923, and *Economica*, February 1924 ' — is apt to be clouded by *ignoratio elenchi* ' (243).

[b] ' Even in scientific works . . . [such as] the Statistical Year-Book of the League of Nations . . ., [support is given to a] false idea [of overpopulation] ' (129).

place in the International Studies Conference's enquiry into population problems. Some of the results of the study will be surveyed in the present chapter; there are, however, three preliminary observations to be made.

In the first place, it is clear that overpopulation, in whatever sense the term may be used, is meaningless save in relation to particular areas and particular points of time.[243] The Conference was not concerned with overpopulation, whether present or future, in the world as a whole,[a] but with the question in its relation to particular countries — the countries with claims for changes in the *status quo* — at the moment of its enquiry.

Secondly, a distinction must be made between the maximum population that can be supported in a given area and the size of the population which can attain maximum welfare in that area.[b] The condition of overpopulation which is relevant to the Conference's study is related to " maximum welfare " and not to " maximum population ". ' One cannot speak of a population exceeding the maximum; this would be a manifest absurdity '.[113] [c] It must be noted, however, that, whereas " maximum welfare " is usually identified in scientific discussions of overpopulation with " maximum economic welfare ", such identification in the context of claims for peaceful change is a fruitful source of confusion. It is true that overpopulation is ' generally considered as an economic problem ', but ' political considerations are a factor in it, such, for instance, as the problem of security and the policies of States tending towards an enlargement of the population and an increase in the birthrate '.[209] [d] Overpopulation must be considered, therefore, not only in its palpable economic and social aspects,

---

[a] ' The earth ', according to one authority, ' can under no circumstances carry something like 18,000,000,000 people ' (i. e. ten times its present estimated population); but those who fear that the world is menaced with overpopulation may find reassurance in his further statement that even to attain, say, 11,000,000,000 would involve (quoting Sir G. Knibbs) ' a perfecting of human knowledge, of human organisation, and of human character, which transcends all our ordinary conceptions of real possibilities . . .; as matters stand ', he concludes, ' there is no real danger of a general overpopulation '; in fact, ' it is hard to see how the earth could possibly double its present population ' (*311*). For a recent discussion of estimates of the world's maximum demographic capacity, see *140*.

[b] See *243* and, in particular, the observations on the ambiguity of the term " supported ".

[c] ' In this connection ', adds the author of this remark, ' I would point out that a population can be said to have reached its maximum when its density is such that the resulting conditions of life cause the death rate to rise to the level of the birth rate — of a birth rate, it need hardly be added, which has not been artificially restricted. It should also be pointed out that this maximum is subject to fluctuation ' (*113*).

[d] Cf. below, chap. 5, § V.

but also in its imponderable political and moral aspects, in so far as they may be amenable to objective analysis. On the other hand, the Conference was concerned essentially with quantitative overpopulation and not with various forms of qualitative overpopulation; thus, however important a bearing ethnic disequilibrium, for example, may have on a country's external relations, it will not be possible to take into account here ' overpopulation in relation to the various elements of a country's population '.[52] [a]

Thirdly, ' demographic experts distinguish between absolute overpopulation and relative overpopulation. By the first is meant the condition of a territory in which the inhabitants, under the existing systems of production and distribution, and in the existing state of technical progress, are unable, by any kind of economic activity, to secure the minimum conditions which are indispensable to physical life.[b] According to these experts, absolute overpopulation exists in only a few parts of the world (China, India). For the world as a whole, there does not appear to be any conceivable possibility of absolute overpopulation ... On the other hand, relative overpopulation has always existed in certain regions, including parts of Europe. The characteristic feature of relative overpopulation is the inability or great difficulty for the inhabitants of certain regions to reach the average standard of living found elsewhere '.[317]

' In the last analysis, absolute overpopulation seems to be an impalpable notion, a phantom that cannot be enclosed within a hard and fast definition. It is only the notion of relative overpopulation that can be justified to a certain extent, in theory and in practice, even in cases where the condition of overpopulation detected at a given moment assumes a permanent character or, at any rate — since it is impossible to see the future course of events — seems to take on such a character '.[127] As a speaker pointed out at one of the Conference's meetings in 1937, ' overpopulation considered as an excess over the optimum is not a condition that we should examine. What we have

[a] For example — it was explained to the Conference — ' antisemitism in Rumania ... is a demographic problem which has arisen because of the unequal distribution of Jews and Rumanians in the different branches of the economic activity of that country ' (52).
[b] Cf. 362 : — ' We must distinguish between two senses of the word " overpopulation ", speaking of *absolute* overpopulation when we mean that, in the world as a whole, or in an isolated community, the point of maximum return has been passed, and of *relative* overpopulation when we mean that, in a particular part of the world's surface, work has to take place under less favourable conditions than elsewhere, so that, other things being equal, a unit of labour is less productive than it would be in another place '.

to consider is overpopulation understood in another sense, namely, the overpopulation of a country as compared with another country '.[200] [a] 'And a country being overpopulated when compared with another, the latter, in turn, will be overpopulated as compared with a third country '.[113] 'If, as a result of its demographic situation, by reason of its density of population, the general conditions of life for the inhabitants of a country are too low as compared with those ruling in other countries, then that country will be tempted to protest, to complain and put forward certain demands that are likely to lead to international conflicts which we are anxious to avoid '.[200] 'If present tendencies of net survival rates continue, the distribution [of labour] will become more and more anomalous. The low reproduction-rate areas, which, broadly speaking, are more richly endowed with natural and artificial resources, will become less populated. The high reproduction-rate areas will become even more overcrowded. Indeed, taking a long view, it is fairly certain that such a situation could not persist. Sooner or later the more fertile peoples, or at least the more vigorous among them, would burst the barriers which hemmed them in and enter into what they regarded as their rightful domain . . .'[346]

'Moreover, even relative overpopulation is a notion resting on a questionable basis; this is proved by the very great variety of the definitions which have been given and which sometimes reach the limits of absolute overpopulation. A distinction is made, for example, between objective and subjective overpopulation; between a state and a feeling of overpopulation; between quantitative and qualitative overpopulation; ever greater extension is given to the territory on which overpopulation can be detected as well as to the notion of overpopulation itself by making a distinction, in the first instance, between local, regional, national, multinational, continental and world overpopulation, and, in the other instance, between agrarian, industrial and mixed overpopulation; and, finally, proceeding by demographic stages, between overpopulation in relation to certain ethnical groups or communities and overpopulation affecting a whole nation or race; or, again, on another

[a] The 'very important view that an overpopulation in our day cannot be regarded absolutely for an isolated country, but must be considered in relation to the conditions in other countries, so that when parallels are drawn between different countries, a form of overpopulation appears in a country when the standard of living which can be attained through a certain amount of work in one country is lower than that which might have been achieved in the other country by doing the same amount of work ' (*134*) was expressed in 1929 in *340*.

plane, between national overpopulation and overpopulation in a universal sense '.[127]

' The problem of overpopulation takes on a vaguer aspect when a study of causes and motives is undertaken. We know that the form, scope and solution of the problem vary according to whether it has arisen as the result of natural phenomena, of political circumstances, of a re-shaping of frontiers, of demological movements, of economic events, of a redistribution of all types of culture, of changes in the standard of living and mode of life . . ., etc. It is no less important to consider the changes that affect the composition of the population, the distribution of the population according to professions and occupations, the transformation of the labour market, the greater difficulty of finding employment; the withdrawal of a territory from the habitual and broader framework of the past, with the resulting diminution of living and working space, and other specific phenomena, such as the barriers suddenly erected in the path of seasonal and alternating movements, of the mobility of the working masses and, most important of all, of the emigration through which a portion of the population seeks to settle in a new country; the changes also that have taken place in production, markets . . . and consumption — so many causes likely to generate overpopulation. There still remain, for consideration, the different forms of relative overpopulation when we turn our attention to the over-crowding of certain professions . . ., the trend of the distribution of the population according to age — particularly in connection with the accumulation of persons of working age — and the pathological distortion of the ratio of workers to supported persons '.[127]

' The fact that, from the dynamic standpoint, it is possible to introduce totally distinct forms of overpopulation further emphasizes the relative character of this notion. The position is different if, for example, overpopulation occurs in the course of the development of the population or if it reflects stagnation in a period of time or, and above all, if it marks the beginning of a period of decadence. Its characteristic features stand out clearly according to the case; and, similarly, the links and inter-relationship with the progress of demographic processes, or with the maintenance or weakening of these processes, vary very considerably from one case to another '.[127]

' But it is not only from the theoretical standpoint that the notion of overpopulation is relative and vague. Defining the degrees of population, and laying down practical criteria for territories that are sparsely, normally or over-populated rests on a still more insecure basis and encounters more numerous obstacles. In point of fact, what destroys the absolute character of the notion and sentiment of optimum population, of the feeding capacity of a territory, of demographic pressure and overpopulation, is no doubt the great number and uncertainty of the pratical methods and possibilities of gauging these factors '.[127]

II. POPULATION DENSITY

' The most popular method of indicating population pressure is to cite statistics of simple density, such as the number of people per square mile of territory, or the number per square mile of arable land '.[55] Accurate figures of the former are available, but ' science has long since demonstrated the vagueness of this concept '[155] of simple or arithmetic density, i. e. the ratio of the number of persons living on a unit of a country's area to the total area of the country. Yet the notion ' still frequently serves as an argument not only in the political discussions of our time,[a] but even in the works of specialists, to characterise absolute " overpopulation " or " underpopulation " '.[155] Thus, among the ' picturesque, though somewhat crude, slogans (presumably coined chiefly for internal circulation)... [used] in German colonial propaganda '[348] as one of the modes of presenting the economic arguments for restoration of the colonies, the following examples illustrate the misleading use of simple density figures :

Germany has a density of 123 inhabitants to the square kilometre, while her former colonial territory had a density of 4 inhabitants to the square kilometre; on this space of 1 square kilometre, Belgium maintains 257 persons and her colonies maintain 6; in France there are 75 inhabitants to the square kilometre as against 5 in French colonies; Great Britain has 45 million inhabitants, while Canada, which is thirty times as large, has only 8 millions; Portugal has 65 inhabitants to the square kilometre and its colonies have 4. Must the evolution of Europe continue in such a way that this disproportion is maintained ? The question supplies its own answer.[388]

[a] Cf. *317* : — ' Demographic questions give rise to unceasing disputes, which at any moment may assume an acrimonious form and thus endanger international good feeling. The adversaries in such disputes almost invariably make arbitrary and absolute statements, based as often as not on a few striking figures illustrating the ratio " man-land ", which are presented as incontrovertible arguments and are accepted as such by the public. These figures become powerful means of agitation without ever being subjected to a critical scrutiny '.

Again,

In Germany there are 136 inhabitants to each square kilometre. In England there are 137, but England has for its 137 inhabitants per square mile [a] one-third of the whole world as a colony.[351]

Yet, ' according to the *International Year Book of Agricultural Statistics*, 1936-37, the density of population per square kilometre (in 1935 or nearest date) was : 141.2 in Germany; 269 in England and Wales; 192.6 in the United Kingdom '.[348]

It is clear that ' the figure representing the size of the population means nothing in itself. Thus, ten men will find it more difficult to live on 10 square kilometres of desert than a hundred men on 100 hectares of fertile land. A figure that is unaccompanied by a commentary of some sort, and next to which no indication is given of such factors as technical organization, standard of civilization and economic conditions, cannot be compared with another figure which leaves us just as much in the dark concerning the concrete realities behind it '.[140]

' Arithmetical density offers only a superficial general view of the demographic condition of the different countries; it can be considered characteristic neither of their economic situation nor of their social level, nor, therefore, of their political and military power '.[155] [b]

Various methods are used by demographers to correct the defects of the crude index of arithmetic density. One of the methods is to express densities in terms of estimated habitable areas by excluding from the ratio of population to area barren surfaces such as ice-bound or desert land and water areas. A further refinement in the comparison of the populations of different countries is to relate densities in regions of equal rainfall. The usefulness of this method is, however, limited. ' For various reasons it is easy to infer too much from such calculations; it is, for instance, not only the total rainfall but also the distribution of rainfall over the year which is important '.[84]

But, whatever be the method employed, ' it must be recognised . . . that surface area is only one, and a decreasingly important, aspect of the natural physical environment which conditions population density. Climate, topography, location, the physical constituents of the soil,

----

[a] *sic.*
[b] ' At most, this density may serve as an indication of overpopulation for nomad peoples or for Indians living in reservations (the Navajos, etc.) ' (*155*).

sub-surfaces, supplies of minerals and fuels and a number of other natural physical factors are equally as important as land area. Moreover, such an index entirely neglects the artificial, physical environment, as well as technological, economic and social conditions of paramount importance in conditioning population growth. To impute under- or over-population by relating the residents of a region to one of many portions of one of many aspects of the total environment would seem on *a priori* grounds to be not only unscientific but misleading '.[102]

As an alternative method of eliminating the errors implicit in comparisons of simple population densities, ' the figure representing the density of population should be followed by another factor which makes it possible to distinguish the demographic differences to be observed in the world. The figure indicating the geographical area should be supplemented by an indication of the economic value of that area. In this way, by taking the ratio of population to a unit of arable land, not merely to a unit of area, it will be possible to draw more practical conclusions '.[140] [a] Yet, even if comparisons are made, not between areas of cultivable land, but between the extent of cultivated land in the various countries, the resulting figures ' unaccompanied by any detailed commentary might give a false idea of the demographic and agricultural situation of the countries considered '.[140] In the first place, ' is it justifiable to include in the denominator of the fraction [population/cultivated land] ... areas of land, whose fertility differs exceedingly on account of the difference of soil and climate ?[b] Must not, at least, the difference in quantity and quality of crops ... be taken into consideration ' ?[129] Secondly, great technical difficulties arise in the interpretation of the national statistics relating to cultivable land,[c] and, even if suitable allowance could be made, ' the agricultural density, i.e. the number of active workers to the unit of cultivable surface, can therefore serve only as a *crude index* of relative overpopulation, even in certain countries where the agricultural population still forms a large proportion of the total population ... It is only in certain regions of the world which are still almost completely isolated, such as Northern China, that the agricultural density taken alone can really show the intensity of overpopulation '.[155]

[a] For a table of " physiological densities ", see *141* or *158*; the figures ' are to be accepted with great reservation ' (*155*).

[b] Cf. *155* : — ' It is not enough to calculate and compare physiological densities; it is likewise necessary to take into account the climate, the quality of the soil, and the intensity of labour '.

[c] A statement of these difficulties is given in *155*.

Density comparisons are also made on the basis of the percentage of the total population engaged in agriculture in the different countries,[a] ' but it is not easy to say who is engaged in agriculture, because many people are engaged part time in agriculture and part time in ancillary occupations such as forestry, in industry, or in domestic work at home; also different countries draw the line between agricultural and other occupations in different places '. Again, in making comparisons of ' the various uses to which land is put [e. g. arable land, permanent grass and pasture, wood and forest, and other land], it must be remembered that temporary pasture is included under arable, though, when laid down for long periods, it occupies as few people as good permanent pasture. Then it is difficult to distinguish between " permanent grass and pasture " and " other land ", that is to say, rough hill grazing shades off by imperceptible stages into barren land '.[84] [b]

' It is, of course, only when environmental conditions are dissimilar that comparisons based on surface density are misleading '; but, since, in practice, no two regions can be found where precisely similar environmental conditions prevail, the point is of academic interest only. ' Yet despite the total inadequacy and obviously misleading nature of surface density figures for the comparison of populations with entirely dissimilar physical, social and economic environments, they still hold an important place in the approved technique of protagonists of colonial expansion by European Powers and of the critics of immigration restriction by the United States and the British Dominions. Their continued use by honest-minded students of population makes one wonder whether there is not more than a little justification for Aldous Huxley's cynical dictum that 20,000 repetitions make one truth '.[102]

The greatest defect of the population-area ratio is that it is a ' very untrustworthy help, if not altogether useless ... [when applied] to non-agrarian territories, where the soil fulfils another economical function than in the rural districts. Everywhere where the population in its activities is not connected with the soil, i. e. everywhere where the population does not seek its means of livelihood in the cultivation of the land, forestry, horticulture or the breeding of cattle, in such

---

[a] Cf. the table of density of population and agricultural employment in Europe in 84.

[b] ' The importance of this latter point can be seen when we contrast Scotland with England and Wales; both countries are recorded as having about the same percentage of permanent grass and pasture [62.6% and 57.1% of the total area, respectively], but we know that in Scotland this is largely sheep grazings on mountain sides, whereas in England much of it is the finest pasture in the world ' (84).

cases the density of population influences prosperity very little. This is most clearly seen in towns '.[129]

In a word, ' agricultural density alone no longer suffices to characterise the alimentary and other conditions of the agricultural population in countries which are even a little more advanced from the industrial standpoint ';[155] and it is ' obvious that besides the figure representing the factor of agriculture, other economic data must be brought into play, to furnish the means of comparing the demographic and economic positions of the different countries '.[140] ' To evaluate the general economic density of a country, it is .... necessary to consider first, in addition to the agricultural density, the various natural resources, independent of that density, namely, the riches and sources of energy in the soil, the sea,[a] and the inland waters. Next, it is necessary to take into account the actual exploitation of this natural wealth ... Furthermore, even primary production depends on the proportional use of the other factors of production, such as capital, on the quantity and the quality of the labour supply ..., [as well as industrialisation][162] and the degree of technical development '.[155] Moreover, ' a new coefficient indicating the industrial equipment of the country must be taken into consideration '.[140] [b]

Nevertheless, ' calculations of density, based on the existing relations between two factors only of production (population and resources) are not adequate to determine the demographic position of a country from the economic or social viewpoint, and cannot serve

[a] ' As is well known, the Japanese eat a great deal of fish and relatively little meat. But few realise how important a part of the food supply sea-products form. The figures show that Japan exports between a fourth and a fifth, by weight, of her takings from the sea. The difference between the catch and the exports is the consumption of Japan. Thus, the Japanese people [whose share of the world's sea-products has increased from 29.4 percent in 1925-29 to 34.5 percent in 1933] in the past ten years have eaten approximately a fourth of all the fish and other sea-products taken by all the nations from all the seas of the world. To get a really accurate picture of the area from which Japanese get their food, therefore, it is necessary to add a large section of the ocean to the dry land of the islands ' (165).
[b] Quoting 142, it is suggested in 140, that this coefficient ' should be composed of certain indices ... such, for example, as : (i) the consumption of machines per capita and in dollars; (ii) the geometric mean of the length of railroads, per capita and per 100 sq. km.; (iii) the tenth of the geometric mean of the number of automobiles, per capita and per 100 sq. km.; (iv) the number of industrial workers per 10 workers in general; (v) one-tenth of the transactions with foreign countries, per capita and in dollars ', and that, ' although it is not possible to embrace the whole of a country's economic activity in a single figure ', a table of figures which is quoted from the same source ' nevertheless has its value in that it serves as a guide in a difficult problem '. While it is admitted that the table ' certainly does not supply the exact formula for the optimum density of population ', it is considered that ' it indicates the path that leads towards its discovery '.

for international comparisons '.[155] Indeed, the conclusions reached from comparisons of population densities expressed in terms of natural resources ' have often been as misleading as those based on simple surface area density figures. The inadequacy of the population-natural-resources ratio derives from several causes. First, most figures on natural resources are at best mere guesses, frequently not even informed guesses ... If it is difficult to secure accurate estimates of physical natural resources it is even more difficult to get satisfactory ... measures [in terms of money]. The resulting uncertainty is increased by failure to distinguish between the actual and the potential. The teaching of geography ... has thoroughly inoculated the present generation with a static conception of natural resources. Modern geographers are attempting to correct this misconception. They are insisting that the resource concept is essentially dynamic. What is a resource to-day may be valueless to-morrow; what is valueless to-day may be a priceless resource a year hence. The only practical method of evaluating a resource is by its income-yielding capacity ... Only to the extent that a natural agent can be made to yield ... [adequate returns to the capital and labour employed] may it properly be said to be a natural resource and can it be counted upon to support population. This brings us to the crux of the problem. How can such increased returns be secured from our natural environment as to warrant its more complete uti-lisation ? ... The old view was that increased population creates new demands sufficient to provide remunerative employment for itself and that the first prerequisite for the conversion of sterile " natural resources " into revenue-producing and population-supporting natural agents is the presence of more people. These notions must be altered in the light of modern research ...[a] Like the man-land ratio, the population-natural-resource ratio is unscientific and misleading as a criterion of [overpopulation or] underpopulation and conditions (other than the presence of population) must be favourable to the increased utilisation of ... natural resources before one may expect any growth of population or any effective addition to ... [a country's] economic capacity to absorb immigration '.[102]

[a] ' The studies of Dr. Jerome [see 88] and others have conclusively demonstrated that business prosperity incident to the discovery of new resources, or changes in the conditions of demand for or in the technique of utilising known natural agents, has preceded rather than followed the great inflows of immigration in recent times ... The causal and temporal sequence which is found to exist in the case of the shorter business cycles might logically be expected to characterise the longer cycles of population growth ... ' (102).

It would seem, therefore, that ' the economic density of a country cannot . . . be studied in our days, generally speaking, without taking into consideration at least the total amount of national income, much of which is obtained by international trade '. Yet, even so, indices purporting to show the economic prosperity of countries which are based on ' the total national wealth or income . . . do not suffice to determine either the static or the dynamic social condition of a population, even in cases where they can be accurately calculated ', because one must also ' take into account the purchasing power of incomes, expenditures of family budgets, etc . . . In reality, the individual incomes of the population are at present extremely divergent. The average cannot, therefore, serve . . . as a basis nor justify conclusions as to the social conditions (importance of the degrees of prosperity or of poverty) of the different strata of the population and particularly of the working popultaion '.[155] [a]

It follows that, ' it must not be assumed that, because we know that there must be a certain density of population which is more desirable than any other in every country at any given time, we can say what it is from our knowledge of the prevailing conditions. We can, in fact, do nothing of the sort; there is no way by which we can even begin to make such a calculation '. And it follows from this that ' there is no infallible and universally applicable test ' which would make it ' possible to say whether any country, as it is now, is under- or over-populated '.[84] This conclusion, however, anticipates the results of the International Studies Conference's study of other methods of testing the presence of conditions of over- or under-population; it suffices here to draw the inference that comparisons of densities are valueless in judging the legitimacy of claims for changes in the *status quo*, for ' the truth is that density of population in particular areas is a response to the economic advantages which these areas have afforded in the past '.[166] [b]

Calculations of population pressure based upon an index of density, whether crude or refined, are a hangover from the earliest scientific efforts to analyse demographic conditions which ' limited themselves

---

[a] Cf. *248*, where it is considered that *per capita* income is not a satisfactory measure in the calculation of demographic conditions; it is rather a question of outgo. But see below, § III, the discussion on standards of living.

[b] Cf. *151* : — ' The territorial distribution of the world's surface exerts a very strong influence on the integration of the population in economic activity. The division of the economic area of the globe into regions is, first of all, a natural necessity, and secondly, the outcome of a long historical-political evolution '.

to ... making clear in a more or less summary way the population of a country or of the world, on the one hand, and the possibilities for subsistence on the other '.[151] This concept of a simple ratio of two quantities purporting to indicate a country's carrying capacity was soon found to be ' quite inapplicable as a scientific measure of comparative population density '.[102] [a] This was so ' for two obvious reasons : first, ... [in many cases] farming is essentially a commercial enterprise producing ... foodstuffs for export; and second, food represents a relatively small proportion of the normal living costs ... Because of the first of these circumstances, it is not the amount of food that can be or is being produced that counts but the amount that can be sold and the price it brings.[b] Because of the second, it is not the quantity of food available that is of vital importance but the quantity of the other products and services which constitute the major part of the family living. *Per capita* foodstuff production is not a suitable measure of the desirable population density for any region engaging largely in the export trade,[c] and potential carrying capacity, whether reckoned in foodstuffs or products of any other kind, is not an acceptable limit of population for countries whose people are accustomed to a standard of living substantially above subsistence '.[102]

III. STANDARD OF LIVING

The foregoing discussion on densities has shown that ' real difficulties arose as soon as an attempt was made to go deeper into ... [the] notion of the possibilities of subsistence. The numerous estimates

[a] Even the later notion of an optimum population (to which reference is made below, § IV) sometimes shows traces of the earlier concept of subsistence, as is shown in the following definition of the optimum : — ' We say there is optimum population in a country when the capacity of production balances the consumption of its inhabitants at a reasonably high standard of living. If the population can be fed without productivity being carried to its full capacity, the country is underpopulated; in the reverse case, there is overpopulation. Optimum population is therefore a state of equilibrium ... In order that an increase in the capacity for production should become a real increase in production, it requires a corresponding growth of the density of population relative to that density which was required to obtain an optimum balance in previous conditions ' (*401*).

[b] Thus ' it would be absurd to conclude that because there are two cattle and 300 sheep for each of the 2½ inhabitants per square mile in the Falkland Islands, that that little corner of the world is underpopulated. The *per capita* foreign trade of the island amounts to $600 a year ' (*102*).

[c] Cf. *179* : — ' The fundamental reason ... why figures based on area and resources per million inhabitants are apt to be misleading is that the industry of any country can utilize foreign raw materials and specialize in occupations such as manufacturing, which require but little space '.

of the present and future food resources of a country or of the world proved to be not only very different but also, and above all, notoriously insufficient for the purposes of comparison.[a] The objection was soon raised that it is impossible to fix a direct relationship between population and food resources. It was, therefore, all the more necessary to agree upon a term of comparison. A scientific examination of the problem showed that there is no magnitude expressible in exact figures that is in constant ratio to the relatively exact figure of the population of a given region; students of the problem were accordingly obliged to go still deeper into the ever-increasing complexity of the questions at issue. First of all, it was sought to solve the problem by making a distinction between absolute overpopulation and relative overpopulation, and by resorting to the auxiliary notions of " temporary overpopulation " and " partial overpopulation ". The main object of the investigations, however, was still to discover a sure measure which would make it possible to say clearly what overpopulation really meant. The notion of the possibility of subsistence was replaced by that of the standard of living.[b] In other words, the question was put whether a growing number of human beings would, while maintaining their level of life, continue to find the means of subsistence in a given region '.[151]

It is clear, however, that, if the standard of living is to be used as a " sure measure " of the quantitative state of the population, it must itself be capable of measurement. It is also clear that, if the standard of living is to be measured, it is necessary to adopt some definite scale of measurement. Furthermore, the scale of measurement adopted must be such as to make it possible to compare the standard of living of one country with that of another for the purpose of determining the relative demographic situations of those countries. In the consideration of demands for changes in the *status quo*, such a

---

[a] ' According to ... [*130*, p. 256] overpopulation begins when *die Bevölkerung dem Nahrungsspielraum gegenüber zu gross ist* (the population is too dense in proportion to the potential food production) ', " *Nahrungsspielraum* " being defined (p. 344) ' as *die zu einer bestimmten Zeit vorhandene Fähigkeit eines begrenzten Gebietes, eines Landes oder auch der ganzen Erde, bei einer gegebenen Lebenshaltung eine bestimmte Volkszahl zu ernähren* ' (the capacity, at a given period, of a given territory, of a country or even of the whole world to feed a given population according to a given standard of living) ... [The author] says (p. 265), however, that this conception is very difficult to lay down in statistics ' (*129*).

[b] Cf., e. g., *340* : — Overpopulation exists ' whenever there are more people than can be supported by a given society without lowering the average standard of living of the masses '.

comparison would be of considerable utility, because ' what makes people feel population pressure, apparently, is not a low standard of living in itself but the degree to which they are aware that under changed conditions this low standard could be alleviated '.[55] [a]   In other words, ' overpopulation may be said to exist, not so much in actual figures as in the consciousness of the country concerned.   Some countries, such as Belgium or the Netherlands, where the arithmetical, physiological and agricultural densities are exceptionally high, have no feeling of being overpopulated, while others with far lower densities experience such a feeling strongly.   This is largely due to differences in the standard of living, which are likely to become a factor of discord and a cause of envy that may prove a menace to world peace '.[317]

As to a scale of measurement, ' it is sometimes said that death rates are an accurate indication of standards of living and hence of population pressure — the higher the death rate the greater the pressure... But clearly these death rates are not directly reflected in *felt* population pressure, leading to demands for changes in the *status quo* '.[55] [b] Moreover, ' the length of life is not always a direct function of the standard of living.   In fact, that standard would be less favourable if the average length of life would be extended to 90 years, for the possibility of earning a living would still cease at the age of 60 to 65...   A high standard of living does not... exclude a low average length of life due to epidemics, wars, etc.' [155]

Alternatively, ' in order to judge the situation of the working classes in the industrial countries, more and more use is being made, with increasingly satisfactory results, of various social statistics and especially of statistics of family budgets '.[155]   But, ' owing to the multiplicity of factors involved and the present inadequacy of the statistical data ',[190] it is difficult ' to make comparisons... between the data furnished by statistics on family budgets and by other social surveys carried out in a country at different times.   It is a still more delicate task to make international comparisons in this field, even in the case of countries lying in the same zone of civilisation.   Family budgets, in particular, have been collected by methods and in settings which differ too widely,

---

[a] ' Cf... [59], pp. 370-1; ... [58], pp. 14-15, 68-69 ' (55).

[b] ' Among the theorists of the optimum population, R. Mukerjee [159] is the most fervent representative of the thesis according to which the " optimum density of population is that where we have the highest expectation of life ".   Wolfe [161] confines himself to the statement that " the true optimum must be consistent with the lowest attainable death-rate " ' (155).

and the cost of living, the degree of culture, customs and social institutions likewise differ in large measure '.[155] [a]

Thus, while it may be true that ' an intimate and comparable knowledge of the respective situations of nations can further their social progress and the cause of peace and, at least, prevent false prophets from hampering a peaceful development ',[197] yet it does not seem to be possible, on the basis of information at present available, to make any scientific comparison of standards of living such as would permit an objective analysis of demographic situations giving rise to claims for change. To say, therefore, that ' overpopulation ... may be defined as that state in a society when the population is too large ... to permit the society to maintain its maximum standard of living '[248] or that ' overpopulation is beginning in a country when any further increase of population, proceeding at the actual rate of increase in that country, would inevitably lead to a *considerable* reduction in the standard of living, [and that] overpopulation exists where this has already happened ',[179] does not explain how, in practice, the standard of living can be used as a test of overpopulation.

When demographers perceived the inadequacy of the standard of living test as a measure of ' the demographic capacity of a given area as a unit of measure ', they were led ' to introduce, besides the standard of living already reached, all the economic and technical data concerning production and, finally, the form taken by the whole of the economic life of a country. In so far as quantitative comparisons are still attempted, in the majority of cases it is now the estimated income and wealth of the people that is brought into relation with the population figure '.[151] Yet, even this method, which has already been touched upon,[b] and to which reference will be made again later,[c] has proved unsatisfactory. In any case, according to one authority, a population optimum test based on *per capita* income of ultimate consumers' goods is useless for three reasons : first, in many cases it is impossible to foresee the trend of the standard of living; secondly, in some countries the

---

[a] It is reported to have been stated at one of the Conference's meetings that, ' in comparing family budgets in the different countries ' for a study on popular food consumption which had been undertaken by the International Labour Organisation, ' it became evident that they were based upon very different elements ' and that ' the calculation of the respective standards of living of two different countries is further complicated by the question of the prevailing mode of life and the preference of the inhabitants ' (53).

[b] See above, pp. 76-77.

[c] See below, p. 83.

standard of living is so high that there is no need to increase it; and, thirdly, the average standard of living may increase in a society in which the wealthy get richer and the masses poorer.   He concludes, therefore, that the standard of living test must be supplemented by others.[313]

In the course of the International Studies Conference's enquiry, it was urged that ' an effort should be made to investigate the matter of standards of living by scientific methods ',[51] particularly in view of the fact that ' the expression " standard of living " was still rather vague '.[53] It was admitted, however, that it might not ' be possible to arrive at more than an approximation of a definition '[51] — an anticipation of the results of the Conference's work which proved to be justified.

IV. OPTIMUM POPULATION

The discussion in the last two sections seems to show that definitions of overpopulation based either on densities of population or on standards of living which do not appear to be self-explanatory without an analysis of the concepts of population densities and of standards of living themselves are not greatly clarified when those concepts in turn are examined.   To get round this difficulty, recourse is now generally had to the auxiliary notion of an optimum population : ' overpopulation exists when the population exceeds the optimum '.   But ' to define overpopulation by introducing this notion of optimum calls for a definition of the optimum itself '.[113]

' In any country under any given set of conditions there may be too sparse a population in the sense that, if the population was more dense, on the average everyone would be better off. . .   On the other hand there may be too many people in the sense that, if there were fewer, every one would be better off . . .   It follows that in any country under any given set of conditions there must be a density of population which it is best to have '.   This density which it is best to have is ' the so-called optimum population '.[84]   In the first case, there is a condition of underpopulation and, in the second, of overpopulation.   Thus, it is the dividing line between underpopulation and overpopulation which marks the point of optimum population.[248]   In other words, ' overpopulation exists when numbers exceed the optimum, and under-population when they fall below it '.[84]   How, then, is the optimum size of the population to be determined ?

' The statement that, with reference to any given area, the optimum population is that population which produces maximum economic welfare is unexceptionable.   Maximum economic welfare is not necessarily the same as maximum real income per head;[a] but for practical purposes they may be taken as equivalent.   Overpopulation exists when numbers exceed the optimum, and underpopulation when they fall below it : in either case real income per head is less than it would be if the optimum prevailed '.[84][b]

It follows that, if it is possible to determine the maximum real income per head in a given country at a given moment, the maximum economic welfare of which it is, in practice, the measure can also be determined in that country; and it follows that, if the maximum economic welfare can be determined, the optimum size of the population can be determined; and it follows again that, if the optimum population can be determined, it will be possible to determine whether the country at that moment is overpopulated, underpopulated or demographically equilibrated.   But it does not follow that, if the real income falls below the maximum, the country is overpopulated; it may be either overpopulated or underpopulated.   Morevover, there is no means of determining the " maximum real income per head " of a population.[c] The concept of optimum alone does not help, therefore, to determine which of the two demographic conditions — overpopulation or underpopulation — is present in a country at a given moment, for, although ' the agencies which govern the optimum ' may be taken to be ' (i) the natural resources of the area, (ii) the constitution, natural endowment, and acquired skill, knowledge, and habits of the inhabitants, and (iii) the opportunities, internal and external, for economic activity . . ., a given kind of change, e. g., increase in skill, does not always shift the optimum in the same direction '.[84]

---

[a] Cf. *156* : — ' The optimum population is that which gives the maximum income per head '.

[b] Cf. *156* : — ' Overpopulation implies an income per head smaller than would have been realised if numbers had been less '.

[c] Cf. *129* : — ' In . . . [the] opinion of [Mombert (*130*) . . ., pp. 266-267] . . ., the gauge of the prosperity of a population (the buying power of the incomes) is the best indicator of overpopulation, if it were not that the changes on the economical conjuncture, the so-called ' konjunkturellen Wandlungen ", influenced the degree of prosperity independent of the ratio of the population to the area.   This last reservation is indeed right : he who attributes the decrease of prosperity since 1929 principally to a rapidly developing overpopulation, shows little understanding of the economic structure of our society '.

The impossibility of expressing in quantitative terms[a] the optimum population as defined above is not the only difficulty which limits the usefulness of this concept in the context of " peaceful change " when the question arises of determining whether a country is overpopulated.

In the first place, the view that ' of the various tests for the existence of overpopulation which have been proposed one only deserves careful consideration, namely, movements in real income '[84] may be " unexceptionable " from the economic standpoint, but it takes no account of the implications in such broader conceptions as the following :

According to a materialist conception, a population reaches its optimum when the number of inhabitants of a given country makes it possible to obtain, in certain conditions, from natural resources, from instrumental capital and from technique, the maximum advantages.

This conception, which is inspired exclusively by the idea of maximum profit, does not take into account interests of the community, cultural and moral interests, or future interests; it has, therefore, steadily lost ground, all the more so since it is impossible to determine exactly the criterion by which this optimum is to be gauged (actual wages, consumption of luxury articles, unemployment, death rate, average span of life, etc.).   There is, in reality, no external sign that can serve as a basis for defining an optimum situation, if conceived from the material standpoint.   What then if an endeavour were made to take into account the interests of the nation or of a group of nations, and also of cultural interests, considered not only from the present but also from the future standpoint ?

These difficulties do not exclude the existence of optimum conditions; optimum population is midway between underpopulation and overpopulation, a situation that will vary according as one wishes to subordinate more or less the purely material conditions of the present to the cultural conditions and conditions of the future, and according as one takes into consideration not only national interests but also international and world interests.[41]

The standard of living is not everything; an optimum population from the point of view of the development of character and of spiritual values might mean keeping the population beyond the point of economic welfare.[375]   ' We hear far too much about raising the standard of living;

---

[a] Cf. *129* : — ' We consider Mombert [*130*, p. 242] is right when he says the social sciences are not yet sufficiently developed to fix such a clear demarcation between under- and over-population '.

what we need is to raise the standard of good citizenship '.[299]   Indeed,
' for the majority of the authors [of the studies prepared for the International Studies Conference's enquiry into " peaceful change "], the notion
of optimum population implies more than the simple maximum economic welfare of the individual'; they held that ' a variety of factors,
many of them of a subjective nature, come into play, so that the ultimate
definition of optimum population depends largely upon the point of
view of the individual author — upon the desiderata on which he lays
most stress '.[190]

Secondly, although it was generally agreed in the International
Studies Conference ' that it is impossible to calculate statistically the
optimum population for any given country — and, consequently, to
measure the degree of absolute over- or under-population ', it was held
' nevertheless, desirable, in considering the problem of peaceful change,
to have some idea of what is meant by the notion of optimum population.
For it is a goal towards which all enlightened nations will strive by
international as well as internal action.   The better the nature of this
goal is understood and the closer it is reached by the individual peoples,
the greater will be the prospects of harmony and co-operation among
the nations '.[190]   Yet, if it is true that the peace of the world is a function
of its apprehension of the concept of optimum population, then the
impalpability of this concept must be as disconcerting ' to scientific
investigators endeavouring to find the right method in the treatment
of the problem of overpopulation ' as the ' uncertainty ' surrounding
the notion of population densities was ' discouraging ' to one of the
Conference's experts.[129]   Moreover, may it not be said that ' no practical purpose would be served by finding a definition for optimum
population, which is something purely theoretical ', because ' it would
be beyond our possibility of control to bring the population of a
country up [or down] to a certain level and to keep it there ' ?[52]

In the third place, is the optimum to be considered from the
point of view of " the masses ", the " working population " as a whole,
or from the separate points of view of the " different strata of the population " or, again, from the point of view of the State which, it has been
suggested,[a] although representing the aggregate of the individuals
under its control, is also responsible, not only for the individuals, but
for posterity ?[260]

---

[a] Cf. the reference to posterity in the passage quoted above, p. 84.

Fourthly, the concept of optimum when applied to the analysis of the demographic situation in a particular country is not useful in any absolute sense but rather in relation to the demographic conditions prevailing elsewhere. Each country when considering its optimum must also take into account the demographic position of other countries.[401]

'The starting-point of any fruitful discussion of population problems to-day is that the population problem for every country is a problem of the distribution of the population of the world as a whole '.[360]

These difficulties all spring from the fact that, as was mentioned above,[a] from the point of view of human welfare, ' fixing the optimum becomes as essentially subjective and therefore arbitrary operation . . . A balance has to be struck between two considerations, that of the quantum of life and that of the standard of well-being. When the population of a given territory increases, it is possible that, as a result of this increase, there will be, for a time, an increase in well-being. But, other things remaining equal and assuming, in particular, that there is no progress in the technique of production, the curve of well-being must, at a certain point, begin to fall. Is it then better to have more life or more welfare ? The point that has to be strongly emphasized is that we must concentrate neither on the quantum of life nor on the standard of well-being. To sacrifice well-being completely would be inhuman; to sacrifice life completely would be absurd. As to the point at which the optimum population is to be fixed, that is a matter which each one will decide for himself '.[113] [b] The optimum size of the population of a given country at a given moment is not capable, therefore, of being determined scientifically; ' the optimum is . . . an intuitive concept, incapable of being calculated '.[317] Hence, the notion of optimum population cannot furnish an objective test of population pressure in the " dissatisfied " countries; ' the optimum theory of population is . . . a speculative construction of little importance for judging actual situations '.[134]

' By a synthetic study of all the quantitative and qualitative

---

[a] p. 85.

[b] ' It is of interest to note ', adds the author of these remarks, ' that the countries where from the point of view which I have indicated, the optimum is fixed at the lowest figure are those which have the highest standard of welfare. One of the wealthiest countries in the world is undoubtedly the United States; and here, when it is a matter of determining the optimum population, the prevailing tendency is to set this optimum much lower than would be done in France ' (113).

" optima ", estimated by the authors who have concerned themselves with this question ',[197] concluded an expert who had been invited by the International Studies Conference ' to analyse in detail and evaluate the different considerations relevant to the establishment of an integrated and balanced notion of optimum population ',[190] [a] he ' arrived at the idea of a realist proportionate optimum which is not an absolute figure, a figure that can be calculated for each country, but one that approximates to the figures desired by the country itself and, taking into account the necessary demographic adjustments, a figure which next makes it possible to determine a relativist optimum — the best condition — as compared with the other countries ... The synthetic optimum of population is closely bound up with certain main objectives of each modern State; its security[b] and prestige, and the social well-being of its population. These two objectives are, moreover, interdependent. From this standpoint, the attitude hitherto adopted by economists in concerning themselves exclusively with the factors and economic structure of the world, on which the optimum population — the yield *per capita* — partly depends, was not inspired by any concern for realities; the demands of social well-being and national security must also be taken into consideration ... Politically, it is not sufficient, as some suggest, to attach importance solely to the optimum social situation, to the standard of a country as compared with that of other countries, because each country has a strong tendency to realize its idea of the optimum by taking into account these different factors in a measure which it considers desirable ... At present, the world optimum cannot be anything but a total of the national relativist optima, that is to say, an *optimum optimorum* '.[197] [c]

Thus, the concept of optimum, like those of population densities and of standards of living, did not help the International Studies

---

[a] See *155*.

[b] An Italian authority considers that, from the point of view of the State, the optimum population varies with the nearness or remoteness of the contingency of war. To a small country, it is of no importance whether its population grows or not, but it is a matter of great importance, for military reasons, to a big Power. ' The population density required to enable a people to expand its aptitudes to the full is highest when external difficulties are greatest, when geographical climatic conditions are the least favourable, and where public order is most difficult to enforce and culture the slowest in developing '. A country with high initiative can reach a high civilisation with a meagre population (e. g. the Scandinavian countries); another may need the stimulus of density (e. g. Italy); while another again may remain torpid and, therefore, suffer from density (e. g. parts of China). See *260*.

[c] For a detailed statement of proposals for the establishment of a " synthetic optimum ", see the special study prepared for the International Studies Conference : *155*.

Conference to formulate any definition of overpopulation in the concrete terms which would have been relevant to its study of " peaceful change ". It does not provide a uniform scale for the measurement of demographic situations in different countries since the situations themselves are not comparable. The optimum population is a variable function of the environment of a people and of the policy of its government. There are other kinds of optima than that of maximum economic welfare; for example, under a régime of self-sufficiency, the optimum population is that number which can live off a territory; in a rural community, the optimum population is that number which can live more or less under rural conditions, etc. It must be concluded, in fact, that, in examining the concept of optimum population, the Conference was pursuing a will-o'-the-wisp, if it is true, as one of its experts suggested, that ' the auxiliary concept of " optimum population ", so often introduced, has developed in connection with the numerous attempts that have been made to find a quantitative expression fixing the elusive moment at which overpopulation occurs '.[151]

V. UNEMPLOYMENT

Some other methods of testing demographic pressure in the dissatisfied countries were suggested in the course of the International Studies Conference's enquiries. Among the tests proposed, unemployment may be considered first, since it is commonly held to be an infallible symptom of over-crowding. Overpopulation, it is said, manifests itself in, *inter alia*, an increase of unemployment.[a]

' The question [of the relation between the population situation and unemployment] was the subject of an elaborate discussion at the World Population Congress at Geneva in 1927. Opinion was divided. On the one hand, it was maintained . . . that obviously there must be some relation and that the great swelling of the ranks of the unemployed was to a certain extent related [in Sweden, for example][b] to the cessation of emigration. On the other hand, it was asserted . . . that in Italy there had been no such effect of the cessation of emigration.[c] Obviously there is nothing to prevent . . . [both opinions having] been right what the effects of the cessation of emigration are to be depends entirely

[a] Cf., e. g., *44* : — ' The criterion of overpopulation is great poverty and unemployment '
[b] See *137*.
[c] See *136*.

upon the economic conditions of the different countries at different times.[a] At the Population Congress in London in 1931, it was maintained ... that the cessation of emigration had had an important bearing upon unemployment in England in recent years '[b] as well as in several other European countries[c] which were described as overpopulated.[134]

' The existence of unemployment does not, of itself, prove that the economic absorption of population is impossible. It merely proves that a certain type or class of population has failed to find employment under exceptionally difficult conditions which may, or may not persist '.[102]

So far as industrialised countries are concerned, ' unemployment is not necessarily, and in fact is not usually, a consequence of overpopulation ... If anyone believes that unemployment is a sign of overpopulation, let him consider two facts. Unemployment has come ... [in Great Britain, for example] in waves; between the waves it was man-power and not work that was lacking. If we graph the unemployment percentage we get a sharply fluctuating curve, whereas the growth of population is represented by a steadily ascending line, and there is no sign of any relation between them. Any one who thinks that the intermittent unemployment crises [in Great Britain] have been due to excessive numbers must hold that ... [that] country has been overpopulated every few years, while in the interval population has been in adjustment '.[84]

' In the United States there has recently been relatively more unemployment than in ... [Great Britain]; but in the United States, which are favoured above all other countries by richness in natural resources, geographical location, and an enterprising population, there are less than 50 persons per square mile as against about 700 in ... [Great Britain]. There cannot be any overpopulation in the United States, and yet unemployment has been more severe there than here '.[84]

' It is evident in fact that there may be overpopulation without unemployment, and unemployment without overpopulation. The United States are an example of the latter, while certain Asiatic countries ..., [where] men work from before dawn until dark for a

---

[a] See below, chap. 7, § V.
[b] See *138.*
[c] See *139.*

pittance . . ., are an example of the former '.[84] [a]   ' It is even conceivable that an appreciable increase in the size of the population, if of the right kind, would *reduce* unemployment in a particular country rather than add to it '.[55]

'Unemployment reveals itself where it occurs as a very variable phenomenon and we observe or understand that it may be due to a great variety of causes : loss of external markets for national production, jamming of the general economic, political and social machinery, which, by raising wages above the marginal productivity of labour, prevents the complete employment of the latter '.[113]

It is difficult, if not impossible, ' to show how great a part of the unemployment that has prevailed in recent years is a result of the downward trend of affairs and how large a share is attributable to the structural changes that have taken place in agriculture as well as in industry '; it is thought probable that, ' owing to the strong rationalisation . . ., part at least of the unemployment and of the lowering of the standard of living that has taken place in some groups of the population in recent years, is due to structural changes in the community '.[134]

Hence, ' when fixing a scale of comparison between overpopulated countries . : ., attention must not be confined to the more or less extensive unemployment prevailing '.[113]   In any case, ' it would seem . . to be a matter of secondary importance whether at a given point of time the designation " overpopulation " can be attached to the population situation of a country or not ', because ' the term itself conveys so little unless combined with a concrete examination of the actual situation '.[134] As a test of overpopulation in industrial countries, therefore, unemployment has to be rejected.

Nevertheless, the view that unemployment cannot be regarded as an effect of overpopulation because ' there is no fixed amount of work to be done in a country . . . [so that], whilst some people increase employment, others are in a position to lessen it ',[b] was questioned in one of the memoranda submitted to the International Studies Con-

[a] ' The nature of unemployment in general may be illustrated by an analogy with a steam-engine in which the steam introduced is the man-power. If the engine is working badly a lot of steam will escape and remain unproductive; this is unemployment. If we reduce the amount of steam entering the engine without improving the mechanism, we may very slightly reduce the amount which escapes; but, however little is introduced, large proportion will continue to escape. In other words, if we reduce the population without removing the causes of friction in the industrial machine, we shall still have unemployment, though perhaps not quite as much ' (*84*).

[b] *134*, quoting Professor Carr-Saunders.

ference. ' It is undoubtedly a fact ', it says, ' that the economic life of a country in point of time represents a dynamic development, where the volume of work to be accomplished can never be said to be constant. But if we consider the different communities at certain times under given states of affairs, it will usually be found that there are relatively narrow limits for the expansion taking place. And if a time with downward tendency in particular be considered, the possibilities of expansion will to a great extent prove to be small, precisely because of the prevailing economic conditions, at least when the conditions are left entirely to themselves. A relatively long time will therefore elapse before the unemployed are able to find place in the process of production once more. In such a period of depression, there will be a nucleus of truth in the popular view that there are too many people in proportion to the amount of work available '.[134]

' It is certain ', maintained the author of another memorandum, ' that a sparsely populated country with a fertile soil and rich in raw materials will be able to settle its economic troubles otherwise and more easily than a poor, densely populated or even overpopulated country '. There is, it was maintained by one of the Conference's experts, a ' close relationship . . . between unemployment and the size of the population. An increase of population does not cause unemployment, but, given a certain social structure and a certain density of population, economic disturbances due to catastrophic events, as was the case in the world economic crisis, result in unemployment that may assume disastrous proportions '.[111]

With the abandonment of the pre-War liberal principle of free movement of goods, capital and labour and with its replacement by a neo-mercantilism and national autarky, ' these new directives of economic policy inevitably affected the bases of the stability of the population in the industrial and agrarian-industrial countries, whether these countries were overpopulated or more or less half-way along the road to overpopulation '.[111] For, according to one view, ' it is impossible to restrict at one and the same time the export of goods and the export of men ',[239] and ' there is only one road across the vast desert of unemployment : a return to the freedom of emigration and immigration of pre-War days, a return to free trade, even if the latter must fail to attain the volume of pre-War years '.[111] On the other hand, ' for . . . a determination of the conception of overpopulation ' implied in the view ' that a country cannot be said to be overpopulated as long as it has unexploited potentialities, which can provide a livelihood for the population . . ., it is vitally important whether the potentialities offered lend themselves to exploitation, or whether their utilisation is rendered impossible by political, economic or other conditions '.[134]

VI. OVERPOPULATION TESTS

Tests of overpopulation are evidently ' hard to come by ', but, ' when dealing with countries the population of which is wholly or mainly engaged in agriculture, we may hope to detect serious maladjustment.　Thus if we find that farms are very small, that the amount of labour applied to an acre is large, that living is poor and less than that won in other countries where skill is no higher but farms are larger, we may suspect overpopulation.　Moreover, since agricultural technique, except in certain countries in very recent times, changes very slowly, we may assume that, if overpopulation exists, it has come about through excessive growth of population and not through any change in the surrounding conditions '.[84]

*　*　*

An interesting method of calculating population pressure ' in agrarian territories inclined to be self-supporting ' was described in one of the papers submitted to the International Studies Conference. Although this method ' is applicable only to virtually self-contained backward regions having an agricultural economy and where the living requirements of the population are absolutely minimum '[190] and may not be relevant, therefore, to the situations giving rise to claims for change with which the Conference was immediately concerned, it will be useful to describe it here as a negative illustration of the difficulties of measuring demographic pressure in agricultural countries which are not self-supporting and, *a fortiori*, in industrial countries having an economic structure based upon a system of international trade.

Overpopulation is defined in this paper as ' such a density of the population that under the existing stage of development in scientific means of production and the present distribution of the means of production, the population is unable to provide itself with the necessities of life ' (i. e. ' the quantities of food, clothing and housing absolutely required to maintain the necessary energy of the population ').

Thus defined, ' overpopulation can only occur if the general standard of prosperity renders the maintenance of the energy of the population impossible . . .; [and] the intensity of population pressure increases proportionally as the population recedes from the attainment of . . . [this] minimum of subsistence '. Applying these principles to certain rural districts of China, the author of the paper examined ' the food value of the products yielded per head of the agrarian population ' for the purpose of fixing ' the ratio between the yield of cultivated grounds and the requirements of their population, which ratio is one of the principal factors that affects a possible overpopulation of China's agricultural provinces '. After calculating the ' food requirement per head of the agrarian population ', the agricultural area per head of the agrarian population and the ' average yield of hectare ', he obtains figures which enable a comparison to be made of ' the available and requisite quantity of cereals ' and to deduce therefrom indications of not only ' where overpopulation exists, but also the intensity of the overpopulation in the various provinces ' (i. e. ' the ratio between the annual grain harvest per head of the agrarian population and the above-stated minimum requirement per agrarian inhabitant '). The results of the investigation refer, of course, to overpopulation ' in the existing stage of scientific production and under the present system of distributing the means of production ' and does not take into account ' future changes in science and society, since these cannot be predicted '; overpopulation, moreover, is considered in relation only to ' the economical and social circumstances of the inhabitants of the territory in question '.[129]

While it may be questionable whether this method of defining overpopulation and calculating population pressure, which is ' based on the minimum standard of living necessary to maintain the vital energy of the population, would be acceptable in countries having a high standard of living and a low population density ',[190] the possibility of using this method may be increased, as its author suggests, owing to ' the now much-favoured self-supporting system, causing a great reduction in the international exchange of goods '.[129]

* * *

' When we come to industrialised countries, it is impossible to find even rough tests ' of the kind suitable in the case of agricultural countries. The difficulty here ' arises from the great complexity of the situation '. Opportunities for external trade, for example, ' may be suddenly expanded and even more suddenly restricted . . . Changes of this nature . . . may cause overpopulation, at least for a time ', but ' such overpopulation is due not to excessive growth of population, but to a recession of conditions leaving the population stranded . . .; this would mean a lowering of the standard of living at least for the time, and might result in unemployment if workers preferred to stand idle rather than accept the lower standard '.[84] To declare, therefore, that ' overpopulation may occur as the result of a deterioration of economic conditions due to natural causes (disasters) or other circumstances (loss of foreign markets, for example) ',[207] is to use the term " overpopulation " in a more restricted sense than that which is contemplated in the statements of claims for relief from population pressure with which the International Studies Conference was concerned.[a]

On the other hand, a speaker at one of the Conference's meetings expressed the view that growth of population not only resulted, in many cases, in overpopulation, but provided a measurable test of demographic pressure. His argument ran as follows :

[In most cases], overpopulation is the consequence of an increase in the density of population to a point above its optimum. If this density subsequently remained constant, the removal of a state of overpopulation by economic means would be an easier problem to solve. Normally, however, the density of population increases continuously with the natural upward trend, and if the economic development of the country is unable to keep pace with it, overpopulation becomes permanent. In these cases, it is the rapidity with which the density of population increases that invariably makes it impossible to reach economic stability. Since this rate of increase depends on the natural increase of population, the latter must be regarded as the essential cause of overpopulation in these cases, the result being demographic pressure.

Obviously, in order to estimate the influence of this rate of increase on demographic pressure, it is not its relative value per 1,000 inhabitants that must be taken into consideration, but the absolute figure representing the annual surplus of births per unit of area . . . This demographic coefficient is proportional to the average density of population and to the rate of natural

[a] Cf. 361 : — ' It is impossible to say whether a highly industrialised country like Great Britain is overpopulated in the strict economic sense . . . What can be asserted of Great Britain is that it is congested, which means that on sociological grounds there are enough, if not too many, inhabitants '.

increase per 1,000 inhabitants. A geographical distribution of the territories characterized by different values of the demographic coefficient makes it possible to indicate those where the absolute surplus of births is greatest and which, therefore, constitute the centres of maximum 'production' of human beings ... Naturally, the relative values of the demographic coefficient will be comparable one with the other if they are calculated for political territorial units incorporating, in the case of colonial Powers, not only the home-country but also the colonies and other possessions dependent on the home-country ...

In 1935, a calculation was made of the excess of births — exact or approximate — per square kilometre for every country of the world, and it was found that there were four countries whose demographic coefficient exceeds one and whose overpopulation was not sufficiently neutralized by the influence of territories dependent upon them. The countries are : China, Japan, Italy and Poland. Next in order came Germany, with a demographic coefficient of 0.99. These countries are known to be over-populated. It seems certain, therefore, that demographic pressure does not exist when there is no great natural increase of population per unit of area.[207]

From the point of view of " peaceful change ", the interest of this argument lies in the support which it gives to claims for colonial expansion based upon demographic needs and, as such, it will be examined again later.[a] Meanwhile, it may be remarked that, in so far as it makes use of the criterion of density to test the presence of demographic pressure, it raises the difficulties which were considered earlier in this chapter.[b]

* * *

In the course of the Conference's study, various other phenomena were indicated as sources of overpopulation, but, since the problem under discussion is overpopulation itself, it would be begging the question to seek a definition of overpopulation by examining it as an effect of certain causes.

[a] See below, chap. 8.
[b] See above, § II.

VII. *OBSCURUM PER OBSCURIUS*

Does the Conference's failure to discover any positive signs which may be accepted as irrefutable proof of the reality of the notion of overpopulation and of the existence of overpopulation in any particular instance suggest that ' overpopulation . . ., properly speaking, has no very definite meaning ' ?[295] ' The social investigator ', wrote one of the Conference's experts, ' has to carry on his work without possessing a clear conception of what overpopulation means '.[129] ' Overpopulation ', stated another, ' is an improper term, whose incorporation alone in geo-human terminology constitutes a danger. Overpopulation is, in the last analysis, the sentiment of a class, of the educated and governing class, in a few of the densely-populated countries '. On the other hand, while showing that ' the earth is still thinly populated ', he admits that ' mankind is unequally distributed over the face of the globe ', but he utters a warning against allowing the idea to gain credit that ' overpopulation is a fact, whereas the situation is still no more than one of tension '. Notwithstanding the high densities of population in certain regions of the world, ' nowhere has saturation been reached, in so far as the economic system remains international. But, in order that international economic relations may " unload " population densities, there must first of all be international peace. Yet, to-day the tendency is to reverse these terms '.[152]

To a speaker at one of the Conference's meetings in 1937, the question of overpopulation appeared ' as one of the most obscure questions of the modern social sciences '. ' How ', he enquired, ' can we discriminate, in the problem of overpopulation, between the reality and the partisan interpretation ? May not a State, at a given moment, in its thirst for prestige, call upon the argument of over-population to justify ambitions which may or may not be avowable ? . . . I wish someone would point out to us the criteria by which it is possible to recognize on the one hand the objective realities, and on the other hand the intensity and the significance of the psychological factor '.[22]

' On the basis of the results achieved so far by science ', stated another authority, ' we are led to believe that no quantitative expression can be assigned to the phenomenon of overpopulation '. But, he adds, it does not follow from this ' that the problem as such is non-existent . . The idea that, in economic life, there is, on the one hand, a certain number of men and, on the other, a certain quantity of goods, is merely a most imperfect theoretical expedient. In reality, we have, on the one hand, a population divided into various superimposed social strata and, on the other, a complex of economic data whose structure is also extremely varied in character. They are bound up one with the other in a variety of respects. It is, therefore, the integration of the population in the economic life of a country that should be taken as the starting-point for any enquiry proposing to pierce through to the decisive problem which the term " overpopulation " does not adequately define '.[151]

' Overpopulation means that there are too many people in relation to a whole set of facts; '[84] the essence of the difficulty in giving precise meaning to the concept of overpopulation is that it is ' relative to economic and social conditions which may change very quickly. '[102] For example, ' the immigrant to whom Canada offers opportunities which his native land denies him cannot think of Canada as overpopulated. The Canadian who, perhaps because he possesses special abilities for which no outlet can be found in Canada, migrates to the United States does so because he believes that, for his purposes, Canada is overpopulated. If migration is not limited by law, men and women move to those districts in which they expect to find the greatest opportunities. For them overpopulation and underpopulation are comparative questions. They do not think of the " highest *per capita* income " but of their own immediate advantage. ' [102]

In the discussion of demographic problems, there would appear, moreover, to be ' a continual oscillation between a fear of population increase and anxiety lest it diminish. These deep contradictions are to be explained by the fact that an essentially qualitative problem is considered from a quantitative standpoint. '[151] The vital question for any society is not how to adjust the mere number of the population but how to find measures of making quantitative adjustments conducive to qualitative improvements.[340] From this point of view there is no contradiction in, for example, the policy of the German government to stimulate the birth-rate,[a] on the one hand, and to welcome the departure of a section of the population of the Reich,on the other hand. ' Malthus himself had already called attention to . . . [the] cardinal error of reasoning [in the quantitative examination of a qualitative problem] — the cause of much confusion in the analysis of the problem. '[151]

* * *

[a] See below, pp. 148-149.

' Demography and political economy are the two branches of the social sciences which have as their object the study of the correlations that exist between men and economic life. The fact that, in reality, they both deal with the same phenomenon was only gradually perceived ... Population and economic life are, indeed, two phenomena that cannot be dissociated; in reality, they are one. This conclusion was first given expression in the idea that somehow there must be a constant balance between the population and the economic life of a country. For the purpose of designating the disturbance of this equilibrium, the expressions " overpopulation " and " underpopulation " were introduced. The concept of equilibrium, borrowed from the natural sciences, was henceforward linked up — in the social sciences — with certain theories on the desirable and proper relationship between population and economic life '[151]

' The integration of population in the economic life of the various parts of the world takes ... the form of an ever-recurring struggle with the natural and political factors of territorial organisation. It is these constant efforts made by mankind to ensure its existence within a given area that should first command attention when it is sought to give the word " overpopulation " its full meaning. It is then immediately realised that it is impossible to reduce the number of problems to be solved simply by bringing the figure of the population of a given region into relation with some other numerical fact. It is far more a question of considering the *manner* in which men apply themselves to the provision of their needs in the various units of area. It is these essentially qualitative problems that really give rise to the question of the surplus or deficit of a given population — a question that is posed in too simple terms because it is considered from a purely quantitative standpoint. In order to understand these various situations, which are usually characterised in public debates by the word " overpopulation, " other considerations must be made to intervene. There is, indeed, another reason why it is impossible to express, as is frequently attempted by doctrinal methods, the relationship between population and economy by a simple ratio of quantitative magnitudes. The fallacy of such a method is immediately revealed when we remember that population and economy are not separate masses of men and property but that both form a single whole composed of elements of social life that are intermingled and closely bound up one with the other '[151]

' Overpopulation cannot be defined quantitatively. The fundamental problems that arise cannot be understood so long as we try to establish a constant ratio between population and some particular magnitude... The questions are of an essentially qualitative character. The auxiliary concept of equilibrium between population and economy, and that of the perturbations which occur in this field in the form of over- or under-population — concepts borrowed from the natural sciences — must be replaced by categories proper to the social sciences. In reality, the economico-social situations to which the term " over-population " is usually applied are the outcome of the manner in which the population is integrated in the economic life of a country and of the continuous and varied conflict with the natural and political factors of territorial organisation. ' [151]

' The phenomenon of overpopulation is, ultimately, nothing but a question of the conflict that goes on between mankind and the natural and political conditions of territorial organisation...; a great variety of solutions can be suggested for the problems that arise here. It will never be possible, however, to carry out such complicated tasks purely and simply by restricting or increasing population. In view of the very important part which the notion of the State plays in the division of the world into different regions, it is comprehensible that the term " overpopulation " often expresses nothing more than the will to dominate manifested by a political group. In that case, there would be no point in enquiring whether, from the scientific point of view, there is actually disequilibrium between population and economic life. But, in the long run, the will to dominate on the part of the State cannot ignore these two fundamental economic and social tendencies which, in all delimited regions of the globe, operate in opposition one to the other ... It is, in fact, a question of a tendency on the part of all regional units, on the one hand, to guarantee their own economic existence, and, on the other, to enter into economic relations with more and more extensive territories. Neither of these two extreme objectives is ever attained and it is for that reason that any unitaleral orientation of State economic policy, either towards the ideal of an international division of labour, or towards that of complete autarky, must be regarded as the mere speculation of Utopian theorists ... The demographic structure should never be correlated with the unattainable ideal of a " closed " or " open " economic system ... It is indispensable that science should succeed in eliminating any notion of value from the concept of overpopulation and base it solely on practical facts.

It will then realise that the notion of overpopulation. . . gives rise above all to three problems : that of the economic framework; that of the development of the various public economies, and, lastly, that of the conflict between men and the natural and political factors of territorial organisation. '[151]

In a word, ' in the majority of cases . . . the figures for population — even when their accuracy is not vitiated by imperfect statistics or bias — cannot be used as a basis for practical conclusions unless various other factors are taken into account, failing which they possess no real significance. Accordingly, if public opinion were more alive to the very uncertain and arbitrary character of the criteria on which the arguments produced in different quarters are based, it might be more inclined to reject radical and specious solutions and devote its attention to possibilities less striking in themselves, but more in keeping with complex realities and to solutions which, by making due allowance for the various factors concerned, might provide effective remedies for certain very difficult situations. '[317]

VIII. CONTEMPORARY DEMOGRAPHIC MOVEMENTS

The elusive character of the concept of overpopulation implies that, if the sympathetic reaction of the man-in-the-street to claims for relief from over-crowding were to be translated into an immediate international policy of action, the result might be merely to confuse the issue. Until the true nature of the problems is understood, the sensible attitude will be to say to the countries lacking in space : 'Formulate your claims but do not threaten us with war ', and to the countries which are more favoured : ' Do not be too stubborn; do not confine yourselves to absolute refusals. '[113]

Although it is unlikely, for reasons put forward in an earlier chapter,[a] that the " dissatisfied " countries would accept this invitation, it is possible that they are, in fact, facing problems of population which, if left unremedied, may be the source of international conflicts. Stated in terms of overpopulation, the present demographic situation in those countries may not tally with popular misconceptions of the nature of overcrowding; stated in terms of the actual direction of present population movements, the real position may be revealed.

* * *

[a] See above, p. 23.

' Up to the period immediately following the war . . ., the lack of adjustment . . . [between] world economic and social policy, more or less controlled to meet the requirements as regards the welfare of the great popular masses . . . [and] the factors of disequilibrium which have their origin in the demographic field . . ., was . . . characterised chiefly by the overpopulation of certain countries, whereas the situation to-day is mainly characterised by the dangers of underpopulation, due to the falling birth rate in the majority of the countries of European civilisation '.[197]

' The Western countries no longer face a steadily increasing menace of overpopulation, merely retarded, from time to time, by an excessive mortality; on the contrary, voluntary limitation of births is raising in these countries the spectre of underpopulation '.[155]

Thus the most striking feature of the present trend of demographic development is not that numbers are still rapidly increasing, but that the rate of population increase is declining almost everywhere, so that, if present movements are maintained, the central problem of demographic policy — ' the chief problem of our age '[241] — will be, not to prevent overpopulation, but to check depopulation.

A brief description of the population histories and prospects of the " dissatisfied " countries will bear out these statements.

GERMANY

Between 1816 and 1936, Germany trebled her population. From about 22 million inhabitants a century and a quarter ago, the population expanded to over 67 millions.[a] ' Germany maintains two inhabitants

---

[a] The following table, based on *391*, shows the ' continuous increase in the number of the inhabitants from 1816 to 1918 within the limits of the territory of the 1871 Empire, and, since 1919, within the new frontiers fixed by the Treaty of Versailles, that is to say, excluding Alsace and Lorraine and the Province of Posen since 1919, and subtracting also Memel, Danzig and the districts ceded to Belgium, to Denmark and to Poland since 1920 and 1922 ' (*376*) :

Years	Population	Inhabitants per sq. km.	Average annual increase in % of average population during each period	
			Periods	%
1816	21,989,000 (?)	—	1816-1834	1.15
1834	27,064,000 (?)	—		
1835	30,802,000	—		
1840	32,621,000	—	1834-1852	0.88
1850	35,312,000	—		
1852	35,864,000	—		
1860	37,611,000	—	1852-1871	0.72
1870	40,805,000	—		

[over

on the area on which France maintains only one to one and a half . . .
This development of the population appears even more striking if the
evolution of the excess of births over deaths is examined . . .[a]   Already
rapid before the war of 1870-71, the increase in the population was
stimulated by the victory, by the foundation of the German Empire
and by the long years of prosperity which followed.   None the less,
after reaching a maximum in 1906, the birth rate fell in Germany as in

1871	40,997,000	—			
1880	45,095,000	—		1871-1890	1.03
1890	49,241,000	—			
1900	56,046,000	—			
1910	64,568,000	124.2		1890-1910	1.38
1913	66,978,000	—			
1914	67,790,000	—			
1919	62,897,000	—		1910-1925	0.54
1920	61,797,000	—			
1925	63,177,000	134.2			
1930	65,084,000	—			
1931	65,429,000	—		1925-1933	0.55
1932	65,716,000	—			
1933	66,027,000	140.3			
1934	66,409,000	—		—	—
1935	67,870,000	—		—	—
1936	67,105,000	142.0		—	—

[a] The following table, based on *391*, shows the natural increase of the population of
Germany between 1851 and 1935 :

Periods	Excess of live births over deaths	Per 1,000 inhabitants	Remarks
1851-1860 i)	326,130	9.0	i) From 1851 to 1935, annual averages
1861-1870	408,333	10.3	
1871-1875	443,914	10.6	
1876-1880	578,154	13.1	
1881-1885	519,444	11.3	
1890 ii)	560,247	11.4	ii) From 1890, annual figures
1895	725,790	13.9	
1900	759,757	13.6	
1905	792,839	13.2	
1906	910,275 iii)	14.9	iii) Maximum
1910	879,113	13.6	
1913	833,800	12.4	
1915	—67,874 iv)	—1.0	iv) Minimum (war)
1920	666,358	10.8	
1925	547,808	8.8	
1930	425,344	6.5	
1931	313,610	4.8	
1932	285,484	4.3	
1933	233,297 v)	3.5	v) Minimum (peace)
1934	472,074 vi)	7.1	vi) Revival due to National-Social-ist policy
1935	469,361	7.0	

all European countries as the result of the changes which took place in economic and social conditions. In Germany particularly, owing to industrialisation and the great amount of migration to the towns (*Verstädterung*), the birth rate fell to the level of that in less prolific nations ... The number of births, which was still 1,600,000 in 1920, had fallen to 937,000 in 1933 '.[376]

In the presence of this decline, a speaker at the World Population Conference in 1927 could declare that ' in Germany it is no longer a problem of surplus population that we have to deal with, but a problem of disappearing population '.[289] The figures certainly seem to indicate that ' Germany has reached a state of virtual depopulation, pending effective depopulation which cannot be far off. Here is a country, therefore, that is sliding down the slope leading towards the extinction of its population ... In 1933, Germany's " reproduction " rate showed a marked deficit, that it to say, the combined action of the two factors in the natural movement of the population — fertility and mortality — were far from ensuring the replacement of the generations '.[113]

It has been thought, therefore, that ' the German population ... is likely to decline at about the same rate as that of Great Britain ',[166] the " net reproduction rate "[a] in the two countries being about the

---

[a] ' A clear conception of how a population is growing can be obtained by the use of two indices. The first is called the gross reproduction rate. To get this, we tabulate the number of births per 1,000 women of a given age for every year of the childbearing period. If we add all these together, we get the number of children which would be born to 1,000 women during the whole of the child-bearing period if fertility remained unchanged. By multiplying this by the proportion of females among all children born and dividing by 1,000 we get the number of girls which would be born per woman if fertility remained at its existing level during their lives. Clearly, if this number, *the gross reproduction rate*, is less than unity, a population is bound to dwindle away unless something happens to raise it. This is true however much may be done to diminish the risk of death to mother and child. The other index of population growth ' — the *net reproduction rate* — ' is obtained by multiplying the birth-rates for each maternal age by the number of survivors of that age given in the life table. On adding the products and multiplying the result by the proportion of females in all births and dividing by 1,000 we get the average number of girls who will themselves survive to become mothers born per woman in the population ' (*297*). ' If ... [the net reproduction] rate is one, it means that the present generation of females will, at their death, have been fully replaced by the girls they have borne, and the population will remain constant. If the rate is above one, the population will increase. If the rate is below one, the population will decrease. If the rate remains below one, the population will eventually die out ' (*312*). ' A net rate of ... [one] is just sufficient to maintain the population figure in the long run ' (*319*).

For more detailed information on reproduction rates, see : *320*, the authors of which ' first made quite clear the influence ... of variations in the age distribution of the population ... upon the virtual evolution of the populations ' (*250*); *321*, the author of which ' has extended the application of this method of demographic forecasting to a large number of European countries ' (*250*); and *322*.

same. ' It is true that the German birth-rate, under the influence of improved business conditions and various official measures,[a] rose by a little more than one-fifth from 1933 to 1934. But this does not mean that a corresponding increase of the net reproduction rate has taken place, an unusual number of the children being the first-born of new marriages. A concentration of marriages in certain years naturally results in a number of such births, but this does not signify a corresponding increase in fertility. It is therefore certain that the German net reproduction rate is still far below . . . [0.9], probably under . . . [0.8]. Pending a change in this respect, the " overpopulation " problem is not likely to arise during the next two decades in Germany, any more than in France, Great Britain or Scandinavia '.[179] On certain assumptions which are ' not by any means improbable ', the future population of Germany (1937 frontiers), exclusive of the Saar, will reach a maximum of seventy millions in 1960, as against sixty-five and a half millions at the end of 1933;[b] ' nobody in his senses can really imagine that an increase of five million people over a period of some twenty-five years is such an acute intensification of the problem that vast territorial revisions are made necessary by it, assuming that such revisions are not already desirable on some entirely different ground. It is quite clear that the growth of demand, owing to an expanding national income, which is due to technological changes, is quite sufficient to take care of a population-increase of this order of magnitude '.[166]

In these circumstances, notwithstanding the assertion by a Polish speaker at a meeting of the International Studies Conference in 1937 that Germany was one of the ' notoriously overpopulated ' countries presenting ' the highest demographic pressure ',[207] ' it is difficult to

---

[a] Cf. below, pp. 152-155.

[b] According to an estimate in *89*, on the assumptions (i) that there will be a 22.7 per cent fall in the number of children born per married couple by 1950 and then stability of fertility, (ii) that there will be a 70 per cent fall in infant mortality and a 20 per cent fall in mortality for older persons, and (iii) that there will be no migration, the population of Germany [which, excluding the Saar territory, stood at the figure of 65.35 millions on December 31, 1933] will reach its maximum size of 65.5 millions in *c.* 1935-1940 and will then fall to under 50 millions by 1975.

According to estimates in *85*, on the assumptions (i) that the annual number of births remains constant at the level of 1927, (ii) that mortality remains as in 1924-26, and (iii) that there will be no migration, the population will reach its maximum of 69.750 millions in *c.* 1960 and will then fall to 69.486 millions by 1970 and to 66.746 millions by 2000; on the assumptions (i) that there will be a 25 per cent fall in fertility between 1927 and 1955 and then stability, (ii) that mortality remains as in 1924-26, and (iii) that there will be no migration, it will reach its maximum of 67.506 millions in *c.* 1950 and will then fall to 62.337 millions by 1970 and to 46.891 millions by 2000.

speak of overpopulation in any real sense in Germany '.[190]   What will probably happen to the German population ' is that during a certain number of years . . ., [it] will remain at about its present level and thereafter decline '.[179]

ITALY

' The Italian people is one of the most prolific in Europe and it does not cease to increase '.[394]   It seems destined, towards the middle of the century, to have doubled itself in a hundred years.[a]

' The development of the population is at present nearly equal to that of Germany in absolute figures, which means that it is proportionally very much greater, since the number of inhabitants of the two countries

---

[a] The table given below, based on 395, gives ' an idea of the movement of increase of the population. For the year 1861, the statistics cover the population of various Italian States, to which have been added those of Venetia, and the Mantuan and Roman districts, in order to have figures comparable with those of the whole kingdom after 1871. Starting from 1921, the population statistics refer to individuals living within the new frontiers ' (394)

Years	Population	Inhabitants per sq. km.
1861	25,017,000	87.2
1871	26,801,000	93.5
1875	27,465,000	—
1880	28,294,000	—
1881	28,459,000	99.3
1885	29,300,000	—
1890	30,351,000	—
1895	31,402,000	—
1900	32,452,000	—
1901	32,475,000	113.3
1905	33,249,000	—
1910	34,547,000	—
1911	34,671,000	121.0
1914	36,120,000	—
1919	36,147,000	—
1921 i)	36,361,000	126.9
1921 ii)	37,973,000	122.5
1925	39,296,000	—
1930	41,069,000	—
1931	41,176,000	132.8
1932	41,809,000	—
1933	42,214,000	—
1934	42,625,000	—
1935 iii)	43,009,000	136.9

i) Old frontiers.   ii) New frontiers.   iii) Provisional figures.

is in the ratio of 1 to 1 ½ '.[394] [a] ' As soon as Italian unity was achieved,
in 1871, the population of the peninsula increased rapidly until about
1900, and then remained stationary for a time, recommencing its upward
movement from 1906 until 1915, the date of Italy's entry into the war.
After the war it gathered force again, and, leaving the year 1932 aside,
the annual increase of births has varied between four hundred and
five hundred thousand souls '.[394]

Italian ' fertility is far above the level of ... [unity]. The net
reproduction rate in 1931 was ... [1.21]. A decline in fertility began
immediately after the war, continuing in recent years at a more rapid
pace; it is therefore probable that the 1936 rate is much below that of
1931, but still well above ... [unity]. The outlook for Italy is that the
population will increase rapidly during the next decade, even though
the actual annual increase may be falling ';[179] the population ' may
be expected to increase by at least an eighth in the next twenty-five
years, that is from 40 to 45 millions '.[81] [b] Yet, ' judged by ... [the]

[a] The following table, based on 395, shows the natural increase of the population of
Italy between 1872 and 1935 :

Periods		Excess of live births over deaths	Per 1,000 inhabitants
1872-1875	(annual average)	170,255	6.3
1876-1880	,, ,,	208,565	7.5
1881-1885	,, ,,	307,420	10.7
1886-1890	,, ,,	306,745	10.3
1891-1895	,, ,,	325,808	10.6
1896-1900	,, ,,	353,011	11.1
1901-1905	,, ,,	351,081	10.7
1906-1910	,, ,,	388,837	11.5
1911-1915	,, ,,	415,532	11.7
1916-1920	,, ,,	—50,143	—1.4
1921-1925	,, ,,	476,058	12.4
1926-1930	,, ,,	436,255	10.9
1930		515,927	12.6
1931		416,792	10.1
1932		380,349	9.1
1933		421,866	10.0
1934		429,627	10.1
1935		402,745	9.4

[b] According to estimates in 87, on the assumption that fertility and mortality remain
at the 1928 levels and that there will be a loss by emigration of 400,000 in each decade after
1921-31, the population of Italy [which stood at the figure of 42.217 millions on December 31, 1933] will rise to 60.589 millions by 1961; on the assumptions (i) that the decline
in fertility shown in 1922-28 continues until 1948, (ii) that there will be no decline in mortality,
and (iii) that there will be the same loss by emigration, the population will rise to 47.337 millions by 1961. According to 41, ' it must be reckoned that in 50 years' time as from 1931,
the population of Italy will have risen by 27 million '.

standard [of the growth in numbers of the population], Italy cannot be said to suffer from overpopulation more seriously than a great number of other European countries that have no overseas territory in temperate climes at their disposal'.[131]

JAPAN

' Nobody can dispute the fact that the demographic situation of Japan proper[a] is extremely serious ... When the evolution of Japanese population for two centuries is examined, one is struck by the contrast between the stagnation of the Tokugawa period and the extremely rapid rhythm of increase since the Meiji period ...[b] The population, which remains stationary at about twenty-six million inhabitants in the 18th and 19th centuries until the arrival of Commodore

[a] That is to say, the four large islands of Honshu, Hokkaido, Shikoku, and Kyushu.

[b] The following table, based on *397* and *399*, shows the growth of the population of Japan between 1721 and 1935 :

| Year | Population | | Inhabitants per sq. km. | Annual increase i) | |
	Family registers	Census		Absolute number	%
1721	26,065,000	—	—	—	—
1732	26,921,000	—	—	—	—
1750	25,917,000	—	—	—	—
1768	26,252,000	—	—	—	—
1780	26,010,000	—	—	—	—
1792	24,891,000	—	—	—	—
1804	25,517,000	—	—	—	—
1828	27,201,000	—	—	—	—
1846	26,207,000	—	—	—	—
1872	33,110,000	—	—	—	—
1879	35,768,000	—	96.2	—	—
1882	36,700,000	—	98.0	—	—
1884	37,450,000	—	100.7	—	—
1894	41,813,000	—	112.4	—	—
1904	47,219,000	—	127.0	—	—
1907	48,819,000	—	—	—	1.36
1910	50,984,000	—	—	730,373	1.45
1914	54,142,000	—	139.5	853,803	1.46
1919	57,223,000	—	147.5	566,195	0.99
1920	57,918,000	55,963,000	149.2	684,700	1.19
1925	62,043,000	59,736,000	162.5	962,500	1.57
1930	66,892,000	64,450,000	174.9	1,000,700	1.51
1931	67,837,000	—	177.4	945,300	1.41
1932	68,865,000	—	180.1	1,028,100	1.51
1933	69,881,000	—	182.7	1,016,000	1.47
1934	70,782,000	—	185.1	900,600	1.43
1935	—	69,254,000	—	—	—

i) On the basis of the number of inhabitants, according to the family registers.

Perry, suddenly begins to increase in a very rapid manner; there are now every year a million more mouths to feed, two hundred and fifty thousand more workers for whom an occupation must be found '.[384]

So far as the population position of Japan in general is concerned, this country ' is to be classed with those countries in eastern Europe where the birth-rate has recently begun to decline[a] and where medical

[a] According to *187*, the annual births in Japan during the last forty years have been as follows :

Year	Average Births
1895-1899	1,323,000
1900-1904	1,472,000
1905-1909	1,563,000
1915-1919	1,796,000
1920-1924	2,005,000
1925-1929	2,092,000
1930-1934	2,107,000

'The decade 1920-30 is the period in which children born between 1890-1900 had entered the child-bearing age-group. The decade 1890-1900 was . . . just the period in which the annual births increased rapidly. Therefore, between 1920 and 1930, the number of women of child-bearing age was increasing rapidly. If young men and women married at the same age as in the foregoing decades and had as many children as before, the annual births of this decade ought to have shown a marked increase, but actually, the births stood at about two million. Marriages did not increase in spite of the growth of adult population . . . The number of births to a family was also falling. Thus, the growth of the child-bearing age-group and the decrease in fertility just offset each other. However, it is not a new fact that the Japanese population have grown less fertile. The refined birth-rate, i. e. the births *per capita* of women in the child-bearing age-group, changes as follows :

Year	Births per capita of women between 15-44	Births per capita of women between 15-29
	(i)	(ii)
1898	0.146	0.250
1903	0.152	0.254
1908	0.160	0.278
1913	0.159	0.285
1918	0.152	0.265
1920	0.169	0.294
1925	0.165	0.277
1930	0.157	0.262

Here, we see the rate (i) had reached a peak already in 1908 and was dropping in the two successive five-year periods, but jumped to another peak in 1920 and dropped again. This irregularity was probably due to the extraordinary boom during the Great War, and it is shown even more emphasised owing to the influenza epidemic in 1918 and abnormal increase in the number of registrations of the hitherto unrecorded births in the first census. But, on the whole, we can safely conclude that the fertility of the nation has entered into a stage of decline. It may be said that the economic depression in the recent years is keeping the number of marriages abnormally low and we might expect to see another rise in fertility when the depression is over. But, it will be unreasonable to imagine a further rise so large as that which followed the tremendous war boom. Contrary to the assumption of some foreign students, the ancient family system of the Japanese nation, although it is rooted in the people's life, does not seem to prevent the birth rate from falling. The Japanese have begun to marry less frequently and to have smaller families in the same manner as Western peoples did. Here, again, we find a reproduction of the population movement in Europe in former times ' (*ibid.*).

and sanitary progress is now reducing the death-rate ... There are certain factors which will make for an increase of population [in the future]. The death-rate is declining and will continue to do so, but it is not very high ... [so that] there is no opportunity for a prolonged or dramatic fall.[a] It is also the case that the pre-reproductive age-group is unusually large ..., a situation which favours a high birth-rate. On the other hand, women are marrying later and, more important still, are limiting their families when they marry.[b] There is little doubt that the latter factors will prove more important than the former ... [It has been estimated that about 1950] the reproductive group will cease to increase relatively to other age-groups, whereas fertility will probably continue to decline.[c] Under these circumstances, the annual number of births will fall well below 2 millions, and the population will cease to grow before it reaches 100 millions and may perhaps never approach this figure '.[84][d]

[a] In recent years, ' the annual number of deaths absolutely declined [in Japan], while the total population was increasing at the rate of one million every year. The death-rate, which stood around 22 per thousand twenty years ago fell to 17 per thousand by 1935. But this statistical result does not mean that men and women of the country live longer now than fifteen years ago, so that life premium may be reduced for that reason. The death-rate for the adult population declined only slightly. The marked drop in the general death-rate is almost entirely due to the improvement in infantile mortality. The life table shows that the mortality among children, and particularly among those under five years of age, is remarkably high in this country even now. The death rate for infants under one year is 16%; for those between one and two years 4.8% and for those between two and three years 2.6%. Of all the babies born, nearly one-fourth are lost before they are five years old. Thus, the proportion occupied by child mortality in the total death roll is very large ... Therefore, even a small improvement in infantile mortality would make a notable decline in the general death-rate. As it happened in fact such improvement was marked in recent years, although the rate is still much above the Western level. Here also the Japanese population movement is following the example of some other countries ' (187).

[b] ' On the whole, we may conclude that the nation is now rearing less children in better conditions than in the past. Lower death rates among children are to some extent making good the decline in natural growth due to the decline of the birth-rate. The future growth of the total population is to be decided between the expanding numbers of the child-bearing age-group on the one hand and the decline of the birth rate counterbalanced to a certain extent by the improvement in child mortality on the other hand ' (187).

[c] ' The Japanese reproduction rate in 1925 and 1930, as calculated by ... [the author of 187], was as follows : — Gross Reproduction Rate : 2.59 in 1925 and 2.37 in 1930; Net Reproduction Rate : 1.64 in 1925 and 1.57 in 1930. Compared with the rates for European countries, the Japanese rate is exceptionally high, although it is probably falling '.

[d] Cf. 179, in which a forecast is made for Japan similar to that for Italy (see above, p. 106). ' Four years ago, when the result of the third national census was published, an estimate of the future Japanese population was made by ... [the author of 187]. As is unavoidable in all such attempts, or estimates, several assumptions had to be allowed ... [He] assumed that the expansion of the child-bearing age-group and fall in their fertility will offset each other and, as a result, the annual births will remain at 2,100,000 for the next twenty years ... [He] also assumed that the death rate for each of the five-year age-groups, including those for children, remain unchanged throughout the period. The third

' While it cannot be decisively proved by figures that Japan is overpopulated, there are various facts relating to the labour expended on the land and to the yields received which strongly suggest that this is so. It is not possible, in fact, to resist the conclusion that there is congestion of numbers in Japan, and that the further increase, which is to be anticipated, though less than sometimes supposed, is a formidable menace '.[84]

POLAND

While ' we may take it that a heavy decline [in the birth rate] has been in progress '[84] in Poland ' the net reproduction rate in 1927 was still as high as 1.3 '[55] a ' At this rate, the population is increasing every generation by 30 per cent ',[55] and ' we may anticipate that ... the population will increase by a quarter at least in the next twenty-five years, that is from 35 to close upon 45 millions '.[84] ' In order to prevent Poland's existing population pressure from increasing, it would

assumption was that there would be no flow of migration, either outward or inward. The estimate obtained under these assumptions was as follows [in thousands] ... :

Year	Total	Increase	Rate of Increase
1920	55,963		
1925	59,736	3,773	0.0674
1930	64,067	4,331	0.0725
1935	68,107	4,040	0.0630
1940	71,850	3,743	0.0549
1945	75,267	3,417	0.0475
1950	78,364	3,097	0.0411
1955	81,155	2,800	0.0357
1960	83,594	2,439	0.0300
1965	85,794	2,200	0.0263
1970	87,753	1,959	0.0228

The estimate of course proved wrong as a prophecy. The actual total population in 1935, according to the result of the latest census, rose to 69,000,000, i. e. about one million above the estimate. The annual births remained so far as an average of 2,100,000 per year, as was assumed. But the number of deaths made a larger drop than that which had been assumed ... There was a considerable improvement in infantile mortality and ... there were more immigrants from Korea ..., while some emigration to Manchuria took place during the five-year period. However, the most important part of the estimate in question is not the calculation of the total population, but that relating to the growth of the age-group between 15 and 60, who may be called the " productive " or " working " population. This group [which] was ... [30,949,000] in 1920, increased to ... [33,223,000] in 1925, and to ... [35,827,000] in 1930, i. e. increased by five millions during the decade, 1920-30, or by 500,000 per year on an average. As calculated in the estimate, the group is to reach ... [45,966,000] in 1950. This means ten millions in the twenty years, 1930 to 1950. The tremendous number of ten millions is to be added to the army of workers, male and female ... '

a Quoting from 57.

be necessary for 30 per cent of her population to migrate each generation. It is possible that places could be found in other countries for this number of Polish emigrants for some time to come, but it is highly doubtful that emigration on such a scale could be kept up indefinitely. Apparently the only permanent solution of a population problem of this kind is a further considerable decline in the birth rate. But it cannot be hoped that the situation will be substantially relieved in this manner for years to come '.[55]

* * *

The inference to be drawn from these observations on the population situation in the " dissatisfied " countries will be clearer when their present demographic movements are set in the wide background of the population trends in the world as a whole.

North and West Europe

' In north and west Europe...,[a] where the [net reproduction] rate is below unity,[b] the population will presently begin to decline unless there is an immediate and considerable rise in fertility ', but ' the prospect is that fertility will decline steadily for some time to come '; hence, ' there is no sign that . . . [the net reproduction rate] is approaching stabilisation '. It may be anticipated that ' there will be no further increase of population of any importance, and that before 1950 the population will be on the decline in most countries in this region '. It is true that ' in no case will the decline be large twenty years from now. For, assuming fertility to decline still farther, the drop in numbers will only become rapid about 1960 '.[84]

South and East Europe

' In the south and east of Europe the prospects are different '.[84] The net reproduction rate is still above unity,[c] and, ' if fertility is stabilised at its present level..., the population will continue to increase '. There is, however, no sign of stabilisation, and, ' in view of the unity of European civilisation and of the evidence that, in respect to size of

[a] Also in Austria and in Hungary (84).
[b] Also in Austria, Czechoslovakia, Hungary, Finland, Estonia and Latvia, but not in Holland and the Irish Free State (312).
[c] i. e., in Italy, Spain, Portugal, Poland, Lithuania and the Balkan States (312).

family as in other matters, the rest of Europe is imitating the west, we may expect that the trend of fertility in the south and east will follow that in the west . . .; it will fall in time to about the same low [replacement] level. Further, since, where fertility has begun to fall latest, it has fallen fastest, we may expect that the time taken to reach this low level will be less in the south and east than in the west '. In south Europe, ' it is probable that the net reproduction rate will fall to unity . . . within two decades . . ., [though], even if this happens, the population will continue to increase for some time to come '. In east Europe, ' the fall of the rate to unity will be still longer delayed in all probability, since it is higher than in south Europe ', but since, as has already been mentioned, ' experience seems to show that, where fertility has begun to fall latest, it has fallen most quickly, we may expect that the decline of fertility in south and east Europe will be rapid '. Thus, as in west and north Europe, the countries of south and east Europe ' are approaching year by year a time when their populations will no longer replace themselves '.[84] [a]

EUROPE OVERSEAS

Similar demographic movements are at work ' in those countries which collectively constitute Europe overseas ', that is, ' those oversea estates, which Europeans have not only acquired but where they do all the work in the fields and in the factories themselves ', namely, Australia, Canada, New Zealand and the United States. ' In the United States the population . . . was only just replacing itself in 1931, while Australia and New Zealand were already below replacement rate in 1932.[b] It is therefore certain that, if present conditions are stabilised, additions to the population of these countries through natural increase will presently cease. The same is almost certainly true of the non-French part of Canada . . . It is . . . probable that, although in the absence of immigration, population will continue to

---

[a] Russia, however, ' is in a different position. The net reproduction rate for the whole country is very high, though there are reasons for thinking that it has fallen recently . . . It is almost certain that fertility will fall very heavily in Russia, and it may fall with a very great rapidity. But it is still so high that the population of Russia may well double itself before it stabilises ' (*84*). If 'continues to grow as, according to the official figures, it has grown from 1924 till 1934, it would by the year 2000 amount to about 650 millions ' (*312*).

[b] ' At present [1935] the [net reproduction] rate is below one in . . . the United States, Australia and New Zealand ' (*312*).

grow in the United States, Australia, New Zealand and non-French Canada for two decades or more, the maximum population will not be more than 10 to 15 per cent larger than the present population. Thereafter decline will set in assuming that fertility does not rise '.[84a]

CENTRAL AND SOUTH AMERICA AND SOUTH AFRICA

In Central and South America and in South Africa, where, unlike the other countries of Europe overseas, there is a smaller proportion of European to non-European inhabitants, the population ' has been increasing rapidly, though it is still sparse '. As to the white population of South Africa, ' the outstanding facts are that the birth-rate and natural increase are high; they have fallen, but not to the same extent as in the other countries [of Europe overseas mentioned above] . . . The net reproduction rate must be well above unity; nevertheless, the indications are that it will slowly fall to unity '. As to Central and South America, ' the position in regard to vital statistics is not unlike that in South Africa. The birth-rate is high, higher than in South Africa for every country for which it is recorded with the exception of Uruguay. But it is everywhere falling. In comparison with South Africa, the death-rates are still higher, and in consequence natural increase in most Central and South American countries is not much above that found in South Africa . . . The prospect is that the population of this continent will grow by natural increase for a long time to come '.[84]

* * *

Thus, throughout the western world (including economically westernised Japan), the rate of population increase is diminishing, and,

a Cf. 102 : — ' It would seem that . . . [the] figure of 10 to 15 per cent as the maximum probable increase in the non-French population of the United States and the British Dominions is likely to prove an underestimate as far as Canada is concerned. A projection of Canada's population on the basis of specific birth rates of 1930-31 and the life tables of the census year 1931 indicates an increase of 20 per cent in the Anglo-Saxon population by the year 1971, of 73 per cent in the population which is neither French nor Anglo-Saxon, and of 224 per cent in the French population, on a self-contained basis. This calculation assumes that there will be no decline in birth rates below the low levels of the base years and no decrease in mortality rates. Neither assumption of course is in accordance with expectation. It is anticipated in particular that non-Anglo-Saxon birth rates will continue to decline materially faster than death rates. Yet, while . . . [the] upper figure . . . [of 15 per cent] may not prove far out for the population of English-speaking origin, it is difficult to accept for other immigrant stocks and . . . [it was] admittedly . . . not . . . [intended] to apply . . . to the population of Canada as a whole . . . '

over the greater part of these areas, there would appear to be a clear prospect of a decline in population within the predictable future.

It has been conjectured that ' only twenty-five years ago . . ., the reaction of public opinion to the prospect of a population decrease in the near future ' would have been one of ' the greatest alarm '; for, ' up to the World War practically all Governments and the great majority of the people viewed a large and increasing population as an economic asset '.   But ' since the World War many Governments and the majority of the people have taken an opposite standpoint.   A large and increasing population is no longer considered an economic asset but an economic burden '.[310]   This is so because, although ' the social, economic, and financial implications from a growing to an at first stationary, and later decreasing, population are manifold . . ., few people so far realise the seriousness of the situation ';[310] if public opinion were aware of the deleterious consequences of declining numbers, the fact that ' the rather remarkable recent trend of population statistics forecasting a definite decline in the population has apparently not yet penetrated the minds of the public '[55] would inhibit public consternation.   For, although ' to-day the decline in the rate of increase is apparent to all, there are few who realise that the net reproduction rate has fallen or is falling below unity; and most people who are troubled about the declining rate of natural increase comfort themselves with the anticipation that, when better times return, the birth-rate will go up '.   Yet, ' a close study of the situation does not reveal any substantial ground for this hope ', inasmuch as ' the course of population has its roots in the previous generation [and] if fertility continues to fall it will be too late to prevent a rapid drop in population if action is delayed until . . . [the drop in numbers becomes rapid] '.[84]

In the meantime, from the point of view of " peaceful change ", the prospect of an early decline in some countries is of immediate importance : as soon as it becomes ' common knowledge to all the world . . ., [it] will (whether for the better or the worse) affect the view taken of these countries, where it is anticipated, by other nations ';[84] and, since the " dissatisfied " nations are among those which are affected by the prospective decline in numbers, public opinion in the " satisfied " countries would no longer lend a sympathetic ear to claims for changes in the *status quo* advanced on grounds of overpopulation.

But whether public opinion is aware or not of the true course of contemporary demographic movements and whether the " dissatisfied " countries are genuinely apprehensive of overpopulation or not, the fact that it may not be possible to show objectively that they are either actually suffering from, or threatened with, demographic congestion does not dispose of the problem.   It is true that, in countries where the net reproduction rate is below unity, 'the problem of " overpopulation " does not exist ' and that ' instead has come the question of the economic effects of a decline of population '; it is also true that ' the number of persons of a working age ' only ' continues to increase for ten or more years after the net reproduction rate has fallen below . . . [unity] '.   On the other hand, ' in countries like Italy, Japan, Russia and certain of the Balkan States ', where the net reproduction rate is still above unity, the number of persons of working age ' is at present growing so rapidly as to constitute a serious problem from the point of view of employment ';[179] while, even those other countries, such as Germany, where the population increase is below replacement rate, still have before them a period of population expansion.   Though the concept of overpopulation must be rejected in the examination of claims, can demands for changes in the *status quo* be based, then, upon demographic pressure due to a *growth* of population, and does the fact that numbers are still rising in all the " dissatisfied " countries explain and justify their expansionist policies and aspirations ?

Chapter 5

The Basis of Population Claims

I. EXPANSIONISM

If it may be correctly inferred from the results of the International Studies Conference's examination of the notion of overpopulation that no convincing tests of the reality of overcrowding in the " dissatisfied " countries are discoverable and, furthermore, that the concept of overpopulation is itself an expedient of questionable utility in the analysis of demographic conditions prevailing in those countries, and that ' even if overpopulation exists . . ., it is, in the modern world, essentially a short-term problem '[166], does it follow that the aspirations and demands which are the subject of this survey are determined, in fact, not by pressure of population, but by ' considerations of another order (ambition, prestige, historical memories, etc.) . . . which are disguised by the pretext of overpopulation ' ?[40] [a]

That there is ' the tendency towards expansion and claims which, formulated on the plea of overpopulation, have really nothing in common with demographic pressure '[207] may be true.' It is possible ', for example, ' for . . . [expansionist] sentiments to arise when the population situation is not in view. Thus colonies may be wanted merely because of the prestige which they confer or because of the access to raw materials which they provide '.[84] Some evidence of cases of this kind will be considered later. There may even be instances where good faith is lacking in some of the claims for relief from demographic congestion and where the real motives for the demands

---

[a] ' The antecedent question whether States which have broken treaty pledges have not thereby forfeited their right to formulate . . . claims ' (176) raises issues of a wider character than can be considered in a survey which embraces only one aspect of the general problem of peaceful change.

are notavowable. ' When, for example, an endeavour is made to recover colonies or to acquire new colonial territories, it is not always for the sole purpose of finding room for a surplus of population or because the country concerned flatters itself that it will derive extra wealth from them; the reason — and possibly the principal reason — may be political and military, the object being to secure naval bases, ports of call on the main lines of world communication, or again for reasons of prestige '.[113] Again, it is said that ' one motive . . . behind the . . . demand for colonies, and . . . a very sinister one . . ., [is] the desire for military power by the use of coloured armies '.[184] [a] Undoubtedly, ' there are demagogues in all countries using the false teachings of population pressure, with the result that we have an intensification of animosities in the world '.[206]

' But it is none the less true that a problem of population pressure really exists ';[113] it is manifestly not the whole truth that this problem is not at the basis of some of the demands for relief from overcrowding. ' The opinion most commonly held is ', rather, ' that differences in the pressure of population have always been a major source of serious international conflicts '.[144] [b] It is reported that, at the meetings of the International Studies Conference, ' there was general agreement among the experts on . . . [their] fundamental premise, namely, that there are serious demographic maladjustments in the world to-day. On the one hand . . ., [there are] countries which are unquestionably over-populated, and, on the other hand, there are regions of the world which are not exploited to the limit of their potentialities and which could, with profit, support a larger population. It was recognised generally by the experts that these demographic maladjustments do constitute a source of trouble and friction in international relations and that, consequently, the means for remedying such a situation, very properly, constitute one of the objects of discussion at a Conference on Peaceful Change '.[226]

These opinions may be illustrated as follows :

Different rates of increase of population (apart from emigration) lead to different rates of growth of different peoples and to changes in their relative

[a] On January 30, 1919, the Council of Ten of the Peace Conference ' discussed an important aspect of the mandates system. From this meeting onwards, the delegates endeavoured to define as explicitly as possible the right of the mandatory Power to recruit native troops in mandated territories. M. Clemenceau, Mr. Lloyd George and President Wilson agreed that it was legitimate to raise troops for the defence of the territory ' (328).

[b] ' Cf., for example, . . . [145, 146, 149, 148] . . .; [the author of 147] is probably alone in upholding the argument that it is difficult to find in the history of the world an undeniable case of aggression knowingly caused by population pressure ' (144).

numerical importance. This in turn produces a different pressure in the economic sphere allotted to them. The recent past provides us with examples of relatives changes in the size of the population as a result of different rates of growth. At the time of the Napoleonic Wars, the population of France formed half of the population of Europe outside Russia; now it forms scarcely a tenth of the population of the same region. In our time the Germanic races have lost ground heavily to the Slavonic races ... The proportion of the Germanic peoples to the total population of Europe fell between 1910 and 1930 from 34% to 30%, while the proportion of the Slavonic peoples rose from 42% to 46%.[a] These are changes affecting every aspect of historical development, not merely external facts, and the struggle for power, but all other fields of human action — especially cultural. Alongside these changes, the different rates of growth usually produce differences in economic pressure. Countries whose population is growing fast are as a rule unable to keep their excess population within their own frontiers and are obliged to transfer them elsewhere. Even when they go to other regions within the same country, this gives rise to political difficulties which present a danger for internal peace ... The consequences are no less dangerous when the pressure of population leads to movements across frontiers ... [In connection with] the demand for colonies on the part of countries with a rapidly increasing population ..., [it is to be noted that] a large number of important authorities are agreed that the limits of subsistence would only be reached with a world population three or four times as great as it is to-day, and that these limits may be extended still further as a result of economic and technical progress. Whether or not this possibility will soon, or indeed ever, be reached, it is of interest to observe the attempts of the powerful nations to procure for themselves as much fruitful land and sources of raw materials as they can in order to make economic provision for the future growth of their people. It is an unpleasant paradox when this growth does not take place and the regions obtained with a view to the expected growth are taken from other countries which owing to their rapid growth stand much more in need of them. This provides a further subject for disputes which may disturb the peace.[81]

If it be held, therefore, that 'as a rule population considerations play a part in the origin of ... [expansionist] sentiments ',[84] it would be but an irresponsible evasion of the problem to dismiss claims based

---

[a] Quoted from F. Burgdörfer.

on the grievance of overpopulation on the ground that, since overpopulation is an artificial notion which does not express any real demographic situation, they cannot be substantiated. Setting aside the postulate of overpopulation, the problem becomes one of discovering the real nature of the " population considerations " which give rise to expansionist aspirations and to claims for changes in the *status quo*. Analysis seems to reveal that such considerations may be grouped under six different headings. There is, first, the circumstance noted in the preceding chapter that numbers are still rising in all the " dissatisfied " countries. This situation may give rise to a belief that a condition of overpopulation is present or threatened and that territorial expansion would relieve or prevent the congestion.[a] Secondly, a consciousness of growing numbers, aided by the doctrine of manifest destiny, may generate a conviction that an expanding population entitles a people to embark on an imperialist policy.[b] Thirdly, a country's apprehension that the acceleration in its rate of demographic growth is declining may provoke a fear of depopulation and hence give rise to a desire to neutralise its detrimental consequences by augmenting the area under the country's sovereign control.[c] Fourthly, there is the deliberate attempt to encourage the growth of population in order to justify or to facilitate imperialist action.[d] The fifth consideration is that wide territories are needed in order to provide a country with greater scope for the self-expression of certain sections of its population.[e] Finally, there is the law of communicating vessels; this physical principle may be drafted into the service of sociology in order to explain why the spectacle of thinly populated areas elsewhere may cause a country overweighted with numbers to give way to the ancient predatory urge to pour down into lower levels of self-protection.[f] Each of these six groups of population considerations will now be considered in turn.

II. THE SPECTRE OF OVERPOPULATION

The first consideration is that of an increasing population. It is said that ' rapid growth of population is especially likely to generate expansionist sentiments] '.[84] It may appear at first sight to be self-evident that, to the extent to which demographic factors are involved,

---

[a] See below, § II. [b] See below, § III. [c] See below, § IV.
[d] See below, §§ V-VI. [e] See below, § VIII. [f] See below, § IX.

it is an expanding population which gives rise to expansionist aspirations, but a proposition of this kind, even if it can be shown to be true so far as it goes, explains nothing.   The question which has to be considered is why expansionist sentiments should develop in countries of growing populations.

As the preceding chapter has shown, although numbers are still rising in all the " dissatisfied " countries associated with claims for relief from population pressure, it does not follow that they are in fact suffering from congestion.   ' Growth of population may or may not lead to overpopulation '.[84]   But, whether growth of population is likely or not to lead to overcrowding, it is not from this angle that the question under consideration can best be approached.   In the first place, as has already been stated,[a] overpopulation, if it exists at all, is a short-term problem; secondly, in view of the present trend of demographic movements in the countries in question, the prospect is that their populations are likely to decline within the predictable future;[b] thirdly, overpopulation, as has been shown, does not appear to be a notion to which any precise meaning can be attached,[c] while, even if this were not so — even if, that is to say, the concept of overpopulation were held to be related to an objectively measurable reality — the demographic phenomenon at present under consideration is, in any case, not " overpopulation " but " growth of population ".

It would appear that the explanation of the generation of expansionist sentiments in terms of growth of population must be sought, in the first place, in the circumstance that countries in which there are visible signs of expanding numbers are apt to believe that conditions of overpopulation are either present or liable to develop in the near or distant future.   It is not the problem of an objectively perceptible condition of demographic pressure, actual or threatened, which nations would try to solve through a policy of territorial expansion; ' indeed, a serious degree of overpopulation is hardly compatible with expansionist sentiment, for it implies internal weakness in the presence of which a people can scarcely picture itself as destined to extend its frontiers '.[84]   It is their subjective belief — springing from a recognition of the symptoms of an expanding population — in the existence of a state of actual overpopulation, and, in particular, the

---

[a] See above, p. 116.
[b] Cf. above, chap. 4, § VIII.
[c] See above, chap. 4, § VII.

apprehension of prospective overpopulation provoked by increasing numbers, which cause them to seek in expansion a psychological remedy for their fears. ' The idea that their country is overpopulated becomes identified immediately in the mind of the masses with the idea of a natural *right* to expansion in less densely populated areas '.[317]   In relation, therefore, to expansionist aspirations and to the claims for changes in the *status quo* to which they may give rise, overpopulation is essentially a state of mind — a condition of '*felt* population pressure '.[55]   If the problem is regarded in this light, it becomes irrelevant to enquire whether overpopulation is an objectively perceived reality in the " dissatisfied " countries, ' for the basis of the trouble is psychological '.[84]   It is ' the sense of claustrophobia which lives in the slogan *Volk ohne Raum* '[341] that may explain expansionist aspirations.

This distinction between the subjective belief in overpopulation and overpopulation as an objectively ascertainable fact might seem to raise the question whether, in the countries concerned, the belief must be entertained by the government or by independent demographic experts or by public opinion in general[a] in order to explain expansionist policies or aspirations.   There does not appear, however, to be any valid reason for lingering over the subtle analytical difficulties which such a question implies, since the regimentation of public opinion in the claimant countries tends to bring about an identification of public sentiment, in so far as expression may be given to it, with the policy of the state, while, by a process of reasoning upon which no comment will be offered here, the expert view in the " dissatisfied " countries appears to be that subjective and objective overpopulation are one and the same thing.   ' The question arises ', states a German author, ' how far the subjective need of revision of a people (national need of revision), to which concepts like that of " nation without space ", " nation without work ", nation without assured food supply, nation without raw materials, nation without security refer, exists only in the mind of its own government, of its politicians, of its public opinion; or how far it can be said to exist also as an objective fact — as a vital lack of a nation or state.   We [Germans] understand the concept of " overpopulation " in the sense of a vital lack implying the co-existence of subjective and objective needs '.[180]

It is easy to conceive how a dread of overpopulation caused by the

---

a Cf. the passage from *192*, quoted above, p. 48.

knowledge of an expanding population may be allayed by a policy of territorial expansion, for, if 'the one unescapable consequence of overpopulation is poverty — greater poverty than there need be in view of the resources of the country and the skill available for exploiting them ',[84] there will be a tendency to presume that the acquisition of territory may provide a way of escape from the lowering of the standard of life which is caused by overpopulation.   Now, while it may be true that absolute overpopulation lowers the standard of living, there can be no such relationship of cause and effect between the impoverishment of a country and its mere belief in actual or prospective overpopulation. It does not follow, however, that nations whose rate of growth of population is regarded by them as an indication that they are suffering from, or threatened with, overpopulation are mistaken in thinking that, ' unless further room for expansion is made available, their rate of improvement of living standards will slow down '.[55]   On the contrary, there can be no doubt that the case does arise when a country with a rapidly expanding population may experience difficulties in providing work for all without lowering the standard of life.   In Russia, for example, ' the annual growth of the population is about 3 millions. This can hardly fail to create a serious situation in a country which is primarily agricultural.   An extremely rapid accumulation of capital will be necessary to ensure a development of the Russian manufacturing industries which will prevent the overcrowding of agriculture with its inevitable corollary, lower standard of living notwithstanding technical progress.   Even the enormous industrial development of the past ten years — based on the " forced saving " of a large part of the national income — has only provided employment for a small proportion of the annual increase in population '.[179]   Similarly, ' in countries like Japan and Italy . . . further expansion of primary industries, i. e. output of raw materials and vegetable foodstuffs, would seem to be difficult.   The annual net increase of the Japanese population is about one million, that of the Italian population, 400,000.   In these cases, it is still more evident that the solution of the employment problem is absolutely dependent upon the rapid progress of the manufacturing industries '.[179]

Thus, owing to a misapprehension of the true nature of their demographic situation, rapidly expanding populations believing that they are menaced with overpopulation ascribe to overpopulation an economic effect of growth of population. This confusion of thought has an important bearing on the question of claims for changes in the *status quo*, for the question arises whether a policy of expansion undertaken in order to solve a hypothetical problem of overpopulation is of any relevance to the true problem of increasing numbers.

The question can be examined by considering how far the successful pursuit of an expansionist policy involving the acquisition or extension of colonial possessions or an enlargement of metropolitan boundaries does in fact afford relief in cases of real demographic congestion and, hence, obviate the economic disadvantages which are thought to be associated with overcrowding. This point will be examined in a later chapter,[a] but the result of that examination may be anticipated here by stating that, in the case of colonial expansion, ' on the basis of past experience . . ., there is little to support the assumption that surplus population flows readily to overseas possessions or colonies '.[55]   On the contrary, the evidence seems to show that, whatever the value of colonial possessions may be, it is not derived from the relief which they afford for demographic congestion at home. ' In the last fifty years the population of Europe increased about 175 millions; there was a *net* emigration of 19 millions, but only 500,000 of them settled permanently in the colonies. People preferred to go to America, especially the United States '.[132]   Nor, it is suggested,[b] does continental expansion appear to offer the remedy which is sometimes claimed.

If, then, the ground for supposing that territorial expansion can provide a solution for absolute overpopulation is so precarious, *a fortiori* it is not an indispensable solution for the less acutely difficult demographic condition of growing population. It would appear, in fact, ' that rapid growth of the population — during a period of technical progress and of large capital accumulation — need not constitute an obstacle to an increase in the standard of living ', that ' the solution of this problem lies in the industrialisation of the countries with increasing population and in the exportation of manufactured goods in order to pay for primary products ', and that ' political control of colonies is not an important, still less an indispensable factor '.[179]

Yet, while the adoption of a policy of expansion does not seem

[a] See below, chap. 8.
[b] Cf. below, pp. 263-4.

to be an appropriate method of meeting the economic difficulties which rapidly increasing numbers may bring about, there is one possible argument in support of a transfer of colonial territories to countries claiming relief from population pressure. Since expanding countries are mistaken when they think themselves to be overpopulated, ' failure to find room for settlement in such colonies as they might claim would do no harm '. On the other hand, ' the mere possession of colonies would provide a cure for the psychological troubles which do arise from the population situation '.[84] The argument is strengthened when it is asked why, ' if possession of colonies in general and [for example] the restoration of the former German colonies to their original owner in particular have so little economic import . . ., the present mandate-holding nations [should] try to be wiser than Germany and retain them, when Germany insists upon their return ' ?[132] This retort has been used by Herr Hitler; if it is true, he said, that colonies have no value, ' this valuelessness would also apply to the other nations, and there is no reason why they should wish to keep them from us '.[296] The argument is still further reinforced when the view is taken that, in the case of the former German colonies, ' although most of the territory in question . . . [is] not suitable for white population, the Germans . . . [are] very energetic in intensive development; they . . . [are] very good at that sort of thing and might develop these territories in a way which would lead to very much greater production than that yet achieved by other Powers '.[234]

These, however, are mere conjectures. When, for example, Governor Schnee himself ' stresses[133] Germany's desire for the return of her colonies, his arguments are based on what Germany *hopes* to do rather than on what she has accomplished in the past or on what is being done now '.[132] Furthermore, against these arguments, ' it may be said that it is impossible to contemplate continual juggling with colonial possessions '[84] — a consideration which seriously impairs the cogency of the argument. ' It is unfortunate ', says an English student of the problem, ' that not only the Germans, but also a large number of people in Great Britain, regard the colonies as a series of material objects which can, by a mere stroke of the pen, be transferred from the ownership of one person into the ownership of another. We know that this is untrue. Colonies are not static pieces of territory; they are living organisms in process of rapid development. To surrender them would not entail merely the signature of some deed of gift; it would

entail a major surgical operation '.[341]   The same consideration has
caused Mr. Winston Churchill, for example, to condemn, in ' picturesque
language . . ., what he stigmatises as " the repulsive talk of handing
over millions of human souls irrespective of their wishes like cattle or
slaves to new sovereignties " ',[176] and a former Prime Minister of France
to declare that ' the cession or sale of one of its colonies would be a
particularly odious act on the part of any European colonial Power . . .
To exchange a colony for some political advantage, that is, to hand over
a number of human beings as if they were cattle or foodstuffs is nothing
less than slave-trading . . .   Germany is constantly talking about her
honour; though England, Belgium and France speak less often of
theirs, they none the less have it at heart '.[333]   As the Deputy Secretary-
General of the Confédération Générale du Travail remarked in a recent
interview, ' to regard colonies as currency exchangeable between the
different capitalist countries is positively repulsive '[332] — a sentiment
which was echoed in a text adopted by the Académie des Sciences
Coloniales.[a]

' The objections to the transfer of colonial territory are indeed
as weighty as they are obvious.   For one thing, would anybody think
it possible to tell the Asiatic peoples who, for centuries, or even for
fifty years, have been under the guidance of Europeans, and in this
manner have developed representative, and in some cases even parliamentary government institutions, that they will be " transferred "
to some other sovereignty, perhaps of a State where no parliamentary
principles are recognised ?   In some African colonies the same objection
would arise, but even where government is still of the patriarchal
type, a transfer of this kind could hardly be considered.   The fact
that a people is " backward " does not mean that it has nothing to lose
by coming under the sway of a dictatorial government.   Without
parliamentary control and criticism in the home country there is little
hope of redress of grievances against colonial administrators when they
are covered by the governor.   Transfer of such a kind would be tantamount to treason, at least in the minds of those whose consent is
necessary, the members of parliament in the countries now governing
these territories.   To say this is not to offer strictures on the dictatorial
form of government, which may suit a given people in a given period.

---

[a] ' It has been rightly said that the transfer of a colony in return for political advantages
would be a revolting action, like trading in negroes . . .' (329).

But it so happens that most of the European colonial Powers govern themselves by parliamentary institutions, and that the dissatisfied Powers are dictatorships; nowhere can a parliamentary vote be expected for transfer under these conditions. Even the most backward tribe, voiceless and unable to make up its mind on the issue, could not be handed over like so many head of cattle '.[131]

' In the case of Germany, especially the National-Socialist race doctrine, with its implications for the treatment of coloured peoples, must be taken into consideration '.[131]   ' Are not the conceptions ... of the new German State as regards the racial problem in conflict with the ideas commonly held on colonisation ' ?[328]   ' It would be a cause of grave disappointment to many Africans were they transferred from the rule of a country which is successfully carrying out the principle of trusteeship, to a country the main and avowed intention of which is exploitation '.[341]

One of the leaders of the German colonial movement has, however, recently given an explanation[330] of Germany's new racial doctrines which, according to him, cannot ' fail to give the Powers the assurances they need.   Every race has its individual biological characteristics : a hierarchy of races should be affirmed but the consciousness of this " racial hierarchy " must not lead to the toleration of the destruction of the inferior races.   National-Socialism will endeavour to further the development of the specific characteristics of the native races by permitting the tribes to live in their traditional environment according to their ancestral customs; racialism rejects only the concept of assimilation, but rejects it vigorously '.[328]

Declarations of this kind, though they cannot well be brought under the heading of " repulsive talk ", may or may not be convincing outside the countries practising a policy of racial discrimination.   But which are these other countries ?   Has not Signor Gayda recently coupled ' Great Britain with France and the United States as a country that is displaying strong racial tendencies ..., [citing] in support of this statement ...   British emigration policy, which, he maintains, favours the Anglo-Saxon and keeps the other races out of an empty Empire ' ?[258]   Without pausing to answer this question, it may be suggested, at any rate, that, as the following discussion which recently took place in Great Britain shows, a moral condemnation of another country's colonial system can be an inconveniently emotional method of disposing of colonial claims :

Miss MARGERY PERHAM said that the amount of attention given to native interests during the discussions of colonial claims showed that it might be in danger of being neglected in any final settlement; yet, however small it might be in the areas and people involved, it was of the utmost importance from the point of view of principle. It was strange that in a country such as Great Britain this point should have been negelcted ... Sympathy with the German claim for the colonies had so increased of late that we were busy clearing Germany's colonial character from the criticisms of Versailles ...[a] The restitution of the former colonial possessions to Germany would not be in the interests of the subjects races. It was impossible to compare the thirty years of German occupation with the twenty years of British rule which had followed ... British administration in Tanganyika, as in Togoland and the Cameroons, was the result of centuries of experience in the government of native peoples ... Even under the most ideal conditions of transfer could any other Power be expected to carry on a system such as this ? ... Probably one of the greatest factors for softening the hard grip of Europe upon native and primitive peoples had been Christianity. Another most potent check was that of free institutions, the greatest amount of publicity, parliamentary discussion, Royal Commissions and all the rest of the British apparatus of public enquiry and reform. In both cases the speaker left the audience to draw the antithesis in the case of Germany. Thirdly, Great Britain had learned how easy it was to expect too much of Africa, to over-exploit, to over-produce. German scientists would be quite capable of dealing with technical matters such as soil erosion, but what about that more dangerous erosion, that of native society crumbling under the pressure of the twentieth-century European industrial exploitation ? ... Dr. Goebbels had said that if the British did not produce very much at present in those colonies Germany would show us how to produce more ... Great Britain was committed to ... [the Mandatory system] not only by her promises under the Covenant but by her own institutions ... Germany had rejected the Mandates system in advance. Hitler had ridiculed our " weak conception " of teaching subject peoples how to do without us. Let us for once face the fact that we were going to do evil that good might come and at best reduce the evil to the smallest possible proportions.[343]

Lord ARNOLD said that he was glad that the moral issue had been mentioned ... [Miss Perham] had indulged in such an assumption of moral rectitude and almost omnipotence on the part of the British that it had made

[a]Cf. below, p. 128, note a.

him gasp. She did not seem to be aware of the fact that there were critics, even in Great Britain, of British government of native races. Sir Edward Grigg had said that the claim that Germany was not fit to govern colonial territory had never been justified and should be removed ... A Lecturer of Manchester University had said that ... Teutonic rule in East Africa had been at least as enlightened as French rule in Equatorial Africa, as Belgian rule in the Congo area, as British government in the East African Protectorate now known as Kenya, and as the government in any of the Portuguese colonies ruled from Lisbon. Then there was for Great Britain the question of the colour bar in South Africa, the confiscation of the political rights of the Cape natives during the last two or three years, the forced labour which was still a part of British policy in certain African territories, and also the loss of the best territory in Kenya by the natives so that the white settlers should be supplied with the best land. The British assumption of moral rectitude must be intolerable to Germany ...[231] [a]

[a] In order to balance Lord Arnold's catalogue of the misdeeds of British colonial administration, it may be permissible to fill a gap in Miss Perham's argument by reproducing here a French writer's recapitulation of the ' brutality with which Prussian methods were applied by the German colonial administration' (*376*). As in his case, ' this discreet and careful reminder of unpleasant facts — which gave rise to just condemnation, even in Germany — is not inspired by any evil desire to revive old quarrels which, on the contrary, one would like to forget. It is the impudence of certain German polemical writers, such as the violent General von Epp, whose sword is still stained with the blood of the Herreros, which has made necessary this reminder of historical events which are not very glorious ' (*ibid.*) :

' The bastinado was an official institution and as long as no harm to the health of the victim was involved, there was no provision against the exercise of the right of punishment of the blacks. For the lightest crimes : imprisonment; for repeated theft : the penalty of death by hanging. When to this unheard-of severity there is added a complete ignorance of the customs and traditions of the natives and a barbarous exploitation of individuals in the plantations and industrial undertakings, the real reason for the perpetual rebellions which took place in the former German colonies are found. If the excesses of the founder of East Africa Carl Peters were such that their author had to be deprived of his duties, and dismissed from the service of the state, the fearful atrocities of General von Trotha at the time of the repression of the rebellion of the Herreros (1904-1906) were considered to be the accomplishment of a divine judgment. Twenty-six thousand natives were massacred. Thirty thousand natives, men, women and children, were driven into the desert and there died of hunger. Professor Schilling has estimated the total number of victims at 150,000. At the same time, the revolt of the Matumbi in German East Africa, was suppressed with equal savagery. The annals of the Reichstag are full of criticisms of the bad treatment inflicted on the natives, of the system of forced labour — that modern form of slavery — and of the brutal methods of government of military leaders like General von Liebert and General Leutwein. Speeches in the debates did not come only from socialist deputies like Bebel, Ledebur or Noske; the voices of leaders of the centre like Erzberger were often heard. Perhaps worse than all this savagery was the moral inferiority in which the natives were confined : they were not allowed to receive higher education, they were forbidden to travel in Europe, their evidence was refused in affairs in which whites were concerned. That is the civilisation which the Wilhelmian German colonisation brought to the colonial peoples ; that is how the Reich understood its mission of education and assistance ' (*ibid.* based on Evans Lewin : *German Rule in Africa* (London), 1918).

It must be admitted, perhaps, that, as the German speaker quoted above[a] suggested to the International Studies Conference in 1937, those who lay down the rule that it is not legitimate to transfer native people like cattle often reason in the abstract. Apparently forgetting that 'that was exactly the way in which people were transferred in 1919', their argument is politically worthless unless it is true 'that there has been a complete change of outlook since then and that the world has moved towards idealism'.[b]

Nevertheless, it is difficult to conceive how any rational system of international relations can be constructed on the principle that territorial revision is the correct cure for a psychological ailment. In any case, does not the demographic argument in favour of meeting claims for colonies break down entirely when it is held that 'to imagine that', for example, 'Germans and Italians are blind to the weakness of their case if based merely on inability to obtain . . . room for settlement would . . . be to underrate their intelligence in view of pre-war statistics of immigration . . . in their colonies'?[176]

III. THE DOCTRINE OF MANIFEST DESTINY

A country's belief that it is suffering from actual demographic congestion or its apprehension of prospective overpopulation in the future are not the only psychological reactions to a perception of growth in numbers expressing itself in expansionist aspirations and policies and in demands for changes in the *status quo*. There may be a causal relation between the numerical growth of a society and its progress and between the decline of a population and its deterioration.[246] It is, perhaps, a view of this kind — that 'depopulation means decadence'[314] — which accounts for 'the nationalist thesis of the essential and transcendent superiority over all foreign peoples . . . [according to which] increase of population is a sign of health, [while] stagnation or decrease marks degeneration . . .; as the future belongs to the healthy, morally and physically, it is the duty of other peoples to make room for . . . them] . . . Obviously, reasoning of this kind has little chance of being accepted by the nations it stigmatises as inferior because they are not so prolific as others',[131] but the stigmatisers are not likely to heed the remonstrances of the stigmatised.

[a] See above, p. 30.
[b] *ibid.*

Furthermore, ' nations which are growing rapidly usually expect the process to continue indefinitely and tend to picture themselves as requiring an increasingly important place in world affairs '.[55] ' A people conscious of rapid growth thinks of itself as unusually vigorous, and believes that it is destined, if not to inherit the earth, at least to inherit the territory of its less dynamic neighbours. Colonies confer prestige ... and countries with growing populations desire that their increasing wealth and importance should be recognised in this fashion '.[84] For example, ' during the period preceding that in which Germany became industrialised, the population of the country was growing slowly; nevertheless, there were signs of overpopulation, for there was congestion in the rural areas and heavy emigration. But of expansionist sentiment there was no trace. As industrialisation became more rapid the rate of population growth increased; signs of congestion vanished, and Germany became a country of immigration. Expansionist sentiment, however, made its appearance and became very prominent;[a] it would be possible to give numerous quotations from German authors in the earlier years of the century who were demanding outlets for Germany's growing millions and who implied, if they did not say, that Germany was overpopulated '.[84]

That German expansionist sentiment has been no less pronounced since the war, and particularly since the rise to power of national socialism is a matter of common knowledge and recent illustration, but one or two quotations may serve to indicate how an expanding population will lead a country to aspire to territorial expansion, not so much as a supposititious solution to a problem of population pressure at home, but rather as the natural right of a people endowed with superabundant energies :

It is an impossible thought for Germans that some day, generations hence, there may be a new kind of Africa in which ... a million white immigrants have transformed everything, without the German people having made their moral and material contribution ...[b]

---

[a] By 1883, ' the dream of a Colonial Empire had taken deep hold on the German imagination ... : we *must* have real colonies, where German emigrants can settle and spread the national ideals of the Fatherland ... To the question, " *Why must ?* ", the ready answer i " a healthy and powerful State like Germany, with its 60,000,000 inhabitants, must expand it cannot stand still, it must have territories to which its overflowing population can emigrate without giving up its nationality " ' (*349*).

[b] *Kölnische Zeitung*, June 17, 1937, quoted in *348*.

[One of the measures by which Germany could be] restored to her old position as a payer of international obligations... would be to place at the disposal of the "people without space" new areas in which this energetic race could settle colonies and carry out great works of peace.[356][a]

Views of this kind find support in a " biological " theory of the evolution of nations which enquires whether ' the countries of Northern, Central and Western Europe [will] throw their doors open in due time to the immigration of the less senescent[b] populations which surround them, and thus share in their demographic evolution ', or whether ' the disparity in the pressure of population [will] go on increasing until it gives rise to a new and yet more tremendous cyclone which will drive the peoples of Eastern and Southern Europe into countries where the pressure of population is less intense '.[262] If this theory is to be taken seriously, the peoples of western and northern Europe may be entitled to retort that ' a nation's lack of demographic foresight must not be described as a divine mission ' and that ' it does not confer upon it the right to multiply and to invade the whole earth '.[124] But a theory which seems to find in zoology an analogy for the conduct of human societies is not one, perhaps, which need unduly abash those against whom it is directed. Even if it were true, for example, that Germany is overpopulated, ' it cannot be admitted that Germany should make a virtue of her faults ' for, although one may understand, as a French writer has suggested, ' that she should envy the equilibrium which France has been able to achieve for herself during the nineteenth century and which brought her so much criticism and sarcasm (country of *petits bourgeois*, country of only sons, a shrunken country, condemned to death by a falling birth-rate) ' yet France, ' *pays de la mesure* . . ., will never admit that she should be charged with a fault which, from a purely objective point of view, may rather be considered as a merit '.[376]

---

[a] ' From the context of the proposal, it would appear that in speaking of " new areas ", . . . [its author] had in mind certain parts of Soviet Russia ' (*348*).

[b] According to a protagonist of this theory, ' it seems as if the birth-rate diminishes, first under the influence of external circumstances outweighing the volitional forces. Then a physiological factor appears, from which it may be supposed that the facility with which considerations leading to the limitation of birth are adopted is only one manifestation of the weakening of genetic instincts, which, in its turn, produces a weakening of the repro-ductive capacity ' (*261*).

IV. THE PROSPECT OF DEPOPULATION

If an expanding population giving rise to a belief in the presence of conditions of overpopulation or to a fear of future overpopulation, on the one hand, or to a sense of natural superiority, on the other hand, is at the root of certain demands for changes in the *status quo*, it is no less certain that the prospect of contracting population giving rise to a fear of ultimate depopulation is an equally powerful motive for the development of expansionist policies.   For example, ' between 1880 and 1900 France pursued a more deliberate and more vigorous expansionist policy than had been followed by any other country in the last hundred years.   In West Africa, the Nile Valley, and the Far East, she sought colonies, and successive French ministries continued to encourage the making of claims by explorers and officials on behalf of France . . .   French policy may be traced primarily to the desire for rehabilitation after the Franco-German war.   But the population situation was not without its influence.   The French were acutely aware of the fact that, while the population of Germany was increasing rapidly, the population of France was almost stationary, and on this account, were rendered more anxious than they would otherwise have been to enhance their position in the world '.   Similarly, ' since the war, and especially in recent years, opinion in Germany has become seriously perturbed about the prospect of a decline in the population of the country, and the German government is now taking energetic measures to avert the decline by stimulating the birth-rate.[a]   Though Germans fear depopulation and not overpopulation, they are again making expansionist claims and are demanding colonies; the present position of Germany is similar to that of France sixty years ago ',[84] though with this difference that the German government, if it invokes the bogy of encirclement, cannot plausibly do so on the grounds that Germany is being enclosed in mounting walls of more rapidly expanding populations.

These illustrations serve to show that ' in the majority of European countries, the demographic problem may be compared . . . with the head of Janus.   It presents one aspect if the concept of overpopulation is regarded not as something chimerical — in spite of the absence of any sound theoretical basis — but as a real eventuality that can and

[a] See below, pp. 148-149.

should be reckoned with. It presents quite a different aspect if the ideal aimed at is a population as large as possible — with quality on a par with quantity — and not ever increasing prosperity (even at the cost of a limitation of development and of births), the former apparently ensuring, in the long run, a better position in the international competition. From the point of view of prosperity, there is a temptation to regard the situation as dangerous when, notwithstanding a falling birth rate, the population or the density of population increases fairly rapidly — especially the population of working age ... On the other hand, the second view of the question implies the conclusion, inspired by the idea of the right to life and regeneration and therefore by a conception more national than human, that anxiety should be felt rather about a declining birth rate and the ever more unfavourable character of the net trend of the population movement '.[127]

'Without going fully into the economic and social implications of a considerable fall in population, it is obvious that such an event may create serious problems '.[263] Indeed, in Great Britain, for example, ' the long-run budgetary outlook opened out by the fall in the birth-rate is extremely formidable, comprising a huge and undiminished national debt, a diminishing national income, and mounting charges for Old Age Pensions '.[294]

In the first place, since a declining population means an ageing population, a society which is contracting will suffer from a ' high degree of invalidity and the burden of state health insurance will be greater. So, too, will be the relative cost of old age benefit. On the other hand, this large section of aged and therefore unemployed people will have to be supported by a relatively much smaller proportion of able-bodied persons ';[263] and ' it makes no fundamental difference whether these elderly dependents are maintained by wage-earning relatives, by the State, or by investment incomes of their own. In any case, their maintenance will be a charge on the productive resources of the rest of the country '.[294] As a result, ' proportionately, the amount of taxation per head will rise, while the ability to bear it will fall '.[263] The following illustration of ' a series of problems which should be studied with regard to the financial consequences of the present population trend ' may be quoted :

To what extent will the decrease in the proportion of children increase the adults' capacity to pay taxes ? To what extent will it reduce public expenses (for schools, welfare institutions, etc.) ? To what extent will the increase in the proportion of old people unable to earn a living increase public expenses (for old-age pensions, etc.) ? To what extent will additional public expenses be caused by the fact that with the decrease of fertility old people unable to earn a living will, in fewer cases than in the past, have children to support them ? To what extent will the changes in the demand for various goods (fewer " cradles ", more " coffins ") affect tax receipts ? To what extent will the reduction of house building activity and the slackening of speculation in urban real estate affect tax receipts ? To what extent will the capacity to meet obligations contracted in the past be affected (civil and military pensions, long-term loans) ? To what extent has the present population trend to be taken into account when issuing new long-term loans and fixing the terms of amortization ?[310]

Secondly, ' the position of industry is likely to be more difficult. In the last century, the industrial system recovered fairly easily from the depressions through which it passed, and one of the major factors in this ease of recovery was, undoubtedly, the growth of population An increase in the numbers of people meant an increase in the demand for the products of industry, and with it the slump period of the trade cycle was shortened '.[263] For 'every individual is a consumer as well as a possible producer. If there were only half as many people in ', for example, ' Great Britain as there actually are, the demand for bread, for clothes, for boots, and shoes, for cinemas and the like[a] would only be about half what it is; so that although there would be fewer people needing jobs there might be proportionately fewer jobs to go round '.[294]

Thirdly, ' we, too, as consumers, may find our standard of life lowered remarkably. The commodities we buy to-day are cheap, largely because they are made by mass-production methods, and such methods are profitable to producers only because large numbers of people demand the goods they make. If our numbers fall, and with them, the extent of the market, the whole costs structure of industry may be changed radically, because it may no longer pay to manufacture goods in such quantities. This in turn may lead to the abandonment of the more efficient large-scale methods of production, with the result that the prices of most goods will rise '.[263]

[a] Some branches of the chocolate and confectionery trade which cater especially for the young people in England are complaining that they are ' beginning to feel the effetcs of the diminishing birth rate ' (327).

Fourthly, although 'there is ... no more widespread impression than that a decline in numbers will diminish unemployment ..., this ... is an illusion' and 'it is a fallacy to suppose that a decline in numbers will make the unemployment problem easier'.[294]   On the contrary, it has been argued that 'if one set out to increase unemployment in a given country for the next fifteen years, one could find no more efficient means than birth-restriction on a very large scale'.[310] [a]   This would be so because 'every individual is a consumer for many years, some fourteen at least, before he enters the labour market.   A reduction in the number of babies born, say, this year could not possibly make any difference to the number of people seeking work until many years later.   In the meantime it might possibly reduce to some extent the demands for goods and services.   From a common-sense standpoint, therefore, the most reasonable assumption would seem to be that a fall in the birth-rate would make unemployment worse for a considerable period, whatever might be its subsequent influence'.[294]

But, 'in order to form a useful idea of the effect which a decline in numbers is likely to have on unemployment ..., the different types of unemployment and the causes that give rise to them' must be considered.   'It is a mistake to suppose that unemployment is due to a chronic and general insufficiency in the demand either for goods and

---

[a] The argument is as follows : 'Let us assume ... that no child would be born ... during the next fifteen years.   What would be the effect upon the labour market ?   Certainly not a single man would find work more easily ...   As a matter of fact the number of persons looking for a job would increase in the next fifteen years as in the past, because there would be more boys and girls reaching the bread-winning age than men and women leaving their jobs on account of old age, death, etc.   The number of job-hunters might increase even more than before, because many young women who, if they had children, would not work might be looking for work if they had no children.   What is still worse, the number of people thrown out of employment would increase at a terrific speed.   The industries catering for the needs of the youngest children would be the first to be ruined.   They would be followed by those supplying the wants of the older children, and so on.   Teachers would lose employment, and so forth.   It may seem at first sight as if the lack of children could not possibly reduce the national income and that, if the total purchasing power remained the same, industry as a whole would not be worse off.   But with the increasing number of unemployed, wages and salaries would necessarily drop so that the national income and the demand for goods would decrease after all.   Conditions might change again when, in fifteen years from now, labour would become scarce because there would not be any young people to fill the positions then becoming vacant by reason of disability or old age ...   Or ... let us assume ... that next year the population of ... [a country] decreases by 10 per cent ...   The heaviest items of public expense — debt-service, defence, etc. — would not be lightened at all and would therefore involve a heavier *per capita* burden.   One-tenth of the dwellings now occupied would become vacant, and real estate would fall in value.   The building trades and all industries producing building material would be paralysed.   Other trades supplying the bare necessities of life would suffer likewise.   While unemployment doubtless would decrease in certain trades it would increase in others' (*310*).

services or for labour.   We all make work for one another.   The more we produce the more we are able to consume.   There is no fundamental reason, therefore, why the demand for goods and services should not be strong enough to provide employment for everyone, if labour itself were perfectly adaptable, however many people there were to be employed.   In practice, moreover, in the periods of active trade which alternate with periods of depression, demand is usually strong enough in the aggregate for this purpose . . .   It is not, therefore, to a chronic insufficiency of demand that unemployment is to be attributed, but rather to *changes* in demand together with change in productive method.   The changes in demand that may give rise to unemployment are of many different kinds.   In some industries the demand for labour varies from season to season, and in a few, such as the docks, from week to week, and even from day to day.   As a result, a considerable number of workpeople are temporarily unemployed . . .   This, however, is of no great consequence.   A far more serious matter is that the demand for labour is apt to shift its direction more or less permanently. Some industries may decline while others grow.   If this happens, it is clearly necessary, if unemployment is to be avoided, that work-people should move from the declining to the expanding industries. But this may prove a slow and painful process.   Many of the work-people who lose their jobs in the declining industries will be elderly and rather unadaptable men or women who cannot easily be absorbed in unfamiliar employments.   Thus a surplus of unemployed labour may remain attached to the industries where employment has declined, even though there may be an unsatisfied demand for labour in other industries . . .   Unemployment of this character is sometimes called " structural " unemployment.   It represents the heart of the un-employment problem in periods of active trade.   The other really serious type of unemployment is, of course, that which results from the periodic occurrence of general trade depressions.   The course of trade is never that of a steady continuous expansion.   It moves in rhythmical series of phases, known as the " trade cycle " from depression to boom and from boom to depression.   These fluctuations give rise to heavy unemployment from time to time which it is convenient to call " cyclical " unemployment '.[294]

' The way in which the change in population trends will affect unemployment is likely to turn mainly, therefore, on the influence it exerts on these two important types of unemployment, structural

unemployment and cyclical unemployment. There is reason to fear
that it will tend to increase unemployment under both these headings.
The fundamental reason is the same in both cases : an obstinate condition
of redundant productive capacity in an important group of industries
is far more likely to develop when numbers are stationary or declining
than when they are growing rapidly. But though the reason can be
expressed in a single sentence, it needs a somewhat lengthy argument to
make its meaning plain ' :

When numbers are growing rapidly there is a strong and fairly steady
increase in the demand for almost every commodity . . . To meet this
increasing demand, the supply of the various commodities must be correspondingly increased. The labour required for this purpose is, of course, readily
available, as a consequence of the growth of numbers. But goods are
not produced by means of labour alone, but by labour in co-operation
with capital equipment and with natural resources. Accordingly a condition
of rapidly growing numbers gives rise to a need for a constant expansion
of capital equipment and natural resouces in almost every branch of production. Additional factories are required in the great majority of industries,
additional land is required for the production of the foodstuffs and raw
materials that are needed in increasing quantities; and additional means
of communication and transportation are required to carry the additional
goods to the consumers. In short, when numbers increase rapidly, there is
need for a steady enlargement of *productive capacity* in almost every part
of the economic system . . . When, however, numbers cease to grow, the
need for a steady increase of productive capacity is neither so great nor
so general. There may still, it is true, be some increase in the demand
for most goods and services and a large increase in the demand for some.
For as the standard of living rises, each individual will be able to consume
more. But the increase in consumption that results from an increase in
the purchasing-power of the individual is likely to be very unevenly spread
over the various objects of consumption. If the population grows by,
say, five per cent in a few years, it is fairly safe to assume that the demand for
each particular type of commodity . . . will also increase by at least five
per cent. But if the population remains stationary, while the purchasing-
power of each individual increases by five per cent, no such assumption
can be made in a country with a fairly high standard of living. It is far
more likely that the demand for some commodities, particularly for basic
necessities . . ., will increase very little if at all, while there will be a big

increase in the demand for goods and services of a semi-luxury character and for novelties. Accordingly if numbers are stationary, while technical improvement is proceeding rapidly, there may be no need at all for an enlargement of productive capacity in many branches of production. On the contrary, it is easy in such circumstances for serious problems of redundant capacity to arise. It is easy, that is to say, to reach a condition in which the capacity available for producing various important commodities is much greater than is required to meet the demand or such expansion of demand as can reasonably be expected in an early future.

The greater likelihood of a prolonged condition of redundant capacity in particular branches of industry ... entails two consequences which are directly relevant to our present argument. First, structural unemployment is likely to be increased. When numbers are growing rapidly, there is such a big increase in the total demand for goods and services, that there is seldom either an absolute decline in the demand for any particular commodity or even an absolute decline in the demand for labour in any particular industry ... In these circumstances there ... [is] no need to move actual workpeople from one industry to another in accordance with changes in the direction of the demand for labour. All that ... [is] necessary ... [is] that the new recruits to industry should go mainly into the more rapidly expanding occupations. When, however, the working population becomes virtually stationary, and the demand for labour continues to shift its direction, an absolute decline in the numbers employed in certain industries is inevitable. Then it becomes far more likely that many workpeople in those industries will lose their jobs and will remain permanently unemployed, unless they are sufficiently adaptable to be able to make good in unfamiliar occupations.

Secondly, it is probable that the same conditions will make trade more unstable and general depressions more severe ... Hitherto, in effecting ... [the] turn round from depression to recovery, the strong normal increase in the demand for goods and services arising from growing numbers has played an important part. When numbers are stationary or declining it seems probable that a longer time may elapse, after the bottom point of a depression has been reached, before the need for fresh capital expenditure on a considerable scale asserts itself. It is true that it is only necessary that this need should display itself in a few important directions to set the wheels of recovery in motion; and sooner or later, this is likely to happen even when numbers are declining. But it seems reasonable to suppose that the interval before this need is felt will be longer when the expansive influence

of growing numbers is removed.   Thus, an increase in the obstinacy of
trade depressions is a likely consequence of the change in population trends;
and this will entail an increase of cyclical unemployment.[294]

Thus ' it is an illusion to suppose that the existence of unemployment is a sign either that a country is overpopulated, or that its numbers
are growing too fast '.[294]

' There are other and perhaps more important consequences . . .
[of declining numbers].   The severe world agricultural crisis of recent
years and the strong movement towards economic nationalism are
largely attributable . . . to the slowing-down that has already occurred
in the growth of Western populations ' :

The rapid growth of numbers in countries like Great Britain in the
nineteenth century was the chief impulse behind the astonishing development of international trade which was characteristic of the period.   It was
really the mainspring of the old Free Trade tradition.   For, as numbers
increased, the demand for food increased correspondingly; and this increase
in demand was greater than could be met by the ordinary progress of technical improvement in agriculture.   For food, as for other commodities,
there was need accordingly for a constant enlargement of productive capacity...
How . . . were the food requirements of the rapidly increasing populations
to be supplied ?   By using less fertile lands, or by cultivating more intensively ?
Either method would be costly; either method would encounter the Law
of Diminishing Returns . . .   The solution was found in the expansion
of international trade . . . by developing the virgin agricultural resources
of new continents.   To make this possible, large sums of European capital
had to be in vested in the building of railways in the United States, in South
America, in the British Dominions; and the investment of capital went
hand in hand with a migration of labour . . .

With the slowing-down in the growth of Western populations, the
whole perspective of international economic relations has been transformed.
The growth in the demand for the more essential foodstuffs is peculiarly
dependent on the growth of numbers, since after a moderate standard of
living has been reached most people do not greatly increase their consumption of food as they become better off.   A position has now been reached
accordingly when the annual increase in the demand for many important
agricultural commodities is perhaps less than can be taken care of by the
ordinary progress of agricultural improvement.   Thus, the need which was

so marked in the nineteenth century for a constant expansion of the world areas of agricultural production has largely disappeared; and the new, and as it would have seemed to thinkers of a hundred years ago, the astonishing phenomenon of redundant productive capacity in many important branches of agricultural production has made its appearance . . .[294]

But — again in countries like Great Britain — ' there are wider and more general consequences to be noted ' :

It was no accident . . . that the Victorian Age, when numbers were growing very rapidly, should have been the heyday of the philosophy of *laissez-faire* . . . For . . . there was then a constant need for an expansion of productive capacity throughout the economic system; and expansion is most easily secured when the freest scope is given to the initiative and enterprise of adventurous individuals. But when problems of surplus capacity arise frequently, unrestricted competition does not work so well . . . and the need is felt for methods of organization which will permit the deliberate adjustment of supply to the demand . . .[294]

It follows that ' an increasing degree of State intervention and control will be required to deal with the difficult problems of economic adjustment which are consequential on the change in population trends '.[294]

' Similarly, thrift was a quality prized as a high social virtue in the Victorian Age . . . Large sums of capital were required to build new factories at home and to develop the communications of agricultural communities overseas; and to supply this capital it was essential that the public should save on a substantial scale. In future, it may well be that . . . capital requirements will represent a smaller proportion of the national income than they did formerly . . . If " over-saving " becomes a serious problem, it will be largely due to the change in population trends '.[294]

* * *

Thus declining and expanding populations alike give rise to economic maladjustments.[a] In the case of contracting numbers,

___

[a] ' A slower rate of population growth, while raising various economic difficulties . . ., none the less facilitates a larger and more rapid improvement in the standard of living . . . From the standpoint of the individual family, a reduction in the number of dependent

however, the economic difficulties which accompany the movement
do not provide an explanation for the expansionist sentiments manifested
by countries with declining populations, for, although they are
objectively ascertainable facts, yet they are of a kind which cannot be
readily perceived.   Unlike the fear of overpopulation generated by
visibly rising numbers and of the economic implications of overpopulation, therefore, a contracting population is not, in relation to policies
of expansion, a subjective, psychological question.   Thus it may seem,
at first sight, to be an unaccountable psychological paradox that the
prospect, whether real or fancied, of a contracting population should
generate the same sentiments of expansion as does the consciousness
of expanding numbers.   But the explanation becomes quite simple
if it is admitted that, wherever demographic movements come within
the sphere of action of the state, governmental attempts to bring them
under control are animated by political rather than by economic
considerations.   In one case, for example, ' it is not an exaggeration
to say that since the rise to power of Italian Fascism, population
encouragement and expansionist aims have been deliberately woven

children means that a given family income goes further than it did . . . From the social
standpoint, productive resources hitherto devoted to other ends are made available for
raising the standard of living.   When numbers are growing rapidly an appreciable part of
the productive resources of the community has to be devoted to equipping the growing
numbers with the capital equipment they require . . .   When numbers cease to grow this
need disappears . . .   This potential gain to the standard of living is, of course, a consideration of the first importance; an advantage which is well worth the price of having to wrestle
with new problems of economic adjustment.   There is, indeed, little doubt that a slowly
growing or a stationary population is, on balance, more favourable than a rapidly growing
population to the economic welfare of society.   From the economic standpoint, therefore,
we have reason to welcome the fall of the birth-rate down to the point at which it is compatible
with a stationary population . . .   But . . . [where] the birth-rate has fallen far below this
point . . . the decline will serve . . . to aggravate the problems of economic adjustment . . .
On the other hand it will contribute virtually nothing, beyond what is given by a stationary
population, to the potential improvement in the standard of living.   Once the position of
a stationary population has been reached, and the age-composition of the community is
adjusted to this position, no productive resources are required to supply growing numbers
with necessary capital equipment, and no further economy is, therefore, to be obtained
from this source.   It is true that there will be fewer people to share the existing stock of
capital goods, but in practice there will be little advantage in that and such advantage as
there may be will almost certainly be outweighed by the greater costliness of production,
which will result in many branches of industry from the consequential contraction in the
size of the market . . .   The other advantage to the standard of living resulting from the
fall in the birth-rate, namely, that a given family income goes further when there are fewer
children to support, is likely to prove ephemeral . . . [in countries where] the proportion of
persons of working age and in the prime of life is . . . abnormally high . . .   Thus the broad
conclusion as to the economic consequences of the fall in the birth-rate is what common
sense would lead us to expect.   Down to a certain point, the fall is to be welcomed; the
advantages preponderate over the disadvantages.   But the further it proceeds the slighter
become the advantages, the more serious the disadvantages . . . ' (294).

together to form one of the main strands of governmental action '.[263] Indeed, ' we know that philosophical and national viewpoints (prestige, military power, cultural supremacy, tradition, political systems) and other imponderables, in the last resort, have hitherto generally decided the attitudes of governments and of peoples in specific demographic situations and in connection with specific demographic changes (war and conquest, migrations, international trade, industrialisation, intensive agriculture, total autarky, etc.) '.[155]

It must also be borne in mind that, ' so long as ... numbers are still on the increase ' even in those countries where the rate of increase is declining, the general public will tend to ' refuse to admit that there is any cause for worry '.[a]   It is only ' when the population has begun to fall and when the rate of decline gets steeper every year ' that this popular view will begin to fade.   Meanwhile, however, an enlightened government, aware of the prospect of a declining population, will not, like the man-in-the-street, ' think it ridiculous to bother about what may happen a generation hence '.[293]

While it may be true that ' it is to avert ... [the] kind of danger [implied in the economic and social consequences of contracting numbers] that ... [certain] European countries ... have for some time been attempting to check the fall in their birth-rates ',[263] [b] it is clear that this danger alone does not suffice to explain why, in some of these countries, an apprehension of declining numbers should have given rise to expansionist sentiments, particularly if it is true that ' in none of the countries ... [in question] does the Government really understand why there is this continuous fall in the birth-rate, or exactly how the fall is making itself felt '.[263]   Are there, then, ' other and less justifiable reasons which have influenced a number of European countries and caused them to make attempts to check the present trend of population decline ' ?[263]

Before passing on to the next section of this chapter, in which this question will be examined, it is important to note that, while an apprehension of depopulation may give rise, as in the case of a fear of over-population, to expansionist sentiments, expansionism is not the only psychological reaction to the fears engendered by the prospect of

---

[a] Cf., e. g., Mr. Neville Chamberlain's admission, when Chancellor of the Exchequer, that he looked ' upon the continual diminution of the birth-rate in ... [Great Britain] with considerable apprehension ' (86) with his declaration, when Prime Minister, that he did not think the time had come to make an enquiry into the question of family allowances (242).

[b] See below, p. 150, note a.

declining numbers. ' Deep in all of us is an instinctive feeling that the most fundamental duty of society is to reproduce itself, that not to do so is a betrayal of life '.[293]

Now there can be no doubt that certain nations have been more deeply impressed than others by the dangers to the future of the race which are implicit in the present trend of population movements, and that it is largely this keener awareness of the perils with which they are confronted that has prompted them to embark upon demographic policies designed to arrest and, if possible, to reverse, the tendency. To the extent that such policies are not dictated by expansionist motives, they would have no bearing — save that of a further nail in the coffin of the concept of overpopulation[a] — on the question of claims for changes in the *status quo* were it not for the circumstance that it is precisely in two of the " dissatisfied " countries — Germany and Italy — that the fear of depopulation is most acute and that a policy of encouraging a rise in the birth-rate has been most sedulously fostered. This circumstance is sometimes seized upon as a ground for resisting claims for relief from population pressure.

Yet, even in cases where claims for relief are put forward by countries which have adopted a positive policy of stimulating a rise in the birth-rate, such an attitude may be difficult to defend in the long run. While it cannot be denied that the claim of an overpopulated country ' is obviously weakened ' if its government hinders ' the spread of birth-control ' and attempts ' to arrest the fall in fertility . . ., there is perhaps something to be said for the... policy of attempting to stimulate the birth-rate which does not appear at first sight... [There is] reason to believe that, once the voluntary small family habit has gained a foothold, the size of family is likely, of not certain, in time to become so small that the reproduction rate will fall below replacement rate, and that, when this has happened, the restoration of a replacement rate proves to be an exceedingly difficult and obstinate problem '.[84b]

---

[a] Cf. *152* : — ' It is true — and this proves the fragility of the overpopulation argument — that there is sometimes a contradiction between the official statements regarding overpopulation and the no less official encouragements given to the production of more children, man being both capital and a force '.

[b] ' It would appear that this has not escaped the observation of Signor Mussolini. " My conviction ", he is reported to have said, " is that even if the laws [i. e. Italian population measures] were shown to be of no avail, it is necessary to try them just as all sorts of medicines are tried when, and more especially when, the case is a desperate one . . . But I think that our population measures, negative and positive, may prevent or retard the decline, provided the social organism to which they are applied is still capable of reaction " ' *84*).

From the point of view of internal policy, the demographic policy of countries complaining of congestion appears, at first sight, as curiously paradoxical as it seemed to be from the point of view of their external relations; but the following explanation[180] of the springs of policy in one of these countries may serve to clarify this further obscurity in a psychological position of great complexity :

... In England, thus far, relatively little attention seems to have been paid to the problem of declining population in Europe, which is demonstrably threatening most seriously the Germanic races ... The English discussion of the population movement in Germany as a revision problem shows that the attempt is made to explain this complex of facts in terms of concepts and theories which were constructed to account for such cases as Japanese overpopulation with its concomitant danger of expansion or the menacing, unrestricted growth of the negroes in South Africa.

Quite different is the German attitude toward the problem of population decline and overpopulation. The German people, under the yoke of the dictated peace of Versailles, has experienced a special connection between the problems of population decline[a] and of " nation without space " and " nation without work ". The German people reacted to the policy of Versailles which destroys and cripples the nation — the hunger blockade, the narrowing of German living space, the robbery of German national property, etc.— at first by an appalling tendency for births to be limited and even to decline and then through the national socialist policy of facilitating and increasing births. For us Germans, the increase in births is a reaction to, and a means of combating, the danger of national extinction and, at the same time, an inward renewal of the national will to live. To the unconscionable Versailles doctrine of " 20 million Germans too many ", German science has replied by research and teaching on the danger of national extinction which is menacing the old civilised nations of Europe and on the closely related problem of the decline of the white race's world supremacy.

... The need of the German people for wider living and working space arose immediately after the *Diktaten* of 1918-1919, which reduced German living and working space; it was accentuated, among other things by the expulsion and elimination of Germans from a number of countries, causing a mass return to the overcrowded homeland.[b] The German people rightly

---

[a] ' In Berlin, for example, the birth rate fell to less than 10 per thousand ' (*245*).

[b] Of ' German population returned from the districts taken from Germany, the most important movement ... [was] that of approximately 600,000 Germans from Pomorze and Posnania under pressure from Poland ... After the Russian Revolution and the end of the

felt this hardship to be an injustice inflicted upon them. As long as the German people were powerless and weary and had a weak government, they met the situation by limiting births, though without abandoning their claim to revision. With Germany's returning strength and her repudiation of national extinction, does the moral basis of her need totally or correspondingly vanish ?

It is nevertheless undeniable that countries with still rising populations do deliberately set out from expansionist motives to foster the movement. This is a third demographic consideration which plays a part in the formation of expansionist policy and which must therefore be analysed in the context of claims for changes in the *status quo*.

V. THE BATTLE FOR NUMBERS : THE HOME FRONT

It would seem that, while ' the reasons which impel nations to seek changes in the *status quo* are ... complex ' and while ' governments are of course concerned with improving the peace-time economic condition of their people ', yet ' there are other ends which ... are seldom publicly announced but which are almost universally regarded as more important than that of a high standard of living ... in peace time ... The first of these ends is power ... There is a constant and vigorous struggle ... to achieve some relative power advantage ... Power in this sense means the ability of a nation to make its will prevail over other nations which have conflicting interests ... Power, which is in fact only a means to enable a state to attain its objectives, becomes itself a major objective of policy. Nations claim things as necessary to their vital interests which in fact are necessary only to build up their power to impose their will upon others. Thus it comes about that the

War many Germans and persons of German origin returned to Germany from the Baltic provinces; many of the prisoners of war held in Russia, estimated at 100,000, were repatriated to Germany; the German armies in the Ukraine returned '. In addition, ' Ostjuden, of whom there were estimated to be 45,000 in Germany in 1914, were increased in number by the 30,000 brought in during the War, and by the migration of a further 70,000 after 1918, of whom about 47,000 were repatriated or emigrated to other countries, leaving approximately 53,000 Ostjuden resident in Germany out of those who entered during and after the War '. Germany also became ' the main concentration and dispersion point for Russian refugees ... [who] included ... large numbers from the German colonies of the Volga, Crimea, Caucasus and Ukraine and other persons of German descent (*Deutschstämmige*) ... By 1925 the German government estimated that the number of Russian refugees in its territory was 50,000 ' (*367*).

things which nations value most highly, and for which they are most readily apt to go to war, are the things which bear upon their power to make war '. A large population is one of these things; a large territory is another. Hence nations with expanding populations will seek to increase their sense of relative power by adding territory to population; while nations with contracting populations will seek, by extending their territorial possessions, to offset any diminution in their relative power which fewer numbers may bring about. ' For power is relative. The strength of one nation can only be measured in terms of the relative weakness of competing nations ... Hence foreign policy becomes directed towards the acquisition of things which enhance state power, and the people attach emotional values to these things quite apart from their effect upon the peace-time standards of living of the country. '[55]

' Everyone is familiar with the paradox that nations which complain the loudest of population pressure are often the ones which work hardest to increase the size of their populations. '[55] While ' it is obvious that the various countries which are making efforts to stimulate the growth of their populations are impelled largely by such motives as the fear of being overshadowed in numbers by other nations, and the desire to maintain a supply of active man-power for industrial and military[a] purposes, '[263] the object in view may be " offensive " as well as " defensive ". If it is offensive in the sense that ' the overpopulation has been voluntarily brought about ... with the ultimate aim of an imperialist war ', then ' it is quite clear that it would be simple-mindedness to try to find ... remedies for it '. [394] But it would appear rather that countries displaying ' a tendency to hurry the process [of rising numbers] by increasing the rate of growth of the population ' are actuated by the belief, on the one hand, ' that other nations will be impressed not only with the needs but especially with the man-power of the nation seeking expansion '[55] and, on the other hand, that they will be enabled either to carry out, or subsequently to justify, a policy of territorial expansion. Thus it has been suggested that in Italy, for example, ' the anxiety to justify an imperialist policy . . . is an addition-

---

[a] Cf. *368* : — ' [One of the arguments in favour of an increase in population], but the one naturally most distasteful to politicians, is that larger armies can be raised from a larger population. But is capacity for defence a mere function of numerical strength ? It would seem that it is becoming less and less so. Mere numbers cannot resist mechanical strength and mechanical strength depends on the wealth of a country rather than its population '.

al factor ' in that country's policy of stimulating the birth-rate.[263]   Some
evidence in support of this suggestion may be found, perhaps, in the
following excerpt from a speech which Signor Mussolini is reported
to have delivered in 1927 :

For five years we have continued to assert that the population of Italy
was like a river overflowing its banks.   That is not true.   The Italian nation
is not growing but diminishing in size . . .   To count for something in the
world, Italy must have a population of at least 60 millions when she reaches
the threshold of the second half of this century . . .   It is a fact that the fate
of nations is bound up with their demographic power . . .   Let us be frank
with ourselves : what are 40 million Italians compared with 90 million
Germans and 200 million Slavs ?   Let us look at our western neighbours :
what are 40 million Italians compared with the 40 millions of France and the
90 millions in her colonies, or with the 46 millions of England and the
450 million inhabitants of her colonial possessions ?[266]

In the same vein is the following utterance by Dr. Goebbels :

We have reversed the phrase of a French statesman.[a]   In our opinion
there are not too many, but too few Germans in the world.   If Germany
wishes to fulfil her great national and international tasks, she cannot do it
with power, living-space and technical means alone.   She needs hands.
That is why the new régime encourages large families . . .   Only peoples
which increase in numbers are young and only young peoples will maintain
themselves in the world.[380]

How determined have been the efforts made in two of the " dissatisfied " countries — Germany and Italy — to raise their birth-rates
will be apparent from the following outline of the essential features of
the measures taken with this end in view.[b]

Italy has ' tried to discourage celibacy and childlessness and to
encourage the raising of large families, by taxing bachelors and married
couples with no or few children; by granting tax reductions and exemp-
tions to State employees with at least 7 children and to other workers

[a] The reference is to Clemenceau's exclamation that there are ' twenty million Germans
too many '.
[b] A detailed account of the measures taken in Germany and in Italy (as well as in Belgium
and France) is given in *263*.   See also *84*, chap. XVI (' Attempts to Raise the Birth-rate '),
and *155*, pp. 89-91.

and employees with at least 10 children; [a] by granting birth premiums and family allowances; by giving preference to married men and women with relatively large families in the allocation of places in the central and local Government services, [b] and in private enterprise, and also in the allocation of cheap houses and flats; and by providing a wide range of services for the protection of mothers and children. ' [310]   Italy has ' introduced also severe laws against birth-control propaganda and deliberate abortion, ' [310c] and she has ' impeded the flow of labour from the country to the towns and initiated a movement in the reverse direction. ' [310]   Recently, a decree designed to enforce the doctrine that a woman's place is in the home has drastically restricted the employment of women, both in Government service and in private enterprise. [280] A newly-created institute for the improvement of the race is to deal, *inter alia*, with the best means of maintaining and increasing the birth-rate. [270]

Germany has, ' in many respects, followed the example of Italy and, in addition, encouraged marriage and provided more employment for men by granting a loan when the woman to be married had been employed for at least nine months in the previous two years. ' [310 d]

---

[a] The facetious have also observed that ' the Duce rewards the mother for every sixth child by sending her his portrait ' (*394*).

[b] On September 1, 1938, the Italian Council of Ministers approved a decree edicting that ' there shall be no bachelors in the senior ranks of the public services. The decree lays down the grade in each group of the three groups of public servants beyond which bachelors may not advance. It also gives the age at which bachelor officials must marry if they want to receive promotion — 30 in the case of executive posts, 26 in the other categories ' (*280*).

[c] ' The law of 1926 . . . punishes contraceptive propaganda by one year's imprisonment, and women who resort to abortion by four years' imprisonment ' (*394*).

[d] ' The loans had at first a twofold object : not only to increase the birth-rate but to reduce unemployment among men by withdrawing women from industry. Consequently they were granted only in cases in which the bride had been a wage-earner for at least nine months in the previous two years, or if doing housework at home was to be replaced by a domestic servant; but since there is now [October 1938] a shortage of labour this condition has been relaxed. The loans, which are financed from revenue raised by income-tax, and vary in amount up to a maximum of 1,000 marks, are given in the form of tokens that may be exchanged for household requisites. No interest is charged, but the loan must be repaid at the rate of 1 per cent a month, and one-quarter of the original sum lent is cancelled at the birth of each child. Up to the end of 1937 loans were granted to 900,000 married couples and the total amount lent was 600,000,000 m. Other measures were adopted. In 1935 lump-sum grants from State funds were made payable on the birth of a child in a needy family with not fewer than four children; and in 1936 family allowances were instituted for persons insured under the social insurance system with annual incomes not exceeding 1,200 m.   The allowances, which are financed from insurance funds, were at first at the rate of 16 m. monthly payable in respect of the fifth and each subsequent child under 16. In 1937 similar allowances, from State funds, were made payable for non-insured persons with annual incomes not exceeding 2,100 m. In April, 1938, the allowance system was considerably extended; the income limits were raised, and for insured persons the monthly

Another measure has been a modification of the law of inheritance in favour of large families; and many towns have adopted a system of sponsorship of third and subsequent children.[376]   An 'important feature of the German population policy is the movement to check the " flight from the land " . . .   Special measures have been adopted to counteract the tendency to increasing urbanization.   The marriage loans are granted on specially favourable terms to persons engaged in agriculture or forestry; under certain conditions such persons may receive the loan almost as a gift; and special facilities are made available for rural housing and the provision of small agricultural holdings, exceptional inducements being offered to persons with large families. ' [281] [a]

In view of these policies, if a ' more or less artificially overstrained increase is adduced as proof of an overpopulation that imposes on other nations the duty of surrendering their independence . . . or part of their territory ', and if it can be shown that, in any particular instance, a

---

rate of 16 m. was made payable in respect of third and fourth children, the rate for the fifth and each subsequent child being raised to 20 m. Herr Reinhardt, Staatssekretär in the Ministry of Finance, on whose initiative the loans scheme was introduced, estimates that the total expended in 1938 on marriage loans, allowances, and lump-sum grants will be 520,000,000 m.   Further extensions are contemplated ' (281).

In September 1937, Italy also instituted a marriage-loans system, whereby loans of one to three thousand lire are granted ' to encourage marriages and the founding of families and a rebate of 10% of the loan is made on the birth of each son ' (394).

[a] Further developments in the system of loans and grants for the agricultural population were decreed in the summer of 1938 with the object of raising working conditions in the country to the level of those ruling in the cities.   The following explanations were given by the Secretary of State in the Finance Ministry : — ' The German food position was such that it was of the highest importance that men and women who " grew up in agriculture or forest work should remain in it ".   As regards the marriage loans . . . agricultural workers would have amortisation payments remitted on application provided that the husband or wife had been employed continuously in agriculture or forestry for at least five years.   The whole debt would be finally remitted if one of the parties stayed 10 years on the land after the debt was contracted.   In the case of marriages contracted after June 30 this year the parties could claim, besides the marriage loan, a loan for equipment.   This, unlike the marriage loan, which is paid in coupons valid only for furniture and household goods, would be paid in cash.   The money could be used not only for setting up a household, but for the purchase of tools, machines, cattle, an allotment, and so on.   If both the man and the wife had been 10 years continuously on the land the loan would amount to 800 m.; where only one of the parties fulfilled this condition it would be 400 m.   The loan would bear no interest and did not need to be repaid at all if the recipient stayed long enough on the land.   At the end of 10 years the State would reduce the debt by 500 m., and thereafter it would be reduced at the rate of 100 m. a year until extinguished.   Then came the grants for equipment, which would amount to 400 m. or 200 m., according to whether both man and wife, or only one of them, had been five years on the land.   There was no means test. The grants were there for all who had worked the prescribed periods in agriculture, forestry, or as agricultural craftsmen and intended to continue in these occupations.   At the end of every further five years on the land the workers could claim additional subsidies . . . The equipment loan and grants did not affect the subsidies for children, which averaged approximately 350 m. for needy families . . .   [Housing conditions being a difficulty in the effort to keep people on the land], land and forest owners may write off for taxation purposes the whole cost of labourers' cottages, built in the years 1937-1941 ' (278).

' rapid increase is not really the cause of the craving for expansion, but that, on the contrary, that increase has been recently, wilfully and artificially, created as a means to enforce, if necessary by war, claims which originated in considerations of national prestige ', then ' the question may well be asked whether the responsibility for the demographic policy . . . should be borne by foreigners who had no influence whatever in the shaping of that policy '.[131] For ' an artificial inflation of the population going beyond . . . [the] goal . . . [of maintaining] at least . . ., by a natural reaction [against depopulation] . . . their present numbers . . ., would lead to a general demographic armament race more violent and costly than ever, and which, coming in addition to material armaments, would produce nervous overstrain and thus lead to a new disaster '.[155] [a]

*   *   *

[a] ' Since the population policies of Germany and Italy have attracted much attention it is sometimes thought that action of this kind is especially associated with authoritarian régimes ' (*84*). The ' direct measures and intensive campaigns [to stimulate a rise in the birth-rate] such as are to be found in Germany and Italy at the present time are not, [however], the only ways of attacking the falling birth-rate ' (*263*) and ' there are two other countries with population policies, France and Belgium, and they are democracies. Swedish opinion is also profoundly disturbed by the trend of fertility; measures are under discussion, and the adoption of a definite policy is only a matter of time ' (*84*). In Belgium and France, however, ' the basic measure in the present population campaign . . . — the family allowance — was not originally introduced for the purpose of raising the birth-rate. It was undoubtedly designed to ease the burden of the married man who was bringing up a family, but it did not aim at offering any real inducement to raise children, and although the allowances have undergone a number of modifications in the last fifteen years, none of these modifications was for the specific purpose of stimulating births ' (*263*). Moreover, while ' the measures applied may . . . have prevented an even steeper decline from taking place . . ., they offer no dependable solution because any possible effects have, up to the present, been imperceptible ' (*ibid.*). (Cf., however, *337*, where it is suggested that in France ' certain private initiatives have shown that the allowances multiply large families. I cannot forget ', adds its author, ' the hairdresser's assistant who said to me : " I have been refused a premium of five hundred francs for my second child; I shall not have a third; they can go and whistle for it " ').

It may be added that ' such indirect means as family allowances ' are in use, in one form or another, in the public services or the private undertakings not only of Germany and Italy and of France and Belgium, ' where they are most firmly established ', but also of Australia, Austria, Bulgaria, Czechoslovakia, Denmark, Esthonia, Great Britain, Hungary, Jugoslavia, Latvia, Netherlands, New Zealand, Norway, Poland, Spain, Sweden, Switzerland and U. S. A. ' (*263*)

Poland is one of the countries having family allowance schemes in private undertakings : ' family allowances are given either through collective agreement clauses or under rules issued by the management (in the case of State monopolies); allowances are given in coal and other mining (collective agreements of November 1929 for Upper Silesia, and June 1929 for Dombrowa and Cracow Fields), certain other industries, and various public utilities and banks; the allowances are paid at the employers' expense ' (*265*). On the other hand, ' the allowances formerly granted to government officials and public servants with large families were entirely abolished . . . a few years ago ' — a measure which a Polish speaker submitted to the International Studies Conference as a proof ' that Poland pursues no demographic policy calculated to increase the birth-rate ' (*207*).

'To what extent', enquired the International Studies Conference's General Rapporteur in the opening phase of its study of "peaceful change", 'should the demographic policy of states be taken into account in judging the legitimacy of their needs' ?[40] There could be no doubt about the answer. 'It is scarcely likely that... claims for expansion will be heard with much sympathy so long as the... [governments in question appear] to be engaged in a campaign to increase the difficulties which... [they ask] that other nations should assist to solve'.[84] 'The claim for room for surplus population is vitiated', it was asserted, 'if special measures are adopted by the State to increase it, e. g., rewards for large families, bonuses for weddings, etc.'.[44] [a] 'We cannot expect a country which is complaining of overpopulation — without ever having defined what it means by that term — necessarily to have the right to send its people abroad, if at the same time it is straining every effort to raise the birth rate and increase its rate of population growth; demanding outlets for its surplus population while at the same time straining every effort (usually unsuccessfully, it is true)[b] to increase its population'.[194] To the extent, then 'that population pressure is related to power considerations, it seems to be beyond the range of procedures of peaceful change. Nations cannot be expected to agree voluntarily to a change in the *status quo* which enhances the claimant nation's power and influence in world affairs at the expense of others... All proposals for changes in the *status quo*, regardless of the grounds on

---

[a] This declaration (by Lord Lugard) provoked the following rejoinder from a German writer : — 'From the individualistic standpoint, a people's will to live, the paralysation of life, the weariness of a people or its extinction, appear merely as subjects of statistical measurement. From the standpoint of the people as a whole, its will to live, its weakness or its growth in strength, are the genuine realities of human life. From the individualistic standpoint, the national regenerative process, as it is effected by National Socialism in Germany, or, in another way, by Fascism in Italy, is a fact that cannot be grasped. The Lugard doctrine, for instance, that overpopulation loses its meaning and its moral implication, when, as in National-Socialist Germany, it issues, *inter alia*, from State measures intended to promote an increase in the birth rate, is based on the questionable assumption that the increased birth rate in the Third Reich is due to governmental measures which are alien to the people. To this it need only be replied that, among the subconscious premises of the apparently purely sociological Lugard doctrine, is the assumption that in National-Socialist Germany there is a separation between people and state, such as exists in the autocratic state; yet this is an erroneous political hypothesis or, at any rate, a biassed interpretation of the relations between people and State' (*180*).

This argument, whether apposite or not as a refutation of Lord Lugard's statement, is not, of course, an answer to the objections against claims arising out of expansionist sentiments deliberately fostered by a policy of increasing the birth-rate; on the other hand, it will be noted with interest in the context of the analysis given above (pp. 141-145) of the internal motives which have prompted that policy.

[b] Cf. below, pp. 152-153.

which they are based, are bound to be assessed first and foremost in terms of their effect upon the power relationships of the nations concerned. Any proposed change which would noticeably alter the existing power ratio to the disadvantage of any state is fairly certain to be resisted tenaciously, regardless of the justice of the claim or of its bearing upon the general welfare of the community. This point cannot be emphasised too strongly ... No nation will willingly agree to a change which will impair its ability to defend its position in a clash with other states ... Of course nations practically never seek changes in the *status quo* openly for the purpose of increasing their war potential at the expense of other states. Such claims are always advanced on some more palatable ground. But whatever the real objective may be, the possible effect of the change on power relationships will be closely scrutinised, and if the effect is perceptible it will be stoutly resisted. This is merely to say that so long as the notion of self-help persists, the aim of maintaining the power position of the nation is paramount to all other considerations. Questions of abstract justice or of internal needs, or demands for equality and independence cannot be expected to prevail over considerations of national power and security '.[55]

There is, however, yet another aspect of state action designed to promote, for expansionist reasons, a rise in the birth-rate which must be taken into account in the consideration of the legitimacy of claims for relief from population pressure. The view that, in cases of this kind, a claim may be vitiated seems to assume that the demographic policies in question are bound to be successful. But it would appear from such evidence of the results of these policies as is already available that this assumption rests on a very insecure foundation. It has been suggested that the measures taken, for example, in Italy, ' since the advent of the Fascist régime ' and in Germany ' since that of the Hitler régime ... have a positive influence on the birth rate ',[141] yet an analysis of the results which may be ascertained so far has been held to show on the contrary, that ' the utmost that can be claimed for these measures is that, if they had not been taken, the Italian birth-rate would have fallen still more rapidly ' than it has and that ' what has so far happened may not ultimately in the least affect the trend of population in Germany '[84] [a] where, although the birth-rate has been raised, ' it remains

---

[a] These conclusions are partly based (see *84*) upon the description and analysis of the attempts to raise the birth-rate in Germany in *263*. The following passages will show the conclusions reached in this and in other studies :

' The rise in the *German* birth-rate, if maintained, is sufficient eventually to replace

to be seen whether this has been achieved by raising fertility or merely by stimulating the appearance of a large number of first-born children in a short period of time '.[a]

the present population by one no smaller in size, though containing a smaller proportion of potentially fertile women. But this rise may have been due largely to the special circumstances following the economic depression of 1930 and 1932, and if that is actually the case, there is little hope of continuing the 1934 level of births. And, in fact, there are already indications that the high rate of 1934 was only temporary ... So rapid a regression does not augur well for the future of the German population ... [In the case of *Italy*], there seem to be no obvious signs of success in encouraging marriages ... Nor does the effect upon the birth-rate appear more noteworthy ... Comparing the situation in 1933, after more than seven years of campaigning against the decline in marriages and births, with that in 1921, it is not easy to find any visible results ' (*263*).

' [*Italy*'s] efforts to increase the number of births were a complete failure. When this policy was inaugurated in 1926, the yearly births numbered 1,095,000. They have been below a million in every year since 1931 ... It is impossible to tell whether ... [*Germany*] will succeed in the long run. The results in the first three years are doubtful. The increase in the number of births was mainly due to an increase of first and second births. If it is true, as is claimed officially, that abortions have diminished conspicuously, the total nuumber of births should have increased much more than it actually has, unless the use of other means of birth-control has expanded ' (*310*).

' The birth and reproduction rates for *Germany* already display the effects of the new population policy ... All the same, the vital statistician F. Burgdörfer states that they are not sufficient to maintain the present population, since the relatively high birth rate is due only to a temporary favourable state of the age-distribution and not to a true healthy reproduction rate of the German people ' (*81*).

' The *German* efforts ... since 1933 are too recent to permit of any conclusions bearing upon the birth-rate over a longer period ' (*179*).

' The measures taken by the *Reich* government, as from 1933, may perhaps have brought about a notable and striking increase in the birth rate, but they have at no time succeeded in eliminating the deficit in reproduction; and now [March 1937] the curve once again shows a downward trend ' (*113*).

' It is to be noted that so far the efforts [made in *Germany* to increase the size of the population] ... do not seem to be meeting with success. Thus ... Germany ... [shows] a declining birth rate ' (*55*).

' In *Italy* ... strenuous efforts were made [from 1926 onwards] to check the downward trend of the birth-rate, which had fallen from 38.0 per 1,000 in 1881-85 to 27.7 in 1926. Nevertheless, the fall steadily continued, and in 1936 the birth-rate was 22.2 per 1,000 ... In *Germany* ... the annual number of births per 1,000 population fell from 34.3 in 1901-5 to 14.7 in 1933 ...; [by 1937 it had risen again to 18.8]. Germany has so far achieved considerable success in her efforts to prevent the onset of depopulation, although the annual number of births is still 10 per cent below the number required for replacement ' (*281*).

It is of interest to note that, according to *81*, the birth and reproduction rates for *Germany* in 1934 ' were above those of the majority of the other sections of the German people ' in Europe. The birth- and reproduction-rate figures were, respectively, as follows : Germany, 18.0 and 7.1; Austria, 13.5 and 0.8; Czechoslovakia, 14.9 and 2.1; Hungary, 17.3 and 4.0; Rumania, 21.9 and 5.5; Carpatho-Ruthenian districts of Czechoslovakia, 12.1 and 14.2.

[a] ' The family allowance system cannot have played an important part, for it was not instituted until 1936 and not extended to non-insured persons until 1937 ... If the marriage loans scheme, which is by far the most important of the special measures, were the main cause of the rise in the birth-rate, it would have taken effect chiefly by increasing the number of first births. But the statistics show that there has been a large increase in second, third, and fourth births, and even an increase in the fertility of marriages of over 10 years'

' That the Italian and German Governments themselves consider their population policies as inadequate is proved by the fact that they have recently announced emphatically the necessity of taking new measures. The most radical feature in the new Italian programme is the suppression of communes and provinces which show a particularly low fertility. The most radical feature in the German programme is the promotion of illegitimate fertility. Whether these measures will have a numerically important effect it is impossible to foretell '.[312]

Moreover, even those who claim to detect an improvement in the movement of population seem to ascribe this result to moral causes rather than to the technical action of governments. A German authority[282] finds the main factors accounting for the increase in the number of marriages and births in Germany since 1932 ' partly in the general social and economic policy of the National-Socialists, which has brought about an enormous reduction in unemployment and created a new sense of social security, but chiefly in the new outlook on life taken by the German people since the Revolution of 1933 '.[281] Here, for example, is his analysis of the rise in the marriage-rate in Germany since the second quarter of 1934 at the International Population Conference held in Berlin in August 1935 :

This change is no doubt partly due to the various kinds of State action to encourage population growth. In particular, the granting of marriage loans has stimulated the marriage- and birth-rates. Sixty per cent of the increase in births comes from marriages which were concluded with the help of loans. But these external measures are not the sole reason for the change. The decisive factor is the new outlook brought about by the National Socialist revolution, the fundamental transformation of the political and moral (*geistigen*) atmosphere, the improvement in the economic situation, clearly shown in the fall of unemployment from over six millions to one and three-quarter

duration . . . A recent book, [282] . . . gives a masterly analysis of the statistical position . . . [It] shows (i) that in the three years 1934-36 there were 900,000 more legitimate births in Germany than there would have been if the number of marriages in 1932 and the specific fertility rates in 1933 had remained constant, and (ii) that 300,000 of these additional births were due to an increase in the number of married couples and the remaining 600,000 to the increased fertility of married couples. [It] . . . shows also that the additional marriages cannot all, or even for the most part, be attributed to the marriage loans; since 1932 the number of marriages has increased in other countries, Great Britain, for example, though not to the same extent as in Germany. And [it] . . . points out that even if all the additional marriages, with their 300,000 additional births, were attributed to the loans, there would remain 600,000 additional births that must be attributed to other factors' (281).

million; in short, the return of confidence on the part of the people in the political and economic government of the nation.[264] [a]

' On the whole . . . [Germany] relies much less on State action than Italy, and rightly expects a striking change in the trend of fertility rather from the spread of new ideals and a spontaneous desire of married couples to have numerous children '.[310]   It is, however, ' impossible to subject all . . . [the] statements [in the above passage] to an exact scrutiny ' for ' there is no means of estimating the effect of a changed political system upon the willingness of German men and women to marry and have children '.[263]   It is sound sense, however, that ' compulsion is no use.   You cannot bribe or terrorize men and women into regulating their most intimate and private lives in a manner contrary to their wishes and to their sense of private duty.   If people are to have more children, they must want more children.   The State can only remove the obstacles to the satisfaction of that want '.[336]

It would seem, therefore, that ' the view that the chief factor in the evolution of the birth-rate . . . [is] probably of a moral order '[114] is not one that can be lightly set aside.   The moral considerations which may play a rôle in this question are of two kinds : ' on the one hand, responsibility before God, and on the other responsibility to society '[114] :

With regard to the first of these factors, it has been statistically proved time and again that invariably more children are born to families whose religious faith calls upon them to multiply and which, moreover, condemns birth control . . .

A similar influence can be exerted by a sense of responsibility towards society.   Illustrations of the part this sense of responsibility can play are afforded by certain societies which, at a given period in history, realised that a declining birth rate was a political and national disaster and that a nation which wished to maintain its position must above all have a large number of citizens at its command.   In order that such a conviction may exercise a real influence, the society must naturally be particularly well disciplined . . .

[a] ' Note that as against . . . [these] contentions, German foreign trade has declined considerably and there is a marked shortage of certain kinds of foodstuffs, while the reduction in the unemployment figure is at least partly due to the transference of unemployed workers to labour camps . . .   All the officials [connected with the application of the various National-Socialist measures for encouraging population growth] admit explicitly that the increase in marriages and births since 1933 and 1934 was due, in a large measure, to specially favourable circumstances ' (263).

Japan is the most striking example in this respect . . . — the most typical example of the influence that can be exerted on the increase of population (which is very often regarded as a natural phenomenon that develops automatically) by a conscious desire to maintain a position of importance. The totalitarian States of Europe have not, so far, furnished an example of such discipline on the part of their nationals. Nevertheless, it is in this sense of responsibility towards society that we can find one of the causes of the fairly strong upward trend in the development of the Italian population. It is this same sense of responsibility which explains the entirely unexpected rise in the number of births in Germany after the Hitlerian revolution.[144]

' On the basis of phenomena of this kind, the theory has been put forward that moral considerations constitute the primary factor from the point of view of the increase or decrease in the number of births. The birth rate should fall in a weak and morally decadent nation, whose citizens are concerned only with their own well-being. In those nations where, on the contrary, the people have the destiny of the State and the future prosperity of the country at heart, the birth rate must inevitably rise and nothing will check it. All considerations, both of economics and of biology, would thus play but an essentially secondary part. The decisive factors would always be moral health and the sense of responsibility of the citizens '.[144]

' During the past few years, this theory has been expounded chiefly by German savants and publicists '.[144] They ascribe ' the decline in the birth-rate . . . not to any loss of the physiological capacity to produce offspring but to the voluntary limitation of offspring. The population question is *eine Willensfrage*. The decline in the birth-rate, it is held, is a symptom of a disease of the will, the decay of faith, the denial of life. [One of them][a] . . . holds that it is a question not of economic but of spiritual values, and that what Germany has done to check the decline in the birth-rate holds out a message of hope to other countries '.[281]

'Hitherto throughout the whole history of the human race replacement has been automatic; indeed the danger has usually been in the direction of excessive reproduction. Replacement is no longer automatic, but of this fact there is no understanding. The most essential thing at the present time is to implant in the members of a modern community a firm grasp of the fact that they are responsible

---

[a] Dr. Burgdörfer.

for its future in the sense that, if they do not replace themselves, the community will be extinguished ... Replacement is a social duty, a fact which at present is entirely unfamiliar to people at large ... In many western communities the average size of family is now such that the duty is not being performed ... Upon attitude to marriage depends the end to which it is directed. No institution has been so degraded and vulgarized as marriage; it would almost seem as though all the artifices known to a sensational press and to a commercialized literature have been employed to emphasise every aspect of marriage except the duties which it imposes and the opportunities of self discipline which it offers ... It is as certain as anything can be that, where families are voluntary, a community, in which marriage is regarded as it is to-day in western civilization, will die out. For it is held up to be no more than a mode of self gratification. Those who are concerned about the small family problem should address themselves earnestly to a reform of the outlook upon marriage ... This is fundamental. It would be a mistake of the first magnitude to suppose that no more is needed than to smooth the path to parenthood by removing the disabilities under which parents suffer ... The transformation of the whole scheme of life ... will gradually have to be accomplished if the inconveniences attaching to parenthood are to be removed ... Nothing less than a social revolution is necessary '.[84]

* * *

Thus the argument that a claim for relief from demographic pressure is vitiated if the congested country is pursuing a positive policy of population expansion derives rather from an automatic reaction of moral indignation than from any cogent relationship to the actual effects of the policy. It must be concluded, in fact, that, from this point of view, ' those countries which are overpopulated cannot be held to be blameworthy, since the present population situation is not the result of policies directly designed to influence the course of population '.[84]

This conclusion, however, does not close the debate; it remains to be seen whether Germany's demographic situation is so different from that of other countries, and particularly from that of the colonial Powers, who are considered in Germany to occupy a position of privilege in the solution of population problems, as to give substance to her colonial claims. Now, while it is true that, in comparison with the colonial Powers of western Europe, 'Germany has by far the largest annual increase of population in absolute figures', yet 'it may be noted that in 1933 she held the last place but one for the coefficient of annual increase.   Doubtless her position has improved since then from the latter point of view.   But it is not certain that this improvement will continue.   Finally her density of population enables her to take only fourth place.   It should be noted that if other European Powers such as Poland which undergo a demographic pressure greater than that in Germany, are taken into consideration, then the position of Germany will be modified to her disadvantage.   The demographic difficulties of which the Reich complains are therefore not an anomaly from which it is the only country in Europe to suffer.   The population of Russia increases by three million souls yearly and the population of Poland by one million.   In these regions the situation becomes continually more serious, whereas in Germany it is at the worst stationary '.[376] [a]   'It cannot be sufficiently emphasised that the position of Germany is not exceptional and that, if it is to be used as a justification for changes in the distribution of colonies, it could equally well be employed by other peoples as a basis for claims of the same kind.   And in fact variations in the birth-rate of the countries of western Europe could become a pretext for periodical revision of the colonial situation. That is clearly a proposal which cannot be sustained '.[376]

Furthermore, it is obvious that, before a country can legitimately ask other countries to make sacrifices in order to relieve it from demographic congestion, 'it must, first of all, endeavour to remedy its position of inferiority unaided ... [that is] by taking steps to increase its production and to improve, by every possible means, the conditions

---

[a] The following figures (see 377) showing the proportion of children born alive per thousand inhabitants in Germany and in the seven European colonial Powers furnish 'conclusive information on   this point' (376) :

Country	1913	1924 to 1929	1932	1933	1934
Belgium	22.4	18.9	17.6	16.5	—
France	19.0	18.4	17.3	16.3	16.2
Germany	26.9	19.3	15.1	14.7	18.0
Great Britain	24.2	17.9	15.8	14.9	15.3
Italy	31.7	26.9	23.8	23.7	23.2
Netherlands	28.2	23.7	22.0	20.8	20.7
Portugal	32.3	33.7	29.8	28.9	28.4
Spain	30.4	29.4	28.2	27.8	26.2

'Germany has returned to the level of Belgium, France and Great Britain.   On the other hand, the Latin countries of the South have a fertility double that of the Germanic countries and if figures were produced for the Slav countries, it would be seen that they have three times the fertility' (see 377).

in which its economic system functions. This is self-evident and there is no need to dwell further on the point '. Moreover, ' it is not sufficient that the standard of living of a given country should be lower than that of another for it to declare that it is overpopulated as compared with that other country and for it to have the right to formulate demands and claims on that ground; these claims could not be recognised as admissible — let us say admissible for the time being; the country in question can legitimately plead overpopulation only in so far as its lower standard of living is not due to its obsolete technique of production, to the inherent indolence of its inhabitants, or again to the incompetence of the government which it has chosen or which it, at least, tolerates. Whether these failings . . . can or cannot be corrected is of little importance; if they exist, they preclude all reference to overpopulation or, at any rate, the right to invoke it in support of claims '.[113]

VI. DEMOGRAPHIC IMPERIALISM

The foregoing account of the ways in which Germany and Italy are exerting themselves to raise their birth-rates does not exhaust the methods designed to ensure an abundant population. Side by side with the policy of directly stimulating natality within the national frontiers there has also been an organised effort to prevent the denationalisation of nationals resident abroad by resisting the processes of assimilation, coupled, in the case of Italy, with a reduction of emigration, and, quite recently, with a policy of repatriation. Attempts to put a check to permanent expatriation are now a part of the general struggle for population. Italy, in particular, has sought to devise a policy of emigration which shall ' tend to maintain as large a population as possible and energetically to prevent absorption by the countries of immigration '.[a] In his passport, the Italian emigrant finds ' instructions and advice reflecting this policy : " Do not fail to have your children educated and, if possible, to send them to an Italian school. Let no Italian ever forsake the privilege and consciousness of being Italian. Let him make it a point of honour to use the products of his national industry, to keep his mother-tongue immutable and alive, to bring his

---

[a] Declaration made by the Italian Minister for Foreign Affairs on the occasion of a request for a credit of 1,100,000 lire ' to be used for combating the " denationalisation policy pursued by certain States " (in this instance, France) '. (117)

children up in a spirit of patriotism, teaching them the language, the history and the geography of Italy " '.[117]

In pursuance of this policy, the emigration of Italian agricultural workers has been prohibited ' on account of its settled character and the facility of assimilation '. The emigration of women and of the families of emigrants has also been restricted ' as being thought conducive to definitive settlement abroad. " Workers' families ", said the rapporteur for the Budget of the Ministry of Foreign Affairs in 1930, " must not leave the home-country, otherwise emigrants would no more think of returning to Italy than of remitting their earnings. Consequently, any worker proposing to stay for a while in a foreign country must sign a declaration undertaking that his family will not accompany him or join him later " '. No better policy could be adopted to impede assimilation. ' Women . . . contribute very largely to the process of stabilisation and adaptation, not only because they make it possible to found a family, but also because their inclination for settling down and for the routine of life is more pronounced than in the case of men, who are more enterprising and more restless. Women are more appreciative of the benefits of a more highly developed material civilisation; they become attached to their surroundings and have less desire to return to their native country '.[117] Experience has shown that, in France, in the United States[120] and in other countries of immigration, ' the foreign population attains more stability as the proportion of the feminine element increases . . .[a] Countries of emigration are fully aware of the stabilising influence of women and girls who may help in the founding of a home. These countries hold the families as veritable hostages who are used as a check to the denationalisation of the emigrant '.[117]

After the war, writes the author of a study on the problem of assimilation in France which was submitted to the International Studies Conference, ' the countries of emigration turned their attention to making the best use of their human resources and to claiming the value of labour as against that of raw materials. Men should no longer be cast — without protection and without the means of obtaining

[a] Cf. *119* : — ' Migration, whether on a large scale or by infiltration, does not result in any permanent alteration of the population map or in racial distribution if the feminine element is lacking or insufficient. Women constitute the element of preservation and stabilisation which attaches a displaced people to its new country . . . Women', state the French authors of these views, ' have been, *par excellence*, the force of assimilation and preservation. It is the feminine contribution to the peopling of our country which undoubtedly explains the composite, yet unified, social group which became ourselves '.

the price of their labour — upon the markets of the world " in the service of the wealth and power of others ". They sought to control their emigrants, to keep them in order and to use them politically. " Those countries ", said Signor Mussolini in 1923, " which nature has endowed with raw materials have shown that they can energetically defend that privilege. Countries of emigration must do likewise : the value of the emigrant must be utilised " '.[117] The Italian government has, indeed, been particularly active in the adoption of ' measures which aim at keeping alive the loyalty of Italians abroad to Italy and at strengthening their attachment to Italian culture '.[84] The following account of the measures which it has taken in France may be quoted here, though it is perhaps to be noted that the intensity of the action pursued by Italy in that country is a function both of the great size of the Italian population in France — in 1931 there were 808,000 Italians in France[117] — and of the fact that Italians, like other Latin groups in France, are more ' easily *francisables* '[117] than certain other national groups :

Italy ... created a number of important services to bring about this " valorisation " ... [to which Signor Mussolini referred]. The General Commissariat for Emigration and, later, the General Department of Italians Abroad were entrusted with the duty of keeping a watch over emigrants " in every respect " by collaborating with the Secretariat of the Fascist organisations abroad and by seeking to make the activities of the various immigrant institutions and associations radiate from the Italian consulates. Emigration counsellors were attached to the Consuls and to the Embassy, since, to quote the Italian report [122], " diplomatic and consular action must not be confined to the function of representation, but must defend and protect emigrants in the political, social and intellectual spheres ". A National Credit Institute was formed to " stimulate thrift and collect the savings of immigrants ". Support and subsidies were given to certain relief agencies, recreational, sports and cultural organisations which " help to maintain the national spirit among immigrants ". These organisations include associations of ex-service men, the Italian Workers' Relief Committee, the Associazione Nazionale Italiana, the Patronato Emigranti Italiani, the Dante Alighieri Society, Fascist clubs, etc. The " Dopolavoro " institutions officially sponsored by the consulates have as their object the employment of spare time " for patriotic ends ". Many of these associations join forces to form regional federations which, very often, have a very extensive radius of action, thereby enabling members to move from one part of the country to another

12

without losing the benefits of their subscriptions.   Every year, the delegates of the Federation of Italian Associations in France hold a general meeting. The majority of these organisations are under the supervision of consular and other official agencies.[117]

Nor is this all.   Pressure is also brought to bear upon the emigrant populations through the clergy, the school and the press. The work of Italian, Polish and other foreign priests and missionaries among their co-nationals in France deserves some attention for it seemed to threaten at one time to give rise to a quasi-competition on the part of the French clergy in which it was difficult to distinguish clearly between the religious and the national motives.   Take, for example, the Italian work of national propaganda carried out in France through the Opera Bonomelli,[a] ' an Italian religious and social welfare organisation subsidised by the Government '[117] :

The missionaries of the Opera Bonomelli — Italian propaganda agents as much as preachers — were the collaborators of the Italian Consuls and their activities were " the complement of the functions assigned to the Commissariat for Emigration in Rome ".[118]   Among the astonishing guiding principles observed by this organisation are to be noted : " energetic action to be taken to prevent the naturalisation of Italian emigrants " and " resolutely to oppose the permanent emigration of Italian peasants ".   This was tantamount to saying that the leaders of this organisation, in spite of the moral dangers which they realised better than anybody else, preferred the temporary emigration of bachelors or unaccompanied married men to permanent and family emigration.[117]

' It may be surprising to see missionaries fulfilling such a rôle under the cloak of welfare work.[b]   In reality, for most of the countries of

---

[a] ' The institution founded by Mgr. Bonomelli and recognised as a public welfare organisation was dissolved in 1929 and replaced by the Association of Italian Catholic Missionaries ' (117).

[b] ' At first sight, it does indeed seem strange that the Church, whose international character has frequently been proclaimed, should act, through the agency of its priests, as the champion of nationalist doctrines.   The reason is that the Church, with so many centuries behind it, is wedded to old formulas and to those old social groups among which it has developed and to which it has given its support.   It accordingly defends, and combats the disintegration of, these groups : the family, the motherland and the nation.   The priest in exile opposes everything likely to denationalise the emigrant and to make him forget his old habits and customs, his ways of thinking and feeling ' (117).   Similarly, ' in the United States, assimilation is difficult only in the case of Catholics, even, if they are Anglo-

emigration — Italy, Poland, Spain — these missionaries and priests are the most active agents of national policies regarding immigrants, and the Papacy has found it necessary to react[a] against these militant clerical nationalists '[117] :

Scattered over the country, in the towns, in workers' settlements or in rural districts, the 150 priests of the Polish Catholic Mission, the 130 to 150 Italian missionaries and priests, and the Spanish and even Flemish missionaries are the most active elements in the ranks of national particularism . . . It would seem that foreign priests living outside their native country are afraid that their flocks will merge and disappear into the adverse national mass. And this fear is all the deeper since, from the religious and moral standpoint, they judge France severely, either because — like the Poles — they confuse " Francisation " with anti-clericalism, " Polonism " with Catholicism, or, like the Italian priests, they regard the French as being " Malthusian, lazy or atheistic ". The priests are, moreover, the only cultured elements in the mass of immigrant workers, for whom they are, in a sense, the leaders and spiritual guides. This explains perhaps the sternness with which they defend an autonomy and a particularism which serve to maintain, among immigrants, the old customs and beliefs on which their authority is based [117].

In France, however, the attempt made by foreign countries to bring influence to bear upon their emigrants appears to have broken down. ' The patriotism and nationalism of foreign priests was bound to come into conflict with French clerical opinion. The French clergy realised that it was just as dangerous to set up no counterpart to the activities of foreign priests as to abandon without leadership or religious guidance the immigrants who were accustomed to such support . . . [for] 75% of the immigrants are not only Catholics but practising

Saxons or Germans. It is as Catholics, clustering around their clergy, that they remain together in isolated communities. Catholicism is the defensive link against assimilation ' (123). A strong tendency to group solidarity running counter to the requirements of assimilation is also attributed to the foreign Jews in France. Cf., for example, the view cited in 337 that Jewish immigrants in France, ' keep their religion, their priests, their customs, have their own newspapers and schools and confide their savings to their own banks '.

a ' In 1929, the pontifical instructions issued to missionaries stated that they (i) must in no place whatsoever practise nationalism; they must practise nothing but Catholicism and apostolic teaching and concern themselves only with souls . . . (ii) Those working in the name of the Almighty must not interfere in secular affairs . . . (iii) God's servants, of whatsoever nationality they may be, must maintain amongst themselves unity of heart, thought and action ' (117).

Catholics . . . who, if left to themselves, would have been dangerously adrift.   They did not wish to see France become a country of foreign missions and they sought to deprive foreign Governments of the argument justifying their intervention, namely, the lack of organisation in the moral and religious life of immigrants.   The work accomplished by the French Church among foreigners is remarkable '.[117]   It ' has set itself, without noise or fuss, quietly and persistently to care for the welfare of immigrants through numerous organisations specially created for the purpose, and has been very successful in its attempt to initiate them into French life '.[84]   ' Foreign clergy have been admitted, as far as possible, within the ranks of Church organisation in France and they have been gradually brought under the control, with more or less difficulty, of the French episcopate . . .   It is to be noted, moreover, that, since 1930, under the influence of Rome, foreign priests have conformed more readily to purely religious discipline and have slightly relaxed their nationalist activity.   The Opera Bonomelli, which was too active politically, has been dissolved [as has already been stated].   The Italian missionaries will henceforward be directly under the authority of the Holy See and under the jurisdiction of the local bishop.   The Rector of the Polish mission receives his powers from the Archbishop of Paris.   The whole of the clergy in France has been made to turn towards a less nationalist and more broadly human aim in religious propaganda.   Understood in this light, the apostolate of these missionaries makes them the collaborators of the French clergy and can contribute to stability and adaptation, since, in the eyes of the immigrant, a priest is not only a spiritual guide, but also an adviser in all the minor problems of life '.[117]

The countries of immigration into France have also recognised the truth expressed in the view that, in the case of the United States, for example, the principal contributive force in the assimilation of immigrants and, in particular, the greatest assimilating influence among children born in America or abroad is undoubtedly the school.[121]

The countries of emigration have tried . . . to react . . . against this strong influence of education . . .   Their efforts have been unsuccessful, since the opening of entirely foreign schools is prohibited by French law.   All they have been able to do is to organise a few independent schools (which are, moreover, subjected to the control of the French authorities), crèches, social clubs, evening classes, continuation classes in foreign languages, lectures, libraries, etc. which affect a total for all nationalities of only 8,000 to 10,000 persons.[a]   Only the Poles have succeeded in obtaining from their employers the building of private schools, with Polish pupil-teachers who, for one half of the time-table, teach the language, history and geography of Poland.   In 1933, there were 150 Polish teachers giving instruction to about 18,000 Polish children '.[117]   ' These pupil-teachers are ... active national propaganda agents.   The tendency is for them to act as agents of liaison and information for the Polish consulates, which keep in close touch with them, give them their instructions and compel them to return to Poland if their work proves to be unsatisfactory '.[117]   That other national groups in France have had less success than the Poles appears to be due partly to their greater dispersion but partly also to the fact that the parents themselves ' prefer to send their children to a French school, where they are more likely to acquire useful knowledge and to learn to fend for themselves later in France.   Thus, private Italian schools, which, incidentally, had been opened in contravention of the law and which were closed by order of the authorities, found it easier to draw French pupils who wished to learn Italian than the children of immigrants '.[117]

It is not easy to assess the propagandist value of the two hundred odd periodicals, reviews and newspapers in foreign languages published in France[117] : it is almost as difficult to choose between condemnation of those which ' conduct veritable campaigns against " Frenchification " and " paper Frenchmen " ', of the Italian journal which gives the names of naturalised Frenchmen under the heading of " renegades ", and of the pamphlet entitled *Tu sei Italiano devi restare Italiano* ' in which France is represented as a thoroughly decadent country ',[117] on the one hand, and admiration for ' the tolerant attitude of the French ',[84] on the other.

Many other methods of preventing denationalisation have been tried out : ' holiday camps for children; repatriation to Italy of women about to become mothers; transfer of savings by special banks; repatriation facilities and encouragement to return home; re-immersion in a Polish or Italian atmosphere; compulsory return for military service by bringing pressure to bear, if necessary, on the relatives at home; difficulties placed in the way of obtaining the necessary papers for the

---

[a] Estimates of the foreign population of France vary between 2½ and 4½ millions — the latter figure including naturalised persons.   (A Paris correspondent dryly informs *The Spectator* (March 25, 1938) that the officers of a newly-constituted " Amicale des Maquilleurs du Cinéma Français " bear the following patronymics : Chakatouny, Tourjansky, Klein, Paltchensky, Arkdelian, Glebov, Safianshikov).

marriage of immigrants in France ... Italy has even endeavoured to use certain immigrants as national leaders and educators of the mass of workers in France and, in particular, to foster in that country a spirit of Fascism '. Again, ' the official control exercised over the majority of [foreign] welfare works and associations by the countries of emigration is manifested not only by grants and moral support, but also by the intervention of special diplomatic or consular agents — veritable workers' attachés similar to military or commercial attachés — whose function it is to protect, guide and group their nationals in France. Some of these consular agents, forgetting that the French authorities are alone competent to issue orders on French soil, have on numerous occasions usurped the latter's powers without causing the public authorities to protest with the necessary vigour against such inadmissible activities. Countries of immigration have sometimes sent to France veritable missions of civil servants, politicians and economists to study on the spot the position and organisation of immigrants '.[117]

Yet ' all these political activities do not always lead to the desired results. They often aggravate dissension among the immigrants, dividing them instead of drawing them together '. This is truer of the Italians than of the Poles. ' Less divided politically, it is easier for them to live in common and to keep up national traditions ... They club together more spontaneously, more naturally, and comprise a far greater number of members in their own organisations than that secured by the superficially created Italian groups. Their influence is consequently much stronger and, more than any other nationality, they contribute to the maintenace of their particularism '. Poland, however, ' has less to gain than the neighbouring countries by seeking to create a minority in France ... It would be an exaggeration to discern, in Poland's action regarding her emigrants in France, nothing but a nationalist policy. Up to a certain point, this action is justified and it is natural that the countries of emigration should take an interest in their emigrants '. Indeed, from the point of view of these countries, the very intensity of their action leads to the paradoxical result that it contributes to ' a diminution of the drawbacks of transplantation ' and hence helps ' to tide over the period of adaptation '. Hence ' the results of the policy pursued by the countries of emigration are not ... commensurable with the efforts made and the expenditure incurred '.[117] But this must be due also to the exceptionally strong assimilative influence which France exerts over her immigrants and it is possible that the lessons of French experience are not applicable to other countries of immigration. This question, however, stretches beyond the scope of the present discussion. Here it must suffice to suggest that ' rarely in history has an ideological principle created with such rapidity so much friction and so many international conflicts as the idea of the political unity, throughout the world, of persons of the same ethnical or racial origin (*Volkstum*), regardless of legal nationality (*Staatsangehörigkeit*) '.[155]

VII. *MAL DU PAYS*

The struggle for population has only just begun. The encouragement of natality at home and the prevention of assimilation abroad are only the first two chapters of the battle for numbers. A new phase in the operation has recently been opened.

In November 1938, the Italian Foreign Minister announced that he was creating a permanent committee for the repatriation to Italy or to Italian possessions of Italians living abroad. The text of the communiqué in which this decision was announced is as follows :

As a consequence of meetings which, by order of the Duce, have been held at the Ministry for Foreign Affairs, under the chairmanship of Count Ciano, and which were attended by the Secretary of the Fascist Party, the Minister of Corporations, the Under-Secretary of State for Foreign Affairs, the Under-Secretary of State for Italian Africa, as well as the Presidents of the various interested confederations and the holders of the most important consulateships abroad, it has been decided to constitute a Standing Committee for the Repatriation of Italians Abroad, the function of which shall be to co-ordinate and facilitate the numerous movements of Italians who have expressed their intention to return to the motherland, especially since the conquest of Abyssinia. The Committee will have its headquarters at the Ministry of Foreign Affairs and will take up its duties immediately[307].

' The constitution of this committee is regarded as an event of exceptional importance. The committee may be called upon to draw up a veritable charter for Italians residing abroad, who, as is known, number several millions.[a] Italy will thus be able to inaugurate a truly

---

[a] According to Italian figures, there are not far short of 10 million Italians abroad (*174*, *173*). This figure is based, however, on an enquiry made by the Italian Government which ' was not restricted to persons of Italian nationality in the legal sense, but covered persons born in Italy, or sometimes even persons of Italian nationality in the ethnic sense who were

imperial policy by gradually calling home all her nationals who have been obliged to leave the too unproductive soil of their native land '.[255]

It will be observed that the communiqué ' mentions simply the " numerous movements of Italians ",[a] without specifying the conditions which they must fulfil. Undoubtedly the standing committee will be obliged to consider the identity of these Italians; but it is also felt that this measure will furnish many of those Italians who have not adhered to the Fascist Party at the time of its formation with an opportunity to return home or to enter the Empire instead of being condemned to permanent exile when they have not engaged in any political activity contrary to the régime '. The creation of the committee cannot be regarded, however, as merely ' a measure of clemency and amnisty '; it is thought that it must also be regarded ' as the beginning of the colonisation of Ethiopia and of a colonial policy on a large scale '.[255] On the other hand, it is stated that this body ' is not intended to encourage the return of emigrants who are well settled and thoroughly satisfied with their lot ';[286] nevertheless, it would seem that ' the serious international crisis which developed at the end of September made the Italian Government realise the extremely precarious position of hundreds of thousands of Italians residing abroad, many of them in countries which might have become enemies '.[255] [b]

Stimulation of the birth-rate at home, prevention of foreign assimilation, repatriation of nationals from abroad — are there any other untapped sources of population increase ?[c]

---

resident abroad, irrespective of the fact that they had been naturalised in some other State ' (172). According to nationality, the number of Italians abroad in 1930 was estimated at about 2 ¼ millions (ibid.).

[a] In July 1938, it was reported, for example, that ' Italians were leaving Brazil in large numbers ' (276).

[b] It was reported from Berlin in July 1938 that ' owing to the difficulty of continuing to live and work [in Brazil] under present conditions ... thousands of Germans and Italians were leaving the country ', and that the exodus seemed ' to be connected with the restrictions placed upon the activities of foreign communities by the decree [May 12] of the Vargas Government ' which is said to have been prompted by National-Socialist political activity (276). Cf. the Berliner Tageblatt's comment : ' The frequent return of German settlers and German technicians to the Homeland has given rise to surprised comment in the Brazilian Press, which is unable to appreciate the simple fact that no German in the world is disposed to let himself be treated as an unwanted guest ' (ibid.).

[c] It has been suggested that Germany should ' be assisted in her attempt to get back German Aryan citizens living abroad by exchanging them against those non-Aryan subjects which she wants — as a matter of internal policy — to get rid of. From a numerus clausus point of view this solution presents no difficulties, since there are many million Germanic Aryans living abroad ' (371). According to 172 about 1930 there were some 2 ¼ million persons of German nationality living abroad. (In the case of Canada, the United States and certain other territories, the figure refers, not to nationality, but to country of birth).

VIII: EQUALITY OF OPPORTUNITY

Finally, ' one of the most important grievances of the non-colonial Powers lies . . . in the opportunity afforded to the colonial Powers for their young men to take part in the technical and administrative services of the colonial areas '.[225] ' We need space ', states General von Epp, ' where our energies will have free play. We want to send out young men to territories belonging to the Reich after they have received a training here '.[350]

It is true that, from a demographic point of view, this ' may be a type of opportunity open to a relatively small proportion of the population ', but it is ' a portion which from the point of view of social and political stability is very important '.[225] ' There are ', for example, ' thousands of splendid young Germans to-day who pine with envy and even rancour at the thought that were they English they would be governing vast provinces with nothing but a fly-whisk in their hands. It is little use explaining to them that the opportunities and delights of colonial service are not quite so lavish as all that. They are convinced in their souls that the present situation implies for them an unjust denial of adventure '.[341] Nor is this conviction wholly groundless. Colonial territories inhabited by native races ' offer particular advantages for the inhabitants of the mother country. The officers obtain promotion more quickly; the soldiers are glad of the change from boring barrack life in Europe. Young employees early feel themselves able to accept a responsibility which would otherwise probably not be offered to them. They have opportunities which Europe no longer gives them and the possibility, if they survive, of saving up capital for their old age. The life is on a large scale, the risks are great but so also are the prospects and the rewards '.[240]

Recalling ' ther emark of the British economist Senior, that the economic value of the Empire to Great Britain was as a form of out-door relief for the younger sons of good families ', one of the International Studies Conference's American experts expressed the view that it constituted ' a very real inequality that the young men of other States should not have similar opportunities '. Pointing out that, under the Mandates system, inadequate efforts had been made to extend the application of the principle of equality of opportunity ' in matters concerning missionary enterprise and archæology . . ., in administrative responsibility or in the recruitment of experts ', and that ' it is the Mandatory Powers themselves who in the main provide experts and administrators for the mandated territories ', he suggested that ' this is a field where equality of opportunity ought to be further extended '.[225]

The suggestion does not appear to have met with any objections in the Conference, though it was pointed out that the " younger son " doctrine rested on a delusion. ' I happen ', said a French speaker, ' to be a " younger son " myself. I should like to clear away certain illusions as to the number and advantages of these positions in the colonies. The number is very limited. I believe that for France, excluding Algeria[a] and speaking of course only of the civilian personnel, the number of colonial civil servants cannot exceed twenty or twenty-five thousand. Now France alone has about a million civil servants. You see the ratio between the two figures, and how much advantage the non-colonial countries might obtain from the admission of some of their citizens to colonial employment : a few hundred positions. Really, when you come right down to the facts, it is insignificant '.[222] It was pointed out, moreover, that ' the difficulties of participation in colonial administration will subsist so long as the present type of individual sovereignty is continued ',[221] because while ' there is no great objection to the employment of foreigners in the technical services

---

[a] ' Speaking personally and as a Frenchman ', said the same speaker on another occasion, ' I wish to say that in no case and under no circumstances does any Frenchman admit that Algeria should figure in a list of colonies. It must be clearly understood that Algeria has always been national territory. Algeria is a French province. Minorities, of course, exist there, but from the constitutional point of view, it is national territory. So much so, in fact, that after a given number of years' residence, a foreigner can become naturalized French without ever having set foot in France . . . I cannot question anybody's right to include Algeria amongst the colonies; one might even add Corsica, on the grounds that this territory is cut off from the rest of France by the sea. Nevertheless, as Frenchmen, we do not admit that point of view ' (222).

Cf. 357 : — ' It is arguable . . . that large parts of the French Empire . . . [are] not strictly colonial in character. Algeria is under the Ministry of the Interior, and Tunis and Morocco are protectorates attached to the Ministry of Foreign Affairs. Not only Algeria, but the older French colonies of Réunion, Martinique and Guadeloupe, are represented in both Houses of the French legislature, and French India, Senegal, Guiana and Cochin China in the Chamber of Deputies. The Conseil Supérieur des Colonies contains representatives from most French colonies. Yet no part of the French Colonial Empire can be said to enjoy fully responsible government, and, indeed, control is as far as possible centralized in Paris. In fact, a comparison with the British figures, which exclude the vast Indian Empire, not yet completely self-governing, is in some respects misleading '. It will be noted that, in so far as this statement might be thought to express a point of view in opposition to that given in the preceding citation, it does not meet the objection contained in the latter since the form of centralised control exercised from Paris over the " province " of Algeria extends equally to, say, Brittany.

of a colony — archæological excavations, geological survey, etc. — ... the same is not true of administrative functions properly so-called '.[220] To one speaker it seemed ' a delicate matter to entrust to foreigners the task of representing the colonial Power before either the general public or the native population ',[220] while another, who conjured up the vision that ' a Brazilian governor ... would be sent to a country under mandate ... aided by a secretary-general from the Republic of San Marino ... [and who] would have to supervise civil servants belonging to all the nations of the world ', enquired whether it was ' possible to hope, by this extraordinary method, to constitute a coherent organization capable of giving to the territory the general and permanent orientation which it must have '. While it did seem to him possible ' to confide certain technical services to citizens of other countries without harmful results ', it appeared to him doubtful whether ' the guardian States would ever permit foreign officials to assume a position of authority and thus to receive by delegation a part of the national sovereignty '.[217]

Lastly, the recent histories of colonial administration have shown that ' the tendency is towards increasing employment of natives in government and other services and that the increase in salaried posts for Europeans is not likely to be great '.[357]

As an alternative to the employment of foreigners in national colonial administrations, it has been suggested that, if colonies were placed under direct international control, the nationals of all nations would have opportunities of participating in colonial work. This suggestion also is open to serious practical objections. ' If it means that an international body should be set up replacing the several Colonial Powers in the control of policy and the appointment of the local staff, a gigantic central office must take over the work which now occupies the various Colonial Ministries. By whom would the prodigious cost be borne, and where would it be located ?[a] Since it is to serve as a means of appeasement the totalitarian Powers will claim an equal — perhaps a predominant — voice. The Colonial policies of the different Powers differ fundamentally; who will decide in a body

---

[a] Cf. 268, the writer of which, having ' had experience of working on international commissions ', does ' not see the need for any " gigantic " office or " prodigious " cost' and feels ' entitled to say quite definitely that loyal co-operation between members of different nationalities in the execution of a specific duty is perfectly practicable and makes outstandingly for good feeling between nations '.

responsible to no one ? The official appointed as Governor in each territory will in practice give effect to the policy of his nation, and, so far as the interests of the local population — European and native — are concerned, the territory might as well be ceded outright to that nation '.[a] It is clear that ' the difficulties of a local staff of mixed nationalities, each favouring the policy of his nation' would be enormous; and ' what would be the official language and currency ? '[324]

The demand for equality of opportunity in the administration of colonial territories is, in fact, not a demand for the relief of sectional pressure of population at home. It is a demand for scope for " cultural " expansion. As such it is no new aspiration. The story of colonial development in the past has been partly written by men and women who, in the pride of their ' national cultural inheritance [have] felt called upon to spread the blessings of their civilisation throughout the world. This " sacred mission " also inspired religious circles wishing to lift backward peoples. Cultural and religious " imperialism " cannot be divorced from economic " imperialism ", because, whereas the latter offered financial allurements, the former gave a moral stimulus to those groups which were not bent on material gain. It would be a great mistake to assume that all those young enthusiasts who shouldered the " white man's burden ", and who devoted their life to the conquest, the exploration, and the economic and cultural development of the colonies, were solely driven by material motives '.[132]

IX. UNDERPOPULATION

The five explanations of expansionism which have been successively examined in sections II, III, IV, V-VII and VIII of this chapter are all related to a given country's internal demographic situation and movements. A sixth demographic consideration which sometimes bears on a country's adoption of a policy of expansion is its belief that certain other regions of the world are either underpopulated or, at any rate, capable of supporting larger populations.

' In general, it seems obvious that the possession of a rich, underpopulated, undeveloped, unassimilated domain . . . by a relatively poor

---

[a] This contingency is, however, rejected by the author of the observations quoted : —
' Tne cession of any Colony or protectorate — save as the result of crushing defeat in war — is simply unthinkable and would never be accepted by the [British] nation ' (*324*).

and weak people . . . is a fact of concern to all nations. The dangers
inherent in such a situation may conceivably become a menace to world
peace '.[60] It is self-evident that, if the free movements of peoples into
habitable but uninhabited or sparsely populated lands are checked by
the political barriers of national frontiers, international friction must
ensue. The spectacle of unoccupied, though not ownerless, land must
be a standing provocation of imperialistic designs. The " dog in the
manger " policy which has been prompted in many cases by ' excessive
fear of competition by immigrants ready to work, temporarily most
often, for low wages . . . was already objectionable before the present
economic crisis began and [it] has become exasperating since then '.[131]

' It is regrettable ', writes an Italian authority, ' to think that in
the present day, after so much progress in scientific and mechanical
civilisation and in lofty intellectual speculations, immense tracts of
land, though not under inclement skies, still lie deserted or barely
touched by primitive forms of human labour; that boundless plains
give scanty grazing to herds of horses and buffaloes and malarial fevers
to their scattered human inhabitants; that large masses of men do not
find means of obtaining on their own land the indispensable necessities
of life and are prevented from seeking them in other lands. And
all this occurs ', he declares, ' while raw materials and products accumulate, while natural forces and powerfully equipped industrial buildings
remain idle; while on the other hand vehicles and ways of communication rapidly increase together with all those other means that facilitate
in every way the life of the human community '. In these circumstances, even ' without venturing upon hazardous prophecies regarding
the future, in which probably man's inventive genius will turn to
account other factors and combinations of factors to provide human
sustenance, it is easy to foresee ', he claims, ' that before very long the
growing density of population in some regions will necessitate a further
investment of producers' goods and of human labour in other
regions '.[178]

It is suggested, then, that ' there are countries living under a
serious pressure of population which renders their labour less fruitful
than it should be . . . and [which] are not adequately provided with
one or both of the two other factors of production, while others, better
endowed with raw materials or capital, are sparsely populated '. ' To
relieve this pressure, to remove the congestion of the overpopulated
countries by transferring their surplus population to thinly populated

lands, means to give to the economic potentiality of the world a power
of expansion and of improvement, to forestall the evils inherent in
technical transformations and in profound mechanical innovations,
to reabsorb with comparative rapidity the serious excess of labour which
is brought about by these innovations'; for, to direct redundant populations 'to new less populated territories, would render more fruitful
at the same time the work of the old countries and that of the new
countries, which on their part have an abundance of land lying idle
through want of labour.   The circle would be completed by directing
the capital resulting from saving, which is sterile on account of its
excessive abundance in over-capitalised countries, towards new
countries which are ready to exploit their energies by the admission of
immigrants who are financially and industrially equipped.   The larger
possibilities of production of this new population would allow of an
extension of its purchasing power and hence of production and of world
trade.   In the plan of this triangular co-operation, one country would
export men and would sell its products to other countries which produce
raw materials, and these latter countries would pay in raw materials
and foodstuffs exported to the first country or to another country, as,
for example, the country which had supplied credit to the first country.
The new countries would be developed, labour would find employment
in those countries and in the old countries in the production of raw
materials and of manufactured products respectively, while the countries
producing capital goods would have raw materials and labour for their
use.   There would be a better division of labour : the old countries
would maintain and increase their production and export goods : the
new countries would be developed, would supply raw materials and
foodstuffs, would extend their consumption and later they would
themselves increase their production of finished goods.   There would
be a parallel increase of production and of world consumption and a
new impulse would be given to general progress.   The relations between
supply and demand, the correspondence between production and
consumption, would find in this world movement what it has irreparably
lost in the narrow play of separate groups lacking co-ordination of
effort.   The protection of the authorities, the corrective political
intervention, would only be a force held in reserve to facilitate the
working of a system which would find the conditions of its equilibrium
in the vastness of its scope.   This is the natural path for the expansion
of industrial civilisation.   Spontaneous, free, unregulated expansion

was useful in the past, when technical progress was within everyone's reach. To-day the difficulties are increasing, while competition is becoming keener among the units which engage in it. Hence the necessity to regulate or to rationalise expansion. The political authorities would strive to restore equilibrium by enlarging the scope of initiative, with particular reference to countries not yet open to profitable economic enterprise. This method is designed to rationalise not only production, but everything it implies, including consumption and exchange, by co-ordinating the energies of separate economic units within the boundaries of each national economic group, and extending this principle to the world as a whole '. The adoption of this triangular plan would signify ' wealth, well-being and the cessation of the most serious causes of convulsive economic and social movements '.[173]

' In the course of the last few decades ', says another writer, ' two States have very forcibly realised the disproportion between their resources in population and in territory. Both of these States first of all sought to adjust this disproportion by peaceful means, by developing their economic life to the maximum and by organising migratory movements on a large scale. But the possibilities of exploiting their territory, which in spite of everything was too small, were used to their extreme limit and emigration ceased owing to the measures taken in the countries of immigration. The attempts that have been made to overcome these difficulties collectively at the international conferences devoted to population and migration problems became lost in obscure phraseology and resulted in nothing more than the settlement of administrative details of third-rate importance. The doctrine of State sovereignty effectively countered the efforts made to find a solution for the fundamental problems. With what consequences ? The Manchukuo affair in 1932, and the Ethiopian affair in 1935-36. If, in the future, international organisation still fails to find an equitable and happy solution for the problems arising out of demographic congestion, such incidents will recur with irresistible regularity. The pressure of population for which no normal outlet has been found will find that outlet by violence. Nothing can prevent this from happening. It is simply the coming into operation of the physical law of communicating vessels '.[144]

Now it may or may not be correct that Manchuria[a] and Abyssinia[b]

[a] Cf. below, pp. 271-273.
[b] Cf. below, pp. 269-270.

have afforded, or will afford, relief for overcrowding in Japan and in Italy, but in relation to the peaceful satisfaction of the claims which are the subjects of the present survey, the question which must be considered is whether there are any underpopulated areas in the world to-day which would be filled up under conditions of free migration. ' The question of the transference of working population from one country to another, for the purpose not only of assuring existence to masses of workers without employment, but more particularly of increasing the economic potentiality and the social well-being of the nations, cannot be separated from *the search for countries capable of receiving this surplus of human forces* '.[178]   This question raises, however, a highly complex series of issues which it would be impossible to consider adequately within the scope of the present volume.[a]

In the case of undeveloped and underpopulated colonial territories, it has been suggested, that the international friction caused by situations of this kind might be softened by placing such territories under the control of some international authority.   Here again, the question cannot be considered in detail;[b] but the following excerpts from the documentation of the International Studies Conference may serve to indicate the conflicting character of expert opinion on this proposal : —

[a] By way of illustration of the type of problem involved, a supplementary chapter has been added to this Survey : it indicates summarily some of the elements of contemporary discussion on the population carrying capacity of Australia.

It may be noted here that the Italian authority quoted in the text seems himself to consider that ' to estimate in the countries where unemployment is serious and in those where population is dense the number of workers available for transfer and permanent settlement abroad ' is a more important task than ' the correlated enquiry into the lands capable of receiving these masses of workers and of undergoing thereby a profound economic transformation '.   ' For the moment ', the first enquiry, which he would confide to the International Labour Office, ' ought to make it possible to determine approximately what transferable contingents can be counted upon for this great work of reconstruction '.   It is also to be noted that his " triangular plan of co-operation " was conceived at a time when, in a geographical division of the Dark Continent into two parts — ' to the east the possessions of Great Britain, to the west those of continental Europe ' — there were still two independent countries in the eastern part, namely, Abyssinia and Egypt; that he considered it might be necessary to limit participation in his plan ' to the continental countries owing to the refusal of Great Britain to take part in it, and, therefore, to do without British co-operation in Africa '; that ' Italy and Germany are naturally indicated for a place in the front rank in this work of development ' because ' they are the countries which combine the conditions of a high density of population and, therefore, of an imperative need for expansion, with a by no means negligible colonial experience and a high level of civilisation '; that ' the other colonial countries, except Belgium ', which, however, has other resources, ' are not overburdened with population '; and that Italy's ' rights to a natural expansion in the neighbouring continent ought not to be any longer impeded ' (*178*).

Japanese projects for settlement in Manchuria are mentioned below, pp. 272-3.

[b] For further information see *185*.

' If something has to be done about colonies ', writes the author of a memorandum submitted to the Conference, ' it would seem desirable to turn our attention to solutions that are really of an international character. Various formulæ have been proposed, whereby an interna-national body, the League of Nations, for example, would according to the most moderate formula be given a " right of access ", or according to the more advanced formula a " right of intervention " in matters concerning the colonial policy of European Powers, or again, to take the extreme formula, it has been suggested that the administration of colonial possessions held by those Powers should be transferred to some international organisation '.[113]

This suggestion was energetically repelled by the author of another Conference memorandum. ' Such proposals ', he declared, are ' not only chimerical, but unsound for other reasons. Colonial adminis-tration involving as it does delicate relations between sovereign and dependent governments and peoples, is complicated and difficult enough without having injected into it the possible intervention of a distant, disinterested and, in one sense, irresponsible authority. If within colonial Powers there can be developed only a small part of the sense of responsibility of world opinion and needs that would be required to accept such an outside control most of the advantages of such a radical, and at present unattainable, readjustment would be secured. At the same time, the disadvantages of outside intervention, with a possible appeal to force, in the colonial affairs of any nation would not be incurred. In this matter, as in many others, international machinery will not take the place of national morality. Systematic, persistent efforts to build up among nations a moral sense upon this subject through the slow process of education (which will show that in the long run morality and self-interest are on the same side) seems . . . to offer the best hope of substituting peaceful for violent changes in world colonial situations that demand remedy '.[60] [a]

---

[a] Cf. *176* : — ' The present Mandates Commission [of the League of Nations] has its hands full in the supervision of twelve mandates. If additional territories were placed under mandate, it is probable that a second Commission would have to be created, at con-siderable cost. It would lack the experience gained during the past fifteen years. The present body, as guardians of the commercial rights of the States which hold no mandate, have become experts in the technical application of the " economic equality clause ", which has given rise to repeated discussions. They could, however, probably undertake to receive any petitions on this one subject, having reference to territories not under mandate '.

13

X. BIRTH-CONTROL POLITICS

To complete this survey of the bearing of population movements on claims for changes in the *status quo*, mention must also be made of a demographic consequence of expansionist action which is likely to be taken into account in the consideration of the legitimacy of such claims. ' A new and prolific people, the circulation of whose men and products is prevented, may consider itself forced into war ',[152] but ' an artificial overpopulation may be produced through the destruction or waste of means of subsistence by the ravages of war or by the burdens of militarism '.[309]

In such a case a claim for relief from congestion will undoubtedly be weakened in the eyes of the countries which are asked to provide the relief; ' it may be argued that this country can still resort to birth control '.[152] It is in cases of this sort that the principle is most likely to be advanced that ' it is legitimate to demand . . . that the government of an overpopulated country should not hinder the spread of birth-control and attempt to arrest the fall in fertility '.[84]

This argument, however, is sometimes vigorously rejected on the ground that ' the moral sense of the community as of the individual may rebel against the adoption of any systematic policy in this matter '.[152] For example :

For my part, if someone said to me " I reject these claims made by overpopulated countries; the remedy lies in their own hands; they have only to develop birth control and arrange matters in such a way that their birth-rate falls; the economic status of individuals will then improve ", I could not agree with him. Similarly, in matters of social policy, if someone opposed the measures taken on behalf of large families, on the ground that " people have only to restrict the number of their children; if they have large families, it is their own fault and they must accept the responsibility ", I would not admit that argument either. We should be grateful to those civilised countries where something is still done to maintain numbers and to perpetuate the human race.[113] [a]

[a] Cf. this vigorous affirmation with the impassive statement made in the course of a discussion of former proposals for state intervention in favour of a restriction of births that ' we do not know whether it is in our interests to accelerate the decrease of the white race by state intervention because from a general point of view we do not know to what extent the tendency to decrease will accelerate itself of its own accord, or to what extent we shall need this population in order to develop the resources of the globe ' (250).

The advocates of birth control expose themselves, moreover, to the retort that ' this restriction has so far been proposed to poor countries of emigration, apparently not disinterestedly, by the wealthier countries of immigration ',[152] and also that ' the neo-Malthusian doctrine contains a cleverly disguised political interest on the part of the countries with a declining birth-rate. Sooner or later, the nations showing a high birth-rate must inevitably become the victorious rivals of those whose birth-rate is falling, in the political, economic and cultural fields. This victory cannot elude them unless they also adopt the policy of birth control. It is for that reason that countries with a low birth-rate seek to inculcate in the others the conviction that any State which adheres to the idea of progress should resort to birth control. It is also for that reason that countries with a high birth-rate should defend themselves against this poison '.[144] [a]

' At the conferences of the Institute of Pacific Relations ', suggests a Polish writer, ' the high birth rate of Japan is constantly a matter of concern to the Anglo-Saxon countries. They very often give Japan " well-intentioned " advice with a view to persuading her to solve her population problem herself — in the restrictive sense, of course . . . Since, however, all nations are not inclined to raise birth control to the dignity of a guiding principle in their policy, the future development

---

[a] These international polemics between the " proletarian " and " bourgeois " nations recall the older quarrel between " labour " and " capital " :

' The introduction of the capitalist system is a sign that the exploitation of the laborer toiling for a bare subsistence wage has become one of the chief arts of life among the holders of tenant rights. It also produces a delusive promise of endless employment which blinds the proletariat to those disastrous consequences of rapid multiplication which are obvious to the small cultivator and peasant proprietor. But indeed the more you degrade the workers, robbing them of all artistic enjoyment, and all chance of respect and admiration from their fellows, the more you throw them back, reckless, on the one pleasure and the one human tie left to them — the gratification of their instinct for producing fresh supplies of men. You will applaud this instinct as divine until at last the excessive supply becomes a nuisance : there comes a plague of men; and you suddenly discover that the instinct is diabolic, and set up a cry of " overpopulation ". But your slaves are beyond caring for your cries : they breed like rabbits; and their poverty breeds filth, ugliness, dishonesty, disease, obscenity, drunkenness, and murder. In the midst of the riches which their labor piles up for you, their misery rises up too and stifles you. You withdraw in disgust to the other end of the town from them; you appoint special carriages on your railways and special seats in your churches and theatres for them; you set your life apart from theirs by every class barrier you can devise; and yet they swarm about you still : your face gets stamped with your habitual loathing and suspicion of them; your ears get so filled with the language of the vilest of them that you break into it when you lose your self-control : they poison your life as remorselessly as you have sacrificed theirs heartlessly. You begin to believe intensely in the devil. Then comes the terror of their revolting; the drilling and arming of bodies of them to keep down the rest; the prison, the hospital, paroxysms of frantic coercion, followed by paroxysms of frantic charity. And in the meantime, the population continues to increase ! ' (365).

of the world's population will probably tend to increase still further the differences already to be noted in the birth rates of the various countries. They will, in an ever increasing measure, constitute a capital problem from the international point of view. Sooner or later, the difference between the various population pressures must in some way or other find an outlet '.[144]

Whether the unflattering imputation to the Anglo-Saxon countries of conscious motives of sinister machiavellism is as perspicacious as it is ingenious may be left here as an open question[a] with the observation that the evidence tends to belie the Polish author's statement. ' The change in the fertility of women as a whole [in Japan] is greater than can be attributed to changes in age at, and amount of, marriage. We cannot obtain specific fertility rates for married women, but if we could we should no doubt find that specific fertility had declined. In fact, birth-control must have been at work. There is abundant evidence that contraception is well known in Japan, and it is reasonable to assume that it is widely practised '.[84] What is this evidence ? In the first place, it is said[91] that ' all the chief contraceptives are made and sold in Japan '.[84] Secondly, ' there are no specific restrictions upon their manufacture or sale '.[84] [b] Thirdly, according to one writer,[92] ' contraceptives are freely advertised in the papers, and . . . birth-control clinics have been opened at Tokyo and Osaka for the poorer classes '.[84] Fourthly, it was implied by a Japanese speaker at a meeting of the International Studies Conference that the practice of birth control is not officially frowned upon; on the contrary, its development is expected. ' It is no easy matter ', he stated, ' to change the customs of

---

[a] Cf. 250 : — ' Immigration into the United States (and to many other overseas countries) was really slowed down by the threat of a fall in the standard of living of the working population and of imperfect assimilation. But, in order to give these interests a theoretical basis, recourse was had to pessimistic notions of neo-Malthusianism. Acute unemployment encouraged these theories in all the Anglo-Saxon countries, which fear an absolute and general overpopulation of the world in the near future. A great part of the public opinion of these countries demands that the countries of emigration should as far as possible follow their example by restricting births in order that they may be able to keep and maintain at home their excess population. The European continental countries, on the other hand, faced wih a declining birth rate, already in their opinion excessive, and as result of their traditional rivalry, practise a policy of encouraging births '. In March 1926 ' a congress of neo-Malthusians held in New York advocated the nomination by the League of Nations of a Committee " for the study of the problem of birth control and for the submission to the States members of proposals with this end in view ", (ibid.).

[b] ' It would seem that the sale of contraceptives and of books about contraception can be brought within the provisions of the Peace Preservation Act, and that occasionally the Japanese police have initiated prosecutions. This has given rise to an erroneous idea that the sale of contraceptives is forbidden ' (84).

a country from one day to the next ... Although contraceptive practices cannot spread in Japan to the same extent as in Western countries, owing to the ideas held on family life[a] and also on account of the manner in which dwelling-houses are constructed, the falling birth-rate must nevertheless be largely attributed to these practices, which are steadily gaining ground ... owing to the development of education and the changes that are being made in domestic architecture '.[210] It would seem, in fact, that ' the attitude of the Government has changed from time to time, but opposition to birth-control has gradually weakened. In 1931 a minister declared that it was a personal matter and that the government would neither oppose nor encourage it '.[84] It is true that the view that changes in the Japanese birth rate are attributable to the practice of birth control is not accepted by all observers;[b] but this does not infirm the effect of the evidence cited.

' It should not be difficult to understand the failure of the attempts to raise the birth rate. All that has been done by those attempts is to deal with a single aspect of a very involved problem and then only in a very inadequate manner. That family allowances ... have been ineffective is no proof that family allowances have no part to play in the reconstruction that must take place. But there is another and very important reason for the failure of these schemes. They have been accompanied by attempts to make birth-control illegal. This is bad tactics. If anything is certain it is that people will resist being driven back under the tyranny of the unlimited family; therefore all measures are suspect which are associated with an anti-birth-control movement But it is much more than bad tactics. It implies a complete misunderstanding of the only possible solution of the small family problem. The solution must begin by welcoming the voluntary small family system, and that means welcoming birth-control. For birth-control is not merely a practice which must be tolerated; it has positive functions of great importance to perform, such as, for example, making possible

[a] ' The traditional attitude that a large family is a sign of uprightness in the parents till subsists..., and this is unfavourable to the spread of a movement to popularise birth control ' (*300*).

[b] ' These measures could not be effective unless they developed on a large scale as a result of a change in opinion and of vigorous governmental action which would recall the iron fist of the Shoguns. But that is not the case. For the moment, therefore, there nothing to be expected ' (*394*). Cf. *250* : — ' With the data at our disposal we cannot timate either the demographic evolution or the economic development of the Asiatic ces, but it appears probable that, even with the expansion of the capitalist system the voluntary restriction of births will spread very slowly among these peoples (see *252* and *1*), while their death-rate will rapidly fall. '

the proper spacing of the family.   Let it be said clearly that the escape
from the unlimited family makes a very great step forward in human
history.   The problem is to adjust outlook to the responsibility involved
by the transition to the voluntary family system '.[81] [a]

This argument is doubtless valid in all countries on the ground
that " proper spacing of the family " diminishes maternal mortality and
perhaps also on the psychological ground that birth control enables
man to conquer nature by an act of volition and to determine, if not the
quality, at any rate the quantity of his offspring.[b]   On economic grounds,
however, the argument loses force when applied to the situation in
those countries where the State tends to take the place of parents in
assuming economic responsibility for children.   It has been suggested,
moreover, that there is a flaw in the argument of those who apprehend
that the declining birth rate may culminate in extinction.   ' The
human race is stronger than human beings ',[236] and ' under the appropriate selective pressure, it would doubtless change its outlook until
current methods of birth control came to be regarded with the same
distaste as is felt towards infanticide by civilized peoples '.[254]   Have
not the prophets of doom who pore so anxiously over vital statistics,
and who see in what is undoubtedly the ' simple and beautiful method '[84]
of probing into the future which the use of the " net reproduction rate "
device affords a new instrument of intelligent control of human way-
wardness, neglected ' the essential fact that the conditions which produce the waning birth-rate ensure the consequent production of more

[a] Cf. *336* : — ' The uncontrolled family has gone, never to return. Voluntary
parenthood has taken its place. But this does not mean cutting down the size of the
family. Control does not mean reduction. It means adjustment to the needs of the
situation, and at present the need is for larger, but still controlled, families '.
[b] It is usual to assume, though perhaps impossible to prove finally, that the agency
immediately responsible for steeply declining rates of population increase in many countries
is the modern method of birth control. This assumption was not discussed by the International Studies Conference, but it is perhaps to be noted here that, as the following dialogue may suggest, it commonly rests partly on a misapprehension :
' The very strong probability... is that the birth-rate will not go back to anything
like the early nineteenth-century level '.
' You mean because contraceptive devices cannot be un-invented ?...
' If you put it like that ...   In the past there were always a considerable number of
unwanted children. The contraceptive is eliminating the unwanted child '.
' A fool-proof contraceptive might ..., but the present hit or-miss gadgets don't
They stop some births, but on the other hand other people, who might otherwise have left
it alone, put their trust in them with disastrous results '.
' Yes, that's true ..., but on the whole unwanted births are decreased. The gadgets
work more often than not '.
' Work more often than not !... That's not much of a recommendation to a man
jumping overboard with a parachute ' (*298*).

fertile generations'? Have they not been too prone to treat 'the members of a population like the molecules of a gas, considering them unchanged in nature by successive expansion and contraction, pressure, and rarefaction of the whole they compose'?[236] An affirmative answer to these questions, based on the principle that 'the characteristic of living creatures is that they change in response to change of their environmental conditions', has recently been stated as follows in regard to the position in England :

Associated with changes in the birth-rate, there have been two great environmental changes in the past 80 years which have profoundly modified the women of England, and will change them much more in the next half-century... From our earliest ancestry until 50 years ago women were married for the most part irrespective of... [their] own preference... Heredity does not commonly maintain a character which has ceased to have survival value... It is not surprising, therefore, that a considerable proportion of... [their] daughters — shall we guess one-third? — neither liked a husband nor to have children... [Since] the revolution of increasing possibilities for women of all classes to earn their living..., the economic change of woman's power to earn money has largely eliminated the compulsion to be a wife; birth-control has largely eliminated the compulsion for a wife to be a mother. We are approaching therefore, for the first time in the history of the world, an environment in which no woman has a child who does not wish to have a child. The desire for offspring is a heritable quality...[a] Men throughout the ages who have not desired women have been eliminated from the race, each new generation has been bred from the men who sought their mates. Now, for the first time, new generations will be bred also almost entirely from women who desire to have children. It therefore follows with certainty that in every successive generation the proportion of women who desire to have children will increase, and the proportion of women who desire to have many children will increase. Now and henceforward there is natural selection of the willing mother.[236]

Are the gloomy forebodings of those who anticipate a catastrophic fall in reproduction rates to prove as shallow as the earlier predictions

---

[a] 'There can be no doubt, in the light of the evidence of recorded pedigrees, that... [it] is right to make the bold claim..., bold..., not because the evidence on which it is based is weak, but because the prejudices it encounters are strong..., that the "desire for offspring is a heritable quality"...' (254).

that mankind was becoming an ant-heap ? If so, will not the future historian look back upon the population " policies " which have been mentioned in this chapter as among the most singularly inept manifestations of state intervention in the private life of the individual ? The answer to these questions seems to depend upon the view taken of the objection to the argument reproduced above that ' the speed with which ... [the postulated environmental] changes are taking place ... [may not be] sufficient to affect the accuracy of the more sober estimates of the future population of ... [the British Isles] '.[254] To the author of the passage quoted above, evolution does not appear to be ' necessarily slow; it may be cataclasmic and even instantaneous when some flood, fire, pestilence, poison, or enemy destroys from a species all the possessors of some dominant character ... In the population problem the destroying agent is the restriction of births, exercised in an increasing degree for 70 years, but only recently approaching the position of being universal. The character eliminated is aversion to parenthood. If it be dominant it will disappear completely wherever the practice is universal; if (as perhaps seems more probable) it is recessive, it will recur in each generation in diminishing proportion. Where universal regulation of families is suddenly attained, unwilling parents commit race-suicide; so the new generation inherits from parents who desired offspring and were not prevented by physical accident from attaining their wish ... However great or small be the inheritance of fertility, its numerical leverage is high not only because of the extinction of the childless family but because, in the remaining families of one child and upwards, the majority of all the children necessarily come from the more fertile half of the parents. Consequently possession of the future by this fertile half is assured '.[237a]

Finally, those who would look askance at the high rate of increase of the populations of certain countries might find that, if rapid demo-

---

[a] ' A small random sample of 60 post-War marriages by Cambridge resident graduate shows an average of 2 1/4 children per marriage (higher than in some other professional circles). Of all the marriages 27 per cent. have one child or none, and are represented by only 6 per cent. of the children; 30 per cent. of the marriages, with two children each possess 27 per cent. of the children; but 67 per cent. of all the children are in the families of three, four, and five, and belong to only 43 per cent. of the marriages. Therefore, if love of children and lack of superstition as to the advantages to them of affluence be alike inherited, we should expect something like three-fourths or four-fifths of the grand children to be descended from the more fertile two-fifths of the present generation. These figures suggest that birth-rate will be noticeably higher in 10 years' time, when a number of these children are married, and substantially so in 40 years, when their children are married ' (237).

graphic expansion is to be stigmatised as improvident and anti-social,. some of their own countries would not have escaped from this charge in the past. In Japan, for example, where, after remaining ' stationary for at least a century . . ., [it] began to expand after the inauguration of the New Régime in 1868 under certain influences, fermented by the events usually called the Industrial Revolution . . ., [the population] doubled in sixty years . . . [and] is still growing at a remarkable pace. The latest national census revealed an increase of 4.8 millions in the five years, 1930-35, or about a million every year '.[187] ' This increase is regarded as extraordinary by European countries ',[210] because, for example, ' England's population in 1933 was only 84,000 larger than in 1932, and that of Germany increased by 233,000 in 1934, [while] the United States, with its total population double as large as that of Japan, made a natural increase annually of 1,100,000 to 1,200,000 in the latest years '.[187] ' But it may be pointed out that England was in the same position during the first half of the 19th century, while the situation in Germany was similar at the end of the 19th and beginning of the 20th century '.[210] ' Germany showed during the first decade of this century an annual increase of 800-900 thousands, although her total population at that time was much smaller than that of Japan at present '.[187] ' It is an inevitable consequence of industrialization. The sole difference between Japan and Western Europe is that, in the case of Europe, the population increased at a time when emigration and foreign commerce were free, likewise colonisation, whereas Japan no longer benefits by such conditions '.[210] ' We do not believe ', states a Japanese authority, ' that the causes of the phenomenal growth of the European population during the nineteenth century have ever been sufficiently explained with scientific accuracy. So it is not yet possible to clarify the causes and effects of every change that took place in the Japanese population in . . . [the period since 1868]. But nobody doubts that the economic development had a fundamental influence on the people's fertility. The Japanese of the Tokugawa Period probably were as fecund in a physiological sense as they are to-day. Their number, which had been limited both by natural calamities and by social habits, found a way for expansion owing to the economic changes due to the coming of the new technique of production and transportation. On the other hand, the Japanese have not shown, as a race, any abnormal fertility. As the Japanese population doubled in sixty years, that of England and Wales jumped from 9 millions in 1800 to 32 millions in 1900 and to 36 millions in 1914, and that of Germany from 23 millions in 1800 to 56 millions in 1900 and to 67 millions in 1914. Thirty to forty years ago, these countries showed a very high birth-rate of 35-37 per thousand, which is just the highest record in ... [Japan] ... The public opinion of this country, just as that of Germany in those days, generally rejoices at each report of larger increase in the number of the fellow countrymen, but, at the same time, feels somewhat uneasy for the future of the people's livelihood ... On the other hand, an enormous change in people's occupations and mode of living has been taking place for two generations and is still going on in a more decisive way. The nation, which originally consisted mainly of peasant families, is being turned into an industrial state '.[187]

XI. PEACEFUL CHANGE LIMITATIONS

These, then, are the demographic factors and considerations which seem to play a part in the formation of expansionist aspirations and policies. No one will deny that, in so far as the aspirations of the " dissatisfied " nations may give rise to demands for colonies, ' the arguments put foward to substantiate the claims ... to the " possession " of colonies which they consider as suitable places of settlement for their surplus population ... deserve the most careful consideration, especially from colonial Powers. It is true that the matter will not be ultimately settled by such consideration or by logical reasoning generally; there is too much irrational, avowedly and wilfully irrational, sentiment in the claims to admit of cool discussion on the basis of facts and figures, profit and loss. Once a nation is led firmly to believe that the honour of the country or its " place in the sun " is at stake, they will not listen to any argument to the contrary, if they are so much as allowed to hear it. But this does not relieve other peoples of the duty to consider whether they could not in justice be called upon to make some contribution to ease the tension caused by the claims, and so to mitigate the danger of conflicts arising from them '.[131]

If the examination of expansionist aspirations, policies and claims made in this survey has revealed anything, it has shown that, in the field of population movements (as, doubtless, in the case of other problems which form the substance of claims for changes in the *status quo*), there is ' a great confusion of values and of attitudes '; that ' things which are valued highly in terms of the national good have often very little to do with the existence and welfare of the people in time of peace ˙; and that ' frequently those who determine government policy are not at all clear in their own minds as to why they seek a particular alteration in the *status quo*, whether it is necessary for the peace-time welfare of the people or whether it is for the purpose of building up the war-time strength of the nation '.[55] That there should be such confusion is not altogether surprising :

The factors at work in the development of population are undoubtedly highly complex, so much so that it is difficult to reduce them to a common denominator. There is, however, one point on which there seems to be no doubt and that is that the laws governing the development of population cannot be expressed by a single immutable mathematical or philosophical formula. The most that can be said is that, under similar natural, economic, technical and moral conditions, different societies behave in similar ways. It is, moreover, impossible to speak of anything more than similar conditions — and not identical conditions — since, in reality, an aggregate of circumstances never has its exact counterpart . . . It is difficult to say which factors play a decisive part and which factors have but a secondary influence. The rôle of each incontestably depends upon the co-existence of the others . . . The inter-play of these various factors is . . . of infinite complexity . . . But . . . it is only their combined action that can have any effect on the development of the population of a given society. They are like the fellow actors filling the principal rôles of a play which cannot be produced unless they all co-operate.[144]

' This situation inevitably limits .the possibilities open to procedures of peaceful change. Where power considerations enter in, it becomes difficult if not impossible to consider claims for changes on their merits. If a claim has a palpable merit aside from the power question, then it is apt to receive due consideration only under four conditions : (i) if it is presented by a strong Power against a weak Power; (ii) if it is presented by a weak Power actively supported by one or more strong Powers; (iii) if it is presented against a Great Power by an alignment of Powers representing an overwhelming force; (iv) if guarantees can be worked out which in effect nullify the power consideration. Otherwise the only possibility is to find some other means of satisfying the needs of the claimant state than by granting the change demanded . . . But in the meantime it must be expected that . . . proposals for alterations in the *status quo* . . . which are designed to give a nation a power advantage over others, or which, although conceived in terms of peace-time needs, would nevertheless upset the existing power relationships, will be strongly resisted '.[55]   'Nations should not be called upon to give in to their neighbours under conditions which cause them to lose face.   The question of prestige . . . is fully as important as the material interests of a nation'.[183]   'Much time and disappointment can be saved by eliminating from consideration the types of situation in which na-tions are not going to be persuaded, except by the actual use of force. . .; this would include all situations which involved a drastic alteration in the power relationships of nations.   The reason why these situations are beyond the reach of mechanisms of persuasion is that self-help is still the ultimate means of making the national will prevail in inter-national matters, and nations will not voluntarily yield up what power they may have either to defend themselves or to exert their will over other nations '.[55]

PART THREE

THE PROBLEM SOLVED ?

Chapter 6

Demographic Remedies for Overpopulation

It was suggested in an earlier chapter that there appears to be little substance in the hypothesis adopted by the International Studies Conference at the beginning of its enquiry into " peaceful change ", namely, that the " dissatisfied " countries are the authors of claims for relief from overpopulation. On the contrary, statements of claims for relief from population pressure frequently seem to raise fictitious issues; as often as not, they appear to have no firmer basis than the artificial inferences of publicists drawn from the popularly accepted but scientifically unverified premise that certain discontented countries with rapidly expanding numbers are given to formulating demands for changes in the *status quo* which would ease their demographic tension.

It has also been suggested in this Survey that, even on the assumption that genuine claims have been made, they invoke a concept of over-population to which it seems difficult to attach any precise meaning; and that it can hardly be possible, in the present state of knowledge of demographic movements and of their real bearing on the course of political action, to determine judiciously whether a claim is legitimate either in the abstract or in relation to the interests of other countries.

It is true that these general conclusions are nowhere explicitly stated in the records of an organisation which is precluded by its rules from formulating positive findings;[a] but it must be left to the reader to decide whether the view is an irresistible one that such conclusions must flow from any attempt to present a synthetic picture of the Inter-

---

[a] Cf., however, the view expressed by a speaker who had been invited to give a summary and criticism of the Conference's discussion of demographic questions (see *208*) that ' it may . . . be that in the troubled times in which we are now living it is impossible to find solutions ' (*209*).

national Studies Conference's enquiry and that they emerge as the dominant feature of its study of population problems.

If this view is accepted, then it must be admitted that, in this respect, the results of the Conference's work are significant in a negative rather than in a positive sense. It would not be justifiable, however, to presume from this circumstance, either that the Conference failed to attain its object or that the problem which it sought to examine does not exist outside the imagination of those who drew up the Conference's terms of reference. Although none of the " dissatisfied " countries can be convincingly shown to be suffering from a pressure of population on its means of subsistence, they are nevertheless facing the difficulties arising out of expanding numbers. ' There are undoubtedly instances of felt population pressure legitimately based on conditions of over-crowding. The patent disparity among the nations in the amount of lands and resources in relation to population is a continuing source of unrest, and is bound to lead to agitation for alterations in the *status quo* '.[55] A problem of this kind is not to be shelved on the facile pretext that its real character is a matter of opinion. It will not be wholly irrelevant, therefore, to review the variety of solutions to the problems arising out of demographic congestion which were suggested in the course of the International Studies Conference's enquiry; nor will it be a wholly idle speculation to enquire whether these remedies are germane to the demographic situations in Germany, Italy, Japan and Poland.

*   *   *

It is obvious that, in theory, an overpopulated country's need for relief from demographic pressure could be satisfied either (1) directly by reducing the size of its population, or, at any rate, by checking its further expansion, or (2) indirectly by increasing the resources available to the population. It will be convenient, therefore, to distinguish between direct, or demographic, remedies for the problem of overpopulation, on the one hand, and indirect, or economic, remedies, on the other hand.

In practice, with one exception, none of the direct demographic methods of relieving population pressure is available. ' Theoretically, there exist four means for checking the population growth in an individual country : reduction of births, increase of deaths, promotion of emigration, and restrictions of immigration '.[310] A reduction of births may be effected in several ways, including celibacy, late marriage, abortion, " birth control " and the Malthusian checks of " moral restraint " and " vice "; but in practice it generally seems to mean artificial birth control in all countries coming under the western system of civilisation (with the possible exception of Ireland).[a] Whatever be the method employed for reducing births, the importance of this measure is, of course, wholly negative in the sense that it may help only to check a further increase in numbers. As a means of reducing existing numbers, it is clearly of no avail. It is, moreover, often rejected on other grounds, as was shown in the preceding chapter where it was sufficiently discussed for the purpose of this Survey.[b]

As for the second direct method of remedying overpopulation — increase of mortality — ' ethical considerations prevent people from advocating [it] '.[310] Moreover, while it may be the case that, in countries where population is pressing upon the means of subsistence in the manner ' which Malthus assumed to be more or less universal in time and space . . ., congestion may reach a point at which deaths will be increased ',[84] mortality has now been brought so effectively under control in the countries specially considered in this Survey that relief is no more to be expected than it would be desired through this means.

There is, thirdly, the method of reducing the size of a population by restricting immigration. This method is to-day almost universally popular, both in countries which complain, or are said to complain, of congestion and in those which appear to be demographically under-developed. Recourse to this method, therefore, is not politically difficult. But the usefulness of immigration restriction as a method of combating overpopulation is, like the method of birth reduction, limited by its negative character. It can prevent further expansion from one of the sources of a country's population growth; it can do nothing to diminish the size of an existing population. Moreover, of the two sources of population growth — natality and immigration — which the overpopulated country must inspect, this method is relevant

[a] After the famine in Ireland, ' the birth-rate was reduced and kept at a low level... by a] mechanism . . . [of] few and late marriages . . . [which implied] great self-restraint and much personal sacrifice . . . [and which is] therefore in sharp contrast with the birth-control mechanism, which, while attaining the same end, permits the enjoyment of mar-ied companionship and home-life ' (*84*).

[b] See above, chap. 6, § X.

only to the one which, normally, is incomparably the less important of the two.

Of the direct, demographic methods suggested for correcting overpopulation, emigration alone, therefore, remains to be considered. It must be examined in this Survey in some detail, not only because it is commonly regarded as the most appropriate method of counteracting an excessive growth of population but because it is the only remedy for overpopulation to which the International Studies Conference devoted any considerable portion of its enquiry.

Chapter 7

Emigration

I. PAST MOVEMENTS AND PRESENT TRENDS

The interest displayed by the International Studies Conference in migratory problems did not spring only, or even mainly, out of the hypothesis that emigration is a solution to the problem of overpopulation. Migration was studied by the Conference, rather, as a problem in itself. The study was prompted by an interest ' in the difficulties which can arise out of migrations from the point of view of countries of emigration and immigration, in other words, in migrations as a direct factor of " peaceful change " '.[49] 'International restrictions on migration ', it was held, ' have given rise to innumerable grievances which, in turn, are a contributory factor in the present world unrest. Various other difficulties and obstacles must be vanquished before the problem of migration can be solved for the better safeguarding of world peace '.[48]

These considerations are probably not open to criticism; but it is clear that this direct approach to the problem of a claim for relief from population pressure is not the same thing as a claim for wider emigration outlets and that this direct approach to the problem of migration from the angle of " peaceful change " bears only remotely on the main theme discussed in the present Survey, namely, the causes of war associated with unsatisfied claims for relief from pressure of population. It is true, doubtless, that ' the situation of the migrant has become considerably worse ', and that ' at the same time as the need to emigrate becomes more pressing in a number of countries the obstacles to migration are multiplied and the difficulties become greater ', but the only pressing needs which can be considered in these pages are those which are felt in the " dissatisfied " countries whose claims,

real or alleged, raise an issue of war or peace. It is not possible, therefore, to endorse the view that ' the countries which close their door
raise . . . an international problem whose importance it would be idle
to conceal and which recent international events — the Abyssinian
war and German territorial and colonial claims — have placed in the
front rank of preoccupations ',[124] unless it can be shown that these
events are attributable to the constriction of emigration outlets and
that such constriction has deprived the " dissatisfied " countries of an
indispensable relief for an intolerable pressure of numbers. To accept
these propositions, however, would be to falsify the whole course of
the argument which has been put forward in this Survey, for it would
have to be recognised that the " dissatisfied " countries allegedly demanding changes in the international *status quo* do so on the grounds, *inter
alia*, that they are overpopulated and that failure to grant them relief
from demographic pressure would imply that they had been placed
in the position of being compelled to resort to war.

That the argument, of course, may have been unsound can be
readily conceded; indeed, it seems likely that, in the last analysis, any
one who reflects on these problems must appeal as much to such complementary sources of decision as political " horse-sense " and an
intuitive judgment of international affairs as to processes of reasoning
when determining for himself, more or less defectively, the true nature
of the problems. Nevertheless, it is manifest that the International
Studies Conference's enquiry into the problem of migrations as such
cannot be brought logically into the compass of this Survey and that
attention must be confined to those aspects of the Conference's study
which bear directly upon emigration as a remedy for demographic
congestion in the " dissatisfied " countries whose position originally
impelled the Conference to study the question of " peaceful change ".
As a speaker reminded the Conference at one of its meetings in 1937 :

The problem of migration, the problem of granting greater facilities
for the movements of men from one country to another, is . . . undoubtedly
very important, but I do not think that . . . [its] importance should be taken
into consideration in relation to what should here be our constant, I would
even say, our sole concern : the examination of the causes of international
conflicts that may exist throughout the world and which we must endeavour
to eliminate as much as possible . . . [The problem of migration is] only
remotely connected with our objective : Peaceful Change. The main interest

of this question of greater facilities to be granted for migration lies elsewhere. If greater facilities are created for emigration, relief will be given to certain countries whose density of population is excessive. The indisputably regrettable inequalities which exist in too marked a degree between the conditions of life in the different countries of the world will be mitigated. Furthermore, the natural resources which, in all parts of the world, are at the disposal of mankind, will be more effectively exploited.[200]

Now although the International Studies Conference, as already stated, did not itself complete an investigation into the validity of the hypothesis that emigration is a remedy for overpopulation, it is, nevertheless, a common belief that emigration is the classic safety-valve for excessively dense populations and the remedy *par excellence* for the economic disequilibria arising out of the demographic maladjustments commonly described as " overpopulation ". The following statement made at a recent international conference of representatives of immigration and emigration countries by the delegate of one of the emigration countries is a typical illustration of this widespread belief :

As in past centuries, there are still a number of overpopulated countries which are unable to make use of their surplus population in industry and which are forced to settle their economic difficulties by emigration. Other countries, inversely, require labour from abroad because they are not yet in a position to develop their vast territories with their available national labour. This state of affairs creates demographic and economic disparities which, before the war, were *automatically eliminated* by international migration.[304] [a]

It is, therefore, proper to include in this Survey some discussion of emigration as a remedy for overpopulation. It will have to be borne in mind, however, that any discussion of this remedy, like the discussion of the remedies mentioned in the previous chapter, must rest upon a fictitious basis, for it will have to be assumed, contrary to the findings which issue from the work of the International Studies Conference, that the " dissatisfied " countries are suffering from a pressure of numbers giving rise to claims for changes in the international *status quo*.

This approach will inevitably beg the question since the notion of overpopulation is not one to which it seems possible to attach any

[a] The writer's italics.

very precise meaning and since, furthermore, none of the suggested tests of overpopulation which were examined in another chapter[a] seems capable of irrefutably demonstrating, in any of the countries which have been associated with claims for relief from overcrowding, the effective operation of a pressure of population on the means of subsistence resembling the true Malthusian congestion from which, for example, Ireland has suffered in the past[b] or which is perceptible to some observers in China or in India to-day.   On the other hand, the discussion will serve the purpose of adding to the tests already considered the further test of emigration, for, if it is true that overpopulation generates an emigratory movement, then, conversely, it may also be true that emigration is a sign of congestion.   Nor will the space devoted to this question have been wholly wasted if it serves to confirm the validity of the thesis running through this Survey.

Since the scope of this chapter must be narrowly confined to a consideration of the bearing of emigration upon the particular instances of demographic maladjustment which have been associated in this Survey with certain " dissatisfied " countries, it is not proposed to enquire here into the theoretical justification for the view that emigration remedies overpopulation.   On the broad question of the nature of the correlation between overpopulation and emigration, it must suffice to point out that several of the Conference's experts themselves questioned the view that there is a causal relation between demographic and migratory movements or that emigration relieves overcrowding. ' To encourage emigration at the moment ', argued a speaker at one of the Conference's meetings, ' in order that the places of the emigrants may soon be filled in the countries of origin accomplishes very little for the ultimate good of these countries '[194].   ' I would ask ', enquired another speaker, ' how many of the movements of population have really lessened the population at home ' ?[206] [c]   ' It is well known ', he affirmed, ' that emigration does not lessen the difficulties of the countries of origin so long as the stimulus to population is on the same lines as before '.[206]   ' If ', wrote the author of one of the Conference's

---

[a] See above, chap. 4.

[b] See below, p. 199, note b.

[c] ' I recall ', the same speaker went on to say, ' some studies I once made of the movement in the population within England at the beginning of the Industrial Revolution, and contrary to popular belief the population in the sheep-growing areas of Southern and Western England did not lessen according to the parochial registers, but continued to increase while Lancaster filled up ' (206).

memoranda, ' the economic pressure which tends to reduce the birth rate is relieved, a desirable and indeed inevitable adjustment is postponed and the danger of overpopulation is increased '.[102] Even in the exceptional case of Ireland,[a] where, after the famine, a ' combination of heavy emigration with a low birth-rate ' reduced the population from more than 8 millions to less than 4 millions, emigration being ' so heavy that it removed more than the natural increase ', it ' could hardly have had this result if the natural increase had not been held down by a falling birth-rate '.[84] [b] As the author of another memorandum who himself presumed ' that migration is desirable ' (though not necessarily for the purpose of relieving overpopulation) declared, ' although the co-existence of certain cases of overpopulation and underpopulation, accompanied by economic and political difficulties, is generally recognised, there is a conflict of opinion over the fundamental question of the necessity and desirability of international migration. This division of opinion ', he noted, ' has at all times manifested itself but ', he added (alluding to " open " and " closed " economies), ' it has never been so acute as it is to-day '.[163]

These, however, are mostly general opinions based upon special cases. It is possible that they are not applicable to the specific demographic situations in the " dissatisfied " countries. Here it seems desirable to consider the remedial properties of emigration empirically in the light of the facts relating to these particular situations. The questions to be considered are whether the demographic movements in Germany, Italy, Japan and Poland reveal any correlation of cause and effect between pressure of population and an emigratory outflow and, if so, whether the outflowing movement effectively relieves the tension by which it is generated.

In theory, it might not be possible to answer the latter question conclusively without enquiring into the indirect effects of emigration,

---

[a] Ireland, it has been said, ' is an exception to most rules ' of demography (*84*). It was pointed out to the Conference by a speaker at its 1937 session that the ' forced emigration from Ireland in the years that followed the Famine ' (*194*) was an abnormal movement. A parallel for the Irish situation is found in the earlier migratory movements from Norway by the author of *134*.

[b] ' Before 1845 . . . the population in Ireland as a whole exceeded 8 millions and has increased with great rapidity since the later decades of the eighteenth century. The country was admittedly grossly overpopulated, and the condition of the people was deplorable. Then came the famine. Since that time the population has steadily declined ' (*84*) until, to-day, it is not much above 4 millions. (According to *319*, the estimated population of Ireland on 31.XII.36 was as follows : Ireland (Eire), i. e., the former Irish Free State, 2,954,000; Northern Ireland, 1,280,000).

since an examination of the size of the population and of the volume
of emigration alone must obscure the important fact that ' migration
is only one aspect of international commerce; the other aspects are
lending and trade, for either they all go together in some measure
or they all cease together. There cannot be movements of people
without lendings of capital and there cannot be lendings of capital
without movements of people to the countries to which the capital is
lent '.[196] [a] In the particular cases under consideration, however, it
is in the highest degree improbabe that the issue will be falsified by
restricting the scope of the present discussion to demographic movements, because, if the trend of this argument may be anticipated, it
will be shown that, taken as a whole, the emigratory movements from
these countries have been quantitatively so inconsiderable in relation
to the magnitude of population growth that the short-run relief which
they have afforded, both directly and indirectly, may be disregarded.[b]

* * *

It is estimated[c] that, between 1846 and 1932, the numbers of
persons who emigrated overseas[d] from Germany, Italy and Japan

[a] Cf. below, p. 257.

[b] If the objection that the long-run economic effects of emigration may have been
substantial can be sustained, the improbability that the argument in the text falsifies the
issue is diminished; on the other hand, the general trend of the argument in the Survey,
namely, that the demographic factor cannot be usefully isolated from the totality of factors
in economic life, is strengthened.

[c] The records show that, between 1846 and 1932, there was a total world inter-continental emigration of 53,450,000 and that, between 1821 and 1932, there was a total world
intercontinental immigration of 59,187,000 (see *84*). ' There are various reasons for supposing that the record of immigrants is more complete than that of emigrants; the total
of 59 millions may therefore be taken as a minimum. But it is certainly an incomplete record,
and it is likely that at least 65 million persons moved overseas in those years ' (*ibid.*). The
real numbers of emigrants from Germany, Italy, Japan and Poland may have been larger
than the figures quoted in the text, since it is reasonable, though arbitrary, to add to the
figures some portion of the difference of 12 millions between the recorded number of
53 million emigrants and the estimated real number of 65 million emigrants; they may
even have been substantially greater; but they cannot have been so much greater as to
detract considerably from the utility of the figures quoted as an indication of the general
order of magnitude of the overseas emigratory movement from Germany, Italy, Japan
and Poland during the 86-year period (12-year, in the case of Poland) in question.

[d] ' Compared with oversea movements the other movements of Europeans have been
numerically of little account ' while ' the intra-continental movements of non-Europeans...,
[although they] have been on a larger scale than their inter-continental movements . . .,
have been of no great significance '. As for intra-continental movements of Germans,
' during the nineteenth century European continental movements were at first on a small
scale; there was some tendency for skilled workers to move from advanced to backward
countries, from Germany to Poland, for instance. After 1880 we begin to notice evidence
of a numerically more important movement of unskilled workers from backward to advanced countries; thus Polish labourers began to enter Germany, but the movements
were largely seasonal ' (*84*).

were, in round figures, five millions,[a] ten millions[b] and half a mil-

[a] Total recorded number of overseas emigrants from Germany : 4,889,000 (see *84*). The folllowing table, reproduced from *376*, shows the course of net overseas emigration from Germany (allowance made for returns to Germany) between 1851 and 1935 :

Years	Number of emigrants [391]	Periods	Losses per thousand inhabitants	Losses in absolute figures [377]
1851-1860	–	1851-1860	– 2.5	–
1861-1870	–	1861-1870	– 2.2	–
1871-1880	625,968	1871-1875	– 1.6 }	– 700,931
		1876-1880	– 1.7	
1881-1890	1,342,423	1881-1885	– 4.3 }	– 1,309,325
		1886-1890	– 1.4	
1891-1900	529,875	1891-1895	– 1.8 }	– 354,685
		1896-1900	+ 0.3	
1901-1910	279,645	1901-1905	+ 0.2 }	– 107,386
		1906-1910	– 0.5	
1911-1913	67,078 }			
1920	8,458 }			
1921	24,173 }			
1922	32,623 }	1911-1925		+ 330,270
1923	115,431 }			
1924	58,328 }			
1925	67,705 }			
1926	? }			
1927	61,379 }			
1928	57,241 }			
1929	48,734 }	1926-1933	– 0 5	– 263,961
1930	37,399 }			
1931	13,644 }			
1932	10,325 }			
1933	12,866 }			
1934	14,232	1934	– 0.21	?
1935	12,226	1935	– 0.18	?

[b] Total recorded number of oversea emigrants from Italy : 10,092,000 (see *84*). The following table, based upon figures given in *84* for the period 1876-1929 and in *395* for the period 1930-1935, shows the course of net emigration from Italy :

Period or Year	Net Emigration	
	Amount (thousands)	Per 1,000 inhabitants
1876-80	54	1.4
1881-85	77	2.8
1886-90	111	3.7
1891-95	128	4.1
1896-1900	155	4.9
1901	265	8.2
1902	286	8.7
1903	241	7.6

[over

lion,[a] respectively.   In Poland, 'before the war, the number of emigrants leaving ... each year was 250,000, in addition to seasonal

1904	145	4.4
1905	438	13.2
1906	465	13.9
1907	384	11.5
1908	37	1.1
1909	356	10.4
1910	342	10.0
1911	155	4.5
1912	343	9.8
1913	477	13.5
1920	414	11.5
1921	57	1.3
1922	163	4.2
1923	265	6.9
1924	186	4.7
1925	90	2.3
1926	85	2.1
1927	79	2.1
1928	51	1.6
1929	34	1.1
1930	151	3.1
1931	58	2.6
1932	10	1.7
1933	17	1.5
1934	19	1.1
1935	18	0.9

The figures for 1930-1935 comprise emigrants 'who have emigrated for the second time (*riespatriati*) and who have thus been enumerated twice' (*394*).

[a] Total recorded number of oversea emigrants from Japan : 518,000 (see *84*).   The following table, reproduced from *398* and *400*, shows the course of net emigration from Japan between 1913 and 1934 :

Year	Emigrants	Returning emigrants	Net emigration
1913	20,966	—	—
1920	13,541	20,376	− 6,835
1923	8,825	10,784	+ 1,959
1924	13,098	15,579	+ 2,481
1925	10,696	13,918	+ 3,222
1926	16,184	14,549	− 1,635
1927	18,041	14,735	− 3,306
1928	19,850	15,004	− 4,846
1929	25,704	14,073	−11,631
1930	21,829	15,432	− 6,397
1931	10,384	12,965	+ 2,581
1932	19,033	13,170	− 5,863
1933	23,317	14,141	−13,176
1934	28,087	—	—

emigration ',[304] [a] while during the 12-year period 1920-1932, some 650,000 persons emigrated overseas.[b]

Thus, in varying degrees, all the " dissatisfied " countries have been centres of emigration in the past and their aggregate contribution to the total flow of emigration has been considerable. The figures quoted, however, are not significant in themselves. ' Neither the gross contribution from any particular country nor the percentage which this contribution forms of the total in any year necessarily corresponds at all closely with the intensity of emigration, as measured by the annual loss per 1,000 inhabitants by emigration '.[84] In order to determine the bearing of emigration upon the demographic situation within a particular country it is necessary to compare the volume of emigration with the size of the population.

Now the records show that, during the period in question, the volume of emigration from Germany was altogether dwarfed by the volume of natural increase of the population,[c] and that, in Japan, ' the movements have been of small importance ',[84] [d] emigration having been but an insignificant dribble beside the immense tide of population expansion.[e] In Italy and Poland, on the other hand, the volume of emigration has been substantial both absolutely and relatively to population increase. In the former country, it is claimed, ' the actual rate of increase of the population . . . was kept down to a low figure

[a] ' Up to 1914 some 600,000 Poles had moved from that part of Poland which was formerly included in Germany, to settle in parts of Germany which were not ethnographically Polish, and over a million Poles had left what was formerly Russian Poland to settle in other pats of Russia. There was in addition a strong seasonal movement of agricultural workers into Germany proper which reached a total of 300,000 in some years ' (*84*).

[b] Total recorded number of oversea emigrants from Poland : 642,000 (see *84*). The following table, reproduced from *167*, shows the course of net emigration from Poland between 1927 and 1934 :

Year	Number of emigrants	Number of returning emigrants	Net emigration (—) or immigration (+)
1927	89,000	73,000	—16,000
1928	122,000	113,000	— 9,000
1929	178,000	98,000	—80,000
1930	172,000	93,000	—79,000
1931	64,000	80,000	+ 16,000
1932	12,000	33,000	+ 20,000
1933	18,000	15,000	— 3,000
1934	22,000	32,000	+ 10,000

[c] See above, p. 101, note a.

[d] ' There are now [1936] about a million Japanese living outside Japan proper but within the Japanese Empire, and another 200,000 in Manchuria ' (*84*).

[e] See above, p. 107, note b.

between 1900 and 1913 because emigration was on so large a scale; in fact in 1905, 1906, 1907 and 1913 the net loss by emigration exceeded the natural increase '.[84] [a]   Yet even in those two countries, the volume of emigration has not been sufficient, in the long run, to keep the population stationary.   There has been nothing comparable with the relatively enormous outflow from Ireland,[b] which, although admittedly exceptional, yet cannot be inexplicable.   Although the total volume of emigration from these countries, considered in isolation as a movement of men across the face of the globe, may seem large because it has to be expressed in figures pertaining to the sensational category of millions, it is but a tiny fraction detached from the main body of the population which has remained behind.

Since the rate and volume of emigration have never caught up (except in one country for a short space of time) with the natural flow of the population, it is difficult to read into the past histories of demographic and emigratory movements in Germany, Italy, Japan and Poland any evidence which would bear out the hypothesis that they have suffered from a chronic condition of local population pressure amenable to no other cure than a flight of their inhabitants into areas of demographic rarefaction.   It would appear, indeed, that the true causes of emigration from these countries must be sought elsewhere.

It would seem that migratory movements are determined rather by the conditions prevailing in the countries of immigration than those obtaining in the countries of emigration, that is to say, that emigration is a movement attracted from without rather than a movement propelled from within.   A study[88] of the relation between the volume of immigration into the United States, for example, and the growth of opportunities for employment in that country has revealed ' strong cyclical and seasonal movements in immigration '[84] and has shown that ' when immigration is not restricted the character of the cyclical variations, at least, is closely similar to the cyclical variations in employment opportunities in the United States. A fairly close similarity is also found in the seasonal movements '.[88]   ' When there was freedom to come and go, the volume of movement corresponded with changes in opportunities for employment in a fashion that was almost uncanny . . .   Emigrants sometimes left when conditions at home were good and sometimes when they were bad . . .   Men left

[a] See above, p. 106, note a.
[b] See above, p. 199.

home, not because things were bad, but because they thought that things would be still better in the United States '.[84] [a]

Nevertheless, before applying the conclusion which springs from this observation to the question under consideration, it will be well to turn from the past to the present trends of population and emigration in the " dissatisfied " countries.

The information given in an earlier chapter[b] has shown that, in each of these countries, the population is at present expanding and that there are no grounds for anticipating that this movement will cease in the near future. It is true that, in the case of Germany, where, until 1933, the annual surplus of births over deaths was rapidly declining and where, notwithstanding the upward trend which has manifested itself since then, the annual surplus is still below replacement rate,

[a] ' How can we explain the fact that ... [intending emigrants] were such excellent judges of the prospects ? There was no attempt on the part of the governments concerned to provide information about conditions overseas; such newspapers as were read by the peasants and workmen of Europe were certainly not of much use to them for this purpose, and in bad times as in good the shipping companies were pressing upon their attention the facilities which they provided for emigration. We can only explain the facts by supposing that the continuous stream of letters from emigrants abroad gave an up-to-date and accurate picture of opportunities in the new countries for those at home who contemplated migration ' (*84*).

' This strong influence on the part of the earlier emigrants is no doubt largely due to their desire to make others share the advantages which they themselves had won, but they may also to a certain extent have had their own interests in view, viz. through fresh emigration to procure for themselves labourers at moderate wages ' (*134*). According to *135*, the circumstances most frequently mentioned as causes of emigration in letters from America to Norway during the second quarter of the nineteenth century ' may be summarized as follows : (i) that there was cheap land, fertile land and plenty of it; (ii) that no distinction was made between people; (iii) that legislation was favourable to the common people; (iv) that there was a complete democracy and that all votes counted equally; (v) that there was no difference between people as regards clothes and privileges; (vi) that there was religious liberty; (vii) that the taxes were low; (viii) that all had to work for a living, but that there was at the same time room for all who would work ' (*134*). ' In a contemporary account an emigrant gives the following circumstances as the chief causes of the emigration : (i) the gloomy prospects in Norway for the future of the rising generation, coupled with the hope of independence and happiness in America; (ii) the fact that for the " producing and working classes " Norway is too circumscribed; that there is not room enough; and that the time is not distant when " a slavish dependence " will become general; (iii) general dissatisfaction with the administration of Norwegian law, especially with reference to relations between debtors and creditors, where the regulations in force work the ruin of the former; (iv) a general feeling that the state does too little to promote agriculture and the welfare of the common people, though it devotes large sums of money to other purposes; (v) dissatisfaction with Norwegian officialdom and the clergy, which form a caste that looks upon an ordinary citizen as an inferior; (vi) failure in Norway to realize the freedom and equality that the constitution of 1814 promised; (vii) the pressure upon the " bonde-stand " (the independent farmers) of poor-relief burdens; (viii) uncertainty of crops and sterility of the soil; (ix) the pressure upon the same class of burdens connected with the Norwegian road system; (x) idealisation of America ' (*134*).

[b] See above, chap. 4, § VIII.

it cannot be said that this country, any more than the other countries
of northern and western Europe, ' is suffering from congestion of
population in the sense that it is experiencing troubles which can only
be alleviated by a change in its population situation '; but it is also true
that Germany, so far from having a stationary population, is still faced
with several decades of demographic expansion. In Italy, although
the annual surplus is diminishing, ' additions to population will remain
considerable for some time to come ';[84] Poland is in a similar position.
Japan also is a country with a population which has not yet reached
its maximum.

On the other hand, emigration from the " dissatisfied " countries
is at present almost at a standstill. Although, apart from the British
Isles,[a] Germany ' was the only . . . country which played a large part
in the earlier phases of the period ' of emigration between 1846 and 1932,
' after 1885 the percentage from Germany markedly diminished '.[84]
Indeed, emigration from Germany practically ceased at the end of
the nineteenth century,[b] and ' was not resumed in any appreciable
degree until 1933 — a year which, for that country, was one of distress
and despair '.[200] Not only was emigration discontinued, but a net
annual average of less than 10,000 emigrants in 1927-1930 was transformed in 1931-1935 into a net annual average immigration of over
30,000.[182] In Italy, the second most important country of emigration
in the past, a net annual average emigration of just under 80,000 in
1927-1930 was reduced in 1931-1935 to less than 25,000.[182] Japan, as
has already been noted, has never been an important contributor to
the flow of emigration. As already indicated,[c] ' there are scarcely
more than a million Japanese outside Japan, whereas there are consider-

---

[a] It is estimated that out of a total overseas emigration of 65 million persons between
1846 and 1932, 18 millions were from the British Isles (see 84).

[b] The following table, reproduced from a table based on 98, shows the percentage of
British, Germans and Italians in the total emigration from Europe to all destinations between
1851 and 1915 :

	British %	German %	Italian %
1851-1860	64.5	23.2	—
1861-1870	56.5	21.8	4.5
1871-1880	51.1	18.6	8.2
1881-1890	35.0	18.7	13.2
1891-1900	26.1	7.5	24.0
1900-1910	23.1	2.3	29.7
1911-1915	26.7	1.2	23.2

[c] See above, p. 203, note d.

ably more than a million Frenchmen beyond the frontiers of France, and the French ... are not regarded as a very migrant nation '.[200] A constriction of the migratory stream even more remarkable than that which has taken place in Italy has occurred in Poland. ' In 1929, the number of persons leaving Poland for oversea countries was still as high as 65,000, but by 1936 the figure had fallen to 24,000. Moreover, as the volume of returning emigrants rose considerably, the actual balance of emigration was reduced to nothing and sometimes even showed a deficit '.[304] A net annual average emigration of not much less than 100,000 in 1927-1930 vanished entirely in 1931-1935.[182] Thus, not only has the outflowing volume of emigration from each of the " dissatisfied " countries been greatly diminished, but, in several of them, the movement has been reversed. A counter-migratory movement is now pumping so strong a stream of migrants back into the alleged countries of emigration that, if it is maintained, the net outflowing current must shortly be reduced to an impotent trickle.[a]

[a] The following table, based upon figures given in *182*, shows in absolute numbers the annual average emigration and immigration in Germany, Italy, Japan and Poland between 1927 and 1935 : —

	Population (in thousands)	Emigration		Immigration		Excess : − emigration + immigration	
	31.XII.35	1927-30	1931-35	1927-30	1931-35	1927-30	1931-35
Germany(α)	67,105	53,262 (β)	14,474 (β)	166,556 (γ)	66,381(γ)	− 9,540 (δ)	+ 31,462(δ)
Italy	42,300(ε)	193,298(ζη)	91,628 (ζ)	114,564(ζη)	67,208 (ζ)	− 78,734(ζη)	− 24,420(ζ)
Poland	33,823	199,018 (ζ)	45,869 (ζ)	101,120 (ζ)	46,509(ζ)	− 97,898 (ζ)	+ 460(ζ)
Japan	69,500(ε)	24,690 (ζ)	21,205 (ζθ)	—	—	—	—

α) 1937 frontiers, including the Saar. β) Not including continental emigration of foreigners. γ) Intercontinental immigration of nationals; continental for foreigners. δ) Intercontinental : nationals. ε) Approximate figure. ζ) Nationals only. η) Average, 1928-30. θ) Average, 1931-34.

For further information on the counter-migratory movement, see *249*. ' By the expression " counter-migration ", we mean a mass migration which takes place in the opposite direction to that of normal migrations (traditional migration) and tends to exceed these normal migrations. Counter-migration, therefore, has a special characteristic at the moment when it takes place; this was, for instance, the case for the period since 1930. It is necessary to distinguish from counter-migration the voluntary emigration of foreigners, their repatriation (particularly when they are without means of support), their enforced deportation as the result of illegal immigration, the extradition of delinquents and the sending back of foreigners even before they have crossed the frontiers of the country of immigration ' (*ibid.*).

This comparison of the present movements of population and of emigration in Germany, Italy, Japan and Poland seems to point, therefore, either to the absence of any correlation of cause and effect between pressure of population and emigration or to the absence of pressure of population in the " dissatisfied " countries. The presumption is that the second hypothesis is valid since it tallies with the conclusions which emerged from the discussion in an earlier chapter on the tests of overpopulation in these countries. In that case, it would be futile to enquire further into the utility of a remedy for a difficulty which does not exist. But, before closing the discussion, it may be useful to inspect the alternative hypothesis a little more closely. The fact that, notwithstanding the expansion of population in the " dissatisfied " countries, the volume of emigration which is at present flowing out of them is no more than a tiny leak out of the vast reservoirs of existing population does not necessarily indicate that those reservoirs are not dangerously filled near to the brim or that a more abundant outflow would not be opportune; for it may be that the outward movement is being obstructed by extraneous impediments or that recourse is being had to alternative remedies. In the latter case, the question would fall outside the scope of this chapter, but in the former case it would be useful to enquire into the nature of the obstructions, the reasons which have caused them to be raised and the possibilities of removing them or of overcoming their effects on the emigratory movement; for it may be that, if the migratory flow were freed from its shackles, it would swell again into an abundant tide.

Now the history of migration throughout the nineteenth century period fails to reveal that any barriers interfered with the free flow of emigration. On the contrary, broadly, emigration was everywhere free and spontaneous. Yet, in spite of this freedom, there was no palpable relation between the expansion of the population and the volume of emigration. Thus the evidence of the past history of demographic and migratory movements seems to indicate that there is no substance in the conjecture that the absence of any visible correlation of cause and effect between population pressure and emigration may be attributable to the intervention of extraneous obstacles. It is possible, however, that the lessons of the past have no bearing upon the present situation and that the mechanics of emigration are now of a wholly different order; and, since freedom of emigration has now, in fact, been replaced by a comprehensive system of limitation, regulation and control, it may be argued that it is the operation of this system which prevents the generation of an emigratory movement.

Turning aside, then, from the main trend of the present argument, a brief description may now be given of the present obstacles to emigration. No attempt can be made, however, to enquire into the complex economic, technical and administrative aspects of the present impediments to emigration and of the methods of overcoming them which have been contemplated both in the International Studies Conference and elsewhere. To do so would be merely to summarise the incomparable wealth of information already available in the publications of the International Labour Office, to which some reference has already been made in these pages, and to draw directly from the unique store of experience and expertise which is pooled in the Office's Migration Section; it would carry the present text, moreover, into a realm of the Conference's enquiry which, as has already been explained,[a] extends beyond the central problem considered in the present Survey. On the other hand, a brief statement can be made of the geographical extent of, and of some of the principal reasons for, the present hindrances with a view to considering the bearing of these data on the position in the " dissatisfied " countries.

II. THE REGULATION OF MIGRATION

The obstacles to emigration are many and diverse. In describing their geographical extent, it will be convenient, therefore, to adopt some conventional system of classification. In the first place, a distinction must be made between (a) the artificial restrictions on emigration which are attributable to the policies of governments and (b) obstacles arising out of other circumstances. Secondly, some of the governmental measures designed to impede emigration are imposed by (1) the countries of immigration; others are imposed by (2) the countries of emigration themselves. The former are geographically far more extensive than the latter and will be considered first. Finally, it is convenient to distinguish between (i) the restriction of the immigration of European peoples and (ii) the restriction of the immigration of Asiatics; Germans, Italians and Poles may be considered together, but the Japanese are subject to disabilities of a special character which modify the nature

---

[a] See above, pp. 195 *sqq.*

15

of the problem. So far as the restrictions on the immigration of
Europeans are concerned, the description will relate exclusively to
immigration into the territories of " Europe overseas ". Immigration
into " colonies " will be considered in the next chapter. Nothing need
be said of the restrictions imposed by European countries upon the entry
of aliens, since, notwithstanding the magnitude of such movements
in the recent past[a] they are far smaller than those which have been
directed overseas; and it is unlikely that a stream of emigration on
a scale relevant to a condition of acute overcrowding could be turned
towards any region in Europe[b]; moreover, it is principally upon the
alleged possession by the overseas countries of considerable areas of
potential settlement that the discussion of emigration hinges in relation
to the problem of " peaceful change ". European Russia may possibly
be an exception to the penultimate statement, but it is more convenient
to assimilate this region to the U. S. S. R. as a whole, which must be
mentioned separately on the grounds that the Ukraine, on which, it
is said, a potential emigratory stream is being focussed, raises issues
which may be comprised more properly in the next chapter, and that

[a] The following table, reproduced from *84* (quoting from the summaries of government
statistics provided by the International Labour Office), shows the volume of continental
emigration from Italy and Poland between 1922 and 1933 :

Year	Italy	Poland
1922	170,155	31,373
1923	229,854	72,058
1924	271,089	26,136
1925	178,208	42,769
1926	141,314	117,616
1927	91,958	89,427
1928	79,173	122,049
1929	88,054	178,132
1930	220,985	171,853
1931	125,079	64,235
1932	58,545	11,772
1933	60,726	18,293

It should be noted that ' there are serious difficulties inherent in any attempt to record
continental movements; it is less easy to keep records of passage across land frontiers than
of a flow through ports. Also there is no uniform system of defining migrants and recording
their movements; therefore national statistics are not strictly comparable ' (*84*).

[b] ' [The countries in the Far North of Europe — Faroe Islands, Iceland, Spitzbergen,
Norwegian coast] untouched by nineteenth century civilisation . . ., remained for a long
time at a fairly low standard of life . . . But the twentieth century brought them modern
civilisation . . ., which raised them in twenty years to a standard of life equal to if not higher
than that of any other people . . . These countries of the Far North appear very rich and
perhaps they have already attracted the attention of countries eager for colonial
expansion ' (*372*).

the main areas of potential settlement in the Union lie in the Asiatic continent.[a]

* * *

(a) GOVERNMENT RESTRICTIONS

(1) *Immigration restrictions*

(i) RESTRICTIONS ON EUROPEANS

United States. — ' The history of immigration to the United States may be divided into four periods : the colonial period, from the time of the first settlement to 1783 . . ., [when] the thirteen colonies became an independent nation . . .; the period of " free immigration ", from 1783 to 1830 . . ., [at about which] time a change in the public attitude toward immigration became noticeable . . .; the period of state regulation, from 1783 to 1882; and the period of federal control, after 1882 . . ., [when] the Federal Government . . . enacted its first important immigration law. During the first three immigration periods and the first decade of the fourth period, that is, until about 1890, the vast majority of the immigrants came from the countries in northern and western Europe.[b] This immigration is referred to as the " old immigration ". From 1890 to about 1923, the sources of immigration shifted to southern and eastern Europe.[c] This is called the " new immigration ". Since 1923, immigration from northern and western Europe has once more exceeded that from other parts of Europe. European immigration, however, has not constituted so large a proportion of immigration since the World War as in earlier years, and immigration from countries in the Western Hemisphere has become increasingly important '.[68] [d]

---

[a] See below, p. 221, note a.

[b] ' Northern and western Europe comprises : Belgium, Denmark, France, Germany, Iceland, Luxemburg, Netherlands, Norway, Sweden, Switzerland, and England, Ireland, Scotland, Wales and " United Kingdom not specified ". Southern and eastern Europe comprises the other countries on that continent ' (72).

[c] ' Since 1882, Italy has sent the United States the largest number of immigrants ' (68).

[d] The following table, reproduced from 68, ' shows the number coming from the most important immigrant-exporting countries during the period 1881-1930, inclusive ' : —

During the colonial period, the largest volume of immigrants next to the Scotch-Irish was the German immigration, ' chiefly from the Palatinate and from Switzerland . . . Desire for religious freedom was a cause of emigration, although civil and economic disabilities contributed. Mennonites, Moravians, and Dunkers formed important groups in the immigration from Germany. It is estimated that the total number of Germans in the colonies in 1750 was about 100,000, and that 70,000 of them were in Pennsylvania '. It has been variously estimated that, in 1790, Germans represented 3.6% and 7.4% of the white population of the United States.[68]

During the period of unrestricted immigration, extending from 1783 to about 1832, ' there were not wanting utterances by the Founding Fathers indicating misgivings about the influx of foreigners and their participation in the government ', but labour shortage led to a demand for skilled workers which exceeded the supply. ' As in colonial times, English, Scotch, Irish and Germans constituted the bulk of the immigration in these years. Persecution on religious grounds and the desire for religious freedom were no longer so important as motives for emigration; economic causes were now predominant. With the exception of the Irish, the newcomers for the most part avoided the cities in the Atlantic States and went West . . . [Thus] they did not come so sharply into contact with a strictly American milieu. During this period, during the last decade especially, there was increasing dissatisfaction because of the lack of regulation of immigration. Certain European countries continued to ship criminals and paupers to the United States. Likewise, owing to the hardships of the voyage, and the exploitation to which immigrants were subjected at all stages of their journey, many arrived in poverty and ill health and became a burden on the American community. The states most concerned therefore enacted legislation to put a stop to certain of these evils '.[68]

Country	1881-1890	1891-1900	1901-1910	1911-1920	1921-1930	Total
Italy	307,309	651,893	2,045,877	1,109,524	455,315	4,569,918
Austria-Hungary	353,719	592,707	2,145,266	896,342	63,548	4,051,582
Russia	213,282	505,290	1,597,306	921,201	61,742	3,298,821
Germany	1,452,970	505,152	341,498	143,945	412,202	2,855,767
Canada	393,304	3,311	179,226	742,185	924,515	2,242,541
Ireland	655,482	388,416	339,065	146,181	220,591	1,749,735
England	664,680	216,726	388,017	249,944	157,420	1,656,787
Sweden	391,776	226,266	249,534	95,074	97,249	1,059,899
Mexico	1,913	971	49,642	219,004	459,287	730,817
Norway	176,586	95,015	190,505	66,395	68,531	597,032
Scotland	149,869	44,188	120,469	78,357	159,781	552,664

In the next period, 1830-1882, ' since the national government failed to regulate immigration, the states with important seaports took over that function '.[68] They enacted various laws restricting the entry of foreign convicts, paupers, mental defectives, undesirables and other persons likely to become a burden on the community, and they sought to protect the community from ill-health and the immigrants from exploitation and fraud.[68] ' During the period 1831-1880, the number of German immigrants entering the country was 3,044,397 . . . After the political upheavals in Germany, emigrating from that country included many intellectuals, who formed a desirable addition to the country's population '. In 1850, ' of the 2,244,602 foreign-born persons in the country . . ., 26 per cent . . . were natives . . . of Germany . . . At the end of this period, in 1880, the natives of Germany formed the largest group (29.4 per cent). in the foreign-born population, which by then had increased to 6,679,943 . . . Natives of Central and South European countries were just beginning to arrive in any numbers; immigrants . . . from Italy . . . formed . . . 0.7 per cent . . . of the foreign-born total. During this period the states encouraged the entry of immigrant labourers and farmers, but fear of the consequences of immigration was already increasing. Immigrants were feared because of their potential economic competition. The growth of foreign colonies and the participation of the foreign-born in politics also aroused apprehension '.[68] The Civil War, however, and consequent shortage of man power put a stop to most of the anti-alien propaganda and some action was taken to stimulate immigration.[68]

But ' state regulation of immigration soon proved unsatisfactory ' and a period of Federal control over immigration began. ' The first general immigration act adopted by Congress after it assumed control of immigration was approved August 3, 1882 . . . It established the selection-by-rejection principle which has since prevailed in United States immigration legislation. It provided for the rejection of certain classes at the lowest rung of the social ladder rather than for the selection of the most skilled and fit in capacity or occupation for meeting the economic or social needs of the country '. This act was followed by numerous other restrictive measures, culminating in the so-called " quota acts " which regulate immigration not only qualitatively but also quantitatively. ' There have been three sets of quotas in force since first the quota method of regulating and restricting immigration to the United States went into effect . . . The first quota act, passed as an emergency measure to stem the threatened exodus to the United States from war-torn Europe, was in force from June 3, 1921, to June 30, 1924 '.[68] It ' limited the number of immigrants of any nationality who might be admitted in any year to 3 per cent. of the number of foreign-born persons of that nationality resident in the United States in 1910 ... The act was restrictive since the total admissions from quota countries could not be more than 357,803; it was also discriminatory because the proportion of the total allotted to southern and eastern European countries was less than the proportion of the total inflow which they were contributing before the Act came into force '.[84] This act ' was superseded by the act of May 26, 1924, an act which at the present time, together with the basic immigration law of February 5, 1917,[a] controls and regulates immigration to the United States '.[68] ' This latter Act ... substituted 2 per cent for 3 per cent and 1890 for 1910. The result was more restriction and more discrimination; for it reduced the total permitted inflow from quota countries ... to 164,667, and allowed only a negligible quota to countries such as Italy whose foreign-born representatives were few in 1890 '.[84] Finally, in 1924, the application of a calculation of the quotas based on national origins[b] resulted in ' slightly more restriction, and a considerable change in the relative sizes of the quotas of certain countries '.[84] The numbers of immigrants permitted under these three quotas to enter the United States from the " dissatisfied " countries in Europe which are under consideration are as follows : — 1921 act : 67,607 from Germany, 42,057 from Italy, and 30,977 from Poland; 1924 act : 51,227 from Germany, 3,845 from Italy, and 5,982 from Poland; 1929 " national origins " quota : 25,957 from Germany, 5,802 from Italy, and 6,524 from Poland.[68] [84] As the figures for Italy and Poland indicate, ' the chief changes occurred when the 2 per cent provisions of the 1924 Act replaced the 1921 Act; they resulted in drastic reductions in the quotas for southern and eastern European countries. Thus the Italian quota was reduced from 42,057 to the derisory figure of 3,845.[c] In

[a] A clause of Section 3 of this Act ' prohibits the entry of any immigrant who is " likely to become a public charge " ' (68).

[b] ' The formula of the National Origins plan is as follows : — *The annual quota of any nationality for the fiscal year shall be a number which bears the same ratio to 150,000 as the number of inhabitants in Continental United States in 1920 having that National Origin bears to the number of inhabitants in Continental United States in 1920, but the minimum quota of any nationality shall be 100* ' (see 68).

[c] ' Italian immigration into the U. S. A. during the decade 1901 to 1910 averaged over 200,000 per annum ' (84).

fact the permitted immigration from southern and eastern Europe was reduced to negligible proportions '.[84]

' After 1929, because of the depression and widespread unemployment, it was quite generally conceded that immigration should be curtailed as much as possible until economic conditions improved. As it did not seem advisable to take legislative action, the drastic enforcement of the clause . . . [of the 1917 act already mentioned][a] was resorted to in reducing the volume of immigration . . . As a result, the number of immigrants admitted per year since 1931 has been lower than at any other time during the past century '.[68]

British Dominions. — In *Canada,* legislation empowers the government to ' lay down whom it will admit, and under what conditions. A list has been prepared of " preferred ", " non-preferred ", and " other countries " '. Germany is included among the " preferred ", whose ' nationals are admitted on much the same terms as British citizens, the chief requirement being that they are proceeding to assured employment or that they have sufficient funds to maintain themselves until they find employment '. Poland is included among the " non-preferred ", whose ' nationals may enter only if they are agriculturists or domestic servants '. The present policy of immigration restriction was initiated in August 1930 following upon the stoppage of Canadian emigration to the United States by American legislation. It limits immigration to certain categories of British subject and American citizen, to certain dependents of residents and to ' an agriculturalist having sufficient means to farm in Canada '.[84]

The result of legislation in *Australia*[b] and *New Zealand* is also restrictive and discriminatory.[84] In *South Africa,* the Quota Act of 1930 ' limits the immigration from non-scheduled countries to 50 a year '; Germany and Italy are among the scheduled countries, Poland among the non-scheduled.[84]

Central and South America. — ' It appears that no country in Central or South America has put legislation into force which either limits the total volume of European immigration or discriminates against particular European nationalities '.[84] But, in Brazil, one of the greatest

---

[a] See above, p. 214, note a.
[b] ' The government of Italy has agreed to restrict the issue of passports [for Australia] to Italians who possess at least £ 40 ' (*84*).

recent obstacles to immigration is constituted by the *carta de chamada*[a],
' which, if it has not completely paralysed immigration, has at least,
unquestionably contributed very largely to the diminution in the number
of immigrants ... Another equally serious obstacle which has made
immigration difficult, if not impossible, lies in the application of para-
graph 6 of Article 121 of the Federal Constitution '. According to
this provision :

The admittance of immigrants to the national territory shall be subject
to the restrictions necessary to guarantee their ethnical assimilability and
physical fitness and their civil status, provided always that the number of
immigrants per year shall not exceed 2% of the total number of nationals
of the respective countries who have been domiciled in Brazil during the last
fifty years.[83]

' During 1936, the provisional number of immigrants admitted ' under
this provision was fixed at 2,318 for Germany, 27,475 for Italy and
2,035 for Poland.[83 b]

(ii) Restrictions on Japanese

The outstanding feature of the restrictions on the migration of
Japanese is that they have been virtually excluded from nearly all the
countries ruled by the white peoples in the Pacific area. ' Japanese
began to arrive in the *United States* shortly before 1900, and anti-
Japanese feeling soon manifested itself '.[84 c] In 1890, there were only
2,039 Japanese in the United States, but by 1900 they had increased to
24,326; by 1910 they numbered 72,157; by 1920, 111,010; and by 1930,
138,834.[68] They ' have concentrated on the Pacific coast; in 1930,
86 per cent of them were there ... As result, numerous discriminatory
measures have been enacted against them, the most serious of them being
probably the California laws prohibiting them from owning land or

---

a ' The *carta de chamada* ..., which involves prolonged and complicated administrative
formalities, is regulated by Decree No. 24,258 of May 16th, 1934 ' (*83*).

b For the reasons which impelled Brazil to apply a quota, ' in spite of the fact that the
country is underpopulated ' (*193*), see below, pp. 237-238.

c ' It is acknowledged in California that the Japanese are unusually law abiding, but ..
[it has been] said [see *73*] of them : " Their good taste, persistent industry, their excellen
qualities and their virtues render their presence among us a pitiful danger " ' (*68*). Cf. the
statement that ' the basis of Chinese exclusion [from the United States] is their virtues, no
their vices ' (*69*).

leasing land and prohibiting the acquisition of land by second generation Japanese (American citizens) under the guardianship of their parents '.[68 a] ' Until 1924, immigration of Japanese was not regulated by law, although in response to agitation in California, many bills proposing their exclusion were introduced in Congress. Largely through the influence of President Theodore Roosevelt, none of them was enacted. Instead, in 1907, a " gentlemen's agreement " was entered into between the United States and Japan, under which Japan bound itself not to issue passports for the United States to Japanese labourers. How carefully the agreement was observed and to what extent it accomplished its purpose are matters of dispute. California and other West Coast states did not find the results satisfactory and kept agitating for more drastic exclusion '.[68] That ' local feeling was not satisfied [was] partly . . . [due to] the entry of " picture brides ", that is of Japanese women who came to marry Japanese already in the United States — a form of immigration not contrary to the Agreement '.[84 b] Complete exclusion was eventually brought about, ' over the protests of the Secretary of State, the Japanese Ambassador and others, [by] a section . . . [of] the immigration act of May 26, 1924, prohibiting the entry of aliens who are ineligible to American citizenship ',[68] the Japanese being so ineligible.

In *Canada*, ' Japanese began to arrive about 1905, and this led to the conclusion of a Gentleman's Agreement in 1908 on the lines of the American arrangement; the agreement remains in force '.[84] ' The maximum number of Japanese allowed to settle in the country has been set at one hundred and fifty per annum '.[108] In *Australia*, ' an arrangement has been made with Japan whereby passports are not granted to Japanese who intend to settle '. In *New Zealand*, ' under an Act of 1920 every person, not of British birth or parentage, is required to obtain a permit to land. This requirement is used to keep . . . Japanese out of New Zealand '.[84]

[a] ' In recent years the " second generation " has constituted a rapidly increasing proportion of the Japanese population group. The sex ratio among Japanese in the United States is far more favourable than that among the Chinese; in 1930, there were 143.3 males per 100 females, the nearest to normal distribution of any of the Asiatic groups. Due to this fact, their rate of increase, in spite of the falling off of immigration, is higher than for any other population group. For the decade 1920-1930, the Japanese . . . rate of increase was 25.1 [per thousand] as compared with 16.1 . . . [per thousand] for the whole population of this country and 15.7 . . . [per thousand] for the native white population ' (*68*).

[b] Cf. *117* : ' China, an intensive emigration country, colonises practically nowhere, because no Chinese women accompany the emigrants '.

The countries of *Central and South America* ' have not all adopted this policy [of exclusion]; in general the less advanced among them have been the most exclusive ... Costa Rica and Guatemala are among the countries which exclude Asiatics; but it would seem that Argentina, Chile, or Brazil have not discriminated against non-Europeans, and the last-mentioned country has in fact encouraged the settlement of Japanese '.[84] [a]

(2) *Emigration Restrictions*

' In the countries of emigration, the individual is being deprived more and more of the right to emigrate of his own free will. Personal liberty in the matter of leaving the country ... no longer exists '.[124] The passport system is now universal, and ' inability to comply with the immigration laws of the countries to which it is desired to go '[84] is a frequent reason for refusing a passport to intending emigrants. ' This restriction is in force in most European countries and operates powerfully to keep down the volume of emigration. It is imposed in order to avoid the trouble and expense consequent upon the refusal by countries of immigration to permit persons to enter; for such persons may have to be brought home by the country whence they came '.[84] This, together with other minor restrictions imposed by the countries of emigration on their nationals by reason of ' the supposed interest of the would-be immigrants or the demands of social justice '[b] but

[a] Under the new quota regulations, the permitted number of Japanese immigrants into Brazil was provisionnaly fixed for 1936 at 3,480 (see *83* and cf. above, pp. 215-6).

[b] That the potential emigrant must still be protected by the State from the unscrupulous exploitation which, in the nineteenth century, was an important source of revenue for shipping companies, is shown in the following warning issued recently by the French Ministry of the Interior : — ' The public is warned against the propaganda conducted by certain groups which seek to recruit emigrants by promising them advantages which they are not in a position to obtain for them. With a view to sparing our fellow-countrymen the regrettable disappointments which they might thus suffer, we advise them to act with the utmost caution when so approached. They should enter into no engagement without previously consulting our diplomatic or consular agents resident in the countries to which an attempt is made to attract them ' (*256*).

' One of the main objects of the regulation of the activities of emigration agencies with regard to the supply of information is to prevent the dissemination of false information concerning possibilities and conditions of emigration. It not infrequently happens that, on the strength of false or misleading statements, would-be emigrants make costly preparations for their departure and even sell up their homes, and only when it is too late learn that emigration permits are no longer delivered for their particular country of destination or that they themselves do not fulfil the conditions of admission. Most post-war legislation therefore forbids the supply of information to emigrants for profit and there is an increasing tendency on the part of emigration countries to prohibit all propaganda. The information which, on the other hand, private agencies may furnish to migrants is subject to strict control ' (*302*).

' the cumulative effect of ... [which] while not negligible, is probably not numerically considerable ',[84] illustrates the tendency for governments to place artificial obstacles in the way of any spontaneous adjustment of demographic disequilibria through emigration.

' In addition to the obstacles ... [set up against emigration] by administrative formalities and the revival of the passport system ... the State subjects the departure of emigrants to a whole series of control measures which may, in some cases, go to the extent of definite refusal. In any case, the State is to-day exerting every effort not to lose such of its nationals whose temporary absence it is obliged to sanction for reasons of necessity. It consents to *lend* them but not to *give* them to a foreign country. It intends to keep an intellectual, moral, political and cultural hold over them ... It opposes any attempt aiming at the systematic denationalisation of its nationals living abroad and claims, on their behalf, all the amenities of a national life : schools, associations, trade unions, theatres, newspapers, the free use of the national language, ministers of religion, etc. This, for example, is the spirit actuating the Italian Government, which has, in a way, banished the word " emigration " from its official vocabulary and replaced the Emigration Department of the Ministry of Foreign Affairs by the Department for Italian Citizens Abroad. This has always been more or less the policy of Germany : the maintenance of German nationality for her nationals naturalised abroad. Poland has frequently formulated a similar opinion ' :[124] [a]

Emigration is a necessity ... But the countries of emigration, after having submitted to the dire obligation of having to authorise it..., now consider it their duty — dictated by their moral and material responsibility — to develop the maximum energy and efforts to mitigate the evils and essential risks of emigration ... In particular, if absolute loyalty to and moral assimilation in the social life of the country of immigration constitute duties for the emigrant, there can be nothing in common between this and the direct or indirect pressure brought to bear on emigrants with the idea of depriving them as rapidly as possible of their national characteristics or religious beliefs ... Recognition of the right of large groups of foreign workers to

---

[a] This attitude is not, of course, confined to the " dissatisfied " countries : ' It would be a bad day for our British people ', states the late Anglican Bishop in Argentina, ' if the nationalism which ... [is] running riot throughout the world ever prohibited the [English] schools [in Latin America] from being conducted in the English language ' (247).

have their own infirmaries, schools and cultural institutions, compatible with their character and national traits, is a postulate that should be freely accepted and loyally applied by the countries of immigration.[125]

'Organised emigration is a veritable drain on the life-blood and economy of a nation. In principle, it should be the ultimate remedy for the evils of overpopulation, at least in countries whose emigrants . . . have no national colonies to go to and who, for the most part, are obliged to expatriate themselves. Economic, national and racial considerations demand that the overflow of the population should be afforded opportunities to go on living in the country even up to, or beyond, the point when practical possibilities are exhausted '.[150]

It is, however, ' only in Italy and Russia[a] that really serious obstacles to emigration exist '.[84] Some of the measures taken by the Italian government have already been mentioned.[b] 'In 1927 regulations were imposed in Italy which laid down that Italian subjects could not leave with the intention of settling abroad unless they were going to join a near relative or possessed a contract of employment. This did not apply to certain classes of professional workers, but it meant that the permanent emigration of unskilled workers was rendered very difficult; the effect of these measures is shown in the drop in Italian emigration in 1927, 1928 and 1929 '.[84] [c] Furthermore, as was stated in an earlier chapter,[d] 'the emigration of families and women was restricted . . . while the emigration of agricultural workers was prohibited '.[117]

(b) PSYCHOLOGICAL OBSTACLES

The foregoing sketch of some of the principal obstacles to emigration may be summarised in a few words. In the traditional countries of immigration the front doors are closed to Japanese emigrants and European emigrants find that they are so slightly ajar that only the

---

[a] ' It would appear that the conditions under which passports are granted in Russia are so strict that there is what amounts to a prohibition upon leaving that country, at least for the ordinary worker ' (84).

[b] See above, chap. 5, § VI.

[c] ' In 1930, however, the regulations were relaxed and the number of emigrants rose sharply ' (84).

[d] See above, p. 160.

thinnest stream can get by,[a] while the side doors can be reached only by a circuitous route which none but the desperate or the pertinacious would care to enter and through which only a few of these can hope to penetrate. Italy, moreover, has barred its own exit by erecting a new principle of politics that expatriation and denationalisation are virtually treasonable. Furthermore, whereas emigration was formerly left to individual initiative, it is now controlled and limited by the state.

These, however, are only the more obvious impediments to the emigratory flow. Apart from the artificial obstacles due to the intervention of governmental measures, a serious difficulty arises out of the attitude of the potential emigrant himself. It is broadly true to say that, before 1914, large numbers of persons in many countries were willing candidates for expatriation. Some were driven by an urge to live under conditions of greater political or religious freedom; others, by grinding poverty[b]; others, again, by the spirit of enterprise. They were not held back by the prospect of discomfort, uncertainty and peril.[c] ' Many of them attached but little importance to a change of nationality; they preferred the opportunity offered to them of improving their lot under another flag to the hopeless life of their own country '.[240] Nowadays potential emigrants ' are less willing than in old days to plunge into the emigration stream, with the vague hope of getting some-

---

[a] According to a speaker at one of the Conference's meetings, Russia, in contrast with these countries, ' actually welcomes immigration ' (203). On the other hand, the author of a Conference memorandum on Austrian emigration states that ' emigration to the U.S.S.R. has become quite negligible; whereas in former years people finding employment in Russia often amounted to more than a thousand a year, at the moment only very occasionally are emigrants to Russia heard of. This is caused by the fact that Russian industry disposes of a sufficient number of qualified workmen and has no longer to rely on supplies from abroad. A suitable amount of workmen has been trained by skilled foreign workers in various branches of industry ' (79). Cf. 61 : — ' Immigration from abroad into USSR has been insignificant and mostly across the Asiatic frontier. The Bolsheviks have always offered asylum to political refugees. Foreign skilled workers also have been welcomed and automatically granted political rights (to vote and be elected to the Soviets). The peculiarity of the Soviet system requires that such immigrants fit into socialist society, and share in its future, which is to forego easy return to their homelands. The most likely immigrants, from the ideological point of view, would be from the Asiatic border countries. Other than the Chinese, Asiatic immigrants generally lack industrial skill. Nevertheless, it is probable that the bars to immigration from abroad would be lowered on the Asiatic frontier before they would on the European '.

[b] ' When people were poorer than they are now, they were willing to be shifted about the world rather like cattle and to accommodate themselves to whatever they found. With a rising standard of living and education, they find it more difficult to do this without encouragement, and, unfortunately, owing to the increase of what many people think of as pseudo-scientific racial theories that encouragement is less forthcoming than formerly ' (196).

[c] ' It is said that only a century ago one emigrant in ten failed to survive the journey ' (344).

where; they are coming to demand a more modern form of transportation, some vessel which will land them at a given spot where a welcome and a job await them '.[84] [a]   Indeed, the reluctance to leave home today is so great in some countries that, for example, a revival of migration for settlement is regarded as obtainable ' only in the measure in which it is found possible to develop and multiply organisations prepared to invest the necesssary capital, granting sufficiently long periods for repayment, and *able to create in the settler's mind the certainty that every effort will be made to ensure his success* ';[b] only in this way is it thought that ' a new impetus may be given to settlement and migration movements '.[303]

* * *

The tide of emigration is thus hemmed in by so strong a combination of obstructions that it seems futile to seek in this direction a remedy for the postulated demographic ailments of the " dissatisfied " countries.   Setting aside the partial but obvious checks to emigration attributable to the restrictions imposed by the countries of emigration and to the psychological change in the attitude of the potential emigrant, it does not follow, however, that the artificial barriers to immigration have been responsible for the constriction of the volume and the slowing up of the pace of emigration; they do not suffice to explain, not merely the relative insignificance of the outward movement, but the recent reversal of migratory movements.   The mere existence of a barricade does not necessarily indicate that anyone is pressing behind it or that, if it were pulled down, the breach would be instantaneously flooded under a tide of migration so ample as to give genuine relief to bursting populations.   New habits may have been formed and it may be that other factors have also been at work and have contributed to the constriction of the migratory movement.   It has been thought, for example, that the reduction of immigration into Canada from about 150,000 in 1927 and 1928 and about 165,000 in 1929 and 1930 to 27,550 in 1931 and to 11,000 in 1935 may have been due as much to the economic

---

[a] For reasons which are stated below (pp. 260-262), the refugee problem must be ignored in this Survey.   But it is pertinent to observe here that, even before 1914, when the emigratory movement was untramelled, a substantial proportion of overseas emigrants were Jews, who are historically more mobile than other peoples. According to the League of Nations High Commissioner for Refugees from Germany, ' before the war, an average of 100,000 Jews left Europe each year for North America and South America ' (*326*).

[b] The writer's italics.

depression as to the initiation in August 1930 of a policy of restriction.[102]
It is possible, indeed, that the need for emigration has gone and that
the condition of pressure of population in the " dissatisfied " countries
which was premised at the beginning of this chapter is, in fact, as
fictitious as has been suggested throughout this Survey.

On the other hand, it is self-evident that no revival of emigration
is possible unless the present impediments are removed. Since an
elimination of the obstacles might not be feasible except in the light of
knowledge of the motives which led to their erection, the next two
sections will be devoted to a rapid sketch of the reasons which have
impelled the immigration countries to protect themselves against an
actual or threatened, real or conjectural, invasion of immigrants from
Germany, Italy, Japan and Poland, and to the circumstances which have
brought about a limitation of the potential flow of emigration in the
emigration countries themselves.

III. THE FRONTIERS OF HOSPITALITY

As the foregoing account of the artificial impediments to freedom
of migration has shown, ' men are free neither to come nor to go.
But they are more free to go, that is to leave the country of which they
are nationals, than to come, that is to enter a country in which they
are aliens '.[84] Attention may be turned first, therefore, to the obstacles
to immigration; the barriers to emigration will be considered in the
next section.

* * *

It may seem strange that, ' at a time when ', as was indicated in
an earlier chapter,[a] ' additions to population by way of a surplus of
births over deaths in the European countries overseas are diminishing ',
these countries should place ' obstacles ... in the way of immigrants;
for, if the population of these countries is to continue to increase, more
reliance must be placed upon immigration in the future than in the past.
It is not the case, however, that, when this policy was initiated, the
likelihood of a serious diminution in the rate of natural increase was
anticipated even by those in the best position to judge '. On the

<hr>

[a] See above, pp. 112-3.

contrary, ' so far as the future course of population was in mind at all, a belief was prevalent that immigration added nothing to population. This belief, so opposed to common sense, was put forward . . . [on the ground that], "instead of constituting a new reinforcement to the population, [it] simply results in a replacement of native by foreign elements ".[a]   In other words . . ., the arrival of immigrants causes the birth-rate of natives to fall, and the loss by decrease in births thus brought about is as large as the gain by new arrivals from overseas '.[84]   Thus a Canadian author[104] ' has advanced the view that the marked decline in the French-Canadian birth-rate following 1840, as well as the concurrent French-Canadian exodus to the United States, was in part attributable to the great influx of immigrants from Great Britain; and the belief is held by some that the heavy immigration from Continental Europe has contributed to the decline of the Anglo-Saxon birth rate in Canada since the beginning of the present century '.[102]   From the point of view of those who believed in this theory, therefore, the imposition of immigration restrictions in countries faced with the prospect of diminishing populations was not paradoxical; on the contrary, it must have seemed to them a legitimate measure of defence against the danger of the replacement of native by foreign stocks. ' Just what part, if any, immigration has had in reducing the native birth rate . . . [in North America] will probably never be precisely determined, but . . .[the author of one of the studies submitted to the International Studies Conference][84] seems to have exploded the notion that the decline which occurred in the United States was large enough to offset the additions to the population of that country through immigration '.[102]

' It is quite possible ', he writes, ' that in certain places the arrival of immigrants has depressed the birth-rate; it is not easy to prove this, but it is also impossible to show that immigration never has this result.[b]

---

[a] This was the opinion of General Francis A. Walker, an official of the United States census bureau and, at that time, ' the leading authority in the field of Federal statistics '. He opposed the view that, for instance, ' the rush of Europeans in large numbers to North America was responsible for the remarkable development of that continent in so short a space of time ' (*167*).

[b] ' That theory had its value as a challenge of the current belief that immigration regularly increased the population by an amount equal to its number. But it is almost equally incorrect to maintain that it did not increase the population at all. In view of the meagre evidence obtainable about the growth of population in the United States in the earlier part of the nineteenth century, it may be doubted whether it will ever be possible to determine where between these two extreme views, both of them apparently incorrect, the truth actually lies ' (*171*).

On the other hand, it is easy to show that the birth-rate in the United States has not fallen to the extent demanded by the theory. An estimate has been made of the American birth-rate at the beginning of each decade since 1800, and we can calculate how many births would have occurred if the birth-rate had remained at that level throughout each decade. By subtracting the actual number of births from the number which would have taken place on this assumption, we discover the decennial loss due to the decline in the birth-rate. It can be shown that in every decade since 1830 the gain by immigration has been larger than this loss. Therefore, even if the whole of the decline in the birth-rate was due to immigration, there was still a net gain from that source. But quite obviously the decline in the American birth-rate was not due wholly, or even chiefly, to the effect of immigration; for in the main it was due to the same causes which have led to a decline in other countries of European civilization. It follows that, even if immigration does at times depress the birth-rate, the result is of small importance, and that, generally speaking, immigration increases population. Thus the common-sense view is correct '.[84]

'In the case of Canada, however, one does not have to take into account any reduction in fertility rates to demonstrate that over the past 80 years as a whole, losses of native Canadians through emigration to the United States and other countries have exceeded gains through immigration; or, to put it in other words, to demonstrate that if there had been no emigration the Canadian population would be at least as large as, and probably larger than, it is to-day even if there had been no immigration from abroad '.[102 a]

It is, in fact, precisely because it is now widely believed that immigration does increase the population that restrictions have been imposed. It is, moreover, always possible that, notwithstanding the present diminishing rate of acceleration of population growth in the European countries overseas, the birth-rate may recover. In Canada, for example, 'there is evidence to show that in the decade of rapid expansion between 1901 and 1911, there occurred a significant increase in the birth-rate of native Canadians;[106] and of an estimated fall of

a '[In the 80 years 1851-1931], 1,740,000 Canadian-born left Canada for the United States, or, if we allow for Canadians who returned after residence in the United States, about 2,250,000 ... It is interesting further to note that the increase in population in the 80 years due to immigration was 1,844,000 and that this about balanced the loss of Canadians to the United States ' (102, quoting from the findings in 105).

16

14.4 per cent in the Canadian birth-rate between 1921 and 1931, as reflected by the ratio of children [in the] 0-4 [inclusive age-group] to women [in the] 15-44 inclusive [age-group], over two-thirds was attributable to less favourable age distribution and delayed marriage. Half of the total decline was attributable to the latter cause alone.[103] With the restoration of prosperity and relief from undue pressure of immigrant competition, some recovery in fertility might reasonably be expected in so far as the decline was attributable to the economic inability to support a home '.[102]

Nevertheless, although it is now generally recognised that immigration increases the population, it is not always publicly admitted; the exploded theory that immigration adds nothing to the population is still used in the agitation for restricting immigration. [a]

* * *

There are two specific grounds on which an increase of population through immigration is resisted. (i) The one is economic and is commonly urged by powerful sectional interests; (ii) the other is social and is usually represented as an emanation of the community as a whole. They may both be illustrated mainly from the American history of immigration restrictions, since it is to the United States that the greatest volume of emigration has flowed in the past.

(i) ' Towards the end of the last century the supply of free land, of a quality that made it desirable for settlement, began to run short in the United States; the same thing happened in Canada at a later date . . . As the process of land settlement came to an end and as industry developed, a larger proportion of immigrants . . . found employment in the towns. Organization of labour followed the expansion of industry, and the aim of trade unionism . . . was to safeguard and raise wages. The most obvious method of attaining this end in the new countries was to reduce the supply of labour by cutting down immigration and so putting up wages . . . To a very considerable extent in all the new countries the restriction of immigration has been due to the political activities of organized labour '.[84] [b]   In the United States, in particular,

[a] Cf. 84 : — ' It is only possible to explain the prevalence of a theory so contrary to common sense and so lacking in factual support by supposing that it is used as a ready-made argument with a respectable ancestry wherewith to attack freedom of entry, which is disliked for reasons that cannot be conveniently disclosed '.

[b] ' It was only prudent, of course, not to emphasize the dominant motive unduly and any convenient argument against immigration has been used, such as the Walker theory [see above, p. 224, note a], the supposed flooding of the labour market, and the alleged difficulties which arise from failure of immigrants to become fully assimilated ' (84).

'there has been established ... a sort of "protectionism" of labour. The workers' unions constitute a kind of monopoly against foreign competition, in the same way as protection against the competition of foreign goods by means of customs tariffs is often demanded '.[211]

(ii) But ' the argument most often used to justify restrictive measures is based on the difficulty presented by assimilation. It is alleged that some peoples cannot be assimilated and that others can only be assimilated with difficulty '.[84] Thus, in the United States, ' it is generally believed that the shift from "old" to "new" immigration in the nineties[a] deepened the opposition [to immigration] ... which had manifested itself to greater or less degree since colonial times. The shift occurred while the United States was changing from a relatively static and rural to a complex industrialized and urbanized social order. While it may not have been responsible for the inevitable disturbance resulting from this change, the addition of a large mass of non-English speaking immigrants, most of them peasants or farm labourers and unfamiliar with urban life, did not ease the process of assimilation. Furthermore, by the time the South and East European immigrants arrived on the scene most of the free or cheap land was gone, and they found employment in the industrial centres, usually in the lowest paid occupations and under the worst working conditions. Forced to live in the slum sections of the cities, they came to be identified more or less with these areas of disintegration and with the delinquency and social inadequacy which such areas produce '.[68]

*　*　*

The economic argument in favour of the restriction of immigration springs from a fear in the more prosperous countries that, if their frontiers are left open, they will be flooded by an inflow of immigrants from the poorer countries and that their standard of living will suffer in consequence of a fall in wages. ' In former times, when immigrants came to develop land, the new-comer was considered as some one who was collaborating in the process of clearing and developing it; now he comes as a wage earner and is looked upon as a competitor '.[196] From the point of view of the wage-earners in the prosperous countries, this difficulty is historically justified. ' In the United States since 1890, and later in the Dominions, the inflow, actual or threatened, of southern

[a] See above, p. 211.

and eastern Europeans has endangered the standards of living of the workpeople in these oversea countries. There is no question but that immigrants from these parts will accept, for a time at least, lower wages than the native-born consider reasonable. The latter have every right to attempt to safeguard themselves '.[84] It is arguable, on the other hand, that the sectional interests of labour do not necessarily coincide with the general interests of the community as a whole, and it is undoubtedly ' a distinguishing feature of advanced communities with complex economic organizations that sectional interests are frequently able to secure mass support from majorities of voters who are unable to see that their general interest in national development is at variance with those of aggrieved sections '.[344] The argument runs as follows[344] :

From the point of view of organised labour, there will appear to be an advantage in keeping labour scarce, for scarcity raises prices and the price of labour is wages. Wages will be kept high, therefore, by diminishing the supply of labour. An obvious way of creating or maintaining scarcity in labour and of thereby defending labour's sectional interest in high wages is to prevent immigration. From the point of view of the community as a whole, however, there can be no advantage in creating a scarcity : on the contrary, every increase in plenty is an increase in prosperity. A shortage in labour resulting in higher wages will attract an inflow of labour from outside. Their arrival reduces a scarcity and thereby raises the general standard of life. This advantage to the general electorate, however, is not so clear to them as the concomitant disadvantage to labour is clear to the latter. ' The benefit is diffused in lower costs and a higher general standard of life, while the disappointment of that section which hoped to do well out of the previous scarcity is concentrated and brought energetically to the public's notice. It is not generally realized that every increase in plenty while raising general standard, will damage those sectional interests which are vested in scarcity. Sympathy with sectional loss is more widespread than appreciation of general interest. The benefits from immigrant labour are, after all, very much like those from the introduction of labour-saving machinery. Such machinery undercuts the wages of the existing workers, who have to get other jobs or accept lower money wages, but it makes the product more plentiful and releases resources for other production, raising thereby the general standard of life '.[344] The validity of this argument largely rests, of course, upon the content of the notion of a " sectional " interest. If the section represents, for example, a major industry, the interests of the section may tend to approximate to the interests of the community as a whole. Thus 'anyone who has the slightest knowledge of the economic distress of the American farmer will know that there would be no alleviation of international tension by allowing a greater degree of intensification of the agricultural distress . . . by sending more farmers to the United States '.[206] Again, ' it is . . . possible to imagine conditions in which a whole community shares a monopoly advantage, in the form of some unique local resource which it exchanges on remunerative terms with buyers outside its boundaries, and in which the entire population might rightly conceive their own interest to demand the exclusion of all immigrants '.[344] In such a case, immigration would make the community worse off. It is clear that the true remedy for the undercutting of wages, however, ' is not mere restriction of numbers, but some system under which undercutting is prevented '.[84] [a] Moreover, it was submitted to the International Studies Conference that the argument upon which the ' demand for the protection of labour is founded . . ., [namely], that labour always competes with labour, and that there results a lowering of wages and of the standard of life in the countries of immigration . . ., [is] partially false '.[211] This result, it was claimed, does not always occur. ' There are, in fact, various categories of labour, which are complementary to each other, which need each other, and which co-operate in the work of production . . . Thus certain low-paid work is often done by immigrants. This was the case, for example, of Polish workers, who immigrated into Germany and the United States. The law of Jean-Baptiste Say, concerning outlets for the exchange of goods, is the basis of liberalism, and an analogous law, concerning the movement of human labour, would be the basis of real liberalism in questions of migration '.[211] The argument was also put forward that, ' from the point of view of peaceful change, however, it cannot be admitted that the maintenance of the standard of living in these countries is the supreme factor that should govern any international population policy ', and that ' it is one of the principles of international justice that the situation of the country of emigration must also be taken into consideration and that an endeavour should be made to arrive at a compromise, that an attempt should be made to bring the

---

[a] The prevention of undercutting is one of the chief objects of the bi-lateral treaties and conventions regulating the collective recruitment and transport of workers which a number of countries have concluded since the war. They are discussed in *84* and in *167*.

standard of living of backward emigration countries into line with that of the developed immigration countries '.[197]   This argument, however, does not meet the sectional objections of organised labour; its effect is merely to place the whole question on a broader basis, and it may be doubted whether, in the present state of international relations, it will carry conviction in those American circles whose attitude has been influential in determining the imposition of immigration restrictions. Moreover, it should be borne in mind that the general attitude of mind in the United States must be coloured by the rise and fall of the curve of prosperity.   On the whole, until the onset of the " depression " in 1929, it was ' quite generally accepted that the supply of unskilled labour made available by mass immigration has been an important factor in the economic development of the country '; but, ' the wide-spread unemployment which followed is generally believed to indicate that immigration is no longer needed for economic development, and there is no doubt that at present at least, popular sentiment is in favour of drastic reductions.   Whether this sentiment will prevail indefinitely it is impossible to foretell '.[68]   Furthermore, although, in the countries of immigration, ' it is obviously possible to point to unused resources . . . which are physically capable of supporting subsistence cultivators at a higher economic level than they are able to reach in certain over-populated countries ', does it follow that they are ' bound to throw these lands open to settlement ' ?[102]   To this question the author of a memorandum on the position in Canada replies that ' most Canadians would say " No ".   They would contend that it is their legal right and the cherished aspiration to maintain and, if possible, raise the material standard of living of the mass of the Canadian people, and that they owe no such duty to foreigners.   They would point out that two standards of living cannot exist side by side for workers in a democratic country like Canada, where choice of occupation is free, where all are entitled to compete for any employment that is offered, and where the movement of citizens from place to place and from employment to employment is and must continue to be unrestricted '.[102]

* * *

The justification of immigration restrictions on the ground that the problem of assimilation raises acute difficulties ' implies the belief that the average representatives of different peoples are unlike, that in some cases the unlikeness persists and that in others it only passes away after a considerable period '.[84]   This belief is expressed, in its extreme form, in ' the race prejudices which, in certain countries represent insuperable obstacles.   Thus the immigration of Asiatics, African negroes, Jews, Levantines, is prohibited, if not explicitly, at least in practice, in certain countries which seek to form a homogeneous nation, composed exclusively of ethnic elements of European origin.   This selection of emigrants constitutes a preventive measure on which the success of every immigration and colonization policy depends '.[83]

When the barriers of prejudice are lowered, it is found that the differences between peoples ' may have their roots either in unlike genetic constitutions or in unlike acquirements, or of course in both at the same time '.[84]   As to the former, the following inferences were drawn from a consideration of genetic physical[a] and mental (intelligence[b] and temperament[c]) differences in one of the studies submitted to the International Studies Conference :[84]

The government of any country has not only the right but also the duty to attempt to ensure that the composition of the population is such that harmonious co-operation is possible between all its elements.   It may be urged that harmony does not demand uniformity and that diversity is a source of vitality.   While this is true, it is also clear that diversity may be such as to render harmony impossible; if this is so, members of diversely gifted groups should remain geographically separate.   There is at least a sufficient possibility that diversities of this kind may exist as to make it doubtful whether the mingling of members of the major groups of mankind in one community is wise.   In other words governments of European oversea countries are entitled to hesitate before they permit the entry of non-Europeans.[84]

[a] ' Unions between all the major groups of mankind are fertile.   As to the implications of so-called racial mixture it is perhaps enough to say that mixture in itself is neither good nor bad; the results depend upon what is put into it . . .   Though there are no grounds for exclusion or discrimination directly on account of . . . genetic physical differences between the average representatives of the major groups of mankind . . ., their existence is indirectly of some importance in relation to the question of assimilation.   For until a physically demarcated group loses its identity through intermarriage, the members are conscious of the possession of common characteristics.   This fact hinders assimilation and makes complete assimilation unlikely, though it does not render it impossible ' (*84*).   ' La vérité ', said Renan, ' est qu'il n'y a pas de race pure. Les pays les plus nobles, l'Angleterre, la France, l'Italie, sont ceux où le sang est le plus mêlé, (quoted in *117*).

[b] ' So far . . . as the evidence derived from intelligence tests goes, there is no reason whatever to suspect the existence of differences in intelligence between the major groups of mankind, with the possible exception of Africans ' (*84*).

[c] ' We observe the enduring differences between the English and the Irish, we can investigate the profoundly interesting evidence offered by the presence of a hundred thousand Japanese in the midst of American civilization; we can ask ourselves why Jewish characteristics remain distinguishable ' (*84*).

As to the acquired differences, ' the immigrants themselves . . ., however anxious they may be to turn themselves into typical citizens in the country of their choice,[a] can never shed all that they acquired in the country of their birth. Thus there is a case for ensuring that unassimilated immigrants do not form too large a fraction of the population. Again, while the complete assimilation of the children is theoretically possible, it does not happen in practice; for alien traditions linger in the households of foreign-born parents. This strengthens the case for regulation . . . Assimilation takes time, and it is proper that the inflow should be restricted to allow sufficient time '.[84] It was partly on this ground that the United States, for example, adopted their policy of cultural exclusion. ' There was a growing feeling that the United States has not been able to absorb and make wholly American the vast multitude of the million immigrants a year coming in just before the war . . . [There are] areas in the United States that are definitely foreign, and while that may increase the interest of . . . [America's] social problems, it also increased the difficulty of the economic, social and moral life of the nation '.[206]

' Since the early days of immigration the people of the United States have customarily regarded the immigrant group which has most recently arrived as the least desirable. The characteristics cited in the early eighteenth century as proof of the undesirability and unassimilability of German immigrants have successively been attributed to Irish immigrants, to South and East European immigrants, and to Mexican immigrants. As the economic situation of such immigrant groups has improved and their " Americanization " has progressed, prejudice against them has gradually subsided. It is probably safe to say that most misgivings about immigration have at all periods of our history been concerned with the social assimilability of immigrants and their alleged criminality and pauperism . . .[b] The World War, with the flare-up of nationalism which accompanied it in the United States

[a] Cf. below, p. 237.
[b] The foreign-born population of the United States are often charged also with a propensity to mental deficiency disproportionate to their numbers. Although the statistics are inadequate and incomplete, such as they are ' they are not indicative of the relative prevalence of feeble mindedness among nativity groups but of the relative extent of institutional care afforded ' (70).

According to recent statistics on inmates of the lunatic asylums in the Department of the Seine, it would appear that mental deficiency is relatively much more frequent among the foreign than among the native population of France (see 339; according to 338, mental patients in France are ' mostly of Slav or Jewish origin ').

as in most other countries, crystallized opposition to further immigration and led to a demand for the " Americanization " of the foreign-born already there. '[68] As to the charges of excessive criminality of the foreign-born, they ' are made in spite of what is generally conceded to be clear proof to the contrary. A number of important, scientifically conducted investigations of the subject have convinced most people that in the words of the so-called Wickersham Commission (1931)[71] in proportion to their respective numbers, the foreign-born commit considerably fewer crimes than the native-born. '[68] As to the alleged pauperism of the foreign-born, reliable statistics are lacking and the available evidence appears to be conflicting.[68]

* * *

This description of immigration restrictions may be summarised by saying that ' it is not only the right but also the duty of the government of any country to regulate immigration on two grounds. In the first place it is proper, in order to avoid the waste, friction, and disappointment, which are inevitable under the old system of individual, hit-or-miss migration, to substitute a system of collective migration. In the second place it is proper to take such steps, as experience may prove necessary, to ensure that such immigrants as are admitted become assimilated. This may involve limiting the annual volume of immigration, special restrictions upon the entry of members of certain groups because they become assimilated more slowly than others, and exclusion of other groups because they cannot be assimilated '.[84]

Applying these conclusions to the policies of immigration restriction which are now in operation, the author of a study which has been frequently cited in this survey does not find that they can all be justified on those grounds. ' The exclusion of non-Europeans from European countries overseas ', he writes, ' is probably wise because the very different traditions of non-Europeans possibly expressing genetic temperamental differences[a], are likely to be very persistent owing to physical differentiation which makes it unlikely that the process of assimilation can be satisfactorily accomplished. But the restriction of the total volume of immigration, at any rate to the low point fixed by the United States, cannot be justified on the grounds that larger numbers cannot be absorbed by the normal expansion of the opportunities for employment.

[a] Cf. above, p. 231.

Nor can the virtual exclusion of southern and eastern Europeans from the United States and the British Dominions (Canada is somewhat more liberal than the other countries mentioned) be fully justified on the ground of the difficulty of assimilation. The action of these countries can partly be explained as due to genuine misapprehension as, for instance, the belief that, when inflow is unregulated, more enter than can be absorbed. But the major part of the explanation is to be sought in motives which are not often openly expressed. Organized labour approves any policy that will make labour scarce; nationalism and the accompanying fear and dislike of foreigners, partly the result and partly the cause of pseudo-scientific " racial " theories, support everything that tends to restriction. Moreover, as is very important to note, the growth of these sentiments itself makes assimilation more difficult; in no small degree, in other words, the assimilation difficulty, which troubles those who are of this frame of mind, is their own creation '.[84]

This argument is not accepted, however, by the author of a memorandum submitted to the International Studies Conference from Canada. Apart from the ' historical major cleavage in the basic population itself — that between the French and the English . . ., [who], contrary to early expectations . . ., have not fused ',[a] he states that ' assimilation between the dominant Anglo-Saxon population outside Quebec and many classes of European immigrant has proved equally difficult, and [that] of all classes of European immigrant the least easy to assimilate are the South, Eastern, and Central Europeans '. He considers that, ' during the first three decades of the present century, immigration which is neither Anglo-Saxon nor French has been far in excess of the social assimilative capacity of both Canada and the United States ', and he declares that any influx of foreign immigrants on a scale bearing an apt quantitative relationship to the annual surplus of births over deaths in the countries of emigration ' would be regarded both in Canada and in the United States as greatly exceeding their social assimilative ability

[a] Cf. *107* : — ' Conflict between nations arises not only from economic causes, but from cultural and ideological friction. In Canada there is an analogy for this as well as for the economic conflict . . . To-day it is probable that among the rank and file of the people hostility and bitterness are as great as, if not greater than, ever before . . . Moreover, the growth of the French population relative to that of the English in Quebec, New Brunswick, and parts of Ontario, has led to exacerbation of feeling and to fear on the part of the English that their standards of living will be lowered, and that the French will become the dominant race. This fear breeds intolerance and hostility. It is doubtful if we can say with any confidence that Canada has today solved the problem of getting peoples of different race, religion and culture to live together peacefully and tolerantly '.

and on that score alone must be ruled out as a possible solution for the overpopulation problem in certain European countries by means of peaceful change '. ' Surely ', he protests, ' Europe has had enough experience with the difficulties engendered by the presence of unassimilated minorities in the Balkans and elsewhere to appreciate the nature of the problems of social assimilation facing the two newly-settled countries on the north American Continent '.[102] [a]

* * *

No attempt can be made here to survey the wide diversity of methods which have been adopted, and the still greater variety of methods which have been suggested, to facilitate assimilation by attenuating the social disharmony caused by the introduction of alien elements into a homogeneous society. They differ from country to country and from case to case. Nowhere, perhaps, have the processes of assimilation been more successful than in France, where, it would seem, an active policy of denationalisation has been eschewed in favour of a régime of liberty and *laisser faire*. ' The unsuccessful attempts which have been made to " Russianise " or " Germanise " the Poles are well known; these failures give all the more importance to the assimilation of these same Poles in the democratic countries of the United States and France. The explanation lies in the fact that, in all psychological matters, compulsion can never bring about what collaboration alone achieves. The same principles operate here as in teaching, where the best methods are those which respect the natural development of the child and which lead him to take an active share in his own education instead of forcing him to learn. The most suit-

---

[a] An appeal of this sort will be robbed of some of its rhetorical effect if it is admitted that, ' in the matter of assimilation, a distinction must be made between two processes '. On the one hand there is the case where ' different races inhabit the same territory ' and where ' assimilation is generally the result of the pressure which one of these races exerts upon the others to ensure a hegemony and to acquire further territory '. On the other hand, ' there is the case where ' a territory inhabited by a population speaking one language receives a contingent of immigrants whose native country is very distant and whose civilisation is of a lower standard '. In such cases ' assimilation is a natural process which is completed in the course of a few generations and gives rise to no territorial conquest, one of the reasons being that the immigrants settle in a country far distant from their native land ' (*126*). If assimilation in the Balkans falls in the first category and assimilation in North America in the second, no analogy can be found in the Balkans for the problem of assimilation in America. It is to be noted, however, that ' the best and soundest' type of immigration from the point of view of assimilation is the ' frontier immigration ', the ' osmotic immigration ' (*117*), which is a notable feature of immigration in countries like France.

able course, therefore, is to let the natural forces of attraction exert their own influence, to develop them and to protect them if necessary against contrary policies '.[117] It is possible, however, that the gentler processes of assimilation which flow from a spirit of liberalism and an attitude of toleration can be successful only in those countries which enjoy the prestige of a higher culture and greater material wealth.[117] Moreover, even in France, a feeling has grown of late that a system of careful selection and regulation of entry may have to replace the open hospitality of the past;[a] and the Prefect of the Department of Seine-et-Oise has apparently found good cause to warn the large numbers of foreigners residing in his area of jurisdiction that they are forbidden to interfere in French politics.[b]

Thus it transpires from an inspection of the motives which have led to the imposition of artificial impediments to emigration by the countries of immigration that the development of a stream of emigration from Germany, Italy, Poland and Japan on a scale comparable with the anticipated annual growth of the population of those countries would imply a radical transformation of the policies of governments. From the point of view of political possibilities, no such reversal of policy can be expected in the near future. It is not safe to anticipate that, in the event of a restoration of prosperity to the standard in force prior to the imposition of the present restrictions, the artificial obstacles to immigration will be removed; for ' reduction of the volume of emigration is a popular policy . . . [and] there may be a reluctance to relax . . . [the] restrictions and to permit even that volume of immigration which was taking place before they were imposed '.[84]

IV. THE END OF EXPATRIATION

It was explained in the second section of this chapter that the obstacles to emigration arise not only out of the restrictions on immigration but also out of a change of attitude on the part of the potential

---

[a] Cf., e. g., the decrees of May and November 1938 governing the position of foreigners in France. For a discussion of the implications of the decree of May 2, 1938, see *337*.

[b] In November 1938, he caused the following notice to be posted up in all the towns and communes under his jurisdiction : ' Foreigners residing in the department of Seine-et-Oise are required to observe the recommendation already addressed to them by the Government, by rigorously abstaining from taking part in any conflicts of opinion which may arise between French citizens, and from participating in any political demonstrations, particularly on the public highway. Any foreigner contravening these orders will expose himself to measures of expulsion ' (*238*).

emigrant himself, on the one hand, and out of a system of state regulation in the countries of emigration, on the other hand. As to the former, many proposals have been made with a view to turning the potential emigrant into an intending emigrant and the intending emigrant into an active emigrant; they are amply treated in the publications of the International Labour Office. As to the latter it is not suggested by anyone that the system of state regulation of emigration which has been developed since the war should be abolished and that a return should be made to the uncontrolled system in operation before 1914.

Apart from these two forms of impediment to emigration arising in the countries of emigration, a new obstacle to emigration has been created as a result of the policies of certain countries of emigration. ' For the most part, until the last few years ..., [the alien immigrant] was almost pathetically anxious ... [to assimilate himself rapidly to his new surroundings]. But things have changed with the rise of aggressive nationalism; and the change is all the more significant when it is fostered by the action of governments '.[84]

The nature of this action, and particularly of that taken by Italy, having already been described,[a] it is enough here to echo the view that ' it is evidently true to say that the object of the Italian government is to hinder or prevent assimilation '.[84] Imperialistic tendencies of this kind have not diminished the anxieties of those who fear massive immigration on the ground of assimilation difficulties. On the contrary, the effect on the attitude of countries of immigration of a policy of regarding emigrants as subject exclusively to the authority of their country of origin has been to stiffen opposition to their admission and to close the doors of entry even more securely. Even those countries which are disposed to welcome an inflow of settlers or of industrial labour now hesitate to run the risk of resorting to an operation calculated to lead to the establishment of foreign enclaves on their territories. Thus Brazil, said a speaker at one of the International Studies Conference's meetings, although ' incontestably an underpopulated country ..., was recently obliged to restrict immigration, not because of economic or financial difficulties but for psychological and, in certain respects, social reasons. These measures are, in a way, the result of instinctive self-defence and of observation of what has happened in the past. Brazil has received a large number of immigrants : Italians, Poles, Germans, Portuguese and, quite recently, a few Japanese ...

---

[a] See above, pp. 219-220.

[She] had to ask . . . [herself] whether, apart from the material contribution to labour they represented, these immigrants would be of value from the cultural and economic standpoint. They had emigrated owing to the high demographic pressure and low standard of living in their own country. These immigrants, however, compete with the native population, which has certain obligations to fulfil — military service, political responsibilities, etc. — with the result that, since they have no such obligations, they reduce the standard of living still further. Again, Brazil has always shown the utmost hospitality towards foreigners, but she does not wish these immigrants to form " cysts " in the country, which might become centres of economic or social difficulties. When a fairly large area of territory is occupied by immigrants of the same nationality, whose numbers increase as children are born and as more immigrants from the same country arrive, a sort of acquired right is established, which soon becomes a source of difficulty for the Brazilian Government. To all intents and purposes, this area is a small part of the foreign country transplanted to Brazilian territory, but without any real fusion with the mass of the national population '.[193]

The fact that ' the legislation of certain countries of emigration seeks to claim the nationality of the sons of emigrants who are settled in the countries of which they themselves consider they form legitimately a part . . . [must give rise to] problems of *jus sanguinis* and of *jus soli* [which] create serious conflicts in international private law '.[83] ' It is essential that some of the emigration countries should change some of their ideas on this subject. I even wonder ', said a Venezuelan speaker at a recent international conference on migration, ' if, in view of the importance taken by the question of population and the necessity of finding a solution for it, jurists will not be forced in the near future to consider whether, in some of its aspects, the law of *jus sanguinis*, all-important in some national laws, is not incompatible with present circumstances '. In his view, ' the existing controversy on the nationality to be retained or acquired by immigrants and their descendants and on the efforts made to impose on them certain links with their native country . . . is one of the most important aspects of the question and one which it is not easy to settle ' : —

Experience shows that the so-called immigration countries are unabel to get over their dislike of seeing compact groups of emigrants establishing themselves on their territory who show no desire to mix with the local population, sometimes even disdain to speak the national language and refuse to send their children to State schools. Such an attitude, it must be admitted, is highly undesirable, the more so as it is a dangerous delusion to endeavour to prolong by artificial means harmful to the nation on whose territory such things occur, the influence of a foreign State on individuals who in the second generation and sometimes even in the first generation at the end of a certain time and when they are left alone, find it in their interests to become part of the local population. A man belongs to the country where he was born and, if no obstacle is put to his education under new surroundings, there can be no nationality problem for him, as in any case he is bound to the country of his parents by various moral, intellectual and even economic ties.[305]

It is, in fact, on the rock of assimilation that the prospect of a revival of mass migration must founder. Insistence on assimilation, on one side, and resistance to assimilation, on the other, set up currents of opposing forces which are not propitious to the smooth flow of a stream of migrants. These ' difficulties of race seem to play a part of ever-increasing importance ';[202] so much so, indeed, that the discussion of migration restrictions cannot be contained within the sphere of demography, but tends inevitably to be ' a mixture of demography and politics '.[206] ' The new ideologies ', writes a Brazilian authority, ' make difficult for those who accept them access to the territories of states having democratic and liberal constitutions with which their régime happens to be in political opposition '.[83]

Thus there is a fundamental conflict of interest between the countries of emigration and the countries of immigration. ' Receiving nations generally endeavour to nationalize immigrants and to assimilate them as a permanent part of the population. The nation of the emigrant, on the other hand, does not like to lose all hold over him, especially if he is still capable of rendering military service to the state '.[55] This conflict gives rise in turn to policies designed to bring the régime of expatriation to an end and to a ' strong desire to provide land under the flag on which the surplus population can settle '.[55] Emigration abroad must be replaced by internal migration, which ' does not result in a loss of the emigrants from the population ',[55] and the scope of internal migration must be extended by the pursuit of policies of territorial expansion designed to secure wider population outlets within the jurisdiction of the congested metropolis. If that policy is successful, the problem of emigration is withdrawn from the

international plane and is transformed into a problem of internal
colonisation. From the point of view of " peaceful change ", therefore,
it is not so much emigration proper which gives rise to international
friction as a policy of territorial expansion contemplated for the purpose
of bringing true emigration to an end — an aspect of the problem
which will be examined in the next chapter.

'One possible way of lessening . . . [the] desire [to provide land
under the flag] would be to provide more adequate safeguards for
immigrant minorities. If nations were prepared to permit immigrants
to retain their nationality and not to try to assimilate them against their
will, the countries from which they migrated might not be so concerned to have them under their own protection . . .; [but] the advantages
of such an arrangement would necessarily have to be weighed against
the problems which it might introduce for the country of immigration '.[55]
There can be little doubt on which side the balance would tip to-day.
Like a speaker at a meeting of the International Studies Conference,
most students of the problem would probably 'be inclined to think
that in the next hundred years the political difficulties in the way of
migration will play a greater part than in the past '.[204] Two principles
of national conduct confront one another : ' on the part of countries
of emigration, to do nothing likely to hinder the adaptation and
assimulation of their emigrants to the populations of the countries of
immigration and, on the contrary, to abstain from any action tending
to consolidate the natural ties which subsist between the emigrant
and his mother country; on the part of countries of immigration, on
the other hand, to do nothing to provoke the compulsory denationalisation of immigrants and to abstain, on the contrary, from taking any
action calculated to hasten their free determination to transform the
country in which they have settled into their country of adoption '.[124]
Each of these reciprocal attitudes is incompatible with the concurrent
satisfaction of contemporary national aspirations both in the countries
of emigration and in the countries of immigration.   If, then, the ultimate
aim of international organisation is to eliminate the sources of international friction, it would seem to follow that, in present circumstances,
wise statesmanship must strive to limit international migratory
movements.

* * *

A desire to prevent assimilation is not, however, the only ground
for a policy of restricting emigration.   Quantitative estimates of the

volume of emigration in the past may be more or less reliable guides to the general magnitude of the movement; qualitative analyses of the composition of the emigratory movements, on the other hand, can be nothing more than rough guesses. There are reasonable grounds for supposing, however, that the emigrant who left his native land in the past was often recruited from the less desirable sections of the community. 'When " remittance men " left England for the Colonies it was for England's good '.[84] Under the modern system of state control of migration, however, the unemployable or sub-normal individual fails to pass through the sieve of migration regulations. Emigration, where it is possible at all, is an outlet available only to the finer types of individual whom the community will strive to keep at home. In a system under which the countries of immigration refuse to receive the dregs of other countries' populations and where the countries of emigration refuse to allow their valuable human resources to leave, none but the cynical can find the marginal room for a substantial flow of emigration.

V. INTERNATIONAL IMMOBILITY

It is now possible to take up again the main thread of the argument. This chapter was opened on the assumption that Germany, Italy, Japan, and Poland are suffering from such intense demographic congestion that they have been led to claim international relief. On this basis, the question was raised whether the population and emigratory movements in those countries are so correlated that the pressure of population might be relieved by a discharge of surplus numbers into other countries. It was found that, notwithstanding the expansion of numbers in those countries, emigration is at a standstill, and an attempt was made to enquire into the causes of the latter phenomenon. It was shown that emigration is impeded by various types of obstacles and it was suggested that there is little prospect of a removal of those obstacles. On the other hand, it was not shown that the artificial barriers to immigration had effectively impeded emigration. It is true that a study of Japanese emigration, for example, tends to show that, if the movement had not been checked by the vigorous measures of exclusion taken in some of the countries in the Pacific, it would have assumed large proportions. Although ' it is, of course, impossible to say what would have happened if entry [into these countries] had been free to non-Europeans . . . [yet] we may hope to discover whether the prospect of a large inflow of non-Europeans was real or imaginary '.[84] In the United States, ' in spite of the virtual prohibition upon immigration since 1907 . . ., the Japanese, who have had their women with them . . ., have increased considerably '.[84] [a] ' The inference is that the United States are attractive to . . . [the Japanese], and that they would have entered in large numbers if they had been allowed to do so. This inference is much strengthened by a study of the Canadian figures[b] . . . [which show] how considerably the Japanese have increased in spite of the Gentlemen's Agreement of 1908 '.[84] It is true, of course, that Japanese emigration before the imposition of restrictions was wholly insignificant, but, as a Japanese speaker pointed out to the International Studies Conference, ' Japan first began to take part in international life only seventy years ago and . . . the country which opened . . . [Japan's] doors and whose climate is the one most favourable to the Japanese, very soon closed its own doors to Japanese emigrants '.[210] It has been conjectured that the western seaboard of America ' would now be the home of millions of Japanese if they had not been prevented from settling '.[84] [c]

Japan, however, is a special case : the restrictions imposed on the immigration of Japanese do not spring from the same motives as those which govern the restriction of European immigration.

In these circumstances the inference that a stream of emigration, strong and ample enough to relieve a genuine condition of population pressure, would be generated if the artificial restrictions on immigration were removed may not be tenable. It is not possible, of course, to give a final answer to a hypothetical question, but it does not seem wholly unreasonable to conjecture that the theoretical consequences of a removal of the artificial restrictions would not occur in practice.

[a] The Japanese population of the United States has grown as follows (see *84*) : — 1890, 2,000; 1900, 24,000; 1910, 72,000; 1920, 111,000; 1930, 139,000. According to another estimate the figures are : 67,744 in 1910; 81,502 in 1920; 70,993 in 1930 (see *172*).

[b] The Japanese population of Canada has grown as follows (see *84*) : — 1901, 4,700; 1911, 9,000; 1921, 15,900; 1931, 23,300.

[c] ' If non-Europeans and especially Asiatics had not been kept out of the United States and the British Dominions they would have entered in very large numbers. By this time the population of the western seaboard of North America would have been largely Asiatic. It seems that Europeans only established themselves in sufficient numbers beyond the Rocky Mountains just in time to be able to secure exclusive possession of this desirable region for themselves ' (*84*). Cf. *109* : — ' The American coast of the Pacific Ocean exerts a magnetic attraction for the yellow race. Owing to their unlimited capacity for work and their low standard of living, they succeed there; and, without doubt, were they allowed to compete freely, they would eventually dominate the western slope of the Rocky Mountains '.

The psychological change in the attitude of the potential emigrant himself alone seems to present an insuperable barrier — in all cases where emigration is not compulsorily forced on a country's citizens[a] — to the development of any powerful flow of emigration.

Moreover, a return to complete freedom of movement is at present inconceivable. In a world in which ' capital and trade have come to be regulated by Governments in a manner formerly unknown and [in which] this regulation is likely to continue, it would seem to follow . . . that migratory movements must come under government regulation also, which means under more than quota restrictions '.[196] But the conclusion of a number of bilateral agreements governing collective migration ' shows that constructive efforts have been made to cope with the migration problem, and it is not the case that government action in this matter is summed up in a lengthy list of restrictions upon the movement of workers. For these agreements contemplate movement and are intended to facilitate it '.[84] In this direction lies the means of a removal of the more irritating obstacles to migration; yet it holds out little hope of a revival of emigration on a scale ample enough to bear relevantly on the solution of a problem of overpopulation.

For what must be the volume of an emigratory stream capable of effectively relieving population pressure ? In the comparison which was made in the opening section of this chapter between the volume of emigration and the size of the population, it was implied that an emigratory flow which does not keep pace with the volume and rate of population expansion cannot be regarded as constituting relief for pressure of population. Indeed, it is obvious that, ' as a remedy of overcrowding . . ., [emigration] would only offer permanent relief in a country of stationary population '.[55] It must be pointed out, however, that, in the context of a study of " peaceful change ", it would be as idle and fantastic as it would be sterile and irrelevant to contemplate a permanent solution. It is only ' from the point of view of the next ten or twenty years . . . [that] we have to look at the matter '.[215 b] It is not permanent relief that is needed, for that would be neither desired nor attainable, but adequate temporary relief of an immediate difficulty. Nevertheless, it is obvious that, if the population is not stationary,

---

[a] Prior to the nineteenth century, important migratory movements were due to mass expulsion. It is believed, for example, that about a quarter of a million Huguenots left France after 1685, and that as many as 20 million Africans were transported to the New World (see *84*).

[b] Cf. *195* : — ' The question . . . is whether and to what extent the countries of immigration can, for a period of ten or twenty years, bring relief to the overpopulated countries '.

even temporary relief will not be adequate unless it is applied continuously and on a substantial scale. In Japan, for example, where
it is estimated, ' from 210,000 to 290,000 men and women come into
the labour market each year to swell the available supply ' and where
this phenomenon ' must be expected to continue for another twenty
years ', it is evident that ' an annual emigration of twenty or fifty
thousand or even a hundred thousand people could not seriously
contribute towards a solution of the population problem '.[363] [a]

It is clear, therefore, that, if emigration is appreciably to counteract during " the next ten or twenty years " such economically deleterious consequences as may flow from the increase in the population
in each of these four countries, it will have to be ' kept up at a high
rate '.[55]

Notwithstanding the difficulties in the way of a removal of the
present obstacles to emigration, it has been authoritatively conjectured
that the emigratory flow will presently revive. Thus, in 1936, the
International Labour Office thought that it might ' be said without
undue exaggeration that the economic recovery, which is now taking
place in many countries, is likely to lead to a modification of the measures
adopted during the depression to restrict the admission of immigrants,
who at that time would not have been able to find employment ';
it was anticipated that ' this period of restriction should be succeeded
by a period of co-operation between those countries which once again
need foreign workers to develop their resources and those which have
a surplus of labour available '.[167]   Again, in 1938, after sounding ' a
certain number of Governments as to their willingness to participate '
in an international conference on migration, the Office felt able to state
that ' the encouraging nature of the response received[b] justified the
hope that the conclusions of the conference will lead to a recovery
of migration for settlement '.[303] [c]   Similarly, in the earlier phases of

[a] The figures of increase in the demand for employment are taken from calculations
made by Professor Uyeda.
[b] The response came from ten " immigration countries " (Argentina, Bolivia, Brazil,
Chile, Colombia, Dominican Republic, Ecuador, Peru, Uruguay and Venezuela) and from eight
" emigration countries " (Austria, Czechoslovakia, Hungary, Japan, Netherlands, Poland,
Switzerland and Yugoslavia). See 303.
[c] Subsequently, the Office again expressed the view that ' migration currents, after
passing through various vicissitudes and being brought almost to a complete standstill
in recent years, have for some time back shown a tendency to revive in many cases ' and that
there are ' signs that public opinion wishes by wise precautions to avoid the risk of being
caught unawares by a possible revival of migration movements among workers ' (302);
but it did not specify the " cases " of a " tendency to revive " nor the " signs " of the wishes
of public opinion.

the International Studies Conference's enquiry, there was some disposition to endorse the view held by ' several of the demographic experts collaborating with the . . . Conference . . . that the time may be ripe for a revival of migratory movements ' and that ' the problem is, therefore, one of actuality '.[48]

It is possible that these judgments may have expressed an acute reading of the trend of international events. It is significant, however, that no definite corroborative evidence supporting these optimistic predictions is to be discovered in the results of the migration conference in Geneva or was adduced in the course of the International Studies Conference's enquiry.[a] On the contrary, such opinions on this question as were expressed at the latter conference all tended to show that there are no reasonable grounds for expecting that any strong movement of emigration can take place within the near future. Thus, a speaker at a meeting of the Conference desired, ' as a historian, to call . . . attention . . . to the fact — one of history as well as of statistics . . . — that only over a limited area of human history have there been migrations of the kind . . . [they were] talking about, i. e. a spreading of the European peoples over the face of the earth. The period — from the era of discoveries to the present day — was relatively very short and one of peculiar quality. Two divisions or sections ', he thought, '[could] be made : one in which Europeans frankly exploited the resources of older civilizations — as in parts of Asia — and another in which they filled the open spaces of the world . . . Looking upon this as a fact of history . . ., [he was] of opinion that both these divisions of the movement of populations . . . [would] be liquidated in the coming period ahead of . . . [them], that they . . . [would] not continue as in the past, and that to address . . . [themselves] to the problem as though there would be a restoration of the old freedom of movement . . . [was] about as practical as to address . . . [themselves] in economics to the bringing back of complete Free Trade '.[206] ' The migratory movement ', another speaker pointed out, ' was an essential part of a much larger process of development in the 19th century, [but] conditions have now changed so as to favour it no longer '.[216] Hence,

---

[a] ' It is . . . not impossible ', wrote the author of one of the International Studies Conference's Canadian memoranda, ' that Canadians may contemplate a vigorous immigration policy. But it will not be a policy of indiscriminate admission. If it is undertaken it will be undertaken for the benefit of Canada and not primarily for the benefit of other countries, and those who advocate it are as insistent as any other Canadians on Canada's right to determine her own immigration policy. Any form of peaceful change which involved renouncing this right would be highly distasteful to Canadians ' (*102*).

' we are not likely ', a third speaker thought, ' to have again the migrations experienced during the last hundred years ';[204] indeed, ' freedom of migration is no longer possible '.[205]

If these expressions of opinion are justified, it would seem that, in the context of " peaceful change " and of national population situations raising problems requiring solutions of an international character, no reliance should be placed upon emigration. Inasmuch as this conclusion is diametrically opposed to the popular belief in the efficacy of emigration as a remedy for overpopulation, it seems desirable, before passing on to other proposed remedies, to return to the point at which the discussion in this chapter began and to consider whether there is any real need for emigration in the " dissatisfied " countries.

Some of the experts who took part in the work of the International Studies Conference were disposed to accept the statement that ' the view . . . that there is practically no further need for emigration . . . is not true, for instance, of Italy, Germany and Poland '.[215] Others, however, were disinclined to endorse this statement without qualification. Moreover, even those who were prepared to admit that ' there certainly exists in the world a need for what is called excess population to emigrate ', made a point of enquiring whether, ' as a counterpart to this need . . ., there . . . are possibilities for this excess population to establish itself elsewhere '.[217] This question will be considered later; here it must be pointed out that, even if it can be demonstrated that emigration is a suitable remedy for redundant population, it would still be necessary to show, in the narrower context of the International Studies Conference's enquiry into the problem of " peaceful change " that there are genuine current claims for relief from overcrowding calling for consideration. Yet, as has been stressed repeatedly in this Survey, the evidence of the reality of any such claims is so tenuous that the effective relationship between the Conference's enquiry into the value of colonies, for example, from the point of view of an inflow of immigrants and concrete cases of dissatisfaction dwindles into insignificance. For ' who ', enquired a speaker at a meeting of the Conference, ' are the claimants ? We have been told ', he said, ' that at the present moment Italy is satisfied. The Duce, speaking for her, has declared, in an interview granted to Mr. Ward Price of the *Daily Mail,* that she was satisfied for thirty years or more, that she had her hands full, that she had joined the ranks of satisfied nations and this was an advantage for everybody '.[a] It was pointed out to the Conference, furthermore, that, ' as regards the demands for colonies, sufficient stress has been placed on reasons of a demographic nature, on reasons connected with raw materials, on reasons of an economic order. Considerations of national honour have also been put forward. As to the reasons of a demographic nature ', it was suggested that ' they have been completely refuted ', and that ' the claimants themselves have abandoned them. They then fell back upon reasons of an economic order '. Yet, it was added, ' these reasons, too, have been refuted . . . Thus there is no longer a demographic question; and there is no longer an economic question; and . . . there remains only the question of national honour '. Consequently ' these questions are not debatable before a conference such as ours ', for ' they are psychological and not scientific '.[222]

For the purpose, however, of stating the facts relating to colonial expansion as a method of furnishing emigration outlets for overcrowded countries, it will now be assumed that such relevant claims as are discoverable merit investigation. The point of view will also be adopted here that, although it may be ' true that the need for emigration is decreasing . . ., that is not the same thing as to say that it has entirely disappeared '.[215] In other words, the intermediate attitude will be taken up that there is a short-term problem to be solved and that, ' if the need exists, even though it be a decreasing one, arrangements nevertheless have to be made to meet it '.[168 b] This method of approaching the question was stated as follows by a speaker at a meeting of the International Studies Conference :

In order to determine the true incidence of the question of emigration on the problem which we are discussing, we must be quite clear in our minds that the trend of emigration varies very considerably from year to year. A few years ago, emigration was an imperative need for a great number of nations. This need is becoming less and less felt. In the case of certain countries which formerly supplied large numbers of emigrants, the problem of emigration has, to all intents and purposes, disappeared. Why has this change taken place ? The explanation is to be found in the increase of industrial capacity, and also in the improvement of living conditions in the countries considered. The more a country is industrialized, the wealthier

[a] Unpublished preliminary record of the Conference's proceedings.
[b] Cf. above, p. 243.

it becomes; it sees the standard of living of its population steadily rise, while its emigration needs and the number of its emigrants decrease. This is easy to explain : (i) a country in process of industrialization can absorb more labour; (ii) the development of industry creates a social class that is treated with ever greater consideration, that becomes more and more exacting and less willing to make sacrifices. Thus, the number of emigrants, even from the ranks of the unemployed, is declining. This phenomenon is to be noted more or less in all countries . . . Another phenomenon to be observed almost generally is the difficulty of inducing a portion of the unemployed industrial population to take up employment in rural areas. " Back to the land " is a problem met with in every country and which encounters serious obstacles because no candidates can be found. I repeat, therefore, that the emigration problem has become less acute in a large number of countries, and it will continue to fall in intensity year by year. This diminution will be proportionate to the social amenities placed at the disposal of the population as a whole. The unemployment policy, in particular, which has become a social necessity in every country, constitutes an obstacle to emigration and, to a certain extent, we may congratulate ourselves on the fact. We must therefore counteract the impression that the world is faced with a poignant problem, because certain countries have closed their frontiers to immigration. In a word, I should say that the problem of emigration is becoming less acute. That does not mean that it has disappeared; and it is certainly indispensable for the peace of the world, that the greatest emigration facilities be granted to the whole of mankind.[218]

' The migratory movement ', stated another speaker, ' was an essential part of a much larger process of development in the 19th century. Conditions have now changed so as to favour it no longer. It is one of the many paradoxes of the present economic situation that it is partly because the growth of population in many parts of Western Europe is much less rapid than formerly, that it is difficult for countries which still have a great pressure of population to secure outlets for emigration . . . The newer countries have great difficulty in accepting immigrants to-day because the opportunities for absorbing large numbers of persons in the agricultural countries of the new world are less than they were. That is largely so because there are no longer very rapidly expanding markets for primary products; that, in turn, is due to the fact that the populations of countries like Great Britain, which used to supply these markets for primary products, are not growing as they used to do. Thus, the very fact that populations in certain parts of Europe are growing much more slowly than formerly, makes it more difficult to relieve the pressure of surplus population in countries like Poland, where it still is a very definite problem '.[216]

From these general statements one may proceed to a consideration of the emigration needs in the individual " dissatisfied " countries.

In the case of Germany, it has already been shown how ' this famous safety valve which emigration is held to have constituted has been gradually closed in proportion as internal pressure has increased. The losses of population by emigration abroad seem to have been keenly resented by the German nation during the period 1871 to 1885 . . . From this moment, at which the excess of births began to be swollen,[a] emigration decreased ',[376] direct action having been taken by the government, such as ' Bismarck's colonisation law for the Polish areas in Prussia'. [97] ' From 1895 to 1905 it was entirely nullified by emigrants returning to the mother-country and the balance of emigration even became positive . . . In this period, however, access to overseas countries was completely free and Germany had all its colonies in full development. The safety valve was functioning in the wrong direction '. [376] The explanation of this reversal in the stream of migration is that Germany was absorbing her increasing population by industrialisation — ' a solution of which there was everyday evidence in the familiar " Made in Germany " trade mark before the war '.[97] ' But how can we explain that, in the period which followed [the war of 1914-1918] and which was a period of great misery, the number of migrants returning to the mother-country was much greater than the number of departures, although the various overseas countries, with the exception of the United States, were not yet closed to foreign emigration and the objections to immigration into mandated territories which were made both by the mandatory authorities and the German nationals, had completely disappeared ? Both under the régime of the Weimar constitution and under the National Socialist régime, which held different opinions on the utility and the opportuneness of emigration[b], this emigration remained infinitesimal in comparison

---

[a] Cf. above, p. 101, note a. See also *100*.

[b] ' Like German statesmen, theoretical economists differed about the value of emigration from the national point of view. While . . . [the author of *387*] believed that it impoverished the country . . . [the author of *381*] held that it enriched it and drew up . . . a vast colonisation and population plan for Germanic emigration ' (*376*).

with the total volume of population . . . and quite similar to that of other countries of Western Europe. '[376] To-day, Germany must apparently remedy a shortage of agricultural labour with the assistance of the Dutch and Italian peasantry.[a]

It is difficult to resist the conclusion that in Germany there is neither a need nor a desire for emigration.

The position in Japan is uncertain, though there is reason to think that she regards emigration as less than a palliative for her demographic maladjustments.[b] ' The Japanese do not desire to emigrate . . . Their natural inclination " is to be a stay-at-home people ",[301] because of their reverence for ancestors and their reluctance to break up the family. If they move at all they prefer to remain within the boundaries of their own country '.[300] The one clear fact is that the number of Japanese who have settled outside Japan proper, the Japanese empire and Manchuria is quite small,[c] but opinion is sharply divided on the question whether this is due to a reluctance on the part of the Japanese people to leave home[d] or to artificial barriers that have been erected against them in certain regions to which, it is thought, they would willingly go. Perhaps both factors have been influential, but it does not seem possible to determine which one has been the stronger. One authority considers that the facts show that the Japanese although ' undoubtedly home-loving people . . . [whose] culture is very distinct, and . . . [who] are deeply attached to their peculiar mode of life . . ., are willing to go far afield under certain circumstances '. He points out that ' the government favours emigration[e] and, unlike the weaker countries of the East, is able to exercise ' organized pressure to secure opportunities

  ^a It was reported from Rome in November 1938 that 30,000 Italian agricultural labourers, having completed an eight-month contract in Germany, were to be brought back to Italy, and that negotiations had been started for sending another large batch to Italy the following summer (see *285*).

  ^b Cf., e. g., above, p. 244.

  ^c The estimates vary between ' about half a million ' (*84*; see above, p. 202, note a) and nearly 2 million. The latter figure is based upon the number of persons of Japanese nationality resident in foreign countries who are shown in the census returns of those countries (see *172*). According to a Japanese enquiry, the number of Japanese abroad is about 1 million (see *170*). This enquiry ' concerned only persons of Japanese race resident abroad (e. g. Koreans and natives of Formosa are not included). Moroever, the enquiry did not include Japanese resident in Japanese colonies. On the other hand, Japanese inhabiting the leased territory of Kwantung (39,885) and the Pacific islands under Japanese mandate (145,629) are included in the total indicated ' (*172*).

  ^d Cf. the view of a Japanese writer that among the difficulties obstructing Japanese emigration is ' the problem of persuading the Japanese to emigrate ' (*342*).

  ^e For example, ' Japan has encouraged and even given financial assistance to emigration to South America ' (*84*).

for emigration ', and that, before the era of immigration restrictions, ' they went freely enough to Hawaii and western America '.[a] He considers that ' the Japanese will go, though perhaps with more reluctance than some other peoples at leaving their homes, to any country where they have not got to compete with others whose standard of living is lower than their own '. In his view, ' there is no evidence . . . [that the Japanese] are unable to live under hard climatic conditions . . .; and such knowledge as we have about the adaptation of peoples to different environments lends no support to the idea '. According to him, ' the difficulty which faces the Japanese is that the countries to which they would willingly go are shut against them '.[84]

Against this view, another writer considers that the only ' areas really suitable to Japanese farmers ' are ' in climates of mediterranean, sub-tropical, and tropical type '.[62] According to a German student of the question ' the Japanese belong . . . to the peoples who are by heredity conditioned to warm climes,[b] and it is clearly apparent that this conditioning, thanks to the preponderance of a strong Malayan section of the populace which originated in the tropics,[c] imposes strict limits upon their political plans . . . A sojourn of undoubtedly more than 50 generations in the subtropic to temperate belt has not yet been sufficient to suppress in these people their tropic-born love of warmth; from which one must assume that they have spent many hundred previous generations in the tropics '.[66] That the climate factor has to be considered does not appear to be a view which the Japanese themselves would repudiate.[d] Moreover, on the question of adaptation, a geographer, who, while agreeing that ' adaptation does, of course, take place ', thought ' that acclimatization is not easy ',[209] informed the International Studies Conference that he had ' noticed, during his

[a] The number of Japanese in Hawaii was 61,115 in 1910, 60,690 in 1920 and 48,425 in 1930 (see *172*); for the United States figures, see above p. 242, note a.

[b] Cf. *62* : — ' From the south, probably by way of the Ryukyu Islands, came the Yamato people, who brought with them Malay blood and old southern cultural elements; from the continent, from China and Korea, came other ancestors of the modern Japanese. The southern oceanic element, however, dominates over the continental strain. This has an effect upon every phase of Japanese life, and has to be taken into account by the leaders and statesmen of the Empire '.

[c] According to *64*, the racial ratios are approximately : Malayan-Mongolian, 60%; Chinese-Mongolian-Tungusian, 30%; Ainu-Palaeoasiatic, 10%.

[d] At one of the meetings of the International Studies Conference, a Japanese speaker, after agreeing ' that the climate of Manchuria is a very hard one ', observed that ' for the emigrants, it would have been desirable to have a climate similar to that of the mother-country '. Japan, he added, ' is, nevertheless, determined to overcome the difficulties ' (*210*).

study of migrations to the United States of America that the European
emigrant generally tended to settle in the United States in regions having
climatic conditions identical with those of the European regions from
which they had come', and he thought 'that this is a normal tendency of
human beings '.[226] [a]   Another speaker held ' that it is not climate acting
directly upon the individual human body that is of importance, it is
rather climate acting indirectly through the environment.   For example,
Italian emigrants to the United States settle in California, not because
it has a Mediterranean climate, but because it has a Mediterranean
culture : the fig, the vine and the olive '.   His view was that ' all evidence
tends to show that the human being is able to adapt himself to virtually
any climate.   He changes, of course — for example, a Dutchman in
Holland is not the same Dutchman as his colleague in Java — but the
change, the natural adaptation which takes place in the human body
when it enters a different climatic region, cannot necessarily be considered
as a degeneration '.[226] [b]

The Italian Government's attitude towards emigration has already
been described.[c]   It is clear that Italy is ' unwilling to avail itself of
this avenue of escape from its difficulties '.[84]   Indeed, Italy has itself
taken steps to block at its own end ' the channels . . . through which
the Italian emigrant stream had hitherto flowed '.[84]   It may be that
' the Italian population would willingly emigrate, but the Italian
Government will not allow it to do so '.[200]   ' If a country suffering from
overpopulation has opportunities for emigration . . . and refuses to
take them, no effective remedy for the trouble can be suggested '.[84]
Yet Italy, like Poland, appears to be ' suffering . . . from difficulties

---

[a] ' I have studied European migrations to the United States in what we call the second
period — between 1870 and 1900 — when the emigrants were mostly from Northern
European countries, and I found that Swedes, Germans, Finns, Norwegians and even Italians
tended to settle almost to a tenth of a degree between the same summer and winter iso-
therms as those of their European homes.   That tendency changed later on, in what we
call the third period of emigration, when the emigrants were mostly from Eastern European
countries and when there were, in the American sense, no frontiers and the emigrants settled
where they could find land.   The problem how far settlement under different climatic
conditions affects emigrants is one more for the physiologist than for the economist or
geographer . . .   Continuing the studies on migrations to America, a pupil of mine found,
as regards Germans settling in that country, that a very high percentage of emigrants from
Mecklenburg, one of the coldest districts in Germany, settled in Michigan, Wisconsin and
Minnesota, whereas emigrants from Wurtemburg — one of the warmest districts of Germany — and a large percentage of other Germans, settled in Ohio, Illinois and Indiana.
This shows that European white people differentiated in their choice of district and tended
to seek climatic conditions similar to those in their original homes ' (209).
[b] For a further discussion of adaptation to climate, see 84.
[c] See above, p. 220.

which can only be alleviated by population changes. To the extent that population increases, these difficulties will become more serious. Therefore . . . [she] would benefit if the loss by emigration was equal to the natural increase, and . . . [she] would benefit even more if it exceeded the natural increase '.[84] Why then does Italy prohibit emigration? ' The explanation is that the only policy which could satisfy the powerful Italian expansionist sentiment was the settlement of Italians in a greater Italy overseas '.[84] This attitude raises issues falling outside the scope of the present chapter, but they will be considered in the next.[a]

There remains Poland which, unlike Italy, who refuses to emigrate, ' shows no such disinclination '.[84] Even Poland, however, while reluctantly admitting that emigration may slightly alleviate her population pressure, loudly decries the tragic dilemma which compels her to claim the need for recourse to the unpalatable remedial properties of a measure which she must fain tolerate as a *pis aller*.[b] Moreover, from the point of view of " peaceful change ", the Polish problem, though more clamorously proclaimed, is not essentially different from the problems of other countries in eastern and south-eastern Europe. The natural population outlet for these countries is eastwards and the fact that a Soviet frontier may present a political and psychological obstacle to this movement is no reason for compelling the countries of Europe overseas to open their doors.

Thus, with one exception of secondary importance from the point of view of the International Studies Conference's enquiry into " peaceful change ", none of the " dissatisfied " countries displays any disposition to claim wider outlets for emigration. ' Japan, Germany and Italy are not claiming greater facilities for the emigration of their nationals. Japan is seeking markets for her industrial production; Germany and Italy are asking for a more abundant and easier supply of raw materials '.[200] It is, moreover, pertinent to remark that, if it must be

---

[a] See chap. 8, §§ I and IV.
[b] ' Despite the need for emigration which is felt at the present time ', said the Polish delegate to a recent conference of experts on international and financial co-operation with regard to migration, ' there can be no question . . . of allowing masses of emigrants to leave the country without any plan, as was the case before the war. Emigration is looked upon more as a necessary evil, and each country considers that its primary duty is to secure a livelihood for its citizens on its own territory. If, as a consequence of difficult economic conditions, a State decides to allow its nationals to leave their native land, it does so in the conviction that their lot will be improved and that they will be in a position in their country of adoption to take up new lines of profitable employment ' (*304*).

concluded that emigration can relevantly be brought within the scope of this Survey on the ground that Poland alone claims without enthusiasm to suffer from a condition of demographic congestion which might be relieved by the direct method of transferring her surplus numbers elsewhere, this, from the international point of view, is a somewhat narrower issue than the grave problems which had been in the mind of the International Studies Conference when it opened its enquiry.

Since the forms of massive emigration which alone can be regarded as relevant to a condition of genuine demographic congestion and which have been such a notable feature of population movements in the past are to-day almost unknown,[a] all substantial migratory movements having come to a standstill, it will seem curious that there should be so widespread a belief, not only that emigration relieves overpopulation, but that Germany, Italy, Japan and Poland are faced with problems of demographic tension in consequence of the constriction of the emigratory outflow. It will seem even stranger that the International Studies Conference should have studied emigration with a thoroughness which it did not devote to its examination of the economic remedies for population pressure which will be mentioned in a subsequent chapter.[b] A brief enquiry into the reasons which impelled it to do so may throw a light upon the question of emigration as a remedy for overpopulation which an examination of past and present emigratory movements from the " dissatisfied " countries has not provided.

It would appear that this belief springs quite naturally out of the general favour which is enjoyed by an operation having the attraction of outward simplicity. Technically, emigration seems the simplest way of coping with a problem of excessive population. Unlike the indirect, economic remedies to be described later, the adoption of a policy of emigration does not call for a difficult and painstaking search for the root of the trouble; it is a frontal attack on the problem itself. Instead of seeking to eliminate the hidden causes of overpopulation, emigration simply removes its visible manifestations. Politically, emigration also has the advantage of still being, in most countries, a readily acceptable remedy. Overpopulation, if it means anything, means poverty. Overpopulation, however, suggests a general affliction, whereas poverty is commonly a sectional malady. A modern com-

---

[a] But cf. below pp. 260-2.
[b] See below chap. 9.

munity suffering from poverty (*alias* overpopulation) will tend, therefore, to favour emigration, which is a solution at the expense of a luckless section, rather than, say, a redistribution of wealth, which is a solution at the expense of the fortunate. In this respect, emigration might be said to lack the feature redeeming the direct method of reducing overpopulation by infanticide and the other methods of increasing mortality, which may be rejected on grounds of unrighteousness or inexpediency[a] — the element of social solidarity.

The effects of emigration are also more immediate and more readily perceptible than those of the indirect, economic remedies. It would not be possible to express in simple quantitative terms the demographic consequence of the modifications of a country's economic system brought about by an application of any of the economic measures designed to remedy a condition of overpopulation. The repercussions of such measures are likely to be manifold and diffused over a period of time; the degree of relief that they might afford to the congested society in which they were adopted could be gauged, perhaps, by the use of mechanical devices such as are employed in the processes of reasoned economic analysis, but it could not be subjected to exact calculation. Emigration, on the other hand, seems to differ from these other remedial measures in this respect because its immediate and palpable effects can be readily detected. Implying as it does the movement of numbers, its effect can be easily measured. Economic changes can be estimated and described with more or less accuracy, but numbers can be counted exactly. If a hundred persons leave a country which has a surplus population of two hundred, then, it may be thought, overcrowding has been reduced by one half. If this is true, then emigration has this advantage over other methods of combating overcrowding — that it is a visible process of a kind that can be physically grasped. In this respect, also, it resembles some of those other numerically measurable methods which were noticed in the preceding chapter among the direct demographic remedies. That this advantage may be, in international life, a real one will not be denied by anyone who believes that perceptible, though possibly shallow, consequences of applied policy may sometimes exercise a more potent influence on the elimination of sources of international friction than deeper effects that cannot be readily apprehended. Nevertheless, the advantage is a

[a] See above, pp. 192-3.

small one and, if the arithmetical properties of emigration have the same kind of intellectual attraction to-day as Malthus's famous mathematical jingle had last century, they resemble it also in that they are misleading abstractions. There are several ways of illustrating this proposition.

A first objection to the popular habit of focussing attention on the arithmetical aspects of migration is that, in the process, its non-demographic functions are assimilated to its demographic functions and tend thereby to be overlooked. The craving for freedom to move, although socially thwarted since earlier ages when roving food-gathering gave way before settled agriculture and urban organisation as the normal way of life for human beings, often appears to be a dominant feature of individual psychology. The right of mobility is still commonly held to be one of the fundamental rights of man. Thus there may be a psychological aspect to the problem of migration, not unrelated to the preservation of peace, which would be overlooked in a consideration of its purely numerical elements. A right to migrate, even when, for various reasons, there is either no desire or no power to exercise it, is manifestly not the same thing, from the point of view of the relations between state and citizen in the first place, and between state and state in the second, as a compulsion to stay at home. From the social point of view as well, migration presents certain features which have a bearing on the maintenance of international peace. For ' universal peace and harmony must needs be based on social justice '[167] [a] and the attainment of social justice has been held to involve, *inter alia*, a system of protection for foreign workers implying a recognition, if not of the utility, yet at any rate of the importance, of the rôle of migration in international social relations.[b] Thus, although the relief of population pressure may be one of the functions of emigration, it is not the only one and perhaps it is not even an important one

---

[a] Cf. the preamble to the *Charter of the International Labour Organisation* : ' Whereas the League of Nations has for its object the establishment of universal peace, and such peace can be established only if it is based upon social justice . . . '.

[b] The equitable economic treatment of all workers legally residing in a given country having been included by the high contracting parties signatories of the *Charter of the International Labour Organisation* among the particularly important and urgent methods and principles for the regulation of working conditions, the International Labour Conference resolved at its first session that ' a special section shall be created in the International Labour Office, to be specially charged with the consideration of all questions concerning the migration of workers and the condition of foreign wage earners ' (*315*) and that ' the International Labour Office shall appoint an international commission, which . . . shall consider and report what measures can be adopted to regulate the migration of workers . . . '.

Emigration also fulfils a social and psychological rôle which a superficial inspection of its numerical attributes fails to reveal.

A second defect of the mathematical approach to an examination of emigration as a remedy for demographic congestion is that it tends to obscure the fact that ' migration only forms part of a whole and that everything in the complex system of exchanges of men, money, and goods is interdependent, so that a change in any one branch of exchange necessarily affects all the others. It has sometimes been thought that a given type of exchange can be isolated, that a liberal policy may be pursued in regard to one type and a policy of restriction in regard to another. Experience has repeatedly shown that this is a fallacy. Since demographic movements, which are both causes and effects, are always preceded or accompanied and followed by movements of capital and goods,[a] not to mention services in the form of transport and commercial and other operations, and since these movements take place either directly between the country of emigration and that of immigration, or, more frequently, between a whole set of countries, each of which is affected in turn,[b] any attempt to restrict migration while encouraging the exchange of capital, goods and services, or *vice versa*, is sure to meet with considerable difficulties... Countries must choose and they cannot expect other advantages or drawbacks than those to which the policy prevailing not only in their own territory, but in all other countries taken as a whole, may give rise, whether that policy be more or less liberal or nationalist, free trade or restrictionist '.[167]

But the principal weakness of the quantitative examination of emigration movements from the point of view of the subject of the present survey arises out of the fallacious assumption on which it rests. While it is certainly true, of course, that the volume of a migratory movement can be measured numerically (though rarely very accurately, owing to the lack of sufficiently sensitive statistical methods), yet the information to be derived from the quantitative measurement of a remedy is not enlightening unless the disease to which it is applied can be brought into the field of a similar scale of measurement. This,

[a] Cf. above, p. 200.
[b] ' Cf... [*168*]; and... [*178*]. As far back as 1885 Sir Robert Giffen pointed out that : " ... in the earlier years of prosperity, a considerable lending of capital from old to new countries goes on, and this lending of capital promotes emigration from the old countries to the new, helping to give greater employment for labour in the new countries than there would otherwise be " (quoted ... [in *169*] ' (*167*).

however, is not possible, for, as was explained in an earlier chapter, overpopulation is not a condition that can be determined scientifically; still less is it possible, therefore, to measure its extent. It follows that, if emigration is to be considered as a cure for demographic congestion, a simple quantitative examination of its volume cannot be usefully related to a discussion of specific claims by particular countries for relief from an imponderable weight of numbers.

If the illusory simplicity of emigration as a remedy for overcrowding is one of the sources of popular belief in the efficacy of this nostrum, the widespread impression that the surface of the globe is still liberally speckled with vast tracts of habitable but unpopulated or underpopulated areas is another. On the one hand, it is thought that colonial territories are capable of absorbing enormous accretions to their populations — a question which will be examined in the next chapter. On the other hand, there are those who consider that the solution of the problem of emigration does not lie in the colonial sphere only but also elsewhere. ' The solution to this problem ', said a speaker at a meeting of the International Studies Conference, ' is to be found all over the world; in other words, it is not only the colonies that must be thrown open to immigration; and we shall see at once that, even if they were opened to the maximum, the colonies could receive but an infinitesimal number of immigrants without incurring the risk of death. If it is really wished to solve this problem of emigration, and a solution must be found, it is the whole world, or at least those countries which, by virtue of their position, can absorb a fairly large number of immigrants, that must be opened '.[218] Although the suggestion that there exist undeveloped but habitable areas, capable of absorbing an inflow of population at a pace which would give effective relief to countries which are at present overpopulated, cannot be examined in the present survey,[a] it may be recorded here that, according to the author of one of the studies submitted to the International Studies Conference, ' only migration to the United States, the British Dominions, and South America can provide opportunity for the movement of substantial numbers ',[b] and that ' the average annual absorption capacity of all

---

[a] See, however, the Supplementary Chapter.

[b] Cf. *218* : — ' In America and particularly in South America, there are territories which, because of the definition we have given to the term " colony ", we cannot classify amongst those which are engaging our attention and which are, nevertheless, territories more specially qualified to receive immigrants; firstly, because they are rich territories more highly developed than most colonies, and secondly, because they are inhabited by ar

the oversea countries taken together is such that they could take about half the natural increase of the countries of south and east Europe '. Moreover, ' as time goes on the absorption capacity of the oversea countries will grow while the natural increase of the European countries will diminish . . . World opinion will probably not admit the right of the inhabitants of any of these countries to continue indefinitely to fail fully to exploit them '. But ' it does not follow that the assimilation capacity of a country is equal to its absorption capacity '.[84] What the assimilation capacity of a country may be is essentially a political question, and any suggestion that ' South, Eastern and Central Europeans . . . [should be shipped] to the United States and the British Dominions by the hundreds of thousands ' is bound to be strenuously opposed.[102] In the deep waters of politics, science can do no more than point a finger of warning against the dangers inherent in policies designed to immobilise men.[a] ' Might we not learn something from the difficulties of internal peaceful organisation ? Have we not learnt that, if we attempt to prevent what might be called social migration within a country, if we attempt to prevent people from pursuing occupations other than those of their fathers and from moving into

extremely small number of Europeans as compared with the total population. There are territories which present the same characteristics in other parts of the world : Australia and New Zealand, for example. There are others which, no doubt, could open their doors a little more widely to immigration in so far as immigration must still be continued '.

[a] It is sometimes suggested that Palestine is an example of ' the opportunities which an under-developed, but not an under-populated, country offers to immigrants ' and of the way in which such a country ' can be made to accommodate within a few years much larger numbers with benefit both to the original inhabitants and to the new-comers '. But the conditions in Palestine are exceptionally favourable. On the one hand, there were large areas of uncultivated but cultivable land awaiting capital and technical resources and large possibilities of developing certain industries. On the other hand, ' the immigrants, though culturally very distinct from the Arabs, are apparently not dissimilar genetically; in any case, the two peoples are not separated by easily observable physical differences . . . [The] religious and cultural differences . . . are not accompanied and enhanced by differences in pigmentation and other physical features . . . [and] there is at least the possibility of the development of a harmonious community because there are no permanent outward marks serving to remind the two sections of the population of their different origins '. Yet ' in spite of these exceptionally favourable circumstances, the success of the experiment is in doubt '. ' The Arabs . . . are increasing rapidly and have lost land . . . As to the Jews, is is doubtful whether, if heavy immigration continues, 20 per cent of them can continue as at present on the land; for to find land for 20 per cent. of a rapidly growing figure means a continual enlargement of land in Jewish ownership . . . Tension between the two peoples is acute, and . . . there is as yet no sign whatever of any growth of understanding one of the other . . . [such as might make it possible] to continue with those industrial and agricultural projects which alone can make the experiment a success. In short, although this experiment is being conducted under very favourable circumstances, it is not yet clear that Palestine can accommodate such rapidly growing numbers with benefit to all concerned ' (84).

other social circles, we build up masses of resentment which finally
overcome the restrictions and lead to internal disorder, to something,
in fact, approaching civil or class war? Is it not also probably true
to say that, if we try to compel people to live and make their living
where they are born, we shall ultimately build up masses of resentment
which they will attempt to relieve by force'?[196] Moreover, 'there
are problems of international justice involved, and it may also be that
opportunities for emigration would have important psychological
results'.[84]

* * *

One general conclusion seems to emerge from this survey of
conflicting views on migration. In the nineteenth century period,
immigration was of great importance to the rising countries overseas;
to-day, it is not necessary to those countries as a whole and it is disadvantageous to certain sections of their populations. Emigration has
never been of great importance to the countries of emigration as a
whole (except Ireland), though it has been useful for certain sections
of their populations; to-day it has become disadvantageous to the
countries of emigration as a whole and of no importance to particular
sections of their populations. Thus there has come about a double
shift in the incidence of the problem of migration. Formerly, it played
a useful international rôle as a movement of immigration; to-day,
it causes international friction as a movement of emigration. In an
age of sprouting autarky, can it not be said that the stimulation of
migration is a paradoxical mutilation of the nation, a gratuitous inci-
tement to international conflict,[a] and a socially untenable admission
that within a community some men are born to be heirs to its benefits
while others are a superfluous charge on their birthplace?

NOTE

Since the conclusion of the enquiry carried out by the International
Studies Conference, public attention has been focussed upon the question of
migration in consequence of the recent re-appearance in Europe of a refugee
problem. The fact that a swelling tide of refugees is to-day one of the
liveliest demographic movements is, however, not of cognate interest to

---

[a] Cf. *326*: — 'In view of the present conditions of the labour market throughout the
world, any migration scheme conceived on a large scale cannot but... arouse hostility'.

the subject of this Survey which is not concerned with political emigration but exclusively with the forms of economic emigration associated with pressure of population. The refugee movement may be ascribed, perhaps, to a form of " qualititative " overpopulation; it clearly does not spring from quantitative overpopulation among the agricultural and industrial working masses of Germany, Poland and Italy. In any case, the forms of political emigration from central Europe which are attracting so much attention to-day are quantitatively insignificant in comparison with the massive movements of men which took place before 1914. Furthermore, whereas the numerically more important elements of the many refugee movements which have occurred since 1929 have raised in an acute form the issues of expatriation and denationalisation mentioned in the text above, the quantitatively smaller, but qualitatively more vociferous, refugee movements which have been attracting wider notice since 1933 because of the manner in which they have been generated and which are of " cultural " rather than of political character, are popular precisely on the ground that, from the point of view of the communities out of which they are flowing, they are not felt to raise those issues.[a] [b]

The refugee problem bears, however, upon emigration as a remedy for quantitative demographic maladjustments in the sense that, in so far as it now dominates the discussion of migration, it reduces the possibility of providing emigration outlets for other potential migrants. It is, for example, with the object of barring the way to a large immigration of Jewish refugees from Central Europe, that certain South American states have recently been impelled to close some of the gaps in their immigration restriction legislation, a step which may be thought to have been immediately prompted

---

[a] In the communities towards which these movements are heading, on the other hand, they are unpopular for the opposite reason that, as the special correspondent of *The Times* at the Evian refugee conference in July 1938 reported of the voluntary organisations invited to the conference, ' some of them seem to envisage the creation of compact settlements almost on an autonomous footing ', in spite of the fact that the Latin American States, the Dominions, and the United States will not ' tolerate the creation of anything that might bear even the appearance of a State within a State ' (*277*).

[b] For a somewhat different view of the nature of the refugee problem, cf. (*367*). ' The refugee problem both in its present form and in its potential form is clearly a world responsibility demanding international action by governments. It is a world problem in the sense that the existence of refugees is a symptom of the disappearance of economic and political liberalism. Refugees are the by-products of an economic isolationism which has practically stopped free migration; they are the products of the population pressures in Europe which result in part from the paralysis of international trade and the restriction of markets; they symbolise in a most tragic way the development of political authoritarianism. The basic real solution of the refugee problem, real or potential, is necessarily therefore related to the solution of the great problems of economic and political adjustment in the contemporary world ' (*ibid.*).

by the foreign publicity which has flooded the predicament in which Jews in Greater Germany and elsewhere are placed, and by the circumstance that, 'foremost among ... the underlying reasons for ... the failures which have attended previous attempted solutions ... [of] the refugee problem ... has been that of using refugee questions as political weapons, instead of treating them as humanitarian problems '.[308]

Chapter 8

Colonial Expansion

I. COLONIAL IMMIGRATION

Territorial expansion ' may assume the form of an increase in the homeland territory or of an extension of colonial possessions. It is very obvious that the two hypotheses cannot be confused. They have the common feature of satisfying the needs of the claimant State only by demanding from one or several other States, the abandoning of territory rightfully possessed; but beyond that, they are very different '.[40]

A discussion of continental expansion would carry this Survey so far beyond the limits of the enquiry made by the International Studies Conference that it must be dismissed here with the remark that, in so far as recourse may be had to such action for the purpose of disposing of surplus population, it does not seem capable of offering to-day the remedy which sometimes appears to be anticipated. It may be, for example, that, from the German point of view, a migratory movement to the Union of Socialist Soviet Republics ' would be much more tempting ',[376] than emigration to tropical colonies or to the regions of European settlement overseas. On the other hand, while ' it might be possible to defend the handing over by Russia of the Ukraine on the ground that a certain country wants to send out thousands of people and settle them on small-holdings . . ., this would certainly involve a fall in the standard of life of those who went there if present technological trends in agriculture continue . . . It may be that Germans if planted in Russia, would be more efficient than the Russians are and so would raise the standard of living in these areas . . .; but the certainty is that Russia itself is by no means empty, and that the net reproduction rate there is higher than . . . [in Germany]; any filling up of Russia,

therefore, should be done by the Russians themselves '.[166]   Again,
' unless the . . . expansion [proposed by Herr Hitler][56] is to take place
on land now uninhabited . . ., [his] programme would seem to imply
that the native population of any land claimed by Germany would
have to be removed or exterminated.   For, how else would it be
possible to establish the " natural and healthy proportion between
the numbers and the increase of the nation and the size and quality of
the land in which they dwell " '[55] which he has contemplated ?

* * *

In undertaking a study of the value of colonies as areas of immigration for the inhabitants of demographically congested metropolitan
countries, the International Studies Conference had in view the common
assumption that colonies provide important outlets for the disposal of
surplus population at home.   The Conference's discussion of this
question was to reveal clearly, however, the fragility of the basis on
which the assumption rests.   Two conclusions seem plainly to emerge
from a consideration of some of the more salient facts relating to immigration in the colonies : first, that there is little supporting evidence
to be discovered behind the contention that colonies have served in the
past as important population safety-valves; and, secondly, that there is
little prospect of expanding their capacity of demographic absorption
in the future.   If such conclusions are accepted, it follows that no
realistic policy of colonial expansion can be directly related to a problem
of overcrowding.   This, indeed, appears to have been the general
sense of the Conference itself; it was summarily expressed by a Belgian
colonial expert as follows : —

We must be careful not to permit the belief that the solution of the
emigration problem lies in the colonies.   It does not.   The contribution
that the colonies can make towards a solution of this problem is a very
small one, for the following reasons : the majority of the colonies which
we have classed under that heading[a] are still but summarily organized; their
development is slow and immigration can be envisaged only in so far as
adequate organization already exists in the country.   Secondly, most of

---

[a] The Conference's discussion of the vexed question of the definition and classification
of colonies is described in *The Colonial Question and Peaceful Change* (Paris : International
Institute of Intellectual Co-operation), in course of preparation.

these territories have a climate which is very unfavourable for mass immigration. It is thought that immigration can be directed chiefly towards the sparsely populated areas of colonial territory. That is a mistake. The areas where there are practically no inhabitants are generally the high plateaux; but these plateaux, which, from the point of view of climate, are certainly suitable for the settlement of groups of immigrants, are not sought after. It is more difficult to carry on economic activity in these regions than elsewhere, because they are generally isolated and still unprovided with means of communication. Considerable expenditure would be necessary for the installation of these means of communication. Markets are rather restricted and any immigrants wishing to devote themselves to some form of industry or to agriculture on a large scale would find no labour.[a] On the other hand, the areas of colonies which can the most easily accommodate certain classes of immigrants are mostly inhabited by the natives, but these areas are low-lying and, therefore, the least healthy. Economically, they are the most highly developed and more urgently need certain categories of settlers, for example : shopkeepers, bankers, engineers, farmers, etc., besides various artisans for trades which the native population has so far been unable to take up.[218]

This commentary was developed by another expert who denounced the misleading character of declarations purporting to show that colonies provided a ready solution for the social problems of Europe :

A large part of the territories of tropical Africa is at present the object of active propaganda declaring with great energy that the European unemployed can establish themselves on the land there, where the density of population is small, that they can live there, prosper and even become wealthy. On the contrary, it must be proclaimed that the tropical regions of Africa are not made to receive unemployed whites, suffering from the crisis in their countries, who are anxious to improve their situation. It cannot be repeated too often that these territories in process of organization are not asking for the addition of every kind of labour but for : (i) directors; (ii) trained labour; and (iii) the capital necessary to build up and put into working order the equipment which is indispensable to production. It would ... be a grave error to continue much longer propaganda tending to turn the white popu-

---

[a] ' The settlement of Europeans in certain colonies, ' said another expert, ' is impossible unless there already exists the labour required for the organisation and development of the country ' (217).

lation towards tropical countries where they would be able neither to live nor to work normally. Colonial governments have understood this for a long time, and all of them have taken the necessary measures to restrict rash immigration. They have been the victims of such propaganda. They have seen arrive on their territories individuals without resources, unspecialized, and without great zeal for work, whom it was necessary to repatriate after a few weeks, at the expense of the local budgets. [217a]

Some attempt, it is true, was made in the Conference by a former Director of the Mandates Section of the Secretariat of the League of Nations to introduce into this sombre picture of the scope for immigration in colonial areas, if not a light of optimism strong enough to shed its beneficent rays on a demographically disequilibrated world, at any rate a glimmer of hope for those portions of the globe which bear the main burden of this inequality : —

Three kinds of obstacles to white immigration in colonial territories appear to emerge [from the Conference's discussion]. They are, first, physical difficulties of habitat; secondly, the lack of economic means — for the modern settler is no longer the pioneer of days gone by — and, finally, administrative obstacles to large-scale immigration. However, conclusions have been drawn from this situation which appear to me rather too definite. For example, it has been affirmed that we must give up all hope of finding in the possession of colonies a solution to the problem of overpopulation, particularly for nations which have certain aptitudes and certain qualities. I agree . . . that we must look for a general solution by economic and political measures. I am not, however, of the opinion that we must exclude the colonial solution, for I think it can help to solve the problem of overpopulation. I have been studying colonial problems too long not to be aware that it constitutes only a relative solution; but as such, it exists all the same . . . It is said that colonies cannot solve the problem of excess population, and that this is proved by statistics . . . But, it is forgotten that the possession of colonies helps the development of the economy of the mother-country, creates employment, etc . . . [It has been] emphasised that the establishment of settlers involved for the colonial power a number of economic measures which constitute for it a very heavy burden and which probably could not be supported by it for the advantage of others. I agree, and that is exactly

----

[a] Cf. *132* : — ' Tropical regions which, if they are worth while, are densely populated, never provided an outlet for European paupers '.

why no country should support this burden of developing colonies if not precisely the country which, suffering from overpopulation, has an interest in colonizing a territory, but on condition that it is subject to its own authority. In conclusion, I repeat that the colonial solution is only a relative solution, but it incontestably constitutes one of the remedies that can be applied to the situation of certain overpopulated countries.[213]

This view, although recognising that emigration to colonies could not take place on a large scale, nevertheless assumes that emigration affords relief to congested areas — an assumption which was shown in the preceding chapter to be of doubtful validity. It may be useful, however, to test this assumption once more by enquiring, into the extent to which colonies have provided outlets for emigration in the past, especially from those countries which were considered more particularly by the International Studies Conference.

II. ITALIAN, JAPANESE AND GERMAN EMIGRATION

In the case of Italy, ' in spite of the individual colonising capacities of Italians, while Italian labour has taken part in all the great works which have changed the face of the world, while she has found suitable fields for her activity in the two Americas and has prospered there, she has not yet been able to establish herself and develop in the African colonies as the following statistics [395] [based on the census of 1931] show ' :[394]

	Total Population	Europeans[a]	Natives	Inhabitants per square kilometre
Tripolitania	543,672	30,901	512,771	0.6
Cyrenaica	160,451	18,506	141,954	0.2
Eritrea	600,573	4,560	596,013	6.0
Somaliland	1,021,572	1,668	1,019,904	2.0
Aegean Islands...	130,842	12,729	118,113	48.5

' Apart from a small fraction of Somaliland, the Italian colonies are deserts and that is why they have not been able to serve as outlets for

[a] ' In 1930, Italy counted hardly 35,000 of her nationals in the colonies ' (249). According to one estimate, ' since 1886, the total net Italian migration to all of Africa has been just about 7,000 '; as in the case of Algeria, ' the number of those who remain out of those who arrive is exceedingly small ' (165).

the excess population of the Kindgom '.[394] The fact that the population of Italy has not overflowed into Italy's colonial possessions in the past does not necessarily mean, however, that those regions are incapable of absorbing excesses in Italian demographic expansion in the future. With Italy's recent acquisition of vast territories in Abyssinia, which, unlike the present made by Monsieur Laval to Signor Mussolini in 1935[a] has not been described by the latter as a desert, this proposition assumes an obvious pertinence. The demographic function of Abyssinia, however, may best be considered when set in the background of the actual and potential rôle of Libya (comprising the two colonies of Tripolitania and Cyrenaica).

In Italy, ' great hopes were based on Libya which was to provide a large and solid demographic foundation ',[394] some Italian authorities having estimated that, in forty or fifty years' time, half a million to a million Italian colonists could be settled here.[396] This is an extreme estimate stretching to the limits of sanguine expectation; even so, it is but a small figure ' with regard to the development of the Italian population if it continues to increase at the rate of four hundred thousand individuals per year'.[394] Nevertheless, ' to the assertion that the country is nothing but a " box of sand " there are at least three replies : first, that it is an exceedingly large box; secondly, that there is a great deal of interest beneath the sand; and, thirdly, that the present owners have shown what can be done with sand by modern irrigation. In addition to reclaiming enormous tracts of desert, sinking wells, and constructing roads the Government have undertaken valuable archæological work . . ., [but] possibly the most striking achievements . . . have been in the sphere of colonisation '.[284] Libya seems to offer, therefore, a prospect of palliating a demographic ailment on a scale which no one would be tempted to belittle. Foreign critics, however, have suggested that the figures mentioned go far beyond the limits of legitimate optimism and that, even ' assuming that the Italian financial position made it possible to sustain so considerable an effort for such a long time[b] and that this effort produced the results expected of it . . ., Libya could only absorb twenty thousand of these four hundred

---

[a] ' The Laval-Mussolini Rome Agreement of January 7th, 1935, redrew the Sahara frontier between French West Africa and Italian Libya so as to place Auzu and Guesenti in Libya, and to leave Bardai and Tecro in the French area ' (357).

[b] It was reported in April 1938 that the Italian Government was proposing ' to allocate credits amounting to 100,000,000 lire a year for five years for . . . public works, land reclamation, housing, and the equipment of rural centres ' (270).

thousand '.[394] [a] Even this figure, moreover, may prove to be an excessive estimate unless Italy is capable of repeating annually ' the most interesting and best organised experiment in mass emigration that has yet been attempted '[269] by following up in 1939 and subsequent years her spectacular despatch of 20,000 colonists in the autumn of 1938. This remarkable triumph of enthusiasm and patient organisation must compel unstinted respect and admiration, but it is permissible to suspend judgment not only on its symbolic demographic significance but also on its immediate economic repercussions.[b]

The not too promising prospects in Libya enhance the interest of Italy's expectations in Ethiopia, where, having ' justified her invasion of Abyssinia partly by her need to find land for settlers ',[357] Italy now ' appears to follow a methodical policy of Italian population '.[394] ' A number of societies were formed in 1936 for the development of Ethiopian agricultural industry[358] and preliminaries for settlement were put in hand, the first being an accurate survey of the country occupied, and the provision of communications. At the end of December 1936, it was estimated that some 100,000 Italian workmen were engaged on the preparatory work for settlement. Companies have been formed for the promotion of stock-raising, cotton-growing, wool-growing, the lumber trade, etc., but it is realised that experimentation is necessary before these agricultural developments are started on a large scale '.[357] Although ' it is possible that the arrival of Italians, men of the country-side by race and tradition, may bring good results for agricultural problems . . ., it is hardly likely that the high Abyssinian plateaux can offer, so generously as is said, healthy conditions of life, existence and work for white settlers . . . Moreover, the industrial revolution tends to extend more and more to agriculture and to diminish the number of workers necessary for cultivation. Furthermore, Italian peasants will not be able to cultivate profitably Ethiopian lands by the intensive methods which they employ in their little estates of Piedmont, Lombardy and Tuscany. They will meet with the

---

[a] Cf. *396* : — ' That is why one thing is certain, namely, that in any event, even under the most favourable hypothesis concerning numbers of men and years, Libya will never be able to absorb more than the surplus in the Italian population for only three or four years. And in the meanwhile ? And afterwards ? ' Cf. also *76* : — ' Libya, costly to maintain . . ., [is not a region] of considerable potential settlement '.

[b] In October 1938, ' the Fascist Grand Council decreed the inclusion of the four provinces of Libya in the national territory of Italy ', a decision which was ' obviously connected with the scheme for the large-scale settlement of Libya with Italian peasants ' (*283*).

competition of industrial processes and the fruits of manual labour will have a cost price too high, even on the internal market. It is, it seems, a naive and dangerous illusion to believe that considerable white labour could be employed in the cultivation of the soil and the extraction of raw materials. Hence, Ethiopia could mitigate only provisionally and very slightly the difficulties resulting from over-population in the Peninsula without solving a problem which must still remain a formidable one '.[394] [a]

' The popular exuberance which followed the conquest of the Empire, and the uninformed statements which represented it as an immediate outlet for thousands of colonists, are things of the past. Time must elapse before large numbers of emigrants can enter the country. At present [November 1938] experiments are being conducted at the agricultural centres near the provincial capitals to ascertain the types of crops and vegetables suited to the soil and the climate at different altitudes and promising prosperity to future farmers. Every effort, too, is being made to induce the natives to improve their primi-tive methods of cultivation and to grow more grain in order to reduce the large quantity which has to be imported to feed the 250,000 resident Italians. Cattle have always represented the chief wealth of the country, hides being one of the most important exports. In some districts, the stock is very poor, and in all districts totally uncared for; veterinary surgeons are trying to stamp out disease and to teach the elements of stock breeding. Three types of colonisation are planned. The first is demographic, in which chosen families from the same districts in Italy will be settled in newly built villages. Three advance parties of about 100 men each have already arrived and are clearing the ground and building houses. The second type is industrial, concessions being given to firms or individuals capable of supplying the necessary capital. The third type may be described as " individual ", small grants of land suitable for market gardening being made to soldiers and road-makers who ask to be demobilized in the country and who have the necessary experience. Two flourishing colonies of ex-Service men already exist near Addis Ababa. The present watchword is " patience " '.[287]

* * *

[a] It was stated in the course of a discussion held at the Royal Institute of International Affairs in London that it had ' been admitted by a distinguished diplomatic representative of Italy at Chatham House that even if Italy had free entry into Abyssinia she would secure at the most the absorption of only one million of her inhabitants ' (see *176*).

The colonisation of Japan's dependencies has been somewhat different in character from the experiments of other countries, Japanese territorial expansion having taken the form of a true centrifugal movement of population into an ever-widening concentric area separated from the homeland only by ownerless (because permanently inhospitable) tracts of water. The movement, however, has not been considerable. 'In the Japanese colonies properly so called (Formosa, Korea, Saghalien, Kwantung . . .) and the islands under mandate in the Pacific Ocean (Caroline, Marianas and Marshall Islands), the number of Japanese, including Koreans and Formosians but excluding soldiers, rose by 519,000 between 1920 and 1932,[a] that is, by 61.4% of the 1920 figures, whereas the increase in the total population of the colonies was 22.21%. For the whole of the Japanese colonies, the number of Japanese amounted, however, to only 5.01% of the total population; in Saghalien, 99% of the population were Japanese as compared with only 2.5% in Korea, 36.1% in the mandated territories and 5% in Formosa '.[214]

The Japanese Empire, together with its politically dependent territories, appears, indeed, to be in an even more unfavourable position than the Italian Empire as an outlet for surplus population in the home-country. 'Will Manchukuo be that territory which Japan has unsuccessfully sought all along the shores of the Pacific Ocean as an outlet for her population? Past experience does not seem to suggest that this region is suitable for Japanese immigration on a large scale. After signing the treaty of 1915 with China, the Japanese Government announced that it would send a million colonists to Manchuria in the space of ten years. Twenty years later, this figure was far from having been reached; in spite of public and private efforts at colonisation, the number of Japanese subjects who had emigrated to Manchukuo was still extremely small (barely 100,000), whereas 800,000 farmers from Chosen had settled there. There are various reasons for this setback : the difficulty experienced by Japanese colonists in acquiring land from Chinese or Manchu owners; competition of Chinese labour at low wages, and, lastly, the inaptitude of the Japanese for mass migration.[b] There

---

[a] Cf. 165 : — 'Between 1925 and 1933 . . ., the total net emigration from Japan to all her colonies [i. e. Formosa, Korea, Kwantung Leased Territory, Japanese Saghalien and South Seas Mandate]... was less than 294,000 ', net emigration being ' calculated by deducting from increase in Japanese population in the colonies, the increase attributable to excess over deaths calculated at 15 per 1,000 per annum '.
[b] Cf. above, pp. 250-252.

is every reason to believe that, for some time to come, Japanese colonists will be chiefly civil servants, traders, clerks and employees — in short, residents rather than colonists. And yet only 12 to 15% of the total area of Manchukuo is under cultivation, whereas 30% could be so utilised. If Japan did not allow herself to be outpaced by the innumerable peasants and coolies from Shantung and Hopei, who are attracted to the country by the security reigning there at present, and if she did not compete with herself by refusing admission to emigrants from Chosen, she could settle a few tens of thousands more colonists in this territory '.[394]

A Japanese writer, who attributes ' the failure of Japanese emigration (to Manchuria and Mongolia) throughout the period prior to the Manchurian affair ... to the insecurity of the country, intervention by the Chinese authorities, legal uncertainty regarding the ownership of land, the absence of institutions for the protection of the immigrants, and their inadequate agricultural experience ', considers that, ' since the creation of " Manchukuo " in 1932 ..., these external reasons for the failure of emigration have been entirely eliminated by the introduction of a new administrative system ', and that ' the future now offers great possibilities '.[342]

In May 1938, the Japanese Oversea Minister announced ' plans for the emigration of 1,500,000 Japanese youths to Manchukuo in the next 20 years ';[271] two months later a Japanese speaker at a meeting of the International Studies Conference stated that ' according to present Government plans, 5 million persons will be transferred to Manchukuo in the course of twenty years, and 100,000 families will settle there during the first ten years '; it was estimated, he added, ' that, in twenty years' time, the population of Manchukuo will have increased from 30 million to 50 million '; Japan, he stated, ' will thus be able to transplant 10% of her population to that territory ' [210 a]. ' Campaigns to enlist likely youths are being conducted in all the rural districts, particularly in the poorer areas. Training institutes have been opened in Japan and training colonies in Manchukuo, where the selected youths receive three years' instruction before being allotted land. It is intended to settle these Japanese in large and comparatively empty areas in North-West Manchuria '.[271] According to the President of the South Manchuria Railway, ' Japanese farmer immigrants into

[a] Cf. above, p. 251, n. d.

Manchukuo may now be counted by tens of thousands . . .; scientific methods of cultivation and the greater use of machinery are enabling the Japanese to farm successfully in Manchuria even in comparison with the Chinese '.[272] [a]

* * *

In the case of Germany, ' with the exception of Kiaochow, which belonged to the category known as *Handelskolonien*,[b] practically all the former German colonies came under the . . . [category of *Pflanzungskolonien*]. Only South-West Africa and a few small territories in East Africa offered some prospect for emigrants. Before the war, however, the settlement of white men in the colonies had become an issue of party politics in which the solution of the problem was sought according to abstract principles, with the result that Germany did not take advantage of her surplus population to hasten the peopling of her colonies. This will be seen from the following figures[376] for white immigration in the three principal colonies ' :[c]

Year	South-West Africa			Cameroons			Togo		
------	Immi-grants	Emi-grants	Differ-ence	Immi-grants	Emi-grants	Differ-ence	Immi-grants	Emi-grants	Differ-ence
1907	4,021	2,955	1,066	631	503	128	119	137	− 18
1908	3,627	2,641	986	448	439	9	171	104	67
1909	5,766	4,835	931	700	532	168	221	179	42
1910	5,052	4,313	739	931	758	171	192	198	− 6
1911	4,308	3,790	518	746	657	89	196	203	− 7
1912	4,648	4,963	− 315	1,170	843	327	219	189	30

[a] ' The immigrants are being settled on the best land available, which happens to be in the north, where, in course of time, they will form a human bulwark against Russia ' (*271*).

[b] ' The German colonial school distinguishes three classes of colonies (see . . . [*382*]) : (i) trading colonies (*Handelskolonien*) . . .; (ii) plantation colonies (*Pflanzungskolonien*) in which the white ruler (*der weisse Herrscher*) is prevented by the climate from doing any work except that of supervision (for this reason, the Germans apply to them the name . . . *Herrschaftskolonien*); (iii) settlement colonies (*Siedlungskolonien*), in which colonists can pursue any occupation without danger, even physical work ' (*376*).

[c] ' See . . . [*384*]. No figures are, unfortunately, available for East Africa. As regards New Guinea, the surplus of immigrants was 144 in 1912; for Samoa, from 1907 to 1912, it varied from year to year between 8 and 33 ' (*376*).

19

' In 1913, the white population (exclusive of troops) of the German colonies was distributed[376] as follows ' :[a]

Colonies	Total white population	Germans	British	British subjects or protected persons	Ratio of number of British to number of Germans
South-West Africa.	14,830	12,292	169	1,630	1.8
East Africa	5,336	4,107	90	321	1.1
Cameroons	1,871	1,643	79	–	1.2
New Guinea	1,427	1,005	51	61	1.2
Togo	368	320	1	–	1.3
Samoa	557	329	132	–	1.25
Kiaochow	4,470	4,438	–	–	
			522	2,012	
Total	24,160	19,696	2,534		

' Such are the actual facts. After nearly thirty years of coloni-sation, twenty thousand nationals at the very maximum had taken up residence in the whole of the German colonial Empire ...[b] — they had " taken up residence "; they were not permanently settled there. German emigration (*Auswanderung*) to the colonies was essentially of a temporary nature and the numbers returning to the fatherland (*Rückwanderungen*) sometimes exceeded those entering the colonies, even in the case of those colonies which were the most suitable for a white population (South-West Africa in 1912). Furthermore, the white immigration was composed of elements of an extremely mediocre quality and in almost every colony ordinances were introduced to restrict their number.[c] Lastly, it will be observed that a large number of British subjects penetrated into the German colonial possessions. These rather poor results of German colonisation ... point to the conclusion that either the German colonies were unsuitable for popu-lation by whites or German emigration deliberately avoided them '.[376]

[a] ' Cf ... [378] and ... [379] '.
[b] ' This is considerably less than half the number of Germans living in 1930 in the Bronx Borough of New York City — the borough which has the smallest German popu-lation of the four principal boroughs ' (165). It is also less than the number of Germans in Paris when the war was declared (see 376).
[c] ' See ... [384] : — As elsewhere, the necessity arose, in territories under German protection, of keeping out undesirable elements, in particular those without means who could become a public charge. The development of a white proletariat in colonies with a native population would be a matter of grave concern. For this reason, in all territories under German protection (except Samoa and Kiaochow), decrees have been enacted whereby the admission of whites without means or without a definite occupation has been, or can be, refused ' (376).

III. THE GERMAN CLAIM

In the light of this record, one may surely echo the conclusion reached in a recent analysis of the economic value of colonies that ' the evidence showing the fallacy of the claim that colonies provide important outlets for population is ... devastatingly clear '.[165] This conclusion, it may be added, is equally applicable to colonial empires other than those which have been considered here.[a] But, although ' the absurdity of claiming that politically controlled colonies have been important as outlets for population ' in the past may be ' obvious ',[165] it is possible to argue in favour of, for example, a return to Germany of her former colonies on the ground that ' the present situation is not comparable to that prevailing before the War, for other outlets, such as the United States, were accessible then, whereas now they are closed '.[50] It is less obviously absurd, therefore, to suggest that Germany's former colonial empire might be capable, in the future, of offering some relief for population pressure. Though it may be true ' that the total number of Germans settled in the pre-War German Empire was less than the number of those Germans who were established in Paris ',[b] yet ' this rejoinder [to Germany's agitation for the return of her colonies] ... is ... ill-considered and unfair... The

---

[a] A comparative study of the economic development of the Scandinavian countries and the Netherlands which was carried out for the International Studies Conference showed that from 1900 to 1930 the net emigration from the three countries without colonies was much greater than from the Netherlands. From the Netherlands the approximate total was 27,000, from Denmark 115,000, from Norway 258,000 and from Sweden 361,000 (see *112*). ' It is, ' concluded the author of the study, ' a mistake, therefore, I think, to believe as many people do, that colonies in general provide an important outlet for surplus population, ' but, he continued, 'I realise, of course, that this statement cannot be generalised and applied to all parts of the world, and that in the particula∵ case in question, we have to do with a small mother-country with large colonies (*199*) ; ' yet the facts suggest that such a generalisation would not be a rash one. ' Between 1865 and 1924, over 17,000 more Hollanders entered the Netherlands from the Dutch colonies than left for these colonies ... All the Europeans of all nationalities, plus the so-called " assimilated " of the local peoples in the French colonies in Africa, to-day [number just over a million and a half] ... Of the 28 millions of all nationalities who sailed to other continents from British ports from 1886 to 1933, precisely 5.0 per cent. went to the British territories other than the Dominion areas; to the regions where Britain had real control, that is to say ... For the 118 years, 1815 to 1933, only 3.5 per cent of those who departed from British ports for overseas destinations had British territories other than the Dominions-to-be as their destinations '(*165*). In the Belgian Congo, ' colonisation is hardly beginning ', the total white population on January 1, 1936, amounting to only 18,683 (12,654 Belgians and 6,029 foreigners), ' which represents barely 7 inhabitants per thousand square kilometres ' (*82*).

[b] Cf. above, p. 274, note b.

true answer to . . . [Germany's claim] is not . . . to dwell upon pre-War statistics, but to examine what the figures would be in ten years time from now '.[341]

It is not easy, of course, to estimate figures of this kind, but it may be said at once that the view that ' it is certain that were the former colonies to be restored to-day, the amount of Germans who would seek to settle in Africa and elsewhere would be enormously increased ',[341] does not appear to tally with such knowledge of the possibilities of habitat in those areas as is at present available.[a] In the first place, although the ' development in the number of Germans . . . in [Germany's former colonies has been] less favourable . . . [since 1919] than when they were directly under German rule ',[214] this does not necessarily prove that it would have been more favourable if those territories had been retained by Germany.   It is true that the German civil population in these areas fell from 19,646 in 1913 (exclusive of Kiaochow to 16,774 in 1930 (exclusive of Kiaochow), but ' the increase in the number of non-German whites (28,300 to 45,000) '[214] was not very great.   ' The decline in the number of Germans is, moreover, partly due to naturalisation '.[214]

Secondly, ' already before the war, the German Ministry for the Colonies estimated that not more than fifty or sixty thousand colonists would find the means for a practicable existence in the German colonies, and even that estimate involved no small a measure of optimism '.[376] This has been admitted by a former German colonial governor, who states that, ' owing to their climatic and sanitary conditions . . ., large proportions of our tropical territories . . ., particularly . . . the regions in the heart of the tropical colonies . . ., were unsuitable for permanent colonisation by Europeans '.[390] [b] Another German colonial expert[385] makes no attempt to ' justify colonisation on the grounds of utility for the purposes of emigration '.[376] According to him, ' the phenomenal development of the German population, which is far greater than that of any other European State except Russia, justifies colonisation for other reasons ',[385] namely, ' the supply

---

[a] ' There are certain " hot-heads " who already picture five million Germans emigrating within the space of four or five years to the restored African colonies ' (376).

[b] Cf. 383 : — ' The colonial territories hitherto governed by Germany do not correspond at all with the former notions of nationally-planned mass emigration; and in so far as these territories may be considered as suitable for white settlement, there can be no question of directing large crowds of emigrants towards them. '

of raw materials '.[376] One of the leaders of the Akademischer Kolonial-bund, who was sent in 1933-34 on a mission of enquiry to the former German colonies by the Notgemeinschaft der deutschen Wissenschaft, the colonial section of the German Ministry of Foreign Affairs, the Prussian Academy of Science, the Deutsche Kolonialgesellschaft and other German learned societies and colonial organisations,[376] is equally emphatic. ' He does not believe in European colonisation on a small scale (Kleinsiedlung) in which the colonist does the same work as he would do in the mother-country. In any case, he has met with no instances of it, except perhaps in a few spots in South-West Africa, and even then in the form of rural colonisation '.[376] ' However ', he writes, ' I should like to warn against imagining that East-Africa or the former German colonies generally, would be in a position to receive a large part of the German surplus population ... The idea of mass settlement in the tropical highlands is based on the assumption of small or peasant holdings for a white and his family, who would produce only sufficient goods for the market to provide him with money to meet current needs '.[393] This view of colonisation, however, ' does not take into account the fact that the country is already inhabited by blacks,[a] or the physical obstacles with which the whites meet '.[376] Moreover, the author himself considers that, ' it has not yet been proved that the European is physically capable of performing continuous heavy manual work in the tropical highlands and of maintaining himself throughout the generations '.[393] Finally, he states that ' the principal question is whether it is desirable from the social and racial point of view that Europeans should perform manual work in the tropical highlands side by side with natives '.[393] Thus, ' from the point of view of settlement, East-Africa is only of limited value. It must no longer be thought of as a region of colonisation, properly so-called : it cannot receive small settlers and, even less, millions of settlers '.[376] He concludes that ' the colonial problem is not a problem of masses in so far as the white settler is concerned ... It is linked up with the pioneer work of individual and vigorous men of action, the fruit of which benefits all the people '.[393]

Some writers consider that certain regions in the former German

---

[a] For information on the size of native populations in colonial territories, see 95. ' The population statistics of most colonies are to-day in a condition similar, in many respects, to that of the population statistics of most European countries 150 years ago ' (ibid.).

colonies might be suitable for a restricted settlement of whites, such as parts of South-West Africa and the high plateau region and mountain slopes of East Africa,[a] but ' no reasonably-minded and cool-headed German can believe in the possibility of transferring a substantial proportion of the surplus population to the former German colonies '.[376][b] In fact, ' the idea of a mass colonisation of overseas countries has now been generally abandoned in Germany, not so much through recognition of the error which such an idea represents as for political, racial and sociological reasons '.[376][c]

On the other hand, while it may be " devastatingly clear " that colonies are of negligible value as outlets for surplus population, it has been held that their possession offers indirect means of relieving population pressure in the metropolitan countries. ' The demographic co-efficient of a home-country ', it is said, ' does not affect its demographic pressure, since its colonies can neutralize this pressure by serving as a direct outlet for its surplus population, or by the influence which they exert on the economic life of the home-country, by permitting a greater density of population to establish itself — a development that would be impossible without the colonies '.[207][d] Thus, ' the Germans . . . claim that if Belgium, Great Britain and the Netherlands can support a population nearly twice that of Germany on an equivalent area of territory, it is because these countries possess vast colonial Empires '. If her former colonies were returned to Germany, they would help to shorten the time-lag between Germany's *Bevölkerungskapazität* and her *Bevölkerungsvermehrung* ' either directly by supplying foodstuffs, or indirectly by ensuring the supply of raw materials

[a] See *376*, the author of which adds that the Cameroons and Togoland, on the other hand, are ' completely out of the question. '

[b] Cf. *341* : — ' No sensible German would claim that, even given the most intensive exploitation and emigration, the return of the colonies would solve either their economic or their demographic problems. '

[c] ' One must not remove from Germany people who could be used here, for the mass colonisation of Africa by the surplus German population. The only colonisation that can be envisaged is . . . qualitative colonisation . . . ' (*386*). Cf. above, chap. 5, § VIII.

[d] Cf. *84* : — ' If the argument . . . is valid . . . [that the] areas which are now administered as colonies or under mandates . . ., which alone can be transferred to another flag, offer very little opportunities for settlement, so limited in fact that migration to them from an overpopulated country of any size could not be on a scale which would afford any appreciable relief, this does not dispose of the case for considering such [territorial] changes, because it may be that certain countries deserve to shoulder the responsibilities and to obtain the prestige which the possession of colonies gives, and also that only in this fashion can access to raw materials be justly apportioned. ' Cf. also *155*, where it is stated as a ' fact ' the ' colonies are at present an essential condition of the relatively favourable economic density of the countries which possess them. '

for national industry and outlets for national commerce '. It is on these grounds that ' abandoning, little by little, the demographic argument which was beginning to show signs of weakening, German propaganda has relied more and more on the economic argument '.[376] This new turn in the colonial claims issue falls outside the scope of the present Survey,[a] but it may be pointed out that the view is also held ' that it is illusory to hope that . . . a transfer [of colonies] will prove the means of providing cheaper supplies of raw materials. What is more probable is that countries having obtained new colonies would prefer more expensive raw materials coming from them to the cheaper materials offered on the world market '. Moreover, even the more tangible ' advantages to be derived from preferential treatment of the goods exported to such colonies ' are not substantial, since ' colonies, with a few exceptions, are such poor purchasers that their markets are of but small interest for the mother-country, even if such colonies — to the detriment of the colonial population — are compelled to discriminate in favour of exports from the latter '. From the economic point of view in general, therefore, it would seem ' that the possession of regions which are at present colonial is not such a powerful factor in the economic prosperity of the manufacturing countries as to warrant the hypothesis that a more even distribution of the political control of such territories would materially further the solution of the " over-population " problem '.[179] [b]

The possession of colonies may also be advocated as an indirect means of affording relief from population pressure on another ground. ' Certain students of the question, who agree on this point, empha-size . . . that colonies may provide an outlet for capital from the manu-facturing countries. Political control, they state, may reduce the risks involved in such investments. This is true. But this fact alone can hardly contribute to the solution of the economic problems of nations with rapidly increasing population, for the latter require for home purposes all the capital they can accumulate. If such nations invest large amounts of capital in colonies, where employment is provided mainly for the native population, this will result in a corresponding

[a] See *Raw Materials and Peaceful Change* and *The Colonial Question and Peaceful Change* (Paris : International Institute of Intellectual Co-operation), in course of preparation.

[b] ' The situation was totally different when the British Dominions and India formed part of a colonial Empire which was of the greatest importance for the industrial develop-ment of the United Kingdom ' (*179*).

decrease in the opportunities of remunerative employment in the home-country. In many cases, the amount of capital invested in the colonies per head of white settlers ... appears to have been several times larger than the sum which would have been required to employ them at home. It is true, of course, that high profits may be derived from such export of capital by the corporations and concerns engaged in exploiting a colony. But, from the national angle this cannot be considered an advantage, if it makes for less favourable conditions of employment in the home-country '.[179] a

* * *

There is no need to dwell here on the legal and political issues which the principle of transfer raises; this is an aspect of the problem of " peaceful change " which outruns the scope of the particular question discussed in this Survey.[b] It will suffice to note here that, whereas the Dutch Chairman of a committee set up by the International Studies Conference in 1937 to consider colonial questions opposed the view that ' it is a delicate matter to ... [discuss in this Conference] questions relating to transfers of colonies ... because it may foster a certain feeling of anxiety in countries which may be directly touched by these problems ' by expressing the opinion that ' discussion in such an assembly as this may serve to re-assure people by demonstrating that even the most delicate questions, which divide the nations' most deeply, can be profitably discussed in a meeting where everyone is animated by a spirit of good faith, and where everybody wishes to contribute to the establishment of universal peace ',[220] a Belgian colonial expert entered a strong plea against the ventilation of a subject which was politically outside the reach of " peaceful change " action : [c]

---

a Cf. 112 : — ' The principal gains which ... the Netherlands [may be supposed to] have acquired from her possession of colonies have been cashed directly by a relatively small number of persons. It is an obvious conclusion, therefore, that the possession of colonies may have caused a somewhat more uneven distribution of wealth in the mother-country than would otherwise have been the case, but it is impossible to say whether this influence on the income structure of the Netherlands has been of importance worth mentioning. '

b See, however, above, pp. 124-129.

c In the discussion in Germany of the return of her former colonies, attention appears to be carefully averted from the South Sea Islands now held under Japanese mandate (cf. 394), but it is of interest to note that, although these islands can never provide an outlet for any substantial stream of emigration, the Japanese themselves have, nevertheless, ' shown their ability as tropical colonisers in the Pacific Mandate ' where ' their number has increased rapidly' (62) and where 'the total native population ..., 50,540, is already outnumbered by the Japanese ' (62). According to 63, the Japanese population in the mandate has increased as follows : 1920, 3,671; 1935, 7,430; 1930, 19,835; 1933, 32,214; 1934,

I do not think there is a single colonial government which would envisage the slightest change in the territorial and political situation of its colonies, and I am convinced that, in this respect, all are supported almost unanimously by the public opinion of their countries. We must leave this kind of solution out of discussions of the colonial problem, as it arises at present. To give it a certain hearing before public opinion and to lead public opinion to believe that the difficulty can be solved by transfer of sovereignty, by the division of colonies, by a new distribution of colonies, or by a system of internationalising colonies, would not be to benefit peace; it would simply be to create one more trouble in the world. It must not be thought that it is selfishness and the desire to defend their economic and political interests which drives colonial Powers to adopt such a downright attitude. The reasons are moral ones. I might also say that political morality and international morality impose on the Colonial Powers, at the moment, a duty not to give way on this point. They cannot do so, because they have to defend the moral prerogatives which they have assumed with regard to native populations, whom they have, at a given moment, taken by the hand, and whom they have already led to a high degree of colonisation. Following upon the work of education and, in a general way, the work of colonisation, which all colonial Powers have carried on with admirable zeal and which every day produce more marked results, a real moral sympathy has been established between the populations of the colonies and those of the mother-countries; it has been established by links which we cannot think of breaking. I repeat : a colonial Power which consented, as a result of discussions taking place around a diplomatic conference table, to give up a part of the colonial population dependent upon it to other countries, and to make them become subject to the cultural, moral and political administration of those countries, would be committing a fault and would incur the blame of all those who really possess a sense of responsibility. I would ask, therefore, that this point should not be insisted upon. I maintain that if we try to create in the public mind the feeling that certain difficulties, which disturb the world at the moment, can be solved by a new distribution of colonies and by a modification in the political and territorial situation of a part of the world, we shall be compromising peace far more than we shall be bringing any appeasement to men's state of mind.[218]

40,215; 1935, 51,606. 'Japanese authorities estimate that there is room for 100,000 Japanese farmers, in addition to whom quite a number of fishermen and tradesmen could be accommodated' (62). 'Japan,' according to an American survey of the limits of land settlement in the world, 'is the only colonial Power that has built up an agricultural industry in a tropical colony, obtaining practically its entire labour force by migration from the mother-country' (62).

IV. COLONIAL POPULATION CARRYING CAPACITY

The above account of territorial expansion in relation to over-population may have shown that demographic decongestion in Germany, Italy and Japan through massive emigration to the colonial areas constituting the former colonial possessions of the first country and the present colonial empires of the two others is a vain dream; but it has not shown, except incidentally,[a] that a form of territorial expansion involving a transfer to these countries of other colonial areas would offer no remedy.

Apart from the general principles implied in a transfer of colonial territories, the question which arises from the demographic point of view is whether the countries suffering from overcrowding do, or could, find in colonial areas outside their own possessions the relief which, as has been shown, does not seem to be available in their present, or, in the case of Germany, former, colonies.

In the course of its session in 1937, the International Studies Conference was informed that the censuses taken in the colonies about the year 1930 showed that, of the total number of French, Dutch, Portuguese and Spanish emigrants, 82%, 49.3%, 38.9% and 26.6%, respectively, went to the colonial possessions of their respective countries.[214] These substantial ratios may seem to suggest that colonies provide important outlets for the emigration from certain countries. The absolute figures, on the other hand, dispel the notion. The total stream of emigration from all countries to all colonial areas has been a tiny ripple in comparison with the great waves of migration which have gone to other regions. ' That colonies do not constitute an adequate, not to say exclusive, remedy for the overpopulation of a country — regardless of the question whether colonies are placed under the sovereignty of this country or not — is proved not only by migration statistics but also by the censuses taken of foreigners '.[214]

As has already been pointed out,[b] however, the fact that colonies have not provided important emigration outlets in the past does not necessarily mean that they cannot absorb larger numbers of immigrants in the future. Nevertheless, current estimates of the remaining regions of habitability in the colonial areas in general seem to show that the

[a] See above, pp. 264-267.
[b] See above, pp. 275-6.

physical possibilities are slight, and that, in the case of Africa, the most positive statement which may be hazarded is that ' the final test of the potentiality of the land ... must remain with the man who tries it out '.[76] Moreover, even if the possibilities were considerable, there would still be, it would seem, two insuperable practical difficulties and one serious political difficulty obstructing any substantial flow of immigration from the metropolitan countries.

In the first place, if the standard of living of the immigrants is high, ' the level of wages in the colony may be forced up, and however beneficial this may be to the inhabitants of the colony, it raises the costs of concerns producing in the colony, and hence affords them smaller profits than would accrue to them if they would employ natives at lower wages, and avoid paying the high wages of persons of metropolitan nationality. Hence, the dividends to investors in the metropolitan country will be relatively lower '.[189]

Secondly, ' should the white man, for instance, undertake to settle in number in Africa, he will not find that disease will clear the way for him. Like other manifestations of culture, the diseases of man have attained the major limits of their possible distribution. On the other hand, the entry of a higher, let us say European civilisation, now means a general improvement of sanitation and a lowering of mortality. The introduction of white settlement tends to be reflected in major benefits of sanitation applied to the native population. In so far as this population has higher reproduction rates than the white colonists, there is, therefore, a tendency for its growth to outstrip the growth of white population and to exert pressure against the European colonist increasingly as time goes on '.[67] [a]

Finally, there is the important question of the protection of native interests. ' Does ... [a removal of restrictions on colonial migration] mean ', enquired a speaker at a meeting of the International Studies Conference, ' that anyone should be able to go to any colonial area without regard to the state of the population or the natural resources of that area, considering nothing but his desire to go or the desire

[a] There is some evidence in the International Studies Conference's documents tending to show that this argument is not applicable to Japanese colonisation. Thus, in the Japanese Mandate, ' it is revealing to compare the statistics of births and deaths during 1934 ' (*62*, quoting from *65*) : Japanese, 1918 births and 538 deaths; Natives, 1211 births and 1100 deaths. Again, in Hawaii, a colonial area not in their possession, ' the Japanese have the most favourable sex ratio among all orientals (16 males; 10 females). This is a guarantee that for a long time to come they will keep the leadership in numbers among the population of Hawaii ' (*62*).

of a country to plant settlers there ' ?[221]   It seemed to him ' that restrictions on immigration . . . [were] necessary, and that . . . [the]
problem . . . [was] not so much their removal as the establishment of
proper restrictions, restrictions that . . . [would] take account of the
state of the population, whether the area . . . [was] adequately or
over-populated, problems of assimilation . . ., problems of natural
resources and so forth '.[221]   ' It must not be imagined ', said another
speaker, ' that immigration restrictions can be entirely abolished.   The
adoption of such a course would lead to nothing but muddle, prejudicial
to certain interests essential to colonial territories '.[218]   ' There is no
colony in the world ', a third speaker pointed out, ' where the immigration of foreigners has not led to what, in many cases, was unfortunate
social and economic disturbance . . .   The colonial Powers have to
shoulder a heavy responsibility, that of the development, transformation
and progress of the native; for that reason . . ., immigration should
always be considered in the light of the repercussions that the arrival
of newcomers can have on the native communities.   The data spread
over what is already a considerable period warn us against a certain
category of foreigners who are not indispensable to the welfare of the
country in which they settle and who may be a danger to the population . . .   [It is] a human and natural fact, [that] when a man or his
family seeks to settle in a new country, in many cases this aim will be
achieved only to the detriment of those who are already established
there '.[217]

Assuming that it is permissible, however, for an overcrowded
people to ' establish itself in a position of domination over a half-civilised
country . . ., where are countries of this kind, open to conquest, to be
found, now that Ethiopia has been conquered by Italy ?   Will any
attempt be made to usurp sovereignty in colonies which, *ex hypothesi*,
are settlement colonies ?   Everybody knows what that means.   In
practice, it is not always easy to draw the line between settlement
colonies and exploitation colonies : for France, Algeria, Tunisia and
Morocco are, up to a certain point, settlement colonies — the term
colony being interpreted in its broadest sense.   A settlement colony
is one to which nationals can be sent, not merely to fill important posts
under conditions of a somewhat exceptional character, but to take
part in every form of economic activity.   Settlement colonies existed
in the past, but it must be noted that those which have succeeded the
best have, in turn, become nations : e. g. the United States and the

British Dominions — Canada, Australia, New Zealand. What remains to-day of settlement colonies' struck the author of one of the papers submitted to the International Studies Conference ' as being insignificant ... Those which come to mind are, at least in part, already peopled by the nation to which they belong. It is scarcely to be expected that the possessor nation, having already made the effort to populate the territory — an effort of particular interest and importance from its point of view — would allow itself to be dispossessed '.[113] [a]

' If room is to be found for immigrants [in the under-developed countries], it can only be provided by reclaiming land, by taking it from its present owners, or by creating new forms of employment. As to reclaiming land, it is very unusual to find any large proportion of land ... which is now quite unused and capable of being rendered fertile; moreover, the cost of irrigation, drainage, clearance ... is very high. ' As to expropriation, unless it ' goes very slowly, the natives will certainly suffer, because it will take a long time for them to learn how to use their remaining land more intensively. But, however land may be acquired for immigrants, it will give little employment for them unless they do the work of the fields themselves. If they merely employ the dispossessed natives, the number of immigrants occupied in supervision will be negligible. But it is impossible to imagine that immigrants will permanently subject themselves to a self-denying ordinance and refuse to employ native labour ... So far as the creation of opportunities for the employment of immigrants, otherwise than upon the land, is concerned, the situation varies greatly from one country to another. ' It would appear that few of the under-developed countries offer much scope. ' Moreover, the same question arises in connexion with work in the factories as in connexion with work in the fields. ' [84]

' There are only three choices; to leave the under-developed countries alone, to put the inhabitants to school but to leave them their possessions, or to take the land and employ the former owners as servants. There can be little doubt that in the interests of the inhabitants the second system is preferable. '[84]

---

[a] Cf. *110* : — ' Why did not Germany and Italy participate in the struggle for the New World when Britain, France, Spain, Portugal and Holland sought to explore the possibilities of the new horizons ? Were they deliberately shut out, or were they satisfied with their inner evolution ? And why did Japan shut itself up and become a hermit kingdom until Commodore Perry broke into its peaceful isolation ? '

Chapter 9

Economic Remedies for Overpopulation

I. ECONOMIC DEVELOPMENT

While any ' change in the population trend is, under any circumstances, a serious matter with far-reaching consequences, good and bad, '[310] the difficulties which arise in the process of adjusting the economic structure of a society to a growth in its size are not necessarily of a lasting character, whereas the deceptively straightforward method of directly overcoming such difficulties through emigration is, in general, marked in its consequences by a feature of permanence which may seem inconsistent with recent apprehensions of declining populations.[a] Moreover, attempts to bring about adjustments through policies of expansion designed to neutralise growth of population through emigration, even if they are successful — which, as was suggested in an earlier chapter, never appears to be the case — in achieving their immediate object, may give rise in turn to new economic difficulties far more acute and of a more lasting nature than those which such policies seek to eliminate. ' Solutions other than territorial solutions (migration being included among territorial solutions) have one advantage over the latter, since they prepare the way for the natural absorption of future excess population, whereas countries with millions of emigrants every year may still remain poor and backward. '[317]

It is evident, moreover, that ' a country sending out large numbers of emigrants must, in fairness, if it wishes reasonable treatment for these emigrants, put its own house in order. If it has a policy of sending its citizens to other countries, it must at home do everything it can to improve the social and economic conditions of its own people.

---

[a] Cf. above, chap. 5, § IV.

If it does that, emigration will be much less, the standard of living will go up, the adjusted birth rate will come down and in time we shall have an equilibrium which will be satisfactory to everyone.' The fact must be emphasised 'that these domestic questions are of equal importance to the question of moving people from one country to another. If in a country the distribution of the national income is such that large numbers of the population receive less than enough to live decently, that country is in no position to demand room for its nationals, room which exists at home, but which it makes its nationals incapable of using or enjoying. A country so governed that its people are unhappy or discontented must put its house in order if it wishes to receive fair treatment from the rest of the world ... The question of migration is not entirely an external question of the country to which the migrant goes, but is equally a domestic question.'[194]

A great protagonist of the intelligent control of migratory movements has himself pointed out that, 'before recourse is had to emigration, it should be seen how far a better organisation of production, increased industry, credit operations, the distribution of the population, internal colonisation, will make possible a solution of the problem;'[374] and it has been authoritatively stated that 'population pressure cannot be relieved by emigration on a sufficient scale' and that 'the only real alternative is vicarious emigration by the export of manufactured commodities embodying the labour provided by dense and growing populations in developing industrial countries'.[154]

These are vast themes. Only one or two of them were touched upon in the course of the International Studies Conference's enquiry into " peaceful change "; others are being considered in connection with a study of economic policies in relation to world peace which the Conference is at present carrying out. A few, brief observations, therefore, must suffice here.

Industrialisation, which, in the case of agricultural countries, is is a ' comparatively slow method of taking care of surplus population ',[55] is a solution which gives rise to a series of other problems. Japan, for example, 'notwithstanding her intensive industry..., remains an agricultural country : 48% of the population are agricultural workers; but the area of arable land represents only 16% of the total area of the country ... Agriculture has been the object of a number of technical reforms, but, from the standpoint of population, it has reached its limit of absorption. The agricultural population fell, in consequence, by about 150,000 between 1920 and 1930 (14,286,592 and 14,131,025, respectively). Japan was, therefore, obliged to adopt a policy of intensive industrialisation — a peaceful solution of the distressing problem of overpopulation. Between 1920 and 1930, however, the industrial population increased by only 14.3 %, that is, by 740,000 persons (5,138,758 and 5,875,991, respectively). In fact, while Japan is obliged to import all her raw materials except silk, she must export her goods in order to pay for these raw materials; on the other hand, however, owing to the customs barriers that have been erected on all sides, she is unable to develop her industry to the extent necessary for her to be able to absorb the surplus population. The greatest number of persons were, therefore, absorbed by commerce ... The result was keen competition, which compels the shopkeepers to be content with very small business profits '.[210]

Nevertheless, ' the economic history of the last hundred years contains many lessons in respect of countries [with a dense and rapidly increasing population] in which ... [the] development [of employment] has taken place without any territorial expansion : '

It is quite clear that the employment of an increasing number of individuals on an area of land with given resources leads to diminishing returns per individual, so long as (i) production is confined to the primary industries — vegetable goods and raw materials — and (ii) technical methods remain unchanged. Even with improved technique, there are strict limits to the amount of fresh labour that can be employed without a decline in its reward, i. e. the standard of living ... This does not apply to the secondary industries — e. g. the finishing industry — where land and other natural resources play a minor rôle compared with skill and organizing capacity and conditions of transport. If the supply of capital keeps pace with the increased quantity of labour, the output per head does not decline. On the contrary, it tends to increase with economies of large-scale production and industrial concentration. With the development of technical progress, *per capita* production and the standard of living may even be subject to a rapid increase. This is what took place in all the industrial countries of Europe during the last half century before the war, including those which acquired no colonies. The natural line of development for a nation whose population has reached a size at which returns in the primary industries tend to fall decisively, is concentration or secondary industries. The output of vegetable agricultural products and of mineral raw materials will then absorb a decreasing proportion of the working population, while manufacturing industries, transportation and various services will employ an increasing proportion.[179]

' Owing to the continuing advance in technique, this is quite compatible with a rising standard of living. '[179] [a]
It is to be noted, however, that ' previous experience was . . . accumulated during a period of relatively free trade ' :

If bilateralism continues to grow and obstacles to international trade continue to increase, countries with a swiftly rising population may not be able to find markets for an increasing output of manufactured goods unless they are prepared to offer such commodities at very low and falling prices. On the other hand, the greater the freedom of trade, the more the chances for such countries to avoid an unfavourable shift in terms of trade.[179]

' Thus, Italy, Japan and other States with rapidly growing population have perhaps a greater interest than others in the removal of the fetters with which international trade is loaded and, more especially, in checking the spread of bilateralism. For these nations an autarkical policy would be even more absurd than for others. '[179] Unfortunately, this hypothesis does not ' appear to fall within the bounds of practical possibilities in any future worth considering. '[179]
Thus, ' industrialisation depends on international trade. ' It is, therefore, ' of vital interest for rapidly growing nations that international trade should be allowed to fulfil this function . . . Nations of rapid growth would lose more than others if the existing state of world trade and finance were to become permanent. They have more than other nations to gain from a liberal Open Door policy . . . and from the elimination of discriminating and bilateral tendencies from world trade. For they are more dependent on suplies of raw materials at reasonable prices and on possibilities of increasing their foreign sales of manufactured goods. Their economic growth depends on such conditions infinitely more than on the political control of certain colonial districts. '[179]
' It is hardly believable that any nation should take the initiative in provoking a general war in order to secure economic advantages in the form of colonies. But a feeling of unfair treatment may breed

[a] ' This is a fact which is frequently forgotten when the question of "overpopulation" is discussed ' (179).

resentment and thus create a situation in which war is difficult to avoid. It is, therefore, of vital importance that discrimination as regards treatment of goods and men, both in colonial and other territories, should as far as possible be avoided. '[179]

In a recent plea that the arrangement of ' an African readjustment that will satisfy Germany once and for all . . . must be tackled with boldness and vision, ' an eminent Asiatic, who has ' no sympathy with " the white man's burden " theory . . . , [considering] it the coloured man's burden, after the model of Sinbad the Sailor, ' has stressed the importance of industrialisation as a remedy for Germany's population problem :

If Herr Hitler lives to be 75, Germany will by that time be a nation of about 100,000,000. Even then her population will be far less to the square mile than the populations of England or Belgium. The Führer and others have said that they need land, but they have also said that the population problem may be solved by their country becoming one of the workshops of the world. We must realize that there are spheres where, for geographical and natural reasons, Germany will be the dominating economic factor. Commercial treaties can be made by which Germany may become one of the great exchanging countries, and history proves that such business intercourse is for the good of all the nations concerned. These economic understandings will be the ultimate solution of Germany's population problem.[233]

Thus, industrialisation is not enough. ' There are two prerequisites for an increase in industrial production : a sufficient supply of raw materials and markets to absorb the products. This implies that, under the new international business codes, if a customer is not willing to accept goods or services as payment for raw materials, industrial countries (and, more particularly, bedtor nations) which do not produce raw materials themselves, must inevitably find limited possibilities of increasing production. If such countries wish to attain autarky and deem it necessary to produce for production's sake regardless of the consuming capacity of the population, they must produce their own (artificial) raw materials and produce for uneconomic purposes '.[132]

Methods of augmenting by internal economic measures the resources available to the population of a country suffering from demographic congestion were considered by the International Studies Conference, therefore, to be ' closely allied to the problem of markets and the distribution of raw materials ',[40] [a] and to the supply of capital. In this connection, however, markets are more important than raw materials and capital. As to the latter, as the author of an International Studies Conference memorandum has pointed out, ' what is said on this subject ... does not seem to call for a long discussion '.[113] It is true that ' there is a relationship between the growth of population and the need for raw materials ', and that the countries where, owing to rapidly increasing populations, industrialisation has become an urgent necessity, ' attach special weight to the question of access to raw materials '; but ' the relationship between population increase and raw materials supply is not so closely connected with the national resources of any given country as with the development of international commercial relations '.[318] In other words, the ultimate remedy for a problem of overcrowding lies in an expansion of export markets. ' If money is available for the purchase of raw materials, they will be supplied; it is only in exceptional cases that the producing countries restrict the exportation of raw materials to the countries that need them '. As for capital, though ' it may be admitted that the organisation of the international circulation of capital is open to improvement ', yet it may be said that ' it goes where it will find, besides the requisite guarantees, a profitable return and a good rate of interest '.[113]

It may be concluded, therefore, that, since ' the rate of economic exploitation of the resources of a given country depends not only on the enterprise of its inhabitants and the available supply of domestic and foreign capital (neither enterprise nor capital is lacking), but upon the opportunities for trade with other countries of the world ',[102] a ' reorganisation of international markets ... is ... necessary if ..., [for example, the] difficulties ... which ... countries like Germany ... find ... at the present time in securing much-needed imports of food and industrial raw materials ... are to be alleviated and ultimately removed '.[154] Yet, while ' an expanding system of international trade is therefore necessary to provide higher living standards for increasing populations ', and while ' international specialisation and national economic development, including population growth, have been postulated upon increasing international co-operation ',[154] ' it seems very uncertain whether any such ... expansion is capable of attainment

---

[a] See the International Studies Conference's special publications on these questions : *154* and *Raw Materials and Peaceful Change* (in course of preparation).

in the face of the recent world-wide revival of seventeenth-century mercantilism '.[102] ' Exportation . . . is to-day very seriously hampered by the intensive protectionism prevalent throughout the world; with regard to some countries even, it is no longer a question of protection but of a policy of autarky, or, at least, of policies with autarkic tendencies. Nearly every country has gone very far in that direction '.[113] ' Such a policy may have served its purpose when the population of the world was much smaller than it is to-day, but it is difficult to see how the greatly augmented world population can be expected to subsist and prosper if it denies itself the full advantages of the geographical division of labour '.[102]

In a word, ' there is no such thing as a surplus population anywhere in the world, except one that is relative to and caused by the existing commercial and economic system. There is no reason why a country should not develop a population as thick upon the ground as in a highly industrialised area and still maintain itself if it could draw freely upon the resources of the rest of the world '.[99]

II. INTERNAL COLONISATION

Since the expansion of international trade, which is the indispensable corollary of industrialisation as a remedy for the economic ailments arising out of expanding populations, is at present blocked by the increasingly autarkical policies of the " dissatisfied " and " satisfied " nations alike, it is possible that the adoption of measures of internal colonisation would provide some relief for demographic congestion. A remedy of this kind is, moreover, clearly indicated wherever the reform of a " country's internal system of land tenure would increase its population-carrying capacity without recourse to changes in the international *status quo* to the disadvantage of other countries.

' In principle, the development of the slightest internal element of subsistence is economically far more valuable to an industrialised country than the colonisation of a sparsely-populated region. This work cannot be compared with the creating of possibilities of work. For, there is here a question, first of all, of creating permanent means of existence; secondly, each new colonisation centre reduces the danger of further overpopulation; it remedies the numerical disproportion between the agricultural and non-agricultural population and mitigates its consequences. Thirdly, since industrial countries never produce enough for them to be self-supporting, each new farm will certainly find a market for its produce and help, at the same time, to maintain the economic status of the country. In principle, therefore, even the industrial countries which are only temporarily overpopulated should make it their imperative duty never to miss the slightest opportunity of organising their territory for the purpose of intensive colonisation and should see therein the ideal means of combating overpopulation '.[150]

' However, methodical recourse to internal colonisation with the object of combating overpopulation meets with a difficulty in the rural problem such as arises in a densely populated country ', and especially in a country where ' the advent of industry has been followed by a notable rise in the standard of living, a circumstance that renders the measures of colonisation relatively costly '. Moreover, where the habit has been adopted ' of demanding in too exacting a fashion that the yield from internal colonisation shall be immediately forthcoming, it has been possible to carry out but a fairly small number of internal colonisation schemes. Some considered these schemes too costly; others hesitated owing to the hardship that all colonising work imposes on the pioneers ... It must be remembered, however, that the countries hit by the crisis and which, in the course of recent years, have carried out vast programmes of internal colonisation (e. g. Italy, Germany, the Netherlands) resolved to do so only by relegating to the backgound their desire to see an early return on their capital '.[150]

' Once the difficulties that prevent ... the utilisation of the last reserves of a country for internal colonisation have been overcome, there will still remain a large number of tasks for it to perform, for example : the extension of the network of colonising centres ...; clearing of all waste land ... where possible ...; creation of agricultural estates outside the industrial areas and of small holdings partly self-supporting and intended for the workers engaged in one or other of the local industries. The object of this work, moreover, will be the more intensive cultivation of land within the former colonisation areas, improvement of the works undertaken in the rural districts, systematic re-extension of agriculture where the nature of the soil presents no difficulty, and the more thorough application of gardening for the development of the land '.[150]

Passing from these general principles to the concrete case of a " dissatisfied " country, the view was expressed in the International

Studies Conference that Poland, for example, had not exhausted the possibilities of internal colonisation. ' The agricultural density is high over the whole country; it is highest in the south, relatively sparse in the east, and relatively moderate in the west. Where the density is high, dwarf holdings of less than five hectares each are numerous; there are over 2 millions of such holdings out of a total of some 2½ millions. Some of those who occupy dwarf holdings have other occupations which they pursue for part of the time, but there are at least a million and three-quarters of such holders whose entire support comes from the land. It has been calculated that the remaining holdings, consisting either of large estates of more than 100 hectares each or of medium-sized holdings, could support not only their present occupiers but also all the landless agricultural workers if they were redistributed. Thus, the problem may be said to centre round the dwarf holdings which do not provide an adequate living for their occupiers '.[84]

Again, in the case of Germany, ' without attributing to the maintenance of the feudal régime[a] alone, the smallness of the population on the eastern borderlands (which is about sixty inhabitants to the square kilometre and which falls as low as thirty-seven inhabitants in Mecklemburg-Strelitz), there is a striking disproportion with the population of Saxony (332 inhabitants per square kilometre) and with that of the Rhineland (495 inhabitants to the square kilometre) and it is impossible to avoid noticing that, if there is lack of space in Germany, it could be remedied much more surely by internal migration than by the possession of colonies.[b] In any case, it would be desirable, after having first applied the remedy, to show that it is ineffective '.[376] [c]

---

[a] ' While the socialist government which had preceded it in the past had undertaken the allotment of the *latifundia* of the eastern provinces (9,000 allotments had been made in 1932), the Hitler government has considerably slowed down the operation (4,500 allotments annually). Of 5½ million rural properties, 7,200 estates have more than 500 hectares. A small number of feudal proprietors continue to own immense estates. The former Emperor, William II, still possesses 97,000 hectares, Prince von Pless, 50,000, Prince von Hohenlohe, 48,000, Prince Hohenzollern-Sigmaringen, 46,000, Prince von Salms, 39,000, etc., and among the smaller proprietors, the Minister of Finance, von Krosigk, 3,900 hectares, and the Minister of War, von Blomberg, 2,300 hectares. The reforms of the new régime stop at the boundaries of these immense estates ' (*376*).

The organ of the S. S. complains that ' the Church takes away . . . a large part of the land from the German national economy ' and that ' it closes to the German people part of its means of maintenance ' (*259*).

[b] It should be noted, however, that it is in East Prussia that ' a large part of . . . [the German post-war land settlement] operations are concentrated ' (*359*).

[c] A law issued in Germany in July 1938 ' announces the abolition (from January 1, 1939) throughout Greater Germany of the so called Familienfideikomiss (Law of Entailment) . . . At the beginning of 1938 there were still 910 entails, covering 1,500,000 hectares of land,

Possibilities of internal colonisation undeniably still exist in a number of congested areas. ' Agriculture, of course, cannot progress indefinitely; nor are the natural conditions and markets unlimited. It is, nevertheless, true that the population living on the land could be appreciably increased by internal colonisation (agrarian reform) '[127] in several countries. On the other hand, in the more acute cases of demographic tension, and even where, contrary to the position in many predominantly agricultural countries, lack of capital does not limit the possibilities of land development,[a] internal colonisation will probably not bring more than temporary relief. In the case of Italy, for example, the Conference was informed that a rough calculation would enable it to ' conclude that the complete execution of the programme for the agricultural development of national territory would, according to the highest estimates, permit the absorption of 17,500,000 persons in 50 years;[b] but, taking into consideration the annual average increase in the population, it must be reckoned that in 50 years' time as from 1931, the population of Italy will have risen by 27 millions '.[41] [c]

which had not been dissolved [under the provisions of the Weimar constitution] . . . It is denied, however, that the law heralds the break-up of the large estates in the interests of a more intensive settlement on the land ' (278).

[a] It is estimated that in Japan ' 6,000,000 acres could be reclaimed, including land now devoted to boundary ridges and pathways that could be saved by the consolidation of small fields '; but ' in most instances the cost of reclamation would be so high that utilization would be an unprofitable business at existing price levels ' (62).

[b] In 1930, the Italian Commissariat for Internal Migration, which had been established in 1926, ' directed and controlled the movement, seasonal and permanent, of 350,000 workers, 295,000 to agrarian occupations (140,000 for wheat harvesting), 55,000 into industry, and 29,000 for roads and building. Internal permanent colonisation by group and family recruitment has also been carried out on reclaimed areas (e. g. Paestum) under the authority of the specially constituted " Comitato Permanente per le Migrazioni Interne ". During the four years of its existence this committee has transferred some 3,246 families from the crowded valley of the Po to the reclaimed districts. Large numbers of Italians have left the Modena and Ferrara districts to be settled in Sardinia . . .; 1,420 families were established . . . in the five years period, 1929-33, in the country round Naples and Bari'; etc. (359).

[c] Cf. above, p. 106, note b.

Chapter 10

International Planning

' Two of the greatest dangers to social tranquility and to political peace to-day in the long run . . . are, first, economic depressions and, secondly, the social pressure of populations '.[323] Neither the one nor the other can be eliminated by independent national action alone. In the course of the work of the International Studies Conference, the suggestion was made that the time had come for international demographic planning : —

' The question . . . [arises] whether it is not necessary to discuss the problem of the necessity of a sort of international machinery whose task it would be to watch questions of population. We are beginning to see the possiblity of a conscious population policy. Since a generation ago there is the new fact of birth control. There is also the far greater and surer knowledge with which we are provided by . . . statisticians . . . It is possible that here we have methods enabling us to follow a continuous policy, but such a policy must be on an international scale '.[201]

' The international organisms have already recognised the ideological unity of economic policy and social policy . . .;[a] unity would, however, remain incomplete if we did not recognise the necessity of

---

[a] Cf. *157* : — ' The intellectual distinction between economic and social questions is already losing its hypnotic influence, which has done so much to divert political thought and action from the path of sensible government. In the face of the facts which have shown the interdependence of economic and social objectives, modern thought is gradually being emancipated from this ancient thraldom. So too the distinction between the economic, social and ethical aspirations of mankind on the one hand and his political activities on the other is dissolving in the light of a more realistic view of history. War is not caused only or mainly by lust for territory or booty or prestige. It is also caused by low standards of living, by the feeling of economic insecurity, by the desire for moral or social emancipation. The founders of the [International Labour] Organisation were right when they discerned an indissoluble connection between peace and social justice '.

taking into account, on the same footing, the demographic factors, and notably the predictable changes in the size and structure of populations. It will, then, depend on the state of the sciences and of knowledge, on the art of statesmen and on the goodwill of the nations whether and when a fair proportion between the different elements of such an integral international social optimum policy can be established in the most satisfactory and constant fashion '.[155] a

ᵃ It was recommended to the International Studies Conference that the following international agreements should be considered (see *155*) :

(1) Agreement concerning the statistical and other criteria of the notion of the synthetic optimum of population (overpopulation and underpopulation);

(2) Agreement concerning the principles and methods of an effort of international collaboration aiming to attenuate the contrasts of standards of living in particularly overpopulated or underpopulated countries ;

(3) Recommendations, and, if possible, an international convention concerning a uniform social policy relative to the distribution of family burdens;

(4) General convention concerning equality of treatment — in the field of social rights — of foreign workers, whose situation is at present a danger for the general standard of living. The conventions concerning post-war emigration by no means suffice ...;

(5) Social principles related to a uniform qualitative policy of population (eugenics, etc.).

The conclusion of these agreements, it was added, would have to be preceded by the following international enquiries :

(1) Comparative international survey of the demographic situation in a certain number of typical countries ... [including] a series of preliminary technical studies, and notably research by methods which have proved particularly satisfactory, into demographic, economic, and social conditions ...;

(2) Optimum population, migration (colonisation) and colonies;

(3) Natural movements of population, internal and external migration;

(4) Counter-migration, standard of living, agrarian reform, industrialisation, international distribution of capital, co-migration, and world trade;

(5) Situation of foreign workers in the world;

(6) Policies in favour of the growth (family policy) or of the control (quantitative or qualitative) of population.

There would also have to be preliminary ' studies concerning the interaction of demographic changes and of the chief problems of social policy which affect the standard of living (employment, unemployment, protection of workers, social insurance, housing, labour hygiene, rural life, etc.) '. The Conference was not informed, however, how it was proposed to carry out so vast an enquiry into subjects many of which have, for nearly two decades, been occupying the attention of the International Labour Office, whose success, for example, ' in stimulating the improvement of record keeping ' is the reason why we now ' possess better figures [of migratory movements] for the post-war than for the pre-war period ' (*84*). It was hinted, however, that a " Standing Committee of demographic conciliation of the League of Nations " might be set up for the purpose, a suggestion which, following upon representations by the Polish delegation to the Assembly of the League of Nations in 1937 that ' it was, paradoxical to deal with the question of the movement of goods and capital and not with that of the movement of human beings ' (*323*), has found concrete expression in a proposal by the Economic Committee of the League of Nations ' that a special demographic committee should be set up to study the demographic problem in its relation to the economic, financial and social situation, and to recommend practical remedies, particular

' The intensity of economic life in very advanced nations . . .
settles the demographic problem as it arises, either within the national
frontiers or beyond them. Hence the importance of international
economic collaboration in dealing with population problems '.[317] As
a step in this direction, proposals for the organisation of international
migrations were brought to the Conference's attention; they are
appended.

Appendix

NOTE ON THE INTERNATIONAL ORGANISATION
OF MIGRATIONS [a]

(*Translation*).

Every policy needs an instrument if it is to be put into practice. A
migration policy can be successful only in so far as it is supported by a machinery of special arrangements, administrative measures and international
agreements. A rudimentary, unofficial, more or less sporadic, organisation
may have been possible in the past. With the general evolution of the modern
world, however, a migration organisation is now inconceivable except as a
complex and systematic mechanism subject to the control of the public
authorities. This is so because, like other forms of exchange, migrations
cannot escape adaptation to the ever greater necessity for foresight and co-
ordination. As national and individual forms of life become more complex,
the adjustment of their activities and needs becomes more difficult and
precarious; and at the same time it becomes increasingly necessary to fortify
society's power to resist crises. The need for the organisation of such
resistance is felt at all points in the commerce of different groups, but the
difficulties involved are sharply intensified by the circumstance that the
organisation must be both national and international.

---

attention being paid to the following points : — (i) various criteria for estimating overpopulation; (ii) the measures adopted in different countries to deal with the increase in population
and possible methods of facilitating the absorption of this increase ' (*316*). In making
this proposal, the Committee was adopting a suggestion from the Secretariat of the League
of Nations that ' since the erroneous or exaggerated opinions which are current in regard to
demographic questions can and do give rise to misunderstandings likely to have an extremely prejudicial effect on international relations, it would be well to set up a " special committee for the practical study of demographic problems " ' (*317*).

[a] See *164* . This document was prepared for the International Studies Conference in
February 1937 by Mr. J. Legouis, of the International Labour Office.

By the force of present circumstances, governments are obliged, *nolens volens*, to regulate migratory movements within their territories and — if they are to avoid disagreeable surprises — to prevent the uncontrolled development or the expansion or the cessation of currents of emigration and immigration. Governments therefore provide, through a variety of internal measures, for the regulation, not only of the volume of migratory movements, but also of their character, their direction and their general behaviour, as well as of the assimilation of immigrants or the repatriation of emigrants.

Experience has shown, however, that the national measures taken in this matter are, in the majority of cases, negative in character; it is far easier for a government, acting alone to restrict or prohibit than to set up or develop migratory currents by balancing supply and demand. It is, therefore, towards agreements between countries directly concerned (countries of immigration and countries of emigration) that the States have very naturally turned their attention.

It should be pointed out first of all that bilateral treaties cannot take the place of a country's internal organisation on the national plane; on the contrary, the former presuppose the existence of the latter of which they are merely the complement. Governments which refrained from intervening in migratory movements would be unable to give one another guarantees as to the volume and composition of the movements, and their conditions of time and place; they cannot even assume reciprocal obligations except in so far as they are in control of migrations from or to their respective territories. The organisation of migration in this bilateral form resting on a national basis has enabled remarkable progress to be made since the world war, particularly in Europe, and it might have been thought that it had taken its final shape. Recent experience, particularly during the crisis years, has, however, revealed serious short-comings and the need, not only for an adjustment of bilateral agreements, but also for a still more developed and comprehensive kind of organisation, which would by no means replace the organisations already existing but would supplement them.

I. The function of the international organisation

The need for an international migration organisation has been stressed by a number of authorities who have studied the problem in its different aspects, approaching it, as it were, from various angles — " national " and " international " experts, authors from emigration and immigration countries, labour writers, independent students, etc., Albert Thomas, M. William Oualid, representatives of countries of immigration such as Senhor de Oliveira

(Brazilian Delegate to the International Emigration Committee, Geneva, 1921), G. Simon (former Polish Minister), Signor De Michelis (formerly Commissioner-General for Italian Emigration), the Workers' Congress on Migration (London, 1926), the International Association for Social Progress, etc.

It is generally expected of an international organisation for migration that, first and foremost, it should contribute to a better adjustment of supply and demand and hence to a return toward equilibrium, to the mitigation of inequalities and, ultimately, to prosperity and peace.

At first sight, and confining myself to a few personal impressions, an international migration organisation should carry out scientific, documentary and practical work for the attainment of these aims. This work, in my opinion, might be outlined roughly as follows :

Scientific work : This would be by way of a preliminary phase, though not the least important The facts to be studied are many and extremely varied, but the instruments of research are very unequal in value and often very defective, so that it is most difficult to make comparisons and to reach accurate conclusions. If we consider the quantitative data available, the statistics relating to migration generally provide only approximately accurate information which needs to be checked against data drawn from a number of sources, and their interpretation can be made only with reserve, particularly because of the frequent gaps in the information concerning occupation, sex and other essential facts. The same may be said with regard to the regulation of migration, much of which is effected by means of administrative circulars and other internal and confidential documents; for, in the matter of migration more than in certain other fields, administrative provisions supplement and go far beyond the legislative texts. In these conditions, the progress that can be made in documentation depends not only on the quantity of material published, but also on the methodological improvements which can be introduced; for example, improvement in the methods of compiling statistics, and in the sources where reliable information can be rapidly obtained on questions of law and practice .

Documentary work : The migration organisation should not confine itself to the investigation of facts, at the risk of remaining purely theoretical or academic; it should endeavour to draw from the documentation analysed concrete conclusions and lessons. Only thus can the States and the other interested parties foresee, as far as may be, the trend of events and plan their migration policy to the best advantage. Purely scientific research should be supplemented by the diffusion of the information collected and, above all, by drawing the attention of the authorities and the general public to important problems, about which so little is known and which are so often imperfectly understood. When the needs and possibilities of the situation are better appreciated, a notable step towards the solving of these problems will have been made.

Before they can be solved, it will still be necessary to create a favourable atmosphere, an atmosphere of collaboration, in which enlightened men of goodwill can be brought together and become accustomed to working in consultation. Committees and conferences do not always achieve this result; some of them even produce the opposite effect; but others, which have the advantage of suitable preparation and of propitious circumstances, can not only solve technical problems, but also promote further efforts and open up new horizons.

Practical work : In my opinion, practical action cannot be envisaged in a vacuum. Not only must it be based on the methods mentioned above, but it is impossible for an international organisation to take any action regarding migration, certain aspects of which touch upon political questions, without paying due heed to what the States want. It would be a mistake to regard such action as a static phenomenon : international activity of this kind is subject to the contingencies of time and place and its limits fluctuate with the ebb and flow of the prerogatives and the idea of national sovereignty. On the other hand, if international organisation — whatever form it may take — must make due allowance for national aspirations, it must, in the last analysis, serve the general interest of the international community and must take as its guide a higher and permanent ideal of justice and equity.

Thus envisaged, practical work can be done in two different fields, according as consideration is given to bilateral relations or to international life in general. In the first hypothesis, it is a question of specific cases, limited in space but apt to be influenced by the existence of other similar cases or to exert an influence on them. Some preparation is necessary for the organisation of *bilateral* systems of migration, and the more thorough this preparation, the easier will it be to gauge the possibilities, to overcome obstacles and to fix the terms of employment and labour contracts, to arrive at the necessary arrangements between unofficial organisations or between public departments, or to conclude treaties, on questions relating to migration and settlement, and the employment and personal status of the workers or colonists concerned. In this respect, a knowledge of similar experiments, and the advice or good offices of experts for the great variety of social, economic, racial, legal and even political questions that arise, which an international organisation is naturally in a position to provide or to obtain, can lead to fruitful results and avoid miscalculations. Moreover, bilateral relations do not generally consist solely in the elaboration of texts of agreements; the application of these texts together with the solving of the practical or legal difficulties to which they give rise is often far more important. In these cases also, the opinion or intervention of experts can be of the utmost assistance.

In *multilateral* relations, a no less important function devolves on the body responsible for the international organization of migrations, and the confidence and co-operation of the States are no less essential. Here again, however, certain fundamental principles remain indispensable.

Very often, the problems which arise in connection with multilateral agreements are very much the same as those which have to be faced by individuals, communities and States in their specific relations, but they are of a more general or even universal character. There are nevertheless certain questions relating to migration which, by their very nature, cannot be settled on a national or bilateral basis. First of all, certain classes of migrants, such as refugees, stateless persons and, in some cases, transmigrants, are not entirely amenable either to national or to bilateral jurisdiction. But it must also be observed that certain national or bilateral problems involve broader relations; for example, a current of migration is rarely set up or revived without the collaboration of a third country in the transport of the migrants, the financing of their undertakings, the marketing of their products, etc. In each of these cases, international organization is a necessity, a visible fact; the only variable factors are the degree and nature — official or unofficial, deliberate or improvised — of that organization.

Multilateral action must also be considered from the point of view of the interests of the international community, and the consideration of these interests must inspire the recommendations and international conventions whereby States are invited to accept the principles which are to serve as a basis for the economic, social and political life and intercourse of societies. Thus, the minimum conditions to be fulfilled in the matter of migration, the treatment of foreigners and the guarantees to be given by the relevant laws and treaties to the various parties concerned might be fixed by international rules. A more positive type of action would be the elaboration of schemes for concerted international action making for economic recovery and peace, by the concerted organization or resumption of migratory movements rationally planned in direct relation to needs and possibilities. It is true that proposals of this kind have hardly taken concrete shape thus far in the general international field, and practical achievements are relatively few; for example, the suggestion for the creation of an " international bank for migration " has never got beyond the stage of theory. The constitution of an international court for the arbitration of disputes arising out of population movements — a " Supreme Court for Migration " — is still no more than a shadowy future possibility. Yet a campaign denouncing the possible creation of such a court succeeded in alarming public opinion in the United States a few years ago. Can anybody predict the fate of these projects ? Will they die a natural death or will they become familiar realities ?

In any case, I think it necessary to point out that the systematic organization of migration can lead to satisfactory results, especially in the international sphere, only if the attendant problems are envisaged as a whole, without isolating them from their social, economic and political causes or reactions. For example, it is obvious that the large majority of migrants leave their country simply because they can no longer find remunerative employment, and that they would abandon their plans if they felt that their subsistence and future were sufficiently assured at home.   In these conditions, a careful study of the general situation, economic and otherwise, prevailing in a given country, can alone make it possible to judge to what extent emigration is necessary or whether it can be avoided by the adoption of an industrial, agricultural or commercial policy, by the undertaking of public works, relief measures, etc. Conversely, a migratory movement, however short its duration may be, can develop only if the country of immigration is enjoying economic prosperity and is satisfactorily organised both socially and politically.

II. A concrete illustration

I have confined myself to giving a broad outline of the organization suggested, because I think that an analytical study would lead us too far and run the risk of departing from immediate realities. It seems preferable to take a concrete example, a method which will be all the more instructive since the example I shall choose is that of the international institution which has made by far the largest contribution to the progress of the international examination of the problem of migration.

There is no need to recite the history of the International Labour Organisation nor to describe its constitution; its fundamental feature is the tripartite collaboration of workers' and employers' delegates and government representatives. An appreciable part of its influence is naturally derived from the relations which States have agreed to maintain with it; but it may well be considered that it draws its main strength from the circumstance that, from the very outset, it was endowed with a constitution setting forth a comprehensive and coherent body of guiding principles, the application of which was entrusted to the Organisation. This programme, founded on social justice, and aiming at the physical, moral and intellectual welfare of workers and the improvement of their condition, which was entrusted to the International Labour Organisation by Part XIII of the Peace Treaties, provides for the regulation of the recruiting of labour, the combating of unemployment and the protection of the interests of workers employed abroad. Article 41 of this Charter further states that the rules enacted in each country concerning labour conditions shall ensure equitable treatment for all workers legally residing in that country.

Thus, not only was the International Labour Organisation provided with an ideological foundation, but this foundation is much broader than any specific problem, such as migration, however vast that problem may be in itself; and, as was seen at the end of the preceding section of this paper, this is an essential condition for dealing with our problem in the light of the facts, and for working out, either in the field of migration itself or elsewhere, solutions of the difficulties encountered. Our approach thus embraces the whole of social life, as well as the economic, moral, intellectual and other factors which influence or are connected with social life.

As soon as it had been created, at its first Conference in 1919, the I. L. O. broached the question of migration; it at once realised the difficulty and complexity of the subject, which permitted neither improvisation nor hasty assumptions. Instead of going into a detailed historical survey, I shall here confine myself to a rapid review of the principal results obtained or at present aimed at by this organization in the particular sphere with which we are concerned.

Scientific work : In 1922, the International Labour Conference recommended that Governments should communicate to the International Labour Office all the statistical or other data in their possession concerning emigration, immigration, repatriation and the transit of emigrants, with details of the measures which they were taking or considering in their respective countries in connection with migration. It further recommended certain improvements in the method of calculating national statistics, mainly with a view to making them internationally comparable. Although nothing more than the communication of existing data was asked for and although the motion adopted was merely a recommendation, a large quantity of interesting information on the volume and regulation of migration regularly reaches the International Labour Office, which has always made a point of selecting and publishing the essential elements of this material. Each year, international statistical surveys of migratory movements in the various countries are issued by the I. L. O. services as an appendix to its year-book; and, from time to time, more detailed booklets give an analysis of these statistics for periods extending over several years, the most recent work in this series being a comparative study of national demographic censuses for 1910, 1920 and 1930, containing a summary of the data relating to foreigners in the different countries of the world.

Similarly, the regulation of migrations is dealt with by the Office in current notes which appear in periodical journals or in general systematic studies devoted either to the problem as a whole (*Migration Laws and Treaties* — three volumes on emigration, immigration and the relevant international treaties and conventions) or to one of its specially important aspects (*The Migration of Workers : Recruitment, Placing, and Conditions of Labour*; *The Organisation of Migration for Settlement*). A mere enumeration of the less extensive studies, those, for example, devoted to particular countries or to questions of a more restricted character, would take us beyond the scope of this memorandum. I would simply point out that migrations and the treatment of migrant workers are also frequently touched upon by the Office in the course of its work as factors arising in connection with other problems : the placing of workers, unemployment and unemployment relief, social insurance, intellectual workers, office workers, labour in the colonies, etc. This list is, in my opinion, sufficient to indicate the policy pursued by the Office, namely that of not artificially separating — even for the purpose of study — the problem of migrations from other social questions, but, on the contrary, of investigating every possible aspect and outgrowth of this problem.

Apart from the scientific value of these investigations, the Office has not overlooked the often thankless task of improving methods of documentation. With regard to statistics, for example, it not only published, as early as in 1922, a booklet on methods of presenting emigration and immigration statistics, but in 1932 it convened a special conference of statisticians which defined the points on which these statistics should be improved, especially with a view to making them more comparable.

International regulation : Among the 58 conventions and 49 recommendations which have so far been drawn up by the International Labour Conference, there is not a single one, whether it deals with working hours,

21

wages, social insurance, industrial hygiene or with some special category of workers (agricultural workers, native labour, professional workers, seamen, etc.), which has not some bearing on the question of migration and the status of migrant workers, if only because the majority of them make no distinction between nationals and foreigners. The ground is thus prepared for an appreciable improvement in the standard of living and for a better organisation of labour in the countries of emigration and immigration, as well as for all that this implies for the improvement of the status of migrants, and in possibilities for the working population to find suitable employment without being forced to emigrate.

Unfortunately, I cannot linger over this very important aspect of the international regulation of labour and I will merely recall that the following points, which directly concern the machinery of migrations and the status of migrants, have been discussed by the International Labour Conference : regulation of the collective recruiting of workers in one country with a view to their employment in another; reciprocity and equality of treatment for foreigners and nationals in respect of the protection of workers' interests and the right to become members of workers' unions; inspection of emigrants and the protection of women emigrants on board ships; equality of treatment regarding workers' compensation for accidents; institution of an international régime for the conservation of pension rights by migrants under disability, old-age and death insurance schemes; regulation of certain special systems for the recruiting of (native) workers. With the exception of those of recent date, these conventions and recommendations are in process of being applied in a number of countries and they account for a substantial fraction of the 732 ratifications of conventions registered by the I. L. O. up to January 1937. Their beneficial effect is, moreover, far from exhausted by number of ratifications or approvals, for even in those countries where such measures have not yet been taken by the competent national authorities, their essential clauses have often been embodied, in some form or other, in the national legislation or in bilateral agreements. Moreover, this remark applies not only to the texts elaborated by the International Labour Conference, but also to the resolutions which, as early as 1921, were voted by the International Migration Committee set up by the I. L. O., particularly with regard to the placing of migrants, equality of treatment, the control of emigration agencies, the collective recruiting of workers for employment abroad and the inspection of emigrants before embarkation.

I would add that the I. L. O., far from considering its task at an end, is actually engaged in preparing a body of rules intended to make possible a more rational organization of the migration of wage-earners . . .

General action : It will perhaps be pointed out that regulation, which is based essentially on statistics, affects only one aspect of life, and that the world economic crisis, by its catastrophic reduction of the volume of migratory currents, tends to render it superfluous. It is no longer sufficient to make good the shortcomings in the system of legal protection and to check abuses; in such circumstances, the fight against poverty and misery calls for efforts to stimulate enfeebled economic activity and thereby to encourage the resumption of international commerce.

From the moment when the first symptoms of the world economic depression made their appearance, these considerations have constantly guided the I. L. O. in its work and they have repeatedly found expression in the resolutions of its Unemployment Committee, in the reports of the Director to the International Labour Office and in the discussions on the economic crisis which have taken place within the Conference. At the International Economic Conference in 1927, the Office presented several reports in which it stressed the paramount importance of demographic and migration problems in the economic life of the world, and it was through no fault of the Office that the Conference failed to discuss these fundamental problems. Whenever the opportunity has arisen, the I. L. O. has not failed to emphasize this same point of view and to offer its collaboration for the solution of these questions.

In its own particular sphere, the Office has, at the same time, intensified its efforts to bring about a resumption of exchanges, in so far as circumstances, especially government policy and the state of public opinion, have permitted it to do so. Without separating migration from other forms of exchange, but, on the contrary, concurrently with the measures requisite for the maintenance of the employment or the consumption of the masses (such as public works and unemployment insurance), it is preparing the conditions conducive to a revival of possible and profitable migratory movements. The favourable reaction already provoked by the proceedings of its unemployment and migration committees, and also of the International Labour Conference, seems to indicate that fresh interest is being taken in this subject. The most conclusive proof is to be found in the resolution whereby the American Labour Congress, in January 1936, asked the I. L. O. to make a special study of European immigration into America and to envisage the problem from the following standpoints : individual immigration, collective recruitment, spontaneous or controlled immigration, relation between immigration and public or private settlement, conditions governing preparatory arrangements for the reception of immigrants. The same resolution also expressed the hope that these studies would lead to the elaboration of international regulations indicating, in particular, the bases for bilateral or multilateral treaties between European and American countries concerning immigration, settlement and labour. This request was all the more significant in that it emanated from new countries whose experience of migratory movements is confined to immigration and which, for many years, have provided considerable outlets for demographic movements.

This request could not fail to find a response. Without relaxing its close study of the migration of wage-earners, which is a question affecting every continent . . ., the Office has actively pushed forward its work concerning settlement, the importance of which is considerable in many respects, particularly as regards relations and exchanges with the New World. In June 1936, the International Labour Conference noted with considerable interest that the question of the establishment of settlers and other independent workers in a foreign country, particularly in overseas countries, had been set down for examination by the Migrations Committee of the Governing Body of the I. L. O.; it was gratified that so vast and so important a problem was to be methodically investigated, and it expressed the hope that the labours of this committee would, as soon as possible, lead to conclusions which would be brought to its notice. Soon afterwards, a mission composed of M. Fernand Maurette, Deputy-Director, and Dr. Enrique Siewers was sent to South America by the I. L. O. to study the position regarding immigration and settlement. On its return, the mission submitted a comprehensive report on the situation in Brazil, Argentina and Uruguay, the fruit of three months' study and research in those States.

As a result of the above resolution and enquiry, the Migration Committee, in the following November, mapped out a very comprehensive programme, the two main points of which were : — (1) The Committee expressed the hope that plans for the development and settlement of certain regions of Latin-American countries would be carefully drawn up by the governments concerned and that the services of the I. L. O. would be placed at the disposal of the governments so desiring it, with a view to undertaking such studies on the spot as might lead to international collaboration; (2) The Committee asked the Governing Body to invite the Director of the I. L. O. to consult, without delay, the States Members of the International Labour Organization on the expediency of convening a conference of experts on settlement migration and to arrange for the holding of this conference as soon as a number of Members sufficient to ensure useful results had expressed the desire to attend. In February 1937, all these proposals were ratified without opposition by the Governing Body, which approved not only the accelerated procedure indicated above, but also the choice of the question of the financing and settlement of the migrants as a suitable subject for discussion by the proposed conference of experts.[a]

There is no need to emphasize the importance of the question of funds and its social aspects (e. g. : guarantees to be given to settlers on the occasion of the purchase of holdings, compensation to be provided for in certain cases for the improvements made by settlers after purchase, the granting of credits, for exploitation and other purposes, etc.). I shall merely point out that it is generaly held that here lies one of the main obstacles to the resumption of migratory movements aiming at the establishment of settlers, even between countries of emigration and immigration which have expressed the desire to increase migratory movements from one to the other. In the report on international settlement migration which it submitted to the Migrations Committee, the I. L. O. noted that this was a problem the solution of which might be very largely facilitated by international collaboration; it added that, at a time when all countries of the world are anxious to see a resumption of international relations, it cannot but be admitted that a revival of settlement movements would contribute, by the re-circulation from country to country of wandering or dormant capital, to the stimulation of currents of exchange from country to country, and that it therefore constitutes an important factor in the restoration of world economy.

Such, very briefly stated, are the few facts which I have thought it of interest to mention at the end of this memorandum, as examples of what an international organization can accomplish in practice in the field of migrations. These efforts — especially as they have the support of attentive and understanding opinion and the active sympathy of experts and public alike — seem to me to justify the hope that positive results will be obtained in the field of international collaboration for peace.

[a] See *303*.

Supplementary Chapter[a]

The Population Carrying Capacity of Australia

With a population of less than 7 millions[b] inhabiting an area of nearly 3 million square miles, Australia is one of the most lightly peopled regions in the world : in 1935, the density of population for the whole Commonwealth was not more than 2.27 inhabitants per square mile.[290] The spectacle of so sparse an occupation of a vast continent, in which, ' in the sixty-four years between the end of 1860 and the end of 1924 . . ., 24 per cent . . . of the growth of the population . . . was due to . . . net immigration ',[84] [c] never fails to hold the attention of the emigration interests. ' To what . . . ', exclaimed the chairman of the inter-governmental committee on refugees which met at Evian in July 1938, ' . . . [does] Australia . . . owe . . . [her] development . . . if not to those constantly renewed influxes of European immigrants, refugees and

[a] The question of habitat, which ' logically precedes any discussion of two of the most important solutions suggested for the problem of overpopulation and underpopulation, namely, migration and colonial expansion ' was included in the International Studies Conference's programme of study, as it was considered ' clear that migration and colonial expansion can only be envisaged as remedies for the lack of demographic balance in the world if the alleged underpopulated regions, whether independent countries or colonial territories, are suitable, by virtue of their climatic and social conditions, for settlement by migrants from the overcrowded areas ' (190). The question was examined incidentally in a number of studies submitted to the Conference and exhaustively for various regions in a symposium submitted by the American Co-ordinating Committee for International Studies (Isaiah Bowman (ed.) : Limits of Land Settlement : A Preliminary Report on Present-day Possibilities (New York : Council on Foreign Relations), 1937); it has likewise been noted in the course of the present Survey. As an illustration of the issues raised in any attempt to answer the Conference's question : What regions seem to offer possibilities of habitat for the different peoples ? a supplementary chapter, in which the problem is related to the Australian continent (one of the regions which most frequently occur in discussions of habitat), is added to the Survey.

[b] According to 290, the population of Australia on September 30, 1937, was 6,846,398.

[c] The contribution of immigration to the growth of population in Australia (excluding aborigines) has been as follows (annual net immigration) : 1871-81, 1.26%; 1881-91, 1.72%; 1891-1901, −0.02%; 1901-11, 0.34%; 1911-21, 0.33%; 1921-31, 0.55%; 1931-32, −0.05% (see 84).

proscribed persons who brought to the new world the precious essences of the old world ' ? ' It . . . [is] therefore in the logic of human history ', he suggested, ' that to-day the initiative and the resources of . . . [this new world] should be offered, by a reversion of history, as it were, to these new clusters of refugees whom revolutions are ejecting from their ancient habitats '.[235]

Now ' it is exceedingly important ', as a memorandum submitted to the International Studies Conference insisted, ' to take the consideration of a subject like this out of the realm of assumption, conjecture, and prejudice. It has been too much the fashion to glance at a map, use loose statistics and then form the opinion that Australia is playing the dog in the manger '.[77] Knowledge of the facts, on the other hand, has led a former Italian Commissioner General of Emigration to declare — in a statement based on ' recent and carefully selected figures regarding the availability and the varied possibilities of the still undeveloped lands ' in which, he thinks, he has ' kept a just mean between general statements, which savour rather of literature for tourists, and a host of statistics which it would have been possible to compile from a series of copious and authoritative documents ' — that ' the physical conditions of this immense territory . . . considerably limit the development of large-scale colonisation '. In his opinion, ' only two areas of Australia may be taken into consideration in this respect : the well-irrigated eastern and south-eastern part of Queensland for intensive agriculture, and the arid zone of the south, suitable for wheat and pasture '.[178] a

' Ignorance of the geography of Australia . . . has led to Australia being singled out as the area *par excellence* which can relieve the pressure of population in other parts of the world '.[77] The fact is often overlooked that about twenty-three per cent of Australia is desert, that is, ' country so arid as to be extremely difficult to settle and develop '. [290] In the remaining habitable area, it is true, the density of population is still only 3.8 per square mile, but, excluding about one million square miles of pastoral country and one hundred thousand square miles suitable for tropical agriculture, there remain only some 600,000 square miles fit

---

a The same authority considers, on the other hand, that, with a change in the present economic conditions, Tasmania, which ' is the part of the Australian Commonwealth that is most favoured by physical conditions . . ., could offer a secure future to the population already existing, and to a by no means inconsiderable number of new settlers . . . The larger part of the area is still untouched, while the mountains contain reserves of gold, silver, lead, zinc and other minerals ' (*178*).

for close settlement.[84] Moreover, ' it is not reasonable to expect more than one-third to be actually arable ', two-thirds being ' affected by (i) poor soil, (ii) rugged mountainous country, (iii) city areas,(iv) forest areas ', while, ' of the 200,000 square miles assumed to be arable, 60,000 square miles of the best land are already farmed '.[77] Consequently, on the basis of these figures and apart from such slight expansion of the population as may be possible in the tropical and pastoral areas,[74] it is only the balance of some 140,000 square miles of arable land, ' considered to be inferior ', which ' represents the scope for expansion '.[77] Clearly, then, " the empty lands " of Australia are a burden to the Commonwealth rather than an asset ', and ' their " vast potentialities " exist only in the mind of the ignorant booster '.[74 a] The truth is that ' the " great open spaces " of Australia are " great " and " open ", not because of any human reluctance to exploit their potentialities, but because of their natural limitations '.[253]

Nevertheless, it would be absurd to pass from one exaggeration to another and to ' suggest that Australia is fully peopled '.[77] This is certainly not the case. ' Nobody thinks that the Commonwealth has reached anything like saturation point '.[373] No one denies that ' the six millions of Australia possess in the south and east of Australia one of the best areas in the world for white settlement '.[74] Here, according to the expectations of the writer of one of the papers submitted to the Conference, ' some twenty millions will dwell, when Australia is developed to the same extent as the United States '.[74 b] If, furthermore, Australia were to adopt ' the lower standards of Central Europe and elsewhere ', and on the assumption ' that the coal is adequately used for manufactures,[c] then ', in the view of the same writer, ' there seems no good reason why this figure should not be doubled or trebled '.[74] For the authors of another memorandum submitted to the Conference,

a According to the special correspondent of *The Times* at the Evian refugee conference in July 1938, ' the supposition that ... Australia ... [has] vast open spaces waiting to be colonised, though fallacious ..., [was] widely held ... [there] ' (277).

b ' If equivalent rainfall areas were as densely peopled in Australia as in the ... western States [of America] ... where there is very little industry ', Australia would have a population of 29.6 millions, or nearly five times its present population; ' it is true to say ', therefore, ' that on a purely agricultural basis Australia is very sparsely peopled when compared with the United States ' (84).

c In view of Australia's large coal resources, ' we may surely forecast a great development of manufactures, based on this cheap power ... Since the chief coalfields of Europe and the eastern United States have led to population densities exceeding 100 to the square mile, we may perhaps indicate three such future centres in eastern Australia at Newcastle [120,000 million tons], Morwell [11,000 million tons], and Ipswich [2,000 million tons] ' (74).

however, ' thirty million would be a liberal estimate . . . of the maximum population which could be sustained in Australia . . ., [but] even . . . [this] estimate . . . presumes a somewhat higher degree of efficiency [in agricultural technique] than that now achieved '.[77] ' The tendency in official circles seems to be at present to accept " at least thirty millions " as the carrying capacity of the continent ',[290] and, while ' those astronomical estimates — reaching as high as sixty million as being both desirable and attainable — which characterised the early post-war thinking '[368] [a] on Australia's population carrying capacity now seem to be generally repudiated, there appears to be common agreement that, whatever the maximum potential population of the Commonwealth may be, not only is Australia capable of carrying a denser population than at present but she even ' stands to gain by having a far larger population '.[77] Indeed, according to one view, ' immigration on a large scale seems necessary at once even to maintain the level of productivity which Australia has already reached '.[325] Thus, while the common assumption that Australia is, to a large extent, an empty continent is literally true, the underlying implication that the Commonwealth is capable of being filled with human beings is meaningless.

The equally frequent assumption that, because Australia has been a major country of immigration in the past, large-scale emigration to the Commonwealth is possible to-day is also based on a misconception. The fact is that ' immigration into . . . [Australia] has always fluctuated in a very marked fashion '[84] [b] and that ' experience . . . suggests that net gain from immigration is largely a function of three variables, economic conditions in Australia, economic conditions abroad, especially in Europe, and the kind and amount of Government assistance rendered '.[290] [c]

It would carry this Survey too far afield to examine these several

[a] Cf. *290* : — ' Estimates of population carrying capacity vary from about 20 millions to about 200 millions '.

[b] The following landmarks in the economic development of Australia in relation to migration movements may be noted : (i) 1840-1 : land boom; establishment of the wool industry; (ii) 1842 : recession; (iii) 1852-4 : gold discoveries; (iv) 1866 : Overend-Gurney crisis in Queensland; (v) 1870 : mining boom in Queensland; (vi) 1883-90 : boom before the collapse; (vii) 1893 : collapse; (viii) 1911-15 and later : assisted migration; (ix) 1931 : the depression. For details of the bearing of these landmarks on migration in Australia see *77*; see also *290*.

[c] For a description of forms of assistance given to emigrants to Australia from the United Kingdom, whence, as is mentioned below, the migratory stream to Australia has been mainly fed in the past, see *94*.

factors, though brief reference will be made later[a] to the internal and external economic conditions which would make it both possible and desirable for an expansion of the population of Australia to take place. Meanwhile, consideration must be given to the present trend of demographic movements in Australia, for it is obvious that, if the population of Australia is growing by natural increase at a rate corresponding with the Commonwealth's economic requirements and possibilities, arguments in favour of a discharge into Australia of the surplus population of other countries are robbed of their moral justification and political force.

Although the population of Australia has grown with very great rapidity,[b] its average annual rate of expansion has nevertheless fallen from 4.47% between 1850 and 1901 to 1.84 between 1901 and 1931.[84] This fall was mainly due to ' the decrease in the average annual gain by natural increase ' which, ' in the sixty-four years between the end of 1860 and the end of 1924 ' had accounted for ' 76 per cent of the growth of the population of Australia . . . Whereas it was well over 2 per cent up to 1890, it was below 2 per cent during the next four decades, and since 1930 has been under 1 per cent; the fall in the gain by births has been dramatic and has not been offset by a corresponding fall in loss by deaths '.[84] [c] ' Since the . . . [death-rate is] very low already,

[a] See below, pp. 317-318.

[b] During the forty-year period from 1881, when ' the early rush of incomers had passed ', to 1921 when the period of immigration restrictions began, ' the average annual rate of increase was . . . 2.2 per cent in Australia ' as compared with ' 1.1 per cent in Japan and 0.9 per cent in England and Wales. In other words, when we omit the early years during which growth was almost inevitably very swift, we find that the rate of growth in . . . [Australia] has been twice that in the old countries ' (84). The following table taken from 75, which is reproduced in 74, shows the dates at which the population passed new " million marks " :

Date	Period in years	Population	Growth	Factors
1788-1834	46	100,000	Very slow	Convicts dominant
1835-1851	17	437,000	Very slow	Squatters; sheep
1852-1858	7	1,000,000	Rapid	Gold rushes
1859-1877	19	2,000,000	Slow	Farming with " selection "
1878-1889	12	3,000,000	Rapid	Approach of land boom
1890-1905	16	4,000,000	Slow	Droughts and slump; W. A. gold
1906-1918	13	5,000,000	Rapid at first	Factories and the war
1919-1926	8	6,000,000	Rapid	Normal immigration, etc.

[c] The annual natural increase of the population of Australia (excluding aborigines), has been as follows : 1871-81, 2.30%; 1881-91, 2.30%; 1891-1901, 1.82% ; 1901-11, 1.62% ; 1911-21, 1.71%; 1921-31, 1.37%; 1931-32, 0.82% (84); 1935, 0.709%; 1936, 0.77% (290).

it would seem that, unless the decline in the birth-rate is halted, natural increase must soon come to an end '.[84]   This expectation is confirmed by the course of the net reproduction rate.   By 1932-33, the net reproduction rate, which stood at 1.539 in 1911[78] and was still as high as 1.319 in 1920-22,[90] had fallen to 0.976 by 1932-33.[90]   It dropped down to 0.956 for the period 1932-34;[292] in 1934, the rate fell as low as 0.939.[78] Since 1932-34, ' the female birth rate has increased ',[290] and the net reproduction rate moved up, in 1935, to 0.940,[78] ' but this can only be interpreted as due to the abnormally low figure of the depths of the depression, not as a reversal of the trend '.[368]   In February 1938, it was found that the net reproduction rate had risen to ' slightly above unity ',[290] but ' it is anticipated . . . that the . . . recovery will be short-lived and that the general downward trend in the natality curve will soon be resumed '.[290 a]   Should this anticipation prove to be correct, then ' the time is not far distant when population will become stationary and begin to decline ',[325] and it may be taken as ' certain that without an increase in the birth-rate, the population of Australia, apart from immigration, will never reach nine millions '.[290]   Indeed, an ' authoritative estimate shows that, without migration, and assuming mortality and natality rates to remain at the 1932-34 level, population will reach a maximum of 7,873,000 in 1978 '.[325 b]   Moreover, even ' on the assumption that immigration of the same volume and age distribution as that which marked the peak of the pre-depression years will be maintained . . ., an estimate of future population [c] . . . based on a reasonably optimistic view of the probable future course of the net repro-

[a] ' We can extrapolate the trend line of the Net Reproduction Rate with some confidence. For the decline is general in all countries for which measurement is possible . . .   Despite the great increase in birth control in recent years, the statistics of illegitimacy as well as the reports of social workers indicate clearly that the practice of contraception can spread much more widely still — and fertility can decline with zero as its limit.   The decline in fertility is to some extent offset by declining mortality.   But mortality certainly has a limit greater than zero, and, moreover, it is only declining mortality amongst women of child-bearing age that contributes to preventing an ultimate decline in the population.   These considerations suggest that to use the fertility and mortality experience of 1932-34 as the basis of an estimate is taking a conservative view of the decline of the Net Reproduction Rate in Australia.   A reversal of the downward trend is only conceivable as a result of strenuous Government action directed to making child-bearing a profitable occupation ' (368).

[b] See also 368, the author of which reproduces (from information both published (see 369) and given to him privately by Mr. S. H. Wolstenholme the following estimates, calculated on the basis of existing rates, of Australia's future population (000's omitted) : — 1933 : 6,630; 1938 : 6,882; 1943 : 7,126; 1948 : 7,353; 1953 : 7,547; 1958 : 7,694; 1963 : 7,788; 1968 : 7,841; 1973 : 7,867; 1978 : 7,873; 1983 : 7,860; 1988 : 7,825; 1993 : 7,770; 1998 : 7,703; 2003 : 7,632.

[c] Prepared by Mr. S. H. Wolstenholme.

duction rate ' shows that Australia will reach ' a maximum population of 8,940,000 in 1981 '.[290]

These figures represent, of course, nothing more than reasoned anticipations based upon current trends. Time alone can verify their worth as a guide to present action. It should not be forgotten ' that a very small excess over unity [in the net reproduction rate] will bring an increase of population, rapid in relation to . . . resources; just as a small deficiency creates an alarming prospect ',[77] nor that ' a decline in population may so affect the causes bringing about the decline that they will cease to operate. Should the net reproduction rate rise to and remain at a little above unity . . ., [Australia will] get all the additional population . . . [she] may be able to absorb '.[290 a] This, however, is sheer speculation. In the face of the clear indications revealed by the analysis of the present direction of demographic movements in Australia, it would be unreasonable to suggest that any considerable expansion of population is likely to occur through natural increase.

Thus, ' a brief survey of present population trends soon disposes of any hope that population is likely to increase in the future at a pace commensurate with the needs of an expanding economy '.[325] Hence, it does not seem unreasonable to emphasise, on the basis of existing trends, ' the great importance of immigration when the future of . . . [Australia] is under review '.[84] This does not mean, of course, that, in order to save themselves from the catastrophe of ultimate extinction, on the one hand, and from the charge of selfish possession, on the other hand, the Australian people must now take steps to ensure a massive immigratory movement. For, ' no matter how many people a country could accommodate in time, using existing technical methods for its exploitation, there is a limit to the rate of increase of population which is desirable. We cannot determine this rate of increase theoretically; but experience shows that the population of . . . [Australia] has increased at an average annual rate of about 2 per cent for the sixty years ending in 1924 . . . We may conclude that the average rate, taking good years with bad, should remain at that level for some considerable time to come. If it does, then, although . . . [Australia] will still be lightly populated for several decades, there will be no substance in the charge that . . . [Australians] occupy territory that they do not use; for they will be making all due speed towards full exploitation. But, if it does not, the charge will lie. ' In order to exculpate Australia from such

---

ᵃ Quoting 291.

a charge, and ' if . . . [Australia] is to continue to grow at an annual average rate of 2 per cent. or even at a much lower rate . . ., [she] will require more assistance from immigration than before '.[84] How much more assistance ? This, from the angle of the International Studies Conference's enquiry, is the crux of the problem.

It has been calculated that ' assuming a slight improvement in natality rates over those of the depression years, an immigration of 7,000 persons per annum of the same age distribution as that which held before 1929, would prevent population declining after 1978 '.[325] This is a small figure in comparison with the average annual gains of 41,690 and 34,911 through net reproduction in, respectively, the seven-year pre-war period 1907-1913 and the ten-year post-war pre-depression period 1920-1929, but it implies a reversal of the migratory stream in the seven-year period 1930-1936 during which there was an average annual loss through net emigration of 2,560.[290 a] Yet, if this stream is not first reversed and afterwards enlarged, then, ' even on the most liberal estimate [of natural increase], there seems little likelihood of Australia's population increasing at a rate which will permit progress at the pace previously reached, unless revolutionary changes occur in productive technique in the near future — changes which will permit a smaller population to maintain its standards of real income, despite increasing difficulty in using the economies of large-scale production '.[325] Since such changes cannot be foreseen, it is legitimate to infer from the present population trends in Australia that there is a clear *a priori* justification for the view that circumstances are propitious for the resumption of a steady, though not necessarily very ample, flow of immigration into Australia. On purely demographic grounds, therefore, Australia cannot resist the claim that she is able to contribute to the operation of a migratory movement out of congested countries. But here the vital question again arises : how many people can Australia absorb from congested areas ?

It was observed above that migration in Australia is a function of a number of factors of which the demographic situation within the Commonwealth is only one. The non-demographic factors would appear to present a formidable obstacle to any considerable stream of immigration into Australia. ' The absorption of population depends upon : (i) agricultural development — and the present situation and

---

a In the six-year period 1914-1919, during which ' emigration was not encouraged from the United Kingdom ', there was an average annual loss through net emigration of 8,260 (*290*).

tendencies of world markets for agricultural products are not encouraging; (ii) the development of mineral resources, which is affected by the formation of companies and the investment of capital . . .; (iii) industrial development, a matter that is under close consideration in Australia at the present time.   It is a significant fact that there has been in Australia a . . . drift of population towards the towns, largely due to industrial development; as a matter of fact, during the post-war decade there was a much greater increase of population in the towns and industrial areas than in the agricultural districts.   [Furthermore], development depends upon capital, and the Australian Government is scarcely in a position to launch further loans as it did from 1920 to 1930, which, in the opinion of Australian economists, contributed very largely to the difficulties which Australia experienced during the depression '.[198] Problems such as these cannot be evaded when consideration is given to the rate of absorption and the magnitude of Australia's population carrying capacity in relation to the problem of peaceful change.

If, however, the assumption may be made here that the internal and external conditions favouring migration will be such as to ensure a sufficient inflow of immigrants into Australia to meet ' what can without exaggeration be called a crisis in . . . [her] population . . . [history] ',[84] is it possible to estimate the extent to which such a movement may affect those particular countries claiming relief from a degree of demographic congestion so acute as to constitute a threat to the maintenance of peace ?   As already noted, it has been suggested[a] that in order ' to secure sufficient immigrants to prevent the population declining after 1978, it may be necessary to import only about 2,000 or 3,000 families per annum '.[325]   This, clearly, is so small a number as to be practically negligible in relation to the problem of peaceful change.   It appears, however, to be generally recognised that it represents only a fraction of the maximum rate of Australia's demographic absorption capacity, though estimates of this rate vary between widely separated extremes.   There are those who consider that Australia's ' absorptive capacity for the next few years is at about the average rate of from 35,000 to 40,000 per annum '.[290] [b]   Others ' would regard a

---

[a] See above, p. 317.

[b] Cf. 77 : — ' The maximum absorptive capacity is not likely to exceed 40-50,000 migrants per annum for some time to come, unless it be at the expense of living standards '; and 368, the author of which, after observing that the conclusions of his ' survey of the Australian problem may appear to be utterly pessimistic ', adds : — ' They are pessimistic about large-scale immigration — of the order, say, of 50,000 immigrants a year. But only as to that. Immigration on a smaller scale could play a distinctly useful part in Australian life '.

mere 35,000 to 40,000 immigrants a year as a ridiculous under-estimate ';
they consider that Australia ' may reasonably expect to absorb about
70,000 in excess of the present natural increase, rising in ten years'
time to about 130,000 in excess of the present natural increase '.
Perhaps most Australians would echo the view that ' the general
principle to be endorsed is infiltration ' and that ' for mass migration no
Australian Government should allow itself to become responsible '.[290]
But, whatever may be Australia's immigration absorptive capacity
on paper, ' past experience suggests that if net immigration tends to
exceed about 40,000 per annum, Governments should study the
economic situation, internal and external, very closely '.[290]

' Those who are advocating peaceful change through migration
can say whether... [migration on this scale] is significant '. To the
authors of one of the memoranda submitted to the International Studies
Conference, it seemed ' a very small contribution of almost negligible
importance ', though they admitted that, ' in view of the probable
decline in European population it might... be very significant '.[77 a]
In the context of the Conference's study of peaceful change, however,
it is not enough to enquire into the ultimate absorptive capacity of
Australia and the present potential rate of immigration into the Commonwealth, on the one hand, and into the future demographic position
of emigration countries, on the other hand. A question which also
arises is the extent to which Australia may be, not merely able, but also
willing to give satisfaction to the countries whose demographic situation
was the subject of the International Studies Conference's enquiry.
In so far as the final answer to this question depends upon the general
political considerations which govern Australian policy, it falls outside
the province of a Survey of the present kind; but there is one political
issue which, although it cannot be judged here, must be stated.

The history of the growth of population in Australia runs counter
to any expectation that the Commonwealth's capacity to absorb a few
tens of thousand immigrants a year means that the countries under
consideration can be annually relieved of a corresponding number of
emigrants. In the first place, ' the people of Australia..., [as Australians have] frequently and proudly stated, are " 98 per cent

---

[a] ' Australia ', said an Australian speaker at the Conference's session in 1937, ' is very
anxious for peaceful change... but her contribution to the solution of demographic difficulties standing in the way of peace cannot be large, but must be strictly limited by reason
of her capacities and the hard facts of her geographic, economic and financial position.
Her contribution will be willing but it cannot be large ' (*198*).

British " ',[290] [a] and ' immigration into Australia has always been over-whelmingly British in character '.[373] [b]   Apart from the geographical

[a] ' If " British " means of British nationality, then in 1933 less than 1 per cent. was " foreign ".   If it means " British by place of birth ", as presumably it does, then included in the 98 per cent. (or thereabouts) were those born in Australia whose parents were foreigners.   But however " British " be interpreted it is certain that the foreign element in the population is relatively very small.   Perhaps 10 per cent. come from foreign parents or grand-parents ' (290).   The following figures (ibid.) show the distribution of the population of Australia by race, nationality and birthplace at the time of the 1933 census : —

(I) Race

European	6,579,993
Non-European	22,780
Half-Caste	27,066
Total	6,629,830

(II) Nationality

British

Born in Australia	5,726,566
Born outside Australia	842,952
Total	6,569,518

Foreign

Chinese	7,792
Italian	17,658
Greek	5,652
Japanese	2,084
Russian	2,055
Yugoslavian	2,826
U. S. A.	2,557
Norwegian	1,238
Polish	1,757
Swedish	1,370
Others	15,270
Total	60,259
Not stated	62
Grand Total	6,629,839

(III) Birthplace

Australia	5,726,566
Norfolk Is.	
Papua	
New Guinea	46,737
Nauru	
New Zealand	
Australasia	5,773,303
England	486,831
Wales	14,486
Scotland	132,489
Ireland	78,652
Isle of Man	964
Channel Is.	1,412
Other British possessions in Europe	2,912
Elsewhere in Europe	89,893
Total	807,639
Asia	24,559
Africa	7,821
America	11,579
Polynesia	2,887
At sea	2,051
Total born outside Australia	903,273
Grand Total	6,629,839

[b] In 1891, by which date ' Germans and Scandinavians had made an appreciable contri-bution to the population ' (84), the apportionment of the European population in Australia by country of origin was as follows : — British (English, 53%; Scottish, 13%; Irish, 23%; other British, 1.5%), 90.5%; non-British (German, 5.2%; Scandinavian, 1.9%; others, 2.4%), 9.5% (ibid.).   ' It is probable that the share of the British has fallen slightly since 1891. While immigration from northern Europe has fallen off, Italians and others, not represented before, have come in, though not in large numbers ' (ibid.).   ' During the period 1921-1925, there was a net gain of 155,569 immigrants of British birth . . .   In 1926-1930, the gain of British-born was 105,358 ' (74).   In 1921-1925, there were 13,628 Italian immigrants; in 1926-30, 10,583 (ibid.).   ' The largest immigration of Italians in any one year was in 1927 when it reached nearly 8,000 ' (84).   ' In the years 1925-1929 the annual average net gain of 33,816 Europeans intending permanent residence in Australia consisted of 26,310 persons of British nationality, 3,713 of Italian nationality, and the remainder divided among a large number of different nationalities ' (373).

and economic factors which govern Australia's population carrying capacity ' another factor limiting European colonisation may be said to be the hostility of the various States to any infiltration of non-Anglo-Saxon elements, such infiltration being regarded as lessening the homogeneity of the population and the permanent influence of the British Government, which seeks to establish British workers. The latter . . . enjoy great advantages, while foreign, non-British workers are subject to many restrictions on admission and may be admitted only in very small proportions '.[178] [a] ' That is undoubtedly the position ', admitted an Australian delegate to the Evian inter-governmental Committee on refugees in reply to a statement that Australia owed her development to the flow of immigration,[b] but, he pointed out, ' that immigration has naturally been mainly British, and it is not desired to go outside that system to any great extent so long as there may be British settlers available '.[402] [c]

[a] ' In 1925 . . . wide powers were given to the Governor-General to prohibit or limit the entry of persons of any race or nationality on grounds so wide that the power was virtually unlimited . . . But in fact these powers have not been exercised. The government, fortified, when it comes to bargaining, by the fact that other governments know that these powers are in reserve, has concluded a number of agreements. The governments of Yugoslavia, Greece, and other eastern European countries have agreed to limit the number of passports issued to their nationals who intend to go to Australia ' (84; see also above p. 215, note b).

[b] See above, p. 310.

[c] It is to be noted that all Australian students of the Commonwealth's demographic position are not indissolubly wedded to the view that a policy of discrimination between British and non-British European immigrants must always be elevated to the status of an axiomatic principle of wise statesmenship. Cf., e. g., 77 : — ' British migration to Australia is ideal for assimilation but it is difficult . . . : (i) there is very little difference between the standard of living of the two countries . . .; (ii) the modern English working man is singularly inadaptable . . . [and] almost useless on the land; (iii) because of the absence of economic stimulus and the need for training to fit the migrant for the new conditions, immigration has to be State organised and the migrant's responsibility for success is diminished . . . Northern Europeans are always acceptable. They are more adaptable than the British and can be readily assimilated, are more willing to take the risk of success. Australia, however, would be sensitive to the formation of enclaves or to any doctrine that the migrant still retained his old allegiance . . . The peasant stocks of the South European peninsulas are undoubtedly inferior in adaptability to the Northern stocks. They are definitely more difficult to assimilate and the difference in living standards between them and the Australian is so great that great discontent is caused '. The view has also been expressed that the predominantly British composition of the population of Australia is open to criticism on sociological grounds : ' Australia is perhaps unduly self-congratulatory on the fact that some 97 per cent of her white folk are of British ancestry. This is satisfactory in so far as it means that there is no language problem in Australia, such as vexes Canada or South Africa. From the racial point of view, Australia differs from Canada or the United States in that there are no immigrants from Central Europe. Hence there is lacking the broad-headed Alpine race, which is so well represented in America. The writer is of the opinion that biologically a strain of Alpine blood would strengthen the future Australian population . . . [Moreover], there is some slight evidence that the darker Mediterraneans may acclimatize more readily in the Australia than the fairer type ' (74).

To the extent, then, that a preference in Australia for British immigrants must restrict the scale of emigration to the Commonwealth from other European countries, the importance of the rôle which Australia could play in relation to this aspect of the problem of peaceful change is diminished since it has not been suggested that a need for emigration in Great Britain raises a "peaceful change" issue. It does not follow, however, that Australia is open to the criticism that, if no immigrants could be attracted from Great Britain, she would prefer to face the contingency of depopulation rather than lower the barriers against the immigration of nationals from other European countries.[a] Yet, it is to be noted that, while, in fact, ' the quantitative effect of the discrimination policy practised by . . . [Australia] against continental Europe has been counterbalanced by the stimulation of emigration from Great Britain ',[84] British emigration has not sufficed to prevent the decline in the total immigration into Australia during the last few years.[b] It is, therefore, of interest to note that the Overseas Settlement Board now suggests, that, failing sufficient settlers from the United Kingdom, the admission of a carefully regulated flow from other countries is to be recommended.[274] At the same time, the Board suggests that such settlers would preferably come from countries whose people are broadly of the same stock as the British and who have a similar outlook,[273] while the Prime Minister of Australia is reported to have stated that, although ' foreigners who were enterprising enough to come and who were acceptable would be welcomed . . ., the Government would make no special concessions, nor would they join in any scheme for assisting migration from any foreign country or make distinctions between European races '.[275] [c] Another objection came

---

[a] While ' it is not possible to bring forward conclusive evidence . . . to show that the immigration . . . [policy] adopted by . . . [Australia has] reduced the volume of immigration in recent years . . ., [yet] it is interesting to notice that there is no sign of any marked increase of immigration into . . . [Australia] following upon the imposition of severe restrictions by the United States, and this is probably explained by the fact that . . . [Australia] was also imposing restrictions . . . That this explanation is correct seems to follow from an analysis of the figures for immigration into . . . [Australia] from those countries whose nationals were virtually excluded from the United States after 1921. The number of immigrants from these countries tended to rise slightly after 1921; but the rise was soon checked. We can probably recognise in this fact the working both of quantitative restrictions and of discrimination in the immigration policy of . . . [Australia]. For it is reasonable to suppose that, had the people of these countries been free to enter, they would have come in fairly large numbers after 1921 ' (84).

[b] Between 1931 and 1935, there was a net *emigration* from Australia of 10,886 (77).

[c] On August 23, 1938, the Australian acting Minister of the Interior was reported to have announced that his Department was ' inundated with applications from German and

from the House of Lords where a Labour peer expressed the hope that 'we should not produce groups of nationalities in the Dominions so that we should have difficulties such as those to which he could point as existing in the world at present ',[370] while to the Under-Secretary of State for Dominion Affairs 'it seemed to be vital that the Empire should be populated, if not by people of our own stock entirely, at any rate by people who could be assimilated to that stock and who held the same kind of ideals '.[244]

But, secondly, 'the most significant feature of this aspect of Australian population history ... relates to ... Asiatics[a] who at one time were beginning to assume an important part in the opening up of some areas of the country.[b] In 1885 there were about 40,000 Chinese and 10,000 Kanakas in Australia, who together formed 2 per cent. of the population. The Kanakas have been deported[c] and the number of Chinese has been reduced to half that present fifty years ago ',[d] while 'an arrangement has been made with Japan whereby passports are not granted to Japanese who intend to settle ... Thus, non-European labourers are excluded from settling in Australia ', and 'the proportion which Europeans form of those engaged in exploiting the country has risen '.[84] [e] It is clear that, whatever prospect there may

Austrian Jews ', that, 'if the present rate of influx continues there will be 50,000 wanting to settle in Australia, but [that] probably only 5,000 will be permitted to come after the application of restrictions on alien immigration ' (see *279*). On December 1, 1938, the Australian Minister of the Interior confirmed in the House of Representatives that 'Australia would receive 15,000 European refugees over three years, including Aryans, Jews, and non-Aryan Christians — namely, persons partly or wholly Jewish of Christian faith '; in arriving at this figure, which the London *Times* noted as 'a characteristically generous contribution to the solution of the refugee problem ', the Australian Government 'had been influenced by the necessity for reconciling with the interests of the refugees the interests of Australia's present population, and of people of British race who desired to establish themselves in Australia ' (*288*).

[a] See *84* for statistics relating to the non-European population of Australia since the middle of the 19th century.

[b] In considering Australia's non-European population, 'we may leave the aborigines out of account since they have taken no part in the exploitation of the country ' (*84*). Moreover, 'the aborigines are almost all to be found along the relatively inaccessible northern coast lands, where they come in contact with only a few hundred whites ' (*74*). The aborigines 'may have numbered 150,000 when Australia was discovered ' (*84*); 'to-day there are about 60,000 full bloods and 20,000 half-castes in Australia ' (*74*).

[c] 'The Pacific Islanders Act of 1901 provided for the deportation with certain exceptions of all Kanakas, the term applied to Pacific Islanders, who were found in Australia after 1906 ' (*84*).

[d] 'The component states of what is now the Dominion of Australia began to impose restrictions upon Chinese immigration at relatively early dates, Victoria in 1855 and New South Wales in 1861 ' (*84*).

[e] 'In the ten years ... [1921-1930] the total number of non-Europeans decreased by 981, the largest number of departures being Chinese ' (*74*).

be of finding an outlet in Australia for the relief of congested populations in Europe, a strict application of the " White Australia " policy[a] stands as a barrier against any substantial stream of emigration from the Asiatic countries. In extenuation of the effects of this policy, however, it has been suggested that, ' since politicians have to a considerable degree dropped their references to the " unlimited potentialities of empty Australia " and have begun to admit that much of Australia is empty because neither British nor Asiatics could do much with it, there is likely to be less objection to the White Australia Policy on the part of foreign nations '.[74]

* * *

The foregoing account of some of the factors conditioning a migratory movement into Australia as a means of alleviating demographic pressure elsewhere is admittedly inconclusive (though doubtless with a tendency to give point to the view that ' migration to Australia cannot be regarded as a sensible contribution to the easing of population problems in other countries');[77] but it is, perhaps, not more inconclusive than might be expected from a survey of conflicting opinions. These opinions are not likely to be replaced by exact knowledge until further enquiry has provided answers to such questions as ' Australia's capacity to produce both in primary and secondary production and ... her capacity to absorb immigrants in both spheres ' and ' the capacity of the home and overseas markets to absorb an increase in primary and secondary production '. A survey of the first question ' would involve, among other things, a study of the cost curves of different types and different quantities of production, problems of transport and communication, and the optimum size of towns and the possibility of developing satellite towns and housing schemes '. A survey of the second question ' would need to consider the whole problem of the standards of living and the diets of different countries, and their economic and political stability ' as well as ' tariff policy generally and in particular the Australian tariff '. ' In short, it would be necessary for Australian Governments to undertake a thorough economic and social survey of Australia '.[325]

---

[a] Cf. 77 : — ' Racial antagonism ... is not mainly based on colour ... The objection to Asiatic or African migration is based really on economic grounds and mainly the difference in the standard of living '; and 74, the writer of which ' has always advocated such a modification of the White Australia Policy as would diminish the friction between Asia and Australia ... This would involve admitting small proportions of Japanese, Chinese and Indians — but not enough to constitute a cultural menace '.

BIBLIOGRAPHICAL INDEX

List of Sources cited in the Survey

The italicised figures in the page-indexing are page references to the sources of the passages in the Survey; in the case of secondary sources, the italicised figures are page references to the corresponding primary sources.

I. I. I. C. = International Institute of Intellectual Co-operation

—————

CONTENTS

* The unpublished mimeographed documents utilised in the Survey are available for reference in the libraries of some of the Institutions represented in the International Studies Conference and in the archives of the International Institute of Intellectual Co-operation.

A. PUBLICATIONS AND DOCUMENTS OF THE INTERNATIONAL STUDIES CONFERENCE

I. Collective Security

Reference
number. *

(1) Preliminary study conference on " Collective Security ", 1934 :

1. *A Short Record of a Preliminary Study Conference on " Collective Security " held in Paris on May 24-26, 1934* (Paris : I. I. I. C.), 1934 (mimeographed document no. C. 93.1934). *Cited on Page* 3.

(2) General study conference on " Collective Security ", 1935 :

(a) Preparatory memoranda submitted by members of the International Studies Conference :

2. MICHEL ANTONESCU : " Respect of International Obligations; Revision of Treaties and International Situations ", in MAURICE BOURQUIN (ed.) : *Collective Security : A Record of the seventh and eighth international studies conferences, Paris 1934 and London 1935* (Paris : I. I. I. C.), 1936. *Cited on Page* 8 *(237-241).*

3. FRANCESCO COPPOLA : " The Idea of Collective Security ", in *ibid. Cited on Pages* 4 *(144-5, 146-7),* 5 *(146-7),* 5 *(147-8),* 7 *(147).*

4. LUDWIK EHRLICH : " Respect of International Obligations; Revision of Treaties and International Situations ", in *ibid. Cited on Pages* 8 *(218-25),* 10 *(223).*

5. LOUIS LE FUR and DE GEOUFFRE DE LA PRADELLE : " The Revision of Treaties ", in *ibid. Cited on Page* 8 *(196).*

6. J. LIMBURG and J. H. W. VERZIJL : " Collective Security ", in *ibid. Cited on Page* 8 *(216-218).*

---

* The reference numbers are printed in small type in the text of the Survey and in italics in the footnotes.

7. C. A. W. Manning : " The Elements of Collective Security ", in " Some British Views of Collective Security ", in *ibid.* *Cited on Pages* 14 (*207-8*), 15 (*207*).

8. David Mitrany : " Peaceful Change and Article 19 of the Covenant ", in *ibid.* *Cited on Pages* 9 (*213*), 9 (*209-215*), 11 (*213*).

9. Alan B. Plaunt (Rapporteur) : " Collective Security ", in *ibid.* *Cited on Pages* 8 (*193*), 8 (*193*).

10. Georges Sofronie : " Means of Ensuring the Progress of Law and the Respect of Justice apart from War ", in *ibid.* *Cited on Page* 8 (*231-233*).

11. Stephan Verosta : " Legal Differences and Conflicts of Interest ", in *ibid.* *Cited on Page* 6 (*191*).

(b) Report on the preparatory memoranda :

12. Maurice Bourquin (General Rapporteur) : " General Report on the Preparatory Memoranda submitted to the General Study Conference on ' Collective Security ' ", in *Collective Security*, etc. (see no. 2). *Cited on Pages* 3 (*6*), 4 (*6*), 5 (*10, 12, 13*), 5 (*8*), 5 (*10*), 6 (*13, 14*), 6 (*8*), 7 (*14*), 8 (*14-15*), 8 (*17*).

(c) Inaugural meeting :

13. Austen Chamberlain, in *Collective Security*, etc. (see no. 2). *Cited on Page* 4 (*34*).

14. Allen W. Dulles (Chairman of the Conference's study meetings), in *ibid.* *Cited on Page* 3 (*40*).

(d) Discussion on the fundamental principles of " Collective Security " :

15. Francesco Coppola, in *Collective Security*, etc. (see no. 2). *Cited on Page* 4 (*166-7, 182-4*).

(e) Discussion on the prevention of war :

16. Fritz Berber, in *Collective Security*, etc. (see no. 2). *Cited on Page* 11 (*281*).

17. Frede Castberg, in *ibid.* *Cited on Pages* 8 (*263*), 9 (*262*).

18. Mircea Djuvara, in *ibid.* *Cited on Page* 10 (*268*).

19. Ludwik Ehrlich, in *ibid.* *Cited on Pages* 7 (*275*), 10 (*273*).

20. José Gascón y Marín, in *ibid.* *Cited on Page* 5 (*259*).

21. Philip C. Jessup, in *ibid.* *Cited on Page* 5 (*270*).

22. Lord Lytton, in *ibid.* *Cited on Page* 9 (*216*).

23. David Mitrany, in *ibid.* *Cited on Pages* 11 (*264*), 20 (*265*).

24.   J. Henry Richardson, in *ibid*. *Cited on Page* 8 (*283*).

25.   Georg Schwarzenberger, in *ibid*. *Cited on Page* 11 (*282*).

26.   Alfred Zimmern, in *ibid*. *Cited on Pages* 11 (*280, 279*), 12 (*280*).

(f) Discussion on the repression of war :

27.   Fritz Berber, in *Collective Security, etc.* (see no. 2). *Cited on Page* 4 (*395*).

(g) Closing meeting :

28.   Maurice Bourquin (General Rapporteur) : " Final Report on the International Studies Conference's study of ' Collective Security ' ", in *Collective Security*, etc. (see no. 2). *Cited on Pages* 5 (*445*), 5 (*447; passim*), 6 (*449*), 7 (*449*), 7 (*449*), 7 (*449*), 8 (*450*).

29.   Allen W. Dulles (Chairman of the Conference's study meetings), in *ibid*. *Cited on Page* 6 (*464*).

30.   Gilbert Murray, in *ibid*. *Cited on Page* 4 (*458*).

II. Peaceful Change

(1) Preparation of the study on " Peaceful Change " :

31.   Philip C. Jessup, in *Minutes of the Meeting of the Programme Committee of the Eighth International Studies Conference held on June 5, 1935* (internal I. I. I. C. document). *Cited on Page* 20.

32.   C. K. Webster, in *ibid*. *Cited on Page* 20.

33.   Alfred Zimmern, in *ibid*. *Cited on Pages* 19, 28.

(2) Preliminary study conference on " Peaceful Change ", 1936 :

(a) Preliminary commentary on " Peaceful Change " :

34.   Maurice Bourquin (General Rapporteur) : " Preliminary Commentary on ' Peaceful Change ' (November 1935) ", in *Preparation and Short Record of the Meetings on the Peaceful Solution of Certain International Problems* (' *Peaceful Change* ') *held at Madrid on May 27-30, 1936* (Paris : I. I. I. C.), 1936 (mimeographed document no. K. 68.1936; 2 vols.). *Cited on Pages* 22 (*10, 16-17*), 24 (*8-9*), 66 (*16*).

(b) Members' observations on the preliminary commentary :

35.   British Co-ordinating Committee for International Studies, in *Preparation and Short Record, etc.* (see no. 34). *Cited on Page* 22 (*75*).

Secondary sources cited :

56. ADOLF HITLER : *My Battle* (Boston edition), 1933. *Cited on Page* 264 (*63, n. 7*).

57. ROBERT R. KUCZYNSKI : " The Decline in Fertility ", in *Economica* (London), May 1935. *Cited on Page* 110 (*72*).

58. WARREN S. THOMPSON : *Danger Spots in World Population* (New York), 1929. *Cited on Page* 80 (*57*).

59. WARREN S. THOMPSON : *Population Problems* (New York), 1930. *Cited on Page* 80 (*57*).

60. JOSEPH RALSTON HAYDEN : *American Experience with Problems of Population in the Philippines and Puerto Rico* (mimeographed document). *Cited on Pages* 173 (*8*), 177 (*27*).

61. BRUCE HOPPER : " Population Factors in Soviet Siberia ", in ISAIAH BOWMAN (ed.) : *Limits of Land Settlement* : *A Preliminary Report on Present-day Possibilities* : A Report to the Tenth International Studies Conference (New York : Council on Foreign Relations), 1937. *Cited on Page* 221 (*118*).

62. KARL J. PELZER : " Japanese Migration and Colonization ", in BOWMAN (ed.), *op. cit.* (see no. 61). *Cited on Pages* 251 (*170-1*), 251 (*163*), 280 (*173*), 280 (*174*), 281 (*175*), 281 (*175*), 283 (*174*), 283 (*175-6*), 295 (*157*).

Secondary sources cited :

63. P. H. CLYDE : *Japan's Pacific Mandate* (New York), 1935. *Cited on Page* 280 (*173*).

64. GUSTAV FOCHLER-HAUKE : *Der Ferne Osten* : *Macht- und Wirtschaftskampf in Ostasien* (Leipzig), 1936. *Cited on Page* 251 (*163*).

65. LEAGUE OF NATIONS : *Annual Report to the Council on the Japanese Mandates, 1935. Cited on Page* 283.

66. K. SAPPER : " Akklimatisation und Rasse ", in *Zeitschrift fur Rassenkunde und ihre Nachtbargebiete*, 1936, vol. 3. *Cited on Page* 251 (*171-2*).

67. CARL O. SAUER : " The Prospect of Redistribution of Population ", in BOWMAN (ed.), *op. cit.* (see no. 61). *Cited on Page* 283 (*19*).

68. MARIAN SCHIBSBY : *The Immigration Policy of the United States* (mimeographed document). *Cited on Pages* 211 (*1*), 211 (*27*), 211 (*27*), 212 (*2, 3*), 212 (*4-5*), 213 (*5*), 213 (*5*), 213 (*6-7*), 213 (*7*), 214 (*8, 9, 10, 12*), 214 (*10*), 214 (*13-14*), 214 (*26*), 214 (*15*), 215 (*26*), 216 (*24*), 216 (*24-5*), 217 (*24-5*), 217 (*25*), 217 (*25*), 217 (*24*), 227 (*28-9*), 230 (*29*), 233 (*29*), 233 (*30*), 233 (*30*).

Secondary sources cited :

69. MARY ROBERTS COOLIDGE : *Chinese Immigration*, 1908. *Cited on Page* 216 (*8-9*).

70. MAURICE R. DAVIE : *World Immigration*. *Cited on Page* 232 (*30*).

71. NATIONAL COMMISSION ON LAW OBSERVANCE AND ENFORCEMENT : " Crime and the Foreign Born ", in *Reports of the Commission*, vol. x. *Cited on Page* 233 (*30*).

72. U. S. A. : *Report of the Commissioner General of Immigration*. *Cited on Page* 211 (*1, n.*).

73. BENJAMIN IDE WHEELER (former President of the University of California) : reported in DAVIE, *op. cit.* (see no. 70). *Cited on Page* 216 (*25*).

74. GRIFFITH TAYLOR : " Possibilities of Settlement in Australia ", in BOWMAN (ed.), *op. cit.* (see no. 61). *Cited on Pages* 312 (*220, sqq.*), 312 (*225*), 312 (*225*), 312 (*226*), 312 (*226*), 312 (*213*), 314 (*204*), 320 (*206*), 320 (*206*), 321 (*204-5*), 323 (*204*), 323 (*204*), 323 (*206*), 324 (*206*), 324 (*206*).

Secondary source cited :

75. *Inlander*. *Cited on Page* 314 (*204*).

76. J. H. WELLINGTON : " Possibilities of Settlement in Africa ", in BOWMAN (ed.), *op. cit.* (see no. 61). *Cited on Pages* 269 (*242*), 283 (*291*).

(ii) Australian Institute of International Affairs :

77. F. W. EGGLESTON and G. PACKER : *The Growth of Australian Population* (Melbourne : Modern Printing Company Pty. Ltd., 18-32 Leicester Street, N. 3), 1937. *Cited on Pages* 311 (*14*), 311 (*3*), 312 (*6*), 312 (*6*), 312 (*3*), 313 (*3, 10*), 313 (*3*), 313 (*16*), 316 (*5*), 318 (*9*), 319 (*3, 13*), 321 (*12*), 322 (*15*), 324 (*14*), 324 (*12-13*).

Secondary source cited :

78. S. H. WOLSTENHOLME : " The Future of the Australian Population ", in *Economic Record*, December 1936. *Cited on Pages* 315 (*4*), 315 (*4*), 315 (*4*).

(iii) Austrian Co-ordinating Committee for International Studies :

79. VIKTOR GUTTMAN : *Individual and Collective Emigration from Austria, and Shifting Population in Austria itself* (mimeographed document). *Cited on Page* 221 (*27*).

80. STEPHAN VEROSTA : *Austria and the Colonial Problem* (mimeographed document). Cited on Pages 60 *(9),* 61 *(7-9).*

81. WILHELM WINKLER : *The Fertility of the Peoples of the Danube Basin* (mimeographed document). Cited on Pages 118 *(1-4),* 153 *(16-17),* 153 *(16;* appendix *4).*

(iv) Belgian Co-ordinating Committee for International Studies :

82. *Le Bassin Conventionnel du Congo Belge* (mimeographed document). Cited on Page 275 *(54).*

(v) Brazilian Co-ordinating Committee for International Studies :

83. ALFONSO DE TOLEDO BANDEIRA DE MELLO : *La Situation demographique des différentes r gions du Brésil...; les conséquences, les remèdes possibles, les pos ibilités d'immigration, les obstacles et les solut'ons proposées* (mimeographed document). Cited on pages 216 *(11-12),* 216 *(14-15),* 216 *(11),* 218 *(14),* 231 *(9),* 238 *(8),* 239 *(8).*

(vi) British Co-ordinating Committee for International Studies :

84. A. M. CARR-SAUNDERS : *World Population* : *Past Growth and Present Trends* (Oxford : Clarendon Press), 1936. Cited on Pages 39 *(144, 322, 333, 142),* 40 *(144),* 40 *(143),* 44 *(143-4)* 45 *(308-9),* 56 *(324),* 72 *(175),* 74 *(140),* 74 *(141, fig. 27),* 74 *(140),* 77 *(137-8),* 82 *(137),* 82 *(330),* 83 *(330),* 83 *(330)* 84 *(330),* 89 *(139, 138),* 89 *(138),* 90 *(138-9),* 90 *(139),* 92 *(140, 138),* 94 *(138, 139-40, 143)* 97 *(139),* 106 *(135),* 109 *(264-5),* 110 *(266),* 110 *(124),* 110 *(135-6),* 111 *(129, 134-5),* 111 *(129),* 111 *(135),* 112 *(129, 134-5),* 112 *(136),* 113 *(160, 178, 179),* 113 *(180),* 114 *(203, 135),* 114 *(135),* 116 *(321),* 118 *(321),* 119 *(321),* 120 *(321),* 120 *(324),* 121 *(328),* 122 *(139),* 124 *(325),* 124 *(328),* 130 *(323),* 130 *(322),* 132 *(321-2),* 143 *(326),* 143 *(327),* 147, 150 *(328),* 150 *(328),* 151 *(327-8),* 152 *(229, 232-3),* 152 *(227),* 157 *(255-7),* 157 *(324),* 161 *(218),* 164 *(159),* 165 *(158),* 178 *(326),* 180 *(263-4),* 180 *(264),* 180 *(264),* 180 *(264),* 180 *(264),* 181 *(264),* 182 *(257-8),* 182 *(123),* 193 *(273, 292),* 193 *(114),* 199 *(114),* 199 *(126),* 199 *(114),* 200 *(49, fig. 9),* 200 *(50),* 200 *(56-7),* 201 *(49, fig. 9),* 201 *(49, fig. 9),* 201 *(199, fig. 46),* 202 *(49, fig. 9),* 203 *(5),* 203 *(57),* 203 *(143-4),* 203 *(49, fig. 9),* 203 *(58),* 204 *(200),* 204 *(206),* 205 *(206-7),* 205 *(207),* 206 *(221),* 206 *(52),* 206 *(49, fig. 9; 50),* 210 *(147, fig. 28),* 210 *(146),* 214 *(191-2),* 214 *(192),* 214 *(192),* 214 *(193, fig. 42),*

214 *(195-6)*, 215 *(194)*, 215 *(196-8)*, 215 *(197)*, 215 *(197-8)*, 215 *(198)*, 215 *(197)*, 216 *(183-4)*, 217 *(184)*, 217 *(185)*, 217 *(185)*, 218 *(186)*, 218 *(148)*, 218 *(148)*, 219 *(149)*, 220 *(149)*, 220 *(147-8)*, 220 *(147)*, 220 *(148)*, 222 *(210)*, 223 *(146)*, 224 *(203-4)*, 224, 225 *(204-5)*, 226 *(208-9)*, 226 *(205)*, 226 *(209)*, 227 *(211)*, 228 *(209)*, 229 *(209)*, 229 *(150 sqq.)*, 231 *(211)*, 231 *(212)*, 231 *(211-6)*, 231 *(216-7)*, 231 *(212-3, 218)*, 231 *(213)*, 231 *(215)*, 232 *(216)*, 233 *(219)*, 234 *(219-20)*, 236 *(191)*, 237 *(217-8)*, 237 *(218)*, 241 *(224)*, 242 *(186)*, 242 *(188)*, 242 *(188-9)*, 242 *(269)*, 242 *(187, fig. 41)*, 242 *(187, fig. 41)*, 242 *(190)*, 243 *(153)*, 243 *(48, 56)*, 250 *(268)*, 250 *(325-6)*, 251 *(268-9, 294)*, 252 *(325)*, 252 *(323)*, 252 *(170 sqq.)*, 253 *(222)*, 252 *(323)*, 253 *(325)*, 259 *(325, 322, 326)*, 259 *(311, 313, 314, 317)*, 260 *(294)*, 278 *(325)*, 285 *(315-6)*, 285 *(318)*, 294 *(143)*, 297 *(146; see also 15)*, 310 *(164)*, 310 *(163, fig. 33)*, 312 *(174)*, 312 *(175)*, 313 *(198)*, 314 *(26, fig. 6)*, 314 *(164-5)*, 314 *(161)*, 314 *(163, fig. 33)*, 315 *(178)*, 316 *(179)*, 317 *(175-6, 179)*, 318 *(179)*, 320 *(169)*, 320 *(168, fig. 37)*, 320 *(169)*, 320 *(169)*, 321 *(197)*, 322 *(202)*, 322 *(198-9)*, 323 *(169, 185)*, 323, 323 *(169)*, 323 *(169)*, 323 *(185)*, 323 *(185)*.

Secondary sources cited :

85.   F. BURGDÖRFER : *Ausblick auf die zukünftige Bevölkerungsentwicklung* : *Statistik der Deutschen Reichs*, Band 401, Part 2, 1930. *Cited on Page* 104 *(fig. 26)*.

86.   NEVILLE CHAMBERLAIN : in a speech in the House of Commons introducing the budget in 1935. *Cited on Page* 142 *(328; see also no. 263, p. ix)*.

87.   CORRADO GINI and B. DE FINETTI : *Calcoli sullo Sviluppo futuro della Popolazione Italiana* (Istituto Centrale di Statistica), 1931, Serie 6, Vol. x. *Cited on Page* 106 *(fig. 26)*.

88.   H. JEROME : *Migration and Business Cycles*, 1926. *Cited on Pages* 204 *(206)*, 204 *(206)*.

89.   E. KAHN : *Der Internationale Geburtenstreik*, 1930. *Cited on Page* 104 *(fig. 26)*.

90.   ROBERT R. KUCZYNSKI : " The Decline in Fertility ", *loc. cit.* (see no. 57). *Cited on Pages* 315 *(fig. 25)*, 315 *(fig. 25)*.

91.   E. F. PENROSE : *Population Theories and their Application*, 1934. *Cited on Page* 180 *(264)*.

92.   M. REQUIEN : *Le Problème de la Population au apon*, 1934. *Cited on Page* 180 *(264)*.

93.   RUPPIN. *Cited on Page* 45 *(308-9)*.

94. DOROTHY HARWOOD : *Organised Emigration from Great Britain and its relation to Unemployment* (mimeographed document). *Cited on Page* 313.

95. ROBERT R. KUCZYNSKI : *Colonial Population* (Oxford University Press), 1937. *Cited on Pages* 277, 277 (*xiii-xiv*).

96. ROYAL INSTITUTE OF INTERNATIONAL AFFAIRS : *Considerations affecting the Transfer of Colonial Territories.* (The substance of this mimeographed document has been published in Chapter VI — " Transfer of Colonial Territory " — of *The Colonial Problem : A Report by a Study Group of Members of the Royal Institute of International Affairs* (Oxford University Press); 1937; the reference is to this publication). *Cited on Page* 23 (*80-81*).

97. ROYAL INSTITUTE OF INTERNATIONAL AFFAIRS : *Raw Materials and Colonies* (Information Department Papers, No. 18). *Cited on Pages* 25, 249 (*7, n. 3*), 249 (*7*).

Secondary sources cited :

98. IMRE FERENCZI : *International Migration. Cited on Page* 206 (*7, n. 2*).

99. ARTHUR SALTER : *Peace and the Colonial Problem* (London : National Peace Council), 1935. *Cited on Page* 292 (*14*).

100. *Statistisches Jahrbuch für das Deutsches Reich* (Berlin : Reimar Hobbing), 1935. *Cited on Page* 249 (*7, n. 4*).

(vii) Canadian Institute of International Affairs :

101. H. F. ANGUS : " Introduction ", in H. F. ANGUS (ed.) : *Canada and the Doctrine of Peaceful Change* (mimeographed document). *Cited on Pages* 14 (*5*), 14 (*5*).

102. W. B. HURD : " The Ability of Canada to Receive Immigration", in ANGUS (ed.), *op. cit.* (see no. 101). *Cited on Pages* 73 (*49-50*), 74 (*52; 52, n.*), 76 (*56*), 76 (*52, 54-6, 58*), 78 (*48*), 78 (*48-9*),78(*48,n. 2*), 89 (*64*), 97 (*64*), 97 (*64*), 113 (*80-1*), 199 (*77-8*), 223 (*68*), 224 (*62*), 224 (*62-3*), 225 (*63*), 225 (*63*), 226 (*79-80*), 230 (*81*), 230 (*81*), 235 (*75-6*), 245 (*65-6*), 259 (*75-6*), 291 (*78*), 292 (*78*), 292 (*78-9*).

Secondary sources cited :

103. W. B. HURD : " The Decline of the Canadian Birth Rate ", in *The Canadian Journal of Economics and Political Science*, February 1937. *Cited on Page* 226 (*80*).

104. GEORGES LANGLOIS : *Histoire de la Population Cana-dienne* (Montreal : Edition Albert Levesque), 1934. *Cited on Page* 224 (*62*).

105. M. C. MACLEAN: *Analysis of the Stages in the Growth of Population in Canada* (Dominion Bureau of Statistics), 1935. *Cited on Page* 225 (*63*).

106. M. C. MACLEAN (Dominion Bureau of Statistics) : unpublished studies. *Cited on Page* 225 (*79*).

107. B. S. KEIRSTEAD : " Peaceful Change within the Canadian Confederation ", in ANGUS (ed.), *op. cit.* (see no. 101). *Cited on Page* 234 (*114-6*).

108. R. A. MACKAY and E. B. ROGERS : " Canada's Attitude in the Past to the General Question of Peaceful Change ", in ANGUS (ed.), *op. cit.* (see no. 101). *Cited on Page* 217 (*20*).

Secondary source cited :

109. ANDRÉ SIEGFRIED : *Canada* (London, 1937. *Cited on Page* 242 (*19*).

110. C. E. SILCOX: " Canadian Opinion and Peaceful Change", in ANGUS (ed.), *op. cit.* (see no. 101). *Cited on Page* 285 (*151-2*).

(viii) Czechoslovak International Studies Centre :

111. ANTONÍN BOHÁČ : *Le Problème Démographique au point de vue de la Tchécoslovaquie* (mimeographed document). *Cited on Pages* 91 (*1-2, 4*), 91 (*10*), 91 (*14*).

(ix) Danish Co-ordinating Committee for International Studies :

112. H. M. GORMSEN : *A Comparative Study of the Economic Development of Small Countries with and without Colonies (Netherlands, Denmark, Norway and Sweden)* (mimeographed document). *Cited on Pages* 275 (*3*), 280 (*16*).

(x) French Co-ordinating Committee for International Studies :

113. ADOLPHE LANDRY : *La Notion de Surpeuplement* (mimeographed document). *Cited on Pages* 36 (*17-18*), 36, 39 (*19*), 40 (*19*), 40 (*19*), 41 (*19-20*), 65 (*20*), 67 (*1*), 67 (*1*), 69 (*3*), 82 (*1*), 86 (*2*), 86 (*2*), 90 (*3*), 90 (*3*), 100 (*21*), 103 (*18*), 117 (*14-15*), 117 (*15*), 153 (*18*), 159 (*5, 4*), 177 (*14*), 178 (*20-21*), 285 (*6-8*), 291 (*12*), 291 (*12*), 291 (*11*)

114. GILBERT MAROGER : *La Question des Matières Premières et les Revendications Coloniales : Examen des Solutions Pro-·posées* (Paris : Centre d'Études de Politique Étrangère). *Cited on Pages* 49 (*27*), 50 (*15-16*), 53 (*27, n. 2*), 54 (*27*), 55 (*27, n. 2*), 55 (*26*), 55 (*13-14*), 57 (*23, 24, 26, 30, 119*), 58 (*38-39*).

115. *Secondary sources cited* :

MARIUS MOUTET : in a statement to the *Echo de Paris*, January 1937. *Cited on Page* 56 (*153*).

116. HJALMAR SCHACHT : in a speech delivered on the occasion of the thirtieth anniversary of the German Colonial Society, reported in *Deutsche Allgemeine Zeitung*, March 26 and 28, 1926. *Cited on Page* 50 (*15-16*).

117. GEORGES MAUCO : *L'Assimilation des Etrangers en France* (mimeographed document). *Cited on Pages* 159 (*8*), 160 (*8-9*), 160 (*8, 46*), 160 (*47*), 161 (*6*), 161 (*3*), 161 (*2*), 162 (*6-8*), 162 (*9*), 162 (*9-10*), 162 (*9, n. 1*), 162 (*10, n. 1*), 163 (*10-11*), 163 (*11-12*), 163 (*11, n.*), 164 (*82-3*), 164 (*83, 85*), 165 (*87*), 165 (*15*), 165 (*89*), 165 (*14*), 165 (*13*), 166 (*16, 12, 14*), 166 (*12-13, 17-19*), 217 (*47*), 220 (*8*), 231 (*44*), 235 (*43*), 236 (*110*), 236 (*66 sqq.*).

Secondary sources cited :

118. MGR. BONOMELLI : Report on the Opera Bonomelli to the first Italian congress on continental emigration assistance, Milan. *Cited on Page* 162 (*9*).

119. JEAN BRUNHES and VALLAUX : *Géographie de l'Histoire*. *Cited on Page* 60 (*46-7*).

120. HERSCHE : *L'Immigration Féminine aux Etats-Unis* (Geneva), 1912. *Cited on Page* 160 (*46*).

121. J. W. JENCKS and J. LANCK : *The Emigration Problem* (New York), 1922. *Cited on Page* 164 (*87*).

122. POLVERELLI : in a report to the Chamber of Deputies, Rome, April 6, 1930. *Cited on Page* 161 (*7*).

123. ANDRÉ SIEGFRIED : *America comes of Age : A French Analysis*, 1927. *Cited on Page* 163 (*10, n. 1*).

124. WILLIAM OUALID : *Les Eléments d'une Solution Internationale du Problème des Migrations Humaines* (mimeographed document). *Cited on Pages* 131 (*8*), 196 (*2, 4*), 218 (*6*), 219 (*6-7*), 240 (*12-13*).

Secondary source cited :

125. INTERNATIONAL ASSOCIATION FOR SOCIAL PROGRESS : 1931 CONGRESS : Report by the Polish Under-Secretary of State for Labour. *Cited on Page* 220 (*7*).

(xi) Hungarian Co-ordinating Committee for International Studies :

126. ETIENNE HOLLOS, with the collaboration of LOUIS THIRRING : *Les Modes Caractéristiques et les Types Principaux de l'Assimilation Nationale* (mimeographed document). *Cited on Page* 235 *(1-2)*.

127. LOUIS THIRRING : *Contributions à l'Etude du Problème et de la Situation Démographiques de la Hongrie au point de vue du Surpeuplement et de l'Espace pour la Vie et le Travail de la Nation* (mimeographed document). *Cited on Pages* 60 *(38, 43-44)*, 66 *(2)*, 68 *(3)*, 70 *(3)*, 70 *(3-4)*, 70 *(4-5)*, 71 *(5)*, 133 *(37)*, 295 *(40)*.

(xii) Institute of Pacific Relations :

128. H. F. ANGUS : *The Problem of Peaceful Change in the Pacific Area : A study of the work of the Institute of Pacific Relations and its bearing on the problem of Peaceful Change* (London and New York : Oxford University Press), 1937. *Cited on Pages* 40 *(190)*, 41 *(190)*, 41 *(190)*, 41 *(35 sqq.)*.

(xiii) Netherlands Co-ordinating Committee for International Studies :

129. F. VAN HEEK : *The Calculation of Population Pressure in Agrarian Territories inclined to be self-supporting* (mimeographed document). *Cited on Pages* 66 *(1)*, 66 *(2)*, 73 *(11)*, 75 *(5)*, 79 *(11-12)*, 83 *(12)*, 84 *(4)*, 85 *(11)*, 93 *(3, 4, 5, 13-14, 15, 17, 22)*, 93 *(24)*, 96 *(13)*.

Secondary source cited :

130. PAUL MOMBERT : *Bevölkerungslehre* (Jena), 1929. *Cited on Pages* 79 *(11-12)*, 83 *(12)*, 84 *(4)*.

131. EMANUEL MORESCO : " Claims to Colonies, Markets and Raw Materials ", in *The New Commonwealth Quarterly* (London), December 1936, vol. II, no. 3. *Cited on Pages* 20, 40 *(319)*, 40 *(319)*, 65 *(318-9)*, 107 *(320)*, 126 *(325-6)*, 126 *(326)*, 129 *(320-1)*, 150 *(320-1)*, 173 *(321)*, 186 *(318)*.

132. B. SCHRIEKE : *The Colonial Question* (mimeographed document). *Cited on Pages* 123 *(7-8)*, 124 *(15)*, 124 *(10)*, 172 *(4)*, 266 *(12)*, 290 *(13-14)*.

Secondary source cited :

133. HEINRICH SCHNEE : " Rohstoffe und Kolonien ", in *Militärwissenschaftliche Rundschau*, I. Jahrgang, 1936. *Cited on Page* 124 *(10)*.

(xiv) Norwegian Co-ordinating Committeee for International Studies :

134. ARNE SKAUG : *Norwegian Emigration, its Fluctuations compared with Fluctuations in Migration from other Countries since 1900, and causes of these fluctuations (development of industries, social conditions, etc.), with special reference to the economic and social difficulties caused for Norway by the American restrictions on immigration* (mimeographed document). *Cited on Pages* 69 (*123*), 86 (*119*), 89 (*121-2*), 90 (*120*), 90 (*121*), 90 (*124*), 91 (*125*), 92 (*124*), 199, 205 (*57*), 205 (*63-4*), 205 (*64*).

Secondary sources cited :

135. BLEGEN, TH. : *Norwegian Migration to America 1825-1860* (Minnesota), 1931. *Cited on Page* 205 (*63-64*).

136. BOLDRINI : in the discussion on ALBERT THOMAS : " International Migration and its Control ", in MARGARET SANGER (ed.) : *Proceedings of the World Population Conference, 1927* (Geneva), 1927. *Cited on Page* 88 (*122*).

137. NILS CEDERBLAD : in the discussion on THOMAS, *loc. cit.* (see no. 136). *Cited on Page* 88 (*121-2*).

138. J. W. GREGORY : in G. H. L. F. PITT-RIVERS (ed.) : *Problems of Population* (London), 1932. *Cited on Page* 89 (*122*).

139. H. L. WILKINSON : " The World Population Problem and a White Australia ", in PITT-RIVERS (ed.), *op. cit.* (see no. 138). *Cited on Page* 89 (*122*).

(xv) Polish Co-ordinating Committee for International Studies :

140. HIPOLIT GLIWIC : " Introduction au Concept de l'Optimum de la Population ", in *Problèmes de Démographie et d'Economie Politique Internationale* (Lwòw : Institut de Droit Constitutionnel et de Droit International, Université Jean Casimir), 1937. *Cited on Pages* 67, 72 (*22*), 73 (*22*), 73 (*23*), 75 (*23*), 75 (*23*), 75 (*25, 27*).

Secondary sources cited :

141. LEAGUE OF NATIONS : INTERNATIONAL ECONOMIC CONFERENCE : GENEVA : MAY 1927 : " Population Density in relation to Cultivated Areas and National Resources on the Surface and Underground ", in *C. E. I. 39. Cited on Page* 73 (*22*).

142. ERNST WAGEMAN : *Struktur und Rythmus der Weltwirtschaft* (Berlin), 1917. *Cited on Page* 75 (*25*).

143.   STANISLAW GRABSKI : " Le Problème de la Population en Pologne et les Intérêts des Etats Surpeuplés ", in *Problèmes de Démographie*, etc. (see no. 140). *Cited on Pages* 46 (*65-66*), 46 (*67*).

144.   STANISLAW EDWARD NAHLIK : " L'Accroissement Naturel de la Population et ses Facteurs ", in *Problèmes de Démographie*, etc. (see no. 140). *Cited on Pages* 46 (*105*), 117 (*103*), 117 (*103*), 152 (*92*), 155 (*94*), 155 (*94*), 156 (*94-6*), 156 (*96*), 156 (*96*), 175 (*105-6*), 179 (*102*), 180 (*102-3*), 187 (*96-8*).

Secondary sources cited :

145.   CARL L. ALSBERG : " The Factors that Govern Population Growth ", in *Problems of the Pacific*, 1927. *Cited on Page* 117 (*103*).

146.   MABEL BUER : in SANGER (ed.), *op. cit.* (see no. 136). *Cited on Page* 117 (*103*).

147.   A. M. CARR-SAUNDERS : " Fallacies about Overpopulation ", in *Foreign Affairs* (New York), 1930-31. *Cited on Page* 117 (*103*).

148.   CORRADO GINI : *Le Basi Scientifiche della Politica della Popolazione* (Catania), 1931. *Cited on Page* 117 (*103*).

149.   WARREN S. THOMPSON : *Population Problems* (see no. 59). *Cited on Page* 117 (*103*).

(xvi) Swiss Co-ordinating Committee for International Studies :

150.   HANS BERNARD : *La Colonisation et la Politique Démographique en Suisse* (mimeographed document). *Cited on Pages* 220 (*24*), 293 (*17*), 293 (*19*), 293 (*20-21*).

151.   RICHARD BÜCHNER: *La Notion de Surpopulation* (mimeographed document). *Cited on Pages* 66 (*2*), 66 (*2*), 77 (*7*), 77 (*2*), 79 (*2-3*), 81 (*3-4*), 88 (*4*), 97 (*4-5*), 97 (*4*), 97 (*4-5*), 98 (*5-6*), 98 (*10-11*), 99 (*14-15*), 100 (*17-18*).

152.   CHARLES A. BURKY: *La Notion de Surpeuplement* (mimeographed document). *Cited on Pages* 96 (*1, 4, 6, 8*), 143 (*4*), 178 (*4*), 178 (*4*), 178 (*4*), 179 (*4*).

153.   PAUL FROSSARD : *L'Emigration Suisse* (mimeographed document). *Cited on Page* 59.

(d) " International " Memoranda :

154.   J. B. CONDLIFFE : *Markets and the Problem of Peaceful Change* (Paris : I. I. I. C.), 1938. *Cited on Pages* 24 (*5*), 36, 41 (*38*), 41 (*38*), 58 (*5*), 287 (*37*), 291 (*37*), 291 (*38*), 291.

155. IMRE FERENCZI : *The Synthetic Optimum of Population :
An Outline of an International Demographic Policy* (Paris :
I. I. I. C.), 1938. *Cited on Pages* 40 *(111, n. 2)*, 71 *(23)*,
71 *(23)*, 72 *(25)*, 72 *(25, n. 1)*, 73 *(29-30)*, 73 *(26, n.
1)*, 73 *(27)*, 73 *(26-27)*, 75 *(30-31)*, 75 *(33-34)*, 76 *(38)*, 77
(40, 49), 80 *(81)*, 80 *(50-51)*, 80 *(80-81)*, 81 *(52-53)*,
87, 87, 101 *(17-18)*, 142 *(115)*, 147 *(89-91)*, 150 *(72)*,
167 *(100)*, 278 *(72)*, 297 *(112-3)*, 297 *(113-114)*.

Secondary sources cited :

156. HUGH DALTON : " The Theory of Population ",
in *Economica* (London), March 1928. *Cited on
Pages* 83 *(44, n. 1)*, 83 *(44, n. 1)*.

157. INTERNATIONAL LABOUR OFFICE : *Report of the
Director*, 1936. *Cited on Page* 296 *(73, n. 1)*.

158. LEAGUE OF NATIONS : INTERNATIONAL ECONOMIC
CONFERENCE, etc. (see no. 141). *Cited on Page* 73
(26).

159. R. MUKERJEE : " Optimum Population and Overpopulation " in *Indian Journal of Economics* (Alla-
habad), 1930, vol. X, part 3. *Cited on Page* 80
(80-81).

160. *Neue Freie Presse*, December 1, 1936. *Cited on
Page* 48 *(64, n. 1)*.

161. A. B. WOLFE : in L. I. DUBLIN (ed.) : *Population
Problems in the United States and Canada* (Boston and
New York), 1928. *Cited on Page* 80 *(44)*.

162. IMRE FERENCZI : French edition of no. 155. *Cited on
Page* 75 *(30)*.

163. J. LEGOUIS : *Migration — An International Problem :
Difficulties and Suggested Solutions* (mimeographed document no. K. 83. 1937). *Cited on Page* 199 *(1)*.

164. J. LEGOUIS : *Notice sur l'Organisation internationale des
Migrations* (mimeographed document no. K. 83. 1937,
annexe). *Cited on Pages* 298 *sqq*.

(e) Other documents and publications distributed to members
of the Conference :

165. GROVER CLARK : *The Balance Sheets of Imperialism :
Facts and Figures on Colonies* (New York : Columbia
University Press), 1936. *Cited on Pages* 75 *(17)*, 267 *(10;
see also 10, n. 11, and 58)*, 271 *(10; 10, n. 15)*, 274 *(10)*,
275 *(9)*, 275 *(10)*, 275 *(11)*.

166.   T. E. GREGORY : "The Economic Bases of Revisionism", in C. A. W. MANNING (ed.) : *Peaceful Change* : *An International Problem* (London : Macmillan), 1937. *Cited on Pages* 51 (*63*), 77 (*66*), 103 (*67*), 104 (*67-68*), 116 (*66*), 264 (*69*).

167.   INTERNATIONAL LABOUR OFFICE : *The Migration of Workers* : *Recruitment, Placing and Conditions of Labour* : Studies and Reports : Series O (Migration), No. 5, 1936. *Cited on Pages* 203 (*23*), 224 (*5*), 229, 244 (*6*), 256 (*2*), 257 (*2-3*), 257 (*3, n. 1*).

168.   *Secondary sources cited* :

FRANCIS DELAISI : *Les Deux Europes*, 1929, quoted in INTERNATIONAL LABOUR OFFICE : *Unemployment* : *Some International Aspects, 1920-1928* : Studies and Reports : Series C, No. 13. *Cited on Page* 257 (*3, n. 1*).

169.   INTERNATIONAL LABOUR OFFICE : "Unemployment and International Migration", in *Unemployment*, etc. (see no. 168). *Cited on Page* 257 (*3*).

170.   JAPAN : MINISTRY OF FOREIGN AFFAIRS : RESEARCH DIVISION : *Distribution of Japanese Nationals in Various Countries, October 1, 1934* (Kaigai Kakuchi Zairyu Hompo Jin Jinko Hyo). *Cited on Page* 250 (*59-60*).

171.   WALTER F. WILLCOX : "Immigration into the United States", in *International Migration* (National Bureau of Economic Research), vol. II. *Cited on Page* 224 (*5-6*).

172.   INTERNATIONAL LABOUR OFFICE : *World Statistics of Aliens* : *A Comparative Study of Census Returns, 1910-1920-1930* : Studies and Reports : Series O (Migration), No. 6, 1936. *Cited on Pages* 168 (*60*), 168 (*168*), 168 (*58*), 242 (*102*), 250 (*168*), 250 (*60*), 251 (*162*).

Secondary sources cited :

173.   *Bolletino mensile di Statistica* (Central Statistical Institute), 1932, no. 5. *Cited on Page* 167 (*59*).

174.   *Censimento degli Italiani all' Estero alla metà dell' anno 1927* (Roma : Ministero degli Affari Esteri), 1928. *Cited on Page* 167 (*59*).

175.   LORD LOTHIAN : in the discussion on ARNOLD J. TOYNBEE : "Peaceful Change or War ? The Next Stage in the International Crisis", in *International Affairs* (London), January 1936, vol. xv, No. 1. *Cited on Page* 38 (*55*).

176. LORD LUGARD : " The Basis of the Claim for Colonies ", in *International Affairs* (see no. 175). *Cited on Pages* 20, 24 (*5*, *6*), 36, 37 (*4*), 38 (*16-17*), 58 (*22*), 116 (*3*), 125 (*14*), 129 (*13*), 177 (*12*), 270 (*22*).

177. C. A. W. MANNING : " Some Suggested Conclusions ", in MANNING (ed.), *loc. cit.* (see no. 166). *Cited on Pages* 14 (*174*), 19 (*170-1*).

178. GIUSEPPE DE MICHELIS : *World Reorganisation on Corporative Lines* (London : Allen and Unwin), 1935. *Cited on Pages* 23, 173 (*77*, *32*), 175 (*32-4*, *237*), 176 (*238*), 176 (*223*, *171*, *181-2*), 257, 311 (*80*, *309-10*), 311 (*310*), 321 (*310*).

179. BERTIL G. OHLIN : " Introductory Report on the Problem of International Economic Reconstruction, " in JOINT COMMITTEE OF THE CARNEGIE ENDOWMENT AND OF THE INTERNATIONAL CHAMBER OF COMMERCE : *International Economic Reconstruction : An Economists' and Businessmen's Survey of the Main Problems of To-day* (Paris : Joint Committee, etc.), 1936. *Cited on Pages* 66 (*143*), 78 (*146*), 81 (*143*), 104 (*147*), 105 (*147*), 106 (*147*), 109 (*147*), 115 (*146-7*), 122 (*144-5*), 122 (*145*), 123 (*153*), 153 (*146*), 279 (*150-1*, *153*), 279 (*153*), 280 (*152-3*), 289 (*148*), 289 (*149*), 289 (*149-150*), 289 (*150*), 289 (*150*), 289 (*154*), 289 (*149*), 290 (*155*).

180. HEINRICH ROGGE : *Das Revisionsproblem : Theorie der Revision als Voraussetzung einer internationalen wissenschaftlichen Aussprache über 'Peaceful Change of Status quo'* (Berlin : Junker und Dünnhaupt Verlag), 1937. *Cited on Pages* 49 (*41*; *41*, *n. 62*), 49 (*40*), 49 (*96*), 49 (*96-7*), 52 (*43-44*), 121 (*38*), 144 (*39-41*), 151 (*42-3*).

Secondary source cited :

181. HJALMAR SCHACHT : *Vortrag auf der Hundertjahrfeier des Vereins für Geographie und Statistik*, December 9, 1936 (reprint). *Cited on Page* 48 (*40*, *n. 61*).

182. E. D. G. RUFF : *Population Statistics of Certain Countries* (Paris : I. I. I. C.) (folder prepared for the Tenth Session of the International Studies Conference, 1937). *Cited on Pages* 206, 206, 207, 207.

183. JAMES T. SHOTWELL : *On the Rim of the Abyss* (New York : Macmillan), 1936. *Cited on Pages* 7 (viii), 24 (*210*), 188 (*201*).

184. LORD STRABOLGI : in the discussion on LUGARD, *loc. cit.* (see no. 176). *Cited on Page* 117 (*17*).

185.   ARNOLD J. TOYNBEE, *loc. cit.* (see no. 175). *Cited on Pages* 20 *(41)*, 20, 27 *(41)*, 35 *(40)*, 36, 37 *(40-41)*, 38 *(see p. 50)*, 176.

186.   C. K. WEBSTER : " What is the Problem of Peaceful Change ? ", in MANNING (ed.), *loc. cit.* (see no. 166). *Cited on Page* 20 *(4)*.

187.   TEIJIRO UYEDA : *The Present Conditions of the Japanese Population* (mimeographed document). *Cited on Pages* 108 *(8)*, 108 *(8-10)*, 109 *(10-11)*, 109 *(11-12)*, 109 *(12)*, 109 *(14-17)*, 185 *(1)*, 185 *(1)*, 185 *(1-2)*, 186 *(7, 2)*.

(f) General Report on the studies and memoranda :

188.   MAURICE BOURQUIN (General Rapporteur) : " Introductory Report presented to the General Study Conference on ' Peaceful Change ', 1937 ", in *Peaceful Change : Procedures, Population Pressure, the Colonial Question, Raw Materials and Markets* : Proceedings of the Tenth International Studies Conference, Paris, June 28th-July 3rd, 1937 (Paris : I. I. I. C.), in the press. *Cited on Pages* 7 *(19, 21)*, 11 *(17-18)*, 11 *(47)*, 14 *(47)*, 15 *(47-48)*, 15 *(48)*, 19 *(17)*.

(g) Report on the colonial studies :

189.   H. O. CHRISTOPHERSEN (Secretary-Rapporteur) : "Report on the Study of Colonial Questions prepared for the General Study Conference on ' Peaceful Change ', 1937 ", in *Peaceful Change,* etc. (see no. 188). *Cited on Page* 283 *(184-5)*.

(h) Report on the demographic studies :

190.   LEONARD J. CROMIE (Secretary-Rapporteur) : " Report on the Study of Demographic Questions prepared for the General Study Conference on ' Peaceful Change ', 1937 ", in *Peaceful Change,* etc. (see no. 188). *Cited on Pages* 80 *(123)*, 85 *(126)*, 85 *(125)*, 87 *(127)*, 92 *(124)*, 93 *(124-5)*, 105 *(135)*, 310 *(138-9)*.

(i) First plenary meeting of the Conference :

191.   LORD LYTTON, in *Peaceful Change,* etc. (see no. 188). *Cited on Page* 9 *(261)*.

192.   C. A. W. MANNING, in *ibid. Cited on Pages* 48 *(271-2)*, 121.

(j) Round-table meetings on demographic questions :

193.   OZORIO DE ALMEIDA, in *Peaceful Change,* etc. (see no. 188)· *Cited on Pages* 216 *(378)*, 238 *(378)*.

194. CARL ALSBERG, in *ibid*. *Cited on Pages* 151 (*409*), 198 (*395*), 199 (*394*), 287 (*409*).

195. ANTONÍN BOHÁČ, in *ibid*. *Cited on Page* 243 (*384*).

196. A. M. CARR-SAUNDERS, in *ibid*. *Cited on Pages* 200 (*377*), 221 (*377*), 227 (*377*), 243 (*407*), 260 (*407*).

197. IMRE FERENCZI, in *ibid*. *Cited on Pages* 81 (*368*), 87 (*363*), 87 (*365-7*), 101 (*368*), 230 (*399*).

198. WILLIAM D. FORSYTH, in *ibid*. *Cited on Pages* 310 (*386*), 319 (*386*).

199. H. M. GORMSEN, in *ibid*. *Cited on Page* 275 (*379*).

200. ADOLPHE LANDRY, in *ibid*. *Cited on Pages* 15 (*362*), 36 (*363*), 69 (*362*), 69 (*362-3*), 197 (*363-4*), 206 (*363*), 207 (*365*), 252 (*363*), 253 (*363*).

201. CHRISTIAN L. LANGE, in *ibid*. *Cited on Page* 296 (*392*).

202. JACQUES LEGOUIS, in *ibid*. *Cited on Page* 239 (*387*).

203. MALCOLM MACPHERSON, in *ibid*. *Cited on Page* 221 (*393*).

204. J. HENRY RICHARDSON, in *ibid*. *Cited on Pages* 240 (*381*), 246 (*381*).

205. B. SCHRIEKE, in *ibid*. *Cited on Page* 246 (*404*).

206. JAMES T. SHOTWELL, in *ibid*. *Cited on Pages* 117 (*403*), 198 (*380*), 198 (*402-3*), 198 (*380*), 229 (*402*), 232 (*402*), 239 (*402*), 245 (*379-80*).

207. JERZY SMOLENSKI, in *ibid*. *Cited on Pages* 94 (*370*), 95 (*370-2*), 104 (*371*), 116 (*310*), 150 (*383*), 278 (*371*).

208. E. C. TARR (Chairman of the Round Table), in *ibid*. *Cited on Page* 191 (*411*).

209. PAUL DE TELEKI, in *ibid*. *Cited on Pages* 67 (*413*), 191 (*413*), 251 (*373*), 252 (*372*).

210. SCHUNZO YOSHISAKA, in *ibid*. *Cited on Pages* 181 (*409-10, 374-5, 410*), 185 (*375*), 185 (*375*), 185 (*375*), 242 (*376*), 251 (*375*), 272 (*375*), 288 (*473-4*).

211. STEFAN ZALESKI, in *ibid*. *Cited on Pages* 227 (*396*), 229 (*396*), 229 (*396*).

(k) Round-table meetings on colonial questions :

212. FRITZ BERBER, in *Peaceful Change*, etc. (see no. 188). *Cited on Pages* 29 (*464-6, 467*), 32 (*479, 480, 481*).

213. VITO CATASTINI, in *ibid*. *Cited on Page* 267 (*440-1*).

214. IMRE FERENCZI, in *ibid*. *Cited on Pages* 271 (*423*), 276 (*423*), 276 (*423*), 276 (*423*), 282 (*422*), 414 (*424*).

215. H. M. GORMSEN, in *ibid*. *Cited on Pages* 243 *(441)*, 246 *(441)*, 247 *(441)*, 247 *(441)*.

216. H. D. HENDERSON, in *ibid*. *Cited on Pages* 245 *(442)*, 249 *(442)*.

217. HENRI LABOURET, in *ibid*. *Cited on Pages* 171 *(474)*, 246 *(443)*, 265 *(443-4)*, 265 *(436)*, 284 *(436, 437-8)*.

218. O. LOUWERS, in *ibid*. *Cited on Pages* 13 *(475)*, 248 *(430-2)*, 258 *(432)*, 258 *(432)*, 265 *(432-3)*, 281 *(445-6)*, 284 *(433)*.

219. LORD LYTTON, in *ibid*. *Cited on Page* 32 *(467-9)*.

220. EMANUEL MORESCO (Chairman of the Round Table), in *ibid*. *Cited on Pages* 171 *(445)*, 171 *(445)*, 280 *(459)*.

221. J. HENRY RICHARDSON, in *ibid*. *Cited on Pages* 16 *(449)*, 170 *(429)*, 284 *(429)*, 416 *(430)*.

222. ANDRÉ TOUZET, in *ibid*. *Cited on Pages* 170 *(471)*, 170 *(425-6)*, 247 *(471-2)*.

223. STEPHAN VEROSTA, in *ibid*. *Cited on Page* 61 *(440)*.

224. BRYCE WOOD, in *ibid*. *Cited on Page* 16 *(455)*.

225. QUINCY WRIGHT, in *ibid*. *Cited on Pages* 13 *(476-7)*, 32 *(476-7)*, 169 *(461-2)*, 169 *(462)*, 170 *(461-2)*.

(l) Second, third and fourth plenary meetings of the Conference :

226. LEONARD J. CROMIE (Secretary-Rapporteur on Demographic Questions), in *Peaceful Change*, etc. (see no. 188). *Cited on Pages* 117 *(487)*, 252 *(490)*, 252 *(490)*.

227. JEAN DE LA HARPE, in *ibid*. *Cited on Pages* 59 *(570)*, 96 *(570-1)*.

228. MALCOLM MACPHERSON, in *ibid*. *Cited on Pages* 3 *(574)*, 3 *(574)*.

229. T. DRUMMOND SHIELS, in *ibid*. *Cited on Page* 26 *(524)*.

III. *Miscellaneous*

230. *The International Studies Conference : Origins, Functions, Organisation* (Paris : I. I. I. C.), 1937. *Cited on Pages* vii *(11)*, 3 *(26)*.

231. *The State and Economic Life : A record of a first international study conference held at Milan on May 23-27, 1932* (Paris : I. I. I. C.), 1932. *Cited on Pages* 3, 19 *(ix; 184, n.)*.

232. *The State and Economic Life : A record of a second study conference held in London from May 29 to June 2, 1933* (Paris : I. I. I. C.), 1934. *Cited on Page* 3.

B. COMPLEMENTARY SOURCES *

Reference
number

233. AGA KHAN (The) : in *The Times*, October 19, 1938. *Cited on Page* 290.

234. ARNOLD (Lord) : in the discussion on HAROLD NICOLSON : " The Colonial Problem ", in *International Affairs* (London), January-February 1938, vol. xviii, no. 1. *Cited on Pages* 124 *(46)*, 128 *(45-46)*.

235. BÉRENGER, HENRY : in an address delivered at the opening meeting of the inter-governmental Committee on Refugees at Evian, 1938, in *Actes du Comité inter-gouvernemental, Evian, du 6 au 15 juillet, 1938* : *Compte rendu des séances plénières du Comité* : *Résolutions et rapports*, July 1938. *Cited on Page* 311 *(16)*.

236. BIDDER, G. P. : in *The Times*, November 3, 1938. *Cited on Pages* 182, 183, 183.

237. BIDDER, G. P. : in *The Times*, November 23, 1938. *Cited on Pages* 184, 184.

238. BILLECARD, ROBERT (Prefect of the Department of Seine-et-Oise) : in a public notice quoted in *Le Temps*, November 29, 1938. *Cited on Page* 236.

239. BOHÁČ, ANTONÍN : in the discussion on THOMAS, *loc. cit.* (see no. 136). *Cited on Page* 91 *(285-6)*.

240. BONN, MORITZ J. : " La Portée internationale du Problème Colonial ", in *L'Esprit International* : *The International Mind* (Paris), vol. 10, no. 38, April 1936 (reprint). *Cited on Pages* 169 *(15)*, 221 *(9)*.

241. CARR-SAUNDERS, A. M. : " The Situation in England ", in *The Population Problem* : *The Experts and the Public* (London : Allen and Unwin), 1938. *Cited on Page* 101 *(83)*.

242. CHAMBERLAIN, NEVILLE : in a reply to a question in the House of Commons, reported in *The Times*, July 1, 1938. *Cited on Page* 142.

243. DALTON, HUGH : " The Theory of Population ", *loc. cit.* (see no. 156). *Cited on Pages* 66 *(30)*, 67 *(30)*, 67 *(30)*.

244. DEVONSHIRE (Duke of) : in a debate in the House of Lords, reported in *The Times*, July 21, 1938. *Cited on Page* 323.

245. DUBLIN, LOUIS I. : *The Population Problem and World Depression* (New York : Foreign Policy Association), January 1936. *Cited on Page* 144 *(18)*.

246. DUPRÉEL, EUGÈNE : in the discussion on H. P. FAIRCHILD : " Optimum Population ", in SANGER (ed.), *op. cit.* (see no. 136). *Cited on Page* 129 *(101)*.

---

* Anonymous publications, periodicals, etc. are listed (in most cases) under the name of the country of issue.

247. EVERY, Dr. E. F. : in an address delivered on the occasion of a collection in aid of a fund for the Fairbridge Farm Schools, reported in *The Times*, May 7, 1938. *Cited on Page* 219.

248. FAIRCHILD, H. P. : " Optimum Population ", *loc. cit.* (see no. 246). *Cited on Pages* 77 *(82)*, 81 *(79)*, 82 *(79)*.

249. FERENCZI, IMRE : " Contre Migration et Politique d'Emigration ", in *Revue Economique Internationale* (Brussels), December 1936 (reprint). *Cited on Pages* 207, 207 *(5, n. 1)*, 267 *(37, n. 31)*.

250. FERENCZI, IMRE : " Les Migrations et les Prévisions démographiques et sociales ", in *Le Assicurazioni Sociali* (Rome : Cassa Nazionale per le Assicurazioni Sociale), vol. vii, no. 2, March-April 1931 (reprint). *Cited on Pages* 103 *(24; 24, n. 3)*, 103 *(24, n. 3)*, 178 *(30)*, 180 *(27-28)*, 180 *(29)*, 181 *(30)*.

Secondary sources cited :

251. ROSS, EDWARD A. : *Raum für Alle ?* (Berlin and Leipzig), 1929. *Cited on Page* 181 *(30)*.

252. WOLFF, JULIUS : *Die neue Sexualmoral und das Geburtenproblem unserer Tage* (Jena), 1928. *Cited on Page* 181 *(30)*.

253. FISHER, ALLAN G. B. : in *The Sunday Times*, August 7, 1938. *Cited on Page* 312.

254. FISCHER, R. A. : in *The Times*, November 8, 1938. *Cited on Pages* 182, 183, 184.

255. FRANCE : *Le Temps*, November 18, 1938. *Cited on Pages* 168, 168, 168.

Secondary source cited :

256. MINISTRY OF THE INTERIOR : Communiqué. *Cited on Page* 218.

257. FRANCE : *Le Temps*, November 21, 1938. *Cited on Page* 43.

258. GAYDA, VIRGINIO : in *Giornale d'Italia*, quoted in *The Times*, August 1, 1938. *Cited on Page* 126.

259. GERMANY : *Das Schwarze Korps*, quoted in *Le Figaro*, November 17, 1938. *Cited on Page* 294.

260. GINI, CORRADO : " Considerations on the Optimum Density of Population ", in SANGER (ed.), *op. cit.* (see no. 136). *Cited on Pages* 85 *(118)* 87 *(118)*.

261. GINI, CORRADO : in the discussion on J. TANDLER : " The Psychology of the Fall in the Birth Rate ", in SANGER (ed.), *op. cit.* (see no. 136). *Cited on Page* 131 *(241)*.

262. GINI, CORRADO : " The Cyclical Rise and Fall of Population ", in *Population* : Lectures on the Harris Foundation 1929 (Chicago University Press), 1930. *Cited on Page* 131 *(77)*.

263. GLASS, D. V. : *The Struggle for Population*, with an introduction by A. M. CARR-SAUNDERS (Oxford : Clarendon Press), 1936. *Cited on Pages* 133 *(14)*, 133 *(14)*, 133 *(14)*, 134 *(14)*, 134 *(15)*, 142 *(33)*, 142 *(15)*, 142 *(88)*, 142 *(15)*, 146 *(33)*, 147 *(33)*, 147, 150 *(50)*, 150 *(88)*, 150 *(87)*, 150 *(51, 122-32)*, 152, 153 *(32, 41, 44, 46)*, 155 *(26, 30)*, 155 *(28, 26)*.

Secondary sources cited :

264. BURGDÖRFER, F. : " Bevölkerungsentwicklung im abendländischen Kulturkreis mit besonderer Berücksichtigung Deutschlands ", in *Bevölkerungsfrage* (Munich), 1936. *Cited on Page* 155 *(26)*.

265. INTERNATIONAL LABOUR OFFICE : *International Survey of Social Services*, 1933. *Cited on Page* 150 *(131)*.

266. MUSSOLINI, BENITO : in an Ascension Day speech, May 26, 1927. *Cited on Page* 147 *(34)*.

267. GOEBBELS, JOSEPH : in an interview reported in *The Times*, November 19. 1938. *Cited on Page* 47.

268. GOODCHILD, W. A. C. : in *The Times*, November 29, 1938. *Cited on Page* 171.

269. GREAT BRITAIN : *The Observer*, October 30, 1938. *Cited on Page* 269.

270. GREAT BRITAIN : *The Times*, April 25, 1938. *Cited on Pages* 148, 268.

271. GREAT BRITAIN : *The Times*, May 7, 1938. *Cited on Pages* 272, 272, 273.

Secondary source cited :

272. MATSUOKA (President of the South Manchuria Railway). *Cited on Page* 273.

273. GREAT BRITAIN : *The Times*, June 30, 1938. *Cited on Page* 322.

Secondary source cited :

274. " Report of the Overseas Settlement Board ", in *Cmd. 5766*. *Cited on Page* 322.

275. GREAT BRITAIN : *The Times*, July 1, 1938. *Cited on Page* 322.

276. GREAT BRITAIN : *The Times*, July 7, 1938. *Cited on Pages* 168, 168. 168.

277. GREAT BRITAIN : *The Times*, July 8, 1938. *Cited on Pages* 261, 312.

278. GREAT BRITAIN : *The Times*, July 11, 1938. *Cited on Pages* 149, 295.

279. GREAT BRITAIN : *The Times*, August 24, 1938. *Cited on Page* 323.

280. GREAT BRITAIN : *The Times*, September 2, 1938. *Cited on Pages* 148, 148.

281. GREAT BRITAIN : *The Times*, October 18, 1938. *Cited on Pages* 149, 149, 153, 154, 154, 156.

Secondary source cited :

282. BURGDÖRFER, F. : *Völker am Abgrund*. *Cited on Pages* 154, 154.

283. GREAT BRITAIN : *The Times*, October 27, 1938.   *Cited on Page* 269.

284. GREAT BRITAIN : *The Times*, November 5, 1938.   *Cited on Page* 268.

285. GREAT BRITAIN : *The Times*, November 14, 1938.   *Cited on Page* 250.

286. GREAT BRITAIN : *The Times*, November 18, 1938.   *Cited on Page* 168.

287. GREAT BRITAIN : *The Times*, November 29, 1938.   *Cited on Page* 270.

288. GREAT BRITAIN : *The Times*, December 2, 1938.   *Cited on Page* 323.

289. HARMSEN, HANS : in the discussion on D. K. DAS : " Population and Food Supply in India ", on CORRADO GINI (see no. 260), on T. N. CARVER : " Some Needed Refinements of the Theory of Population ", and on L. MARCH : " Differential Increase in the Population in France and in the World ", in SANGER (ed.), *op. cit.* (see no. 136). *Cited on Page* 103 (*197*).

290. HARRIS, H. L. : *Australia's National Interests and National Policy* (Melbourne University Press), 1938. *Cited on Pages* 310 (*14*), 310 (*131*), 311 (*11*), 313 (*17*), 313 (*30*), 313 (*21, n. 7*), 313 (*30, n. 15*), 314 (*138*), 315 (*21*), 315 (*21-22*), 315 (*21-22*), 315 (*22*), 316 (*22*), 316 (*22, n. 13*), 317 (*29*), 317 (*29; 30, n. 15*), 318 (*31*), 319 (*31, 35*), 319 (*32*), 320 (*15*), 320 (*15*), 320 (*140*).

Secondary sources cited :

291. EGGLESTON, F. W. *Cited on Page* 316 (*22, n. 13*).

292. WOLSTENHOLME, S. H. : " The Future of the Australian Population ", *loc. cit.* (see no. 78). *Cited on Page* 315 (*21*).

293. HENDERSON, H. D. : " Causes and Remedies ", in *The Population Problem*, etc. (see no. 241). *Cited on Pages* 142 (*143*), 143 (*143*).

294. HENDERSON, H. D. : " Economic Consequences ", in *ibid. Cited on Pages* 133 (*106*), 133 (*106*), 134 (*84-5*), 135 (*84, 95*), 135 (*85*), 136 (*85-8*), 139 (*88-94*), 139 (*95-6*), 140 (*96-8*), 140 (*100-1*), 140 (*101*), 140 (*101-2*), 141 (*103-6*).

295. HERSCH, L. : in the discussion on THOMAS, *loc. cit.* (see no. 136). *Cited on Page* 96 (*282*).

296. HITLER, ADOLF : in a speech to the Reichstag, January 30, 1937, reported in *The Times*, February 1, 1937. *Cited on Page* 124.

297. HOGBEN, LANCELOT : *Mathematics for the Million : A Popular Self-Educator* (London : Allen and Unwin), 1936. American edition : *Man and Mathematics* (W. M. Norton, Inc.). *Cited on Page* 103 (*623*).

298. HOLLIS, CHRISTOPHER : *We Aren't So Dumb* (London), 1937. *Cited on Page* 182 (*87*).

299. INGE (Dean) : reported in *The Observer*, November 6, 1938. *Cited on Page* 85.

300. INTERNATIONAL LABOUR OFFICE : *Industrial Labour in Japan* : Studies and Reports : Series A (Industrial Relations), No. 37, 1933. *Cited on Pages* 181 (*9, n. 2*), 250 (*8*).

Secondary source cited :

301. NITOBE, I. : " The Question of Food and Population in Japan ", in *World Outlook*, April 1927. *Cited on Page* 250 (*8*).

302. INTERNATIONAL LABOUR OFFICE : INTERNATIONAL LABOUR CONFERENCE : TWENTY-FOURTH SESSION : GENEVA : 1938 : REPORT III : *Recruiting, Placing and Conditions of Labour* (*Equality of Treatment of Migrant Workers*), 1938. *Cited on Pages* 218 (*4*), 244 (*xi*).

303. INTERNATIONAL LABOUR OFFICE : *Technical and Financial International Co-operation with regard to Migration for Settlement. Technical Conference of Experts* : Studies and Reports : Series O (Migration), No. 7, 1938. Pages 222 (*32*), 244 (*7*), 244 (*vii*), 309.

Secondary sources cited :

304. MAZURKIEWICZ, W. *Cited on Pages* 197 (*97*), 203 (*97*), 207 (*97*), 253 (*98*).

305. PEREZ, C. PARRA. *Cited on Page* 239 (*107-8*).

306. INTERNATIONAL LABOUR OFFICE : in an editorial summary of SEISHI IDEI : " Japan's Migration Problem ", in *International Labour Review*, December 1930, vol. xxii, no. 6. *Cited on Page* 40 (*773*).

307. ITALY : Press communiqué, quoted in *Le Temps*. November 18, 1938 (cf. no. 255). *Cited on Page* 167.

308. JOHNSON, T. F. : in *The Times*, July 14, 1938. *Cited on Page* 262.

309. KOULISHER, A. : " Some Aspects of the Migration Problem ", in SANGER (ed.), *op. cit.* (see no. 136). *Cited on Page* 178 (*306*).

310. KUCZYNSKI, ROBERT R. : *Population Movements* (Oxford : Clarendon Press), 1936. *Cited on Pages* 114 (*61-62*), 114 (*61*), 134 (*77*), 135 (*65*), 135 (*65-66, 67-68*), 148 (*59-60*), 148 (*60*), 148 (*60*), 148 (*59-60*), 153 (*60-61*), 155 (*60*), 192 (*68*), 193 (*68*), 286 (*78-79*).

311. KUCZYNSKI, ROBERT R. : " The World's Future Population ", in *Population*, etc. (see no. 262). *Cited on Page* 67 (*283, 255-6, 302, 286-7*).

312. KUCZYNSKI, ROBERT R. : " World Population ", in *The Population Problem*, etc. (see no. 241). *Cited on Pages* 103 (*113*), 111 (*113*), 111 (*115*), 112 (*116*), 112 (*113-4*), 154 (*112-3*).

313. KUCZYNSKI, ROBERT R. : in the discussion on FAIRCHILD, *loc. cit.* (see no. 246). *Cited on Page* 82 (*109-10*).

314. LANDRY, ADOLPHE : *La Révolution Démographique* (Paris : Sirey), 1934. *Cited on Page* 129 (*107*).

315. LEAGUE OF NATIONS : *International Labour Conference* : *First Annual Meeting*, October 29, 1919 — November 29, 1919 (Washington : Government Printing Office), 1920. *Cited on Page* 256 (*276*).

316. LEAGUE OF NATIONS : ECONOMIC COMMITTEE : " Report to the Council on the Work of its Forty-Eighth Session, held at Geneva from July 4th to 9th, 1928 ", in *C. 233.M.132.1928.II.B.*, July 11th, 1938. *Cited on Page* 298 (*6-7*).

317. LEAGUE OF NATIONS : SECRETARIAT : " Preliminary Observations on the drawing-up of a scheme of work for the study of demographic problems ", in LEAGUE OF NATIONS : ECONOMIC COMMITTEE, etc. (see no. 316). *Cited on Pages* 58 (*9*), 68 (*11*), 71 (*9-10*), 80 (*11*), 86 (*8*), 100 (*10*), 121 (*11*), 286 (*13*), 298 (*12*), 298 (*13*).

318. LEAGUE OF NATIONS : " Report of the Committee for the Study of the Problem of Raw Materials ", in *A.27.1937.II.B.*, September 1937. *Cited on Page* 291.

319. LEAGUE OF NATIONS : *Statistical Yearbook of the League of Nations*, 1937-38. *Cited on Pages* 103 (*57*), 199 (*20*).

Secondary sources cited :

320. DUBLIN, LOUIS I. and LOTKA, ALFRED J. : " On the True Rate of Natural Increase ", in *Journal of the American Statistical Association*, September 1925. *Cited on Page* 103 (*57*).

321. KUCZYNSKI, ROBERT R. : *The Balance of Births and Deaths* (Washington), 1928 and 1931. *Cited on Page* 103 (*57*).

322. KUCZYNSKI, ROBERT R. : *The Measurement of Population Growth* (London), 1935. *Cited on Page* 103 (*57*).

323. LOVEDAY, ALEXANDER : " The Economic and Financial Activities of the League ", in *International Affairs* (London), vol. xvii, no. 6, November-December 1938. *Cited on Pages* 296 (*799*), 297 (*805*).

324. LUGARD (Lord) : in *The Times*, November 23, 1938. *Cited on Pages* 172, 172.

325. MADGWICK, R. B. : " Migration ", Paper no. 3 in *Australian Population : Supplementary Papers, Series A*, prepared for the British Commonwealth Relations Conference 1938 by the Australian Institute of International Affairs (Sydney), 1938 (mimeographed). *Cited on Pages* 313 (*11*), 315 (*11*), 315 (*11*), 316 (*11*), 317 (*11, n. 5*), 317 (*11*), 318 (*12, n. 6*), 324 (*15*).

326. MALCOLM, Sir NEILL : in an address to the third public meeting of the inter-governmental Committee on refugees at Evian, 1938, in *Actes du Comité inter-governemental*, etc. (see no. 235). *Cited on Pages* 222 (*33*), 260 (*33*).

327. MANUFACTURING CONFECTIONERS' ALLIANCE, PRESIDENT OF THE : in a speech at the Chocolate and Confectionery Exhibition, Earl's Court, September 1938, reported in *The Times*, September 1, 1938. *Cited on Page* 134.

328. MAROGER, GILBERT : *L'Europe et la Question Coloniale : Revendications Coloniales Allemandes — Aspirations Coloniales Polonaises*, with a preface by SÉBASTIEN CHARLÉTY (Paris : Sirey), May 1938. *Cited on Pages* 20, 42 (*249*), 42 (*249-50*), 42 (*250*), 42 (*250*), 42 (*249, n. 1*), 43 (*250-1*), 44 (*251-2*), 44 (*252*), 45 (*252-4*), 45 (*225*), 46, 48 (*193*), 55 (*195-6*), 55 (*196, 208*), 56 (*197-8*), 56 (*218*), 117 (*42, n. 23*), 126 (*306*), 126 (*307*).

Secondary sources cited :

329. ACADÉMIE DES SCIENCES COLONIALES : in *L'Afrique Française*, January 1938. *Cited on Page* 125 (*292*).

330. VON EPP, General RITTER : in *Europäischer Revue*, September 1936, and in *Westdeutsche Beobachter*, October 23, 1936. *Cited on Page* 126 (*307*).

331. LOUWERS, O. : *Le Problème Colonial au point de vue international* (Brussels), 1936. *Cited on Page* 59 (*265, n. 19*).

332. RACAMOND : in *Vigilance*. *Cited on Page* 125 (*287*).

333. SARRAUT, ALBERT. *Cited on Page* 125 (*286-7*).

334. *Le Temps*, January 11, 1938. *Cited on Page* 43 (*250*).

335. WIESENDANGER, PAUL : " Auch die Schweiz hat Kolonialansprüche anzumelden ", in *Nationale Hefte*, February-March 1937. *Cited on Page* 59 (*265, n. 21*).

336. MARSHALL, T. H. : " General Conclusions ", in *The Population Problem*, etc. (see no. 241). *Cited on Pages* 155 (*175*), 182 (*175*).

337. MILLET, RAYMOND : *Trois Millions d'Etrangers en France* : *Les Indésirables — Les Bienvenus* (Paris : Médicis), 1938. *Cited on Pages* 150 (*23*), 163 (*109, 55*), 236 (*61 sqq.*).

Secondary sources cited :

338. OLLIVIER, Dr. JEAN. *Cited on Page* 232 (*86*).

339. *Bulletin Officiel de la Ville de Paris*, May 12, 1938. *Cited on Page* 232 (*149-151*).

340. NASU, SHIROSHI : " Population and the Food Supply ", in *Population*, etc. (see no. 262). *Cited on Pages* 69, 79 (*143*), 97 (*169*).

341. NICOLSON, HAROLD : " The Colonial Problem", *loc. cit.* (see no. 234), *Cited on Pages* 53 (*38-39*), 56 (*39-41*), 121 (*35*), 125 (*36*), 126 (*36*), 169 (*35*), 276 (*34-35*), 276 (*35*), 278 (*35*).

342. OGISHIMA, TORU : " Japanese Emigration ", in *International Labour Review* (Geneva), November 1936, vol. xxxiv, no. 5. *Cited on Pages* 250 (*651*), 272 (*651*).

343. PERHAM, MARGERY : in the discussion on NICOLSON, *loc. cit.* (see no. 234). *Cited on Page* 127 (*42-44*).

344. PLANT, ARNOLD : " Population Trends and International Migration ", in *The Population Problem*, etc. (see no. 241). *Cited on Pages* 221 (*122*), 228 (*131*), 228 (*132 sqq.*), 228 (*132-3*), 229 (*134*).

345. POLAND : *Wieczór Warszawski*, quoted in *Le Figaro*, October 28, 1938. *Cited on Page* 42.

346. ROBBINS, LIONEL : *Economic Planning and International Order*, 1937. *Cited on Page* 69 (*72*).

347. ROBERTSON, MALCOLM : in the discussion on NICOLSON, *loc. cit.* (see no. 234). *Cited on Pages* 53 (*44*), 55 (*45*).

348. ROYAL INSTITUTE OF INTERNATIONAL AFFAIRS : *Germany's Claims to Colonies* : Information Department Papers, No. 23 (London), May 1938. *Cited on Pages* 20, 49 (*25*), 49 (*28*), 51 (*47*), 71 (*33*), 72 (*34, n. 1*), 130 (*32*), 131 (*29*).

  Secondary sources cited :

349. CROWE, Sir EYRE : in *British Documents on the Origins of the War*, vol. iii. *Cited on Page* 130 (*9*).

350. VON EPP, General RITTER : reported in *Daily Telegraph and Morning Post*, December 7, 1937. *Cited on Page* 169 (*36*).

351. GOERING, HERMANN : in a speech reported in *The Times* and in *The Manchester Guardian*, October 29, 1936. *Cited on Page* 72 (*34, n. 1*).

352. HITLER, ADOLF : *Mein Kampf* (1930 edition). *Cited on Page* 54 (*25*).

353. HITLER, ADOLF : in a speech to the Reichstag, January 1937, reported in *The Times*, February 1, 1937. *Cited on Page* 49 (*28*).

354. HITLER, ADOLF : in a speech at the Harvest Thanksgiving Festival, October 3, 1937. *Cited on Page* 49 (*35*).

355. HITLER, ADOLF : in a speech at Augsburg on November 21, 1937, reported in *The Times*, November 22, 1937. *Cited on Page* 49 (*38*).

356. HUGENBERG : in a report outlined in June 1933 to the London Economic Conference as given in *The Times*, June 17, 1937. *Cited on Page* 131 (*29*).

357. ROYAL INSTITUTE OF INTERNATIONAL AFFAIRS : *The Colonial Problem*, etc. (see no. 96). *Cited on Pages* 170 (*11*), 171 (*342*), 268 (*83*), 269 (*361*), 269 (*364*).

  Secondary source cited :

358. *Business and Financial Reports* : *A Monthly Survey of Italian Trade and Industry* (Rome : Fascist Confederation of Industrialists; Association of Italian Corporations), October 1936. *Cited on Page* 269 (*364*).

359. ROYAL INSTITUTE OF INTERNATIONAL AFFAIRS : *Unemployment* : *An International Problem* : A Report by a Study Group of Members of the Royal Institute of International Affairs (Oxford University Press), 1935. *Cited on Pages* 294 (*329*), 295 (*244, 329*).

  Secondary sources cited :

360. BEVERIDGE, Sir WILLIAM : *Unemployment* : *A Problem of Industry* (London), 1931. *Cited on Page* 86 (*197*).

361. CARR-SAUNDERS, A. M. : " Migration Policies and the Economic Crisis ", in *Foreign Affairs* (New York), July 1934. *Cited on Page* 94 (*197*).

362. ROBBINS, LIONEL : " The Optimum Theory of Population ", in *London Essays in Honour of Edwin Cannan.* *Cited on Page* 68 (*235, n. 2*).

363. SATO, NAOTAKE : *The Problem of Population and Industrialisation in Japan* (Tokyo : The International Association of Japan), 1936. *Cited on Page* 244 (*6, 9*).

364. SCHACHT, HJALMAR : " Germany's Colonial Demands ", in *Foreign Affairs* (New York), January 1937, vol. xv, no. 2. *Cited on Pages* 49, 50 (*234*), 50, 50 (*227*).

365. SHAW, G. BERNARD : " The Basis of Socialism : Economic ", in *Fabian Essays in Socialism* (London : Walter Scott Publishing Co. Ltd.), 1908 (reprint). *Cited on Page* 179 (*21-22*).

366. SHIELS, T. DRUMMOND : in the discussion on NICOLSON, *loc. cit.* (see no. 234). *Cited on Page* 24 (*47*).

367. SIMPSON, Sir JOHN HOPE : *Refugees* : Preliminary Report of a Survey (London : Royal Institute of International Affairs), 1938. *Cited on Pages* 145 (*134*), 261, 261 (*193*).

368. SMITHIES, A. : " The Future of the Australian Population " : Paper 2 in *Australian Population,* etc. (see no. 325). *Cited on Pages* 146 (*5-6*), 313 (*17*), 315 (*3*), 315 (*3*), 315 (*1-2*), 318 (*17*).

Secondary source cited :

369. WOLSTENHOLME, S. H. : " The Future of the Australian Population ", *loc. cit.* (see no. 292). *Cited on Page* 315 (*1-2*).

370. SNELL (Lord) : in a debate in the House of Lords (see no. 244). *Cited on Page* 323.

371. SPIER, EUGEN : in *The Times,* July 15, 1938. *Cited on Page* 168.

372. STROWSKI, FORTUNAT : Paper read before the French Academy of Moral and Political Sciences, reported in *Le Figaro,* November 7, 1938. *Cited on Page* 210.

373. TAIT, D. CHRISTIE : " Migration and Settlement in Australia, New Zealand and Canada ", in *International Labour Review* (Geneva), vol. xxxiv, no. 1, July 1936 (reprint). *Cited on Pages* 312 (*31*), 320 (*3*), 320 (*3*).

374. THOMAS, ALBERT : in the discussion on THOMAS, *loc. cit.* (see no. 136). *Cited on Page* 287 (*269*).

375. THOMPSON, WARREN S. : in the discussion on FAIRCHILD, *loc. cit.* (see no. 246). *Cited on Page* 84 (*101*).

376. TOUZET, ANDRÉ : *Le Problème colonial et la Paix du monde* (Paris : Sirey) : Vol. I. : *Les Revendications coloniales allemandes,* 1937. *Cited on Pages* 20 (*xxxvii*), 20, 35 (*xvii*), 35 (*xvii*), 36 (*xxxi*), 37 (*xxxv, xl-xli*), 42 (*xxxiii*), 42 (*xxxiii*), 43 (*xxxiii-xxxiv*), 43 (*xxxiv*), 44 (*xxxiv*), 45 (*xxxv*), 59 (*xxxii*), 101 (*108*), 103 (*109-111*), 128 (*283*), 128 (*285*), 128 (*283-4*), 131 (*123*), 149 (*111*), 158 (*124*), 158 (*126*), 158 (*125*),

201 (*115*), 249 (*116*), 249 (*116*), 249 (*116*), 250 (*117*), 263 (*128-9*), 273 (*130*), 273 (*128-9*), 273 (*129, n. 3*), 274 (*131*), 274 (*131-2*), 274 (*131*), 274 (*132, n. 1*), 276 (*132-3*), 276 (*135*), 276 (*133*), 277 (*146*), 277 (*140*), 277 (*140*), 277 (*142*), 277 (*142*), 278 (*143*), 278 (*145*), 278 (*136*), 279 (*126, 146*), 294 (*127-8*), 294 (*127*).

Secondary sources cited :

377. BURGDÖRFER, F. : *Aufbau und Bewegung der Bevölkerung* (Leipzig : Barth), 1935. *Cited on Pages* 158 (*125*), 158 (*125*), 201 (*115*).

378. " Deutsche Schutzgebiete ", in *Deutsches Kolonial Lexicon*, vol. I. *Cited on Page* 274 (*131*).

379. " Engländer in den Kolonien " in *ibid*. *Cited on Page* 274 (*131*).

380. GOEBBELS, JOSEPH : in a speech delivered on June 7, 1937, at Frankfurt-am-Main to the congress of large families, reported in *Le Temps*, June 8, 1937. *Cited on Page* 147 (*112-3*).

381. LIST, F. : *Système National d'Economie Politique*. *Cited on Page* 249 (*116*).

382. RATHGEN : " Arten der Kolonien " in *Deutsches Kolonial Lexicon*, vol. II. *Cited on Page* 273 (*129*).

383. RATHGEN : " Auswanderung ", in *ibid*., vol. I. *Cited on Page* 276 (*134*).

384. RATHGEN : " Einwanderung ", in *ibid*. *Cited on Pages* 273 (*129*), 274 (*132, n. 1*).

385. RATHGEN : " Volkswirtschaftliche Bedeutung der Kolonien für Deutschland ", in *ibid*., vol. III. *Cited on Pages* 276 (*135*), 276 (*135*).

386. ROHRBACH, PAUL : *Deutschlands Koloniale Forderung* (Hamburg : Hanseatische Verlangsanstalt). 1935. *Cited on Page* 278 (*145*).

387. ROSCHER : *Economie Politique* (Traduction Wolkonski), vol. II. *Cited on Page* 249 (*116, n. 1*).

388. SCHACHT, HJALMAR : in a speech delivered in 1927. *Cited on Page* 71 (*119*).

389. SCHACHT, HJALMAR : in a speech delivered on the occasion of the centenary of the Geographical and Statistical Society of Frankfurt-am-Mein, reported in *Berliner Börsen Zeitung*, December 8, 1936 (cf. no. 181). *Cited on Page* 49 (*120, n. 1*).

390. SCHNEE, HEINRICH : *Braucht Deutschland Kolonien?* *Cited on Page* 276 (*134*).

391. *Statistisches Jahrbuch für das Deutsche Reich* (Berlin : Reimar Hobbing), 1936. *Cited on Pages* 101 (*108*), 102 (*110*), 201 (*115*).

392. TIERNEY, MICHAEL : " Colonies Policy and European Peace ", in *Studies : An Irish Quarterly Review*, 1935. *Cited on Page* 59 (*xxxiii, n. 1*).

393. TROLL, C. : *Das deutsche Kolonialproblem. Cited on Pages* 277 *(141-2)*, 277 *(142)*, 277 *(142)*, 277 *(143)*.

394. Vol. II. : *L'Expansion coloniale italienne : Para-colonisation nipponne de l'Asie orientale*, 1938. *Cited on Pages* 20, 105 *(66)*, 105 *(66)*, 106 *(68)*, 106 *(69-70)*, 108 *(227, 233, 235)*, 146 *(234)*, 148 *(73)*, 148 *(72)*, 149 *(72-73)*, 181 *(257)*, 202 *(75, n. 1)*, 267 *(83)*, 268 *(84)*, 268 *(84)*, 268 *(85)*, 269 *(85)*, 269 *(87)*, 270 *(89)*, 272 *(281-2)*, 280 *(167-8)*.

Secondary sources cited :

395. *Annuario Statistico Italiano*, 1936. *Cited on Pages* 105 *(67)*, 106 *(69)*, 201 *(75)*, 267 *(83)*.

396. DI CAMEROTA, D'AGOSTINO ORSINI : " Da un decennale a l'altro ", in *Rivista di Politica Economica*, 1933. *Cited on Pages* 268 *(84-5)*, 269 *(85)*.

397. *Financial and Economic Annual of Japan*, 1936. *Cited on Page* 107 *(234)*.

398. *The Japan Yearbook*, 1935. *Cited on Page* 202 *(247)*.

399. KOKUSEI (National Census Council), Tokyo. *Cited on Page* 107 *(234)*.

400. YANO, TSUNATA and SHIRASAKI, KYOICHI : *Nippon 1936* (Tokyo : Kokuseisha), 1936. *Cited on Page* 202 *(247)*.

401. VARLEZ, LOUIS : in the discussion on FAIRCHILD, *loc. cit.* (see no. 246). *Cited on Pages* 78 *(93-94)*, 86 *(95)*.

402. WHITE, Lieut. Col. T. W. : in an address to the second public meeting of the inter-governmental Committee on refugees at Evian 1938, in *Actes du Comité inter-gouvernemental*, etc. (see no. 235). *Cited on Page* 321 *(19)*.

ANNEX :

ALPHABETICAL LIST OF SOURCES
CITED IN THE SURVEY*

* The figures correspond with the reference-numbers in the Bibliographical Index.

SUBJECT INDEX [1]

---

[1] See also the Alphabetical List of Sources cited in the Survey, pp. 360-3 above.

Imprimé en Belgique

12120 - Impr. Vaillant-Carmanne, S. A., Liége.
Un adm.-dir. L. DALLEMAGNE, 4, place St-Michel, Liége.

PRINTED

BY

H. VAILLANT-CARMANNE, S. A.

LIÉGE (BELGIUM)

MCMXXXIX